THE DYNAMICS OF POWERS IN THE EUROPEAN UNION

Separation of powers is the time-tested touchstone of the legitimate exercise of power in modern democracies. This collection examines decision-making in the EU's multi-layered and polycentric constitutional structure through this lens.

The focus on separation of powers reveals how strong executive powers collaborate in the EU as a single source of public power, which is not sufficiently counterbalanced by parliaments or the judiciary. The collection explores three policy fields marked by crisis: the economic and monetary union (EMU), migration, and trade. Drawing on expertise from across these sectors, with a strong conceptual thread linking all the contributions, this important work illustrates how different branches of government co-determine each others' powers.

Volume 126 in the Series Modern Studies in European Law

Modern Studies in European Law

Recent titles in this series:

Judicial Authority in EU Internal Market Law: Implications for the Balance of Competences and Powers
Vilija Velyvyte

The Changing European Union: A Critical View on the Role of Law and the Courts
Edited by Tamara Capeta, Iris Goldner Lang and Tamara Perisin

The Structural Transformation of European Private Law: A Critique of Juridical Hermeneutic
Leone Niglia

The Future of EU Constitutionalism
Edited by Matej Avbelj

The Changing Role of Citizens in EU Democratic Governance
Edited by Davor Jancic

The EU and the Baltic Sea Area
Edited by Allan Rosas and Henrik Ringbom

The Evolving Governance of EU Competition Law in a Time of Disruptions: A Constitutional Perspective
Edited by Carlo Maria Colombo, Kathryn Wright and Mariolina Eliantonio

The European Integrated Border Management: Frontex, Human Rights, and International Responsibility
Giulia Raimondo

Private Autonomy in EU Internal Market Law: Parameters of its Protection and Limitation
Rufat Babayev

Free Movement and Welfare Access in the European Union: Re-Balancing Conflicting Interests in Citizenship Jurisprudence
Victoria Hooton

EU Trade and Investment Treaty-Making Post-Lisbon: Moving Beyond Mixity
Gesa Kübek

The Normative Foundations for EU Criminal Justice: Powers, Limits and Justifications
Jacob Öberg

EU Neighbourhood Law: Wider Europe and the Extended EU's Legal Space
Alessandro Petti

The Dynamics of Powers in the European Union
Edited by Christina Eckes, Päivi Leino-Sandberg and Anna W Ghavanini

For the complete list of titles in this series see www.bloomsbury.com/uk/series/modern-studies-in-european-law/

The Dynamics of Powers in the European Union

Edited by
Christina Eckes
Päivi Leino-Sandberg
and
Anna W Ghavanini

•HART•
OXFORD • LONDON • NEW YORK • NEW DELHI • SYDNEY

HART PUBLISHING

Bloomsbury Publishing Plc

Kemp House, Chawley Park, Cumnor Hill, Oxford, OX2 9PH, UK

1385 Broadway, New York, NY 10018, USA

29 Earlsfort Terrace, Dublin 2, Ireland

HART PUBLISHING, the Hart/Stag logo, BLOOMSBURY and the Diana logo are trademarks of Bloomsbury Publishing Plc

First published in Great Britain 2024

A catalogue record for this book is available from the British Library.

A catalogue record for this book is available from the Library of Congress.

ISBN: HB: 978-1-50997-159-6
ePDF: 978-1-50997-161-9
ePub: 978-1-50997-160-2

Typeset by Compuscript Ltd, Shannon

ACKNOWLEDGEMENTS

This edited collection is the result of the research carried out in the project 'Separation of Powers for 21st Century Europe', which is a joint project by the Amsterdam Centre for European Law and Governance at the University of Amsterdam, the Erik Castrén Institute of International Law and Human Rights (ECI) at the University of Helsinki, and the Department of Law at the University of Gothenburg. The project was funded by the Norface Network, as part of the 'NORFACE Democratic Governance in a Turbulent Age programme.'

We thankfully acknowledge the organisational support of Ellysia van der Werf, who has provided invaluable assistance during events throughout the project. We also acknowledge the research assistance of Camilla Pedersen, Izel Karahan, and Sarah Kaddar, who coded the judiciary database, and the editorial assistance of Tessa Trapp and Mariam van der Horst in preparing this volume for publication.

We would also like to thank our collaborators, who participated in many of our discussions and generously shared their time and thoughts with us: Thomas Beukers, Marta Božina Beroš, Filipe Brito Bastos, Deirdre Curtin, Piet Eeckhout, Joana Mendes, Daniel Naurin, René Repasi, Tuomas Saarenheimo, Annette Schrauwen, Maria Weimer, and Jonathan Zeitlin. Finally, we appreciated the insights of all other scholars that contributed to our thinking on separation of powers.

TABLE OF CONTENTS

PART III
THE RELATIONSHIP BETWEEN THE JUDICIARY AND THE EXECUTIVE

PART IV
CROSS-CUTTING CONSIDERATIONS

LIST OF CONTRIBUTORS

Laurens Ankersmit is assistant professor at the University of Amsterdam, Netherlands.

Nik de Boer is associate professor at the University of Amsterdam, Netherlands.

Merijn Chamon is professor at the Vrije Universiteit Brussel, Belgium.

Florin Coman-Kund is associate professor at the Erasmus University Rotterdam, Netherlands.

Christina Eckes is professor at the University of Amsterdam, Netherlands.

Cristina Fasone is assistant professor at the Luiss University, Rome, Italy.

Anna W Ghavanini is associate professor at the University of Gothenburg, Sweden.

Davide Gnes is a postdoctoral researcher at the University of Amsterdam, Netherlands.

Piotr Krajewski is a PhD researcher at the University of Amsterdam, Netherlands.

Päivi Leino-Sandberg is professor at the University of Helsinki, Finland.

Panu Minkkinen is professor at the University of Helsinki, Finland.

Christoph Möllers is professor at the Humboldt-University Berlin, Germany.

Marta Morvillo is assistant professor at the University of Amsterdam, Netherlands.

Allison Östlund is a senior lecturer at the University of Gothenburg, Sweden.

Antti Ronkainen is a PhD researcher at the University of Helsinki, Finland.

Milka Sormunen is a postdoctoral researcher at the University of Helsinki, Finland.

Anna Waldenström is a senior lecturer at the University of Gothenburg, Sweden.

Martin Westlund is a PhD researcher at the University of Gothenburg, Sweden.

PART I

Conceptual Considerations

1

Introduction

CHRISTINA ECKES, PÄIVI LEINO-SANDBERG
AND ANNA W GHAVANINI

The democratic crisis is also an institutional crisis. Democracy is in decline, globally but also within the European Union. A high level of informalisation allows the circumvention of institutional powers and prerogatives. The executive branch is structurally overreaching. Parliaments are weakened. The judiciary is sidelined and sidelines itself. The law is at times delegitimised as just another political position. These trends are also often, but not always, related to externalisation of decision-making. What we can witness more broadly is that current institutional practice is unable to provide the mechanisms that channel political conflict to fora that ensure collective will-formation supported by the many rather than the few. As governance takes on new forms and dimensions, it is rendered ever more complex and further removed from the people in whose name public power is exercised. Separation of powers is under pressure.

These dynamics are particularly apparent in the multilayered and polycentric construction of the EU, which does not follow a classic conception of separation of powers. We can identify the European Court of Justice and the European Parliament as exercising central functions of the judiciary and the legislature, respectively. The Commission may be regarded, and describes itself, as the principal 'executive organ' of the EU, and exercises various functions that 'according to the classical doctrine of the separation of powers, are within the province of the executive'.[1] However, neither the Council of the European Union, consisting of national executives but exercising legislative and quasi-legislative functions within the EU, nor the European Council, fit easily into that framework. Furthermore, while the Parliament and the Council are commonly referred to as the 'EU's co-legislature', the Commission holds the monopoly power to initiate legislation. The Court of Justice therefore convincingly included the Commission as a 'key player in the legislative process'.[2]

State-of-the-art of research on the EU has pointed out that the multilayered polycentric legal order of the EU by its very construction strengthens executive power.[3]

[1] Case T-562/12, *John Dalli v Commission* ECLI:EU:T:2015:270 [133]–[134].

[2] Case C-57/16 P, *Client Earth v Commission* ECLI:EU:C:2018:660 [88].

[3] P Dann, 'European Parliament and Executive Federalism' (2003) 9 *European Law Journal* 551; D Curtin, *Executive Power of the European Union – Law, Practices, and the Living Constitution* (OUP, 2009); R Schütze,

Additionally, executive powers in the EU are gaining through crisis measure, informalisation and externalisation, ie moving policy-making from the domestic institutional setting to international relations. However, there is more to the executive dominance in the EU legal order than meets the eye. Democratic scrutiny and deliberation remain a challenge in the EU. This is the case not only because of the Union's constitutional and institutional set-up, but also because of the tasks that the institutions assume or do not assume and their own understanding of their roles in the system. Our research project on the Separation of Powers in 21st Century Europe (SepaRope) mirrored these practices against the ideal of separation of powers and identified how institutional interactions amongst both the EU institutions and between the EU institutions and Member States' authorities shift powers between the three branches. The 14 chapters of this volume present different challenges to establishing and maintaining a convincing conception of separation of powers within the EU.

The EU's particularities are often understood to lead to democratic deficiencies. Criticisms of this sort are regularly countered by reference to how the EU is 'special' and that it therefore 'cannot be measured by reference to traditional nation-State standards'.[4] However:

> Make no mistake: it is perfectly understood that the Union is not a State. But it is in the business of governance, and it has taken over extensive areas previously in the hands of its Member States. … Democracy is not about the States. Democracy is about the exercise of public power—and the Union exercises a huge amount of public power. We live by the credo that any exercise of public power has to be 'legitimated' democratically …[5]

While recognising the EU's specificities, this edited collection is based on the presumption that the need to debate the limits of its powers is even greater *because* the EU is different from nation-states and not a deeply rooted political community. The EU exercises state functions with direct implications both for the rights and obligations of individuals and for the scope of manoeuvre of democratic decision-making within the Member States. The traditional example is the empowerment of national courts vis-à-vis the other branches.

The EU's democratic problems derive not only from its atypical institutional design, but also from its strong emphasis on efficiency and functionalism that have enabled the transformation of essentially political questions into legal and technical ones. While much has been achieved in terms of joint or at least coordinated problem-solving, this has happened at the cost of the democratic anchoring of EU policies. In 2000, Joschka Fischer described quite pointedly how the process of European integration is called into question by many people: 'it is viewed as a bureaucratic affair run by a faceless, soulless Eurocracy in Brussels – at best boring, at worst dangerous'.[6] Since then, little

'From Rome to Lisbon: "Executive Federalism" in the (New) European Union' (2010) 47 *Common Market Law Review* 1385.

[4] K Lenaerts, 'The Principle of Democracy in the Case Law of the European Court of Justice' (2013) 62 *ICLQ* 271.

[5] JHH Weiler, 'Europe in Crisis — On "Political Messianism", "Legitimacy" and the "Rule of Law"' (2012) *Singapore Journal of Legal Studies* 248, 251.

[6] J Fischer, 'From Confederacy to Federation – Thoughts on the finality of European integration' Speech at the Humboldt University in Berlin 12 May 2000, at ec.europa.eu/dorie/fileDownload.do?docId=192161&cardId=192161.

has changed. The EU continues to lack a deeply integrated political community, and suffers from a 'persistent, chronic, troubling democracy deficit, which cannot be talked away'.[7]

I. The Three Branches of the EU

The EU builds its democratic legitimacy on a two-pronged institutional basis: directly via the EU institutions and indirectly via national institutions.[8] This two-pronged approach is reflected in the principle of democracy under the EU Treaties and confirmed by the approach of national constitutional courts.[9] Yet, there remains a disconnect between the two layers that strongly contributes to the persistent democratic deficiency. The Union has failed to adopt 'even the imperfect habits of governmental control, parliamentary accountability and administrative responsibility that are practiced with different modalities in its various Member States'.[10] Although the Union institutions insists on the EU's *sui generis* nature and autonomy from the Member States' legal orders, its authority 'remains almost entirely normative and regulatory, even as EU judges, lawyers, and law professors use a "constitutional" vocabulary to describe it'.[11] Despite many declarations on the EU's commitment to democracy and the rule of law, democratic principles continue to be directed more at others and continue to be enforced more stringently towards the Member States than the EU's own institutions.[12] They matter more at the level of values than daily practice. As a result, the EU continues to rely on democratic legitimacy from the Member States.[13] Member States and EU institutions interact within the EU in a complex framework that transcends national constitutional structures but depends on them.

National parliaments are the central organ of the parliamentary democracies of the Member States. The European Parliament continues to lack the same democratic legitimacy and influence as national parliaments, because of the lack of a unified procedure, structurally low voter turnout, and its more limited grip on the adoption of legislation in the EU. It is struggling to exercise consistently political control over the EU's course of action and its interventions are at times perceived as erratic and

[7] Weiler (n 5) 251.

[8] Fundamentally: J Habermas, 'Citizens and State Equality in a Supranational Political Community: Degressive Proportionality and the Pouvoir Constituant Mixte' (2017) 55 *Journal of Common Market Studies* 171; F Scharpf, 'Legitimacy in the multilevel European polity' (MPIfG Working Paper no 1, 2009), at www.econstor.eu/bitstream/10419/41652/1/610149423.pdf.

[9] See Arts 2, 10, 12 and 14 TEU and see eg the *ultra vires* test applied by the German Constitutional Court: BVerfG, PSPP Judgment of the Second Senate of 5 May 2020, 2 BvR 859/15, paras 1–237, at www.bverfg.de/e/rs20200505_2bvr085915en.html.

[10] Weiler (n 5) 251.

[11] P Lindseth, 'The Law of the European Union in Historical Perspective' in H Pihlajamäki, MD Dubber and M Godfrey (eds), *The Oxford Handbook of European Legal History* (OUP, 2018) 1115, 1117.

[12] K Lenaerts, 'On Checks and Balances: the Rule of Law within the EU' (2023) 29 *Columbia Journal of European Law* 2.

[13] C Eckes and P Leino-Sandberg, The EU–UK Trade and Cooperation Agreement – Exceptional Circumstances or a new Paradigm for EU External Relations? (2022) 85 *MLR* 164.

unpredictable when they are triggered by the political salience of one issue while invisible on others.

Given the current state of integration in the EU, Member States must remain in the position to exercise substantial influence within the decision-making process of the Union. An illustrative example, also discussed in several chapters of this collection, is the frequent choice for mixed agreements,[14] which gives a voice to national parliaments alongside the EU institutions in the conclusion of international agreements. Another example, albeit more indirect, is the control and oversight of the national representatives in the Council by national parliaments.

The Member States are in the Council represented in a hybrid EU institution that forms part of both the legislature and the executive. In the European Council, they are represented in the top-level 'federal' executive organ setting out general guidelines and addressing political conflict above all between Member States as 'federate' units. While federal states usually ensure representation of the federate entities in the federal legislature, they typically do not include the federate entities directly in the federal (top-level) executive. The strong inclusion of Member States, including in its top-level formation (ie, the European Council and the Council) entails that the EU unlike (other) federations also has a top-level split executive. In administrative procedures, the tight interlocking of national and EU executive actors results on occasion in a 'hybrid' form of decision-making that blurs responsibilities and undermines effective control and balancing possibilities of the legislature and the judiciary.[15] The lack of clarity about responsibilities and powers to take autonomous decisions has been particularly apparent in the context of the withdrawal from the Energy Charter Treaty (ECT). The picture is further obscured by the unwillingness to take a public position on the allocation and also boundaries of responsibilities and powers.[16]

Sufficiently clear allocation of responsibilities is of crucial importance in the context of contemporary governance, where executives have become ever more powerful, assisted by crisis governance, informalisation, technocratisation and increasing polarisation. The EU's polycentricity and the attempt to give both the EU and the Member State executive a place in decision-making (top-level and administrative) creates more cumbersome procedures constructed to integrate the autonomous voices into the federal decision-making. It also raises the question as to whether the different executive actors could be seen as offering mutual control mechanisms or whether they primarily collaborate in a way that sidelines the other branches. Executive power has emerged beyond the institutional structures set out in the founding Treaties. It has taken dispersed forms

[14] Ankersmit (chapter 5) and Eckes (chapter 12) in this volume. See also C Eckes and P Leino-Sandberg (ibid); L Ankersmit, 'Opinion 2/15 and the future of mixity and ISDS' (European Law Blog, 2017) at europeanlawblog.eu/2017/05/18/opinion-215-and-the-future-of-mixity-and-isds.

[15] C Eckes and R D'Ambrosio, Composite administrative procedures in the European Union. European Central Bank (ECB) 2020; FB Bastos, 'Judicial review of composite administrative procedures in the Single Supervisory Mechanism: Berlusconi' (2019) 56 *Common Market Law Review* 1355.

[16] P Leino-Sandberg and C Eckes, 'The European Commission's Assessment of EU Withdrawal from the Energy Charter Treaty: Legal analysis or confidential strategy?', Blogpost 41/2022, at europeanlawblog.eu/2022/09/28/the-european-commissions-assessment-of-eu-withdrawal-from-the-energy-charter-treaty-legal-analysis-or-confidential-strategy.

bringing to the fore the internal tensions *within* the executive.[17] This tension is captured and maintained by the adoption of various forms of 'fuzziness', under which 'creative' use of legal tools fabricate an appearance of legality that masks the lack of effective limitations of power.[18]

The Court is probably the most distinct 'branch' in the EU system, sharing its task of 'ensur[ing] that in the interpretation and application of the Treaties the law is observed' (Article 19 TEU) with national courts. On the one hand, the ECJ is given exceptional powers, eg the power to review envisaged international agreements pursuant to Article 218(11) TFEU; on the other, the ECJ heavily depends on the support and cooperation of both the other branches and the national judiciary in order to be able to exercise these powers. The distinction of the judicial branch has also been diminished by the establishment, alongside the formal judiciaries, of the Ombudsperson and the Court of Auditors both in law and in practice. Both fulfil quasi-judicial powers in scrutinising in particular the actions of the executive, but lack the effectiveness and enforcement powers of the judiciary and rely on parliaments to give effect to their findings.

Together with the Commission, the Court of Justice acts as a 'guarantee institution', as strong and independent organs capable of making sure that all Member States comply with the common rules in the same way.[19] This is also a cooperative relationship, as the Commission fulfils a quasi-judicial role in enforcing EU law obligations against the Member States, is responsible for bringing cases for the Court, and routinely participates in all Court litigation. In practice, the Commission and its Legal Service self-identify as experts in the Court's service.[20] This institutional collaboration contributes to blurring the boundaries of the powers of the executive and the judiciary. The Court of Justice is commonly seen as a driver of integration and has structurally given much weight to the 'unity, primacy, and effectiveness of EU law'.[21] This is one reason why judicial control of the acts of the EU executive and legislative and of the boundaries of the competences of the EU is often considered weak or deferential; indeed, these boundaries have at times been expanded through the Court's case law, giving rise to accusations of judicial overreach.[22] At the same time, the Court is treated more as a solution to problems that are extraneous to the Court: it solves problems that the politicians have been unable to tackle efficiently.[23]

The EU is a particular example of the trend towards technocratic governance, which generally renders democratic decision-making and judicial control more

[17] M Cohn, *A Theory of the Executive Branch – Tension and Legality* (OUP, 2021).

[18] ibid.

[19] LS Rossi, 'The Principle of Equality among Member States of the European Union' in LS Rossi and F Casolari (eds), *The Principle of Equality in EU Law* (Springer, 2017) 3–42, 16.

[20] L Romero Requena, 'La Commission devant la Cour de justice: l'exemple de la procédure préjudiciell' in *The Court of Justice and the Construction of Europe: Analyses and Perspectives on Sixty Years of Case-law – La Cour de Justice et la Construction de l'Europe: Analyses et Perspectives de Soixante Ans de Jurisprudence* (TMC Asser Press, 2013) 160–61.

[21] Illustrative: Case C-399/11 *Stefano Melloni v Ministerio Fiscal* ECLI:EU:C:2013:107 [57]–[64].

[22] M Dawson, B de Witte and E Muir (eds), *Judicial Activism at the European Court of Justice* (Edgar Elgar Publishing, 2013).

[23] Weiler (n 5) 263.

difficult. Knowledge production in the process of EU law-making and implementation has a crucial impact on the division of powers. The Commission, for example, relies, when proposing or amending legislation, on public consultations and the involvement of expert groups both from the private sector and civil society, and carries out an information-gathering function. The growing 'expertisation' of decision-making leads to an empowerment of the executive branch when it comes to policy-relevant knowledge production. This is commonly justified on grounds of technical complexity and specialised knowledge.[24] The Commission's expertise-based determinations are also one reason for the demands on greater transparency of evidence collection during Commission's preparatory work. The EU executive has great framing powers, but also has the effect of shifting the burden of argument. It places the legislature on the back foot, having to overcome a presumption established by 'evidence' if it wants to go another way.

It is generally acknowledged that the EU evolves through crises, and the last decade has offered crises of many kinds. Instead of a return to normalcy after the passing of the acute stage of the crisis, crisis measures in the EU gradually tend turn into the 'new normal' when the measures become an established part of the *acquis* and the EU toolkit.[25] This seems to echo the Giorgio Agamben's description of a 'permanent state of exception' in which necessity is first invoked as a ground for not following the law and then, with time, transforms the 'exception' into the 'rule'.[26] These developments have affected all three branches and the balance of their powers. The EU's executive institutions have taken on new tasks, making the exercise of executive power more difficult to control. For example, in the area of economic governance, through the supervision and control of imbalances post Euro-crisis, the EU has disregarded the principle of enumerated powers while disrespecting the democratic legitimacy of national institutions, in particular the budgetary powers of parliaments.[27] Similarly, the breadth and depth of issues dealt with in international trade and investment agreements has expanded tremendously. However, even after the continuous expansion of the role of the European Parliament in the negotiation and conclusion of international agreements,[28] international treaty-making firmly remains under the control of EU executive actors, namely the Commission and to a more limited extent the Council. In other words, when the range of policy issues expands and the regulatory effects of these agreements deepen, powers shift into a realm where the legislature and the judiciary are on the back foot. Moreover, crisis solutions have also strengthened actors formally falling outside the EU's normal institutional framework (such as the Eurogroup)

[24] C Holst and A Gornitzka, 'The Expert-Executive Nexus in the EU: An Introduction' (2015) 3 *Politics and Governance* 1; M Weimer and A De Ruijter, 'Regulating Risks in the European Union: The Co-production of Expert and Executive Power' in M Weimer and A de Ruijter (eds), *Regulating Risks in the European Union: The Co-production of Expert and Executive Power* (Hart Publishing, 2017).

[25] On this, see eg P Leino-Sandberg and M Ruffert, 'Next Generation EU and its constitutional Ramifications' (2022) 59 *Common Market Law Review* 433.

[26] See G Agamben, *State of Exception* (The University of Chicago Press, 2005).

[27] See eg C Joerges and M Weimer, 'A Crisis of Executive Managerialism in the EU: No Alternative?' in G de Búrca, C Kilpatrick and J Scott (eds), *Critical Legal Perspectives on Global Governance: Liber Amicorum David M Trubek* (Hart Publishing, 2014) 314.

[28] C Eckes, 'How the European Parliament's participation in international relations affects the deep tissue of the EU's power structures' (2014) 12 *International Journal of Constitutional Law* 904.

or acting jointly with EU institutional actors exercising their functions formally outside the formal EU Treaty framework.

When emergency powers and crisis measures are used, mechanisms of judicial scrutiny are particularly important from the perspective of the substantive conception of the rule of law.[29] The permanent effect of various crisis solutions, justified at the time of their adoption with 'exceptional circumstances', on the EU's institutional relationships and power structures has so far received far little attention, nor has the Court proved particularly wiling to scrutinise them. The role of the European Court of Justice has changed as the level of review it exercises has remained low in crisis situations.[30] During crises the European Council has often taken a leading role in solving political deadlocks. This has also led to a debate about the effect of its conclusions on executive and legislative work in the EU.[31] As a body entrusted with no formal legislative powers, the European Council escapes procedural rules. The executive and legislative actors have nevertheless found their discretion significantly reduced by solutions already found at the highest political level.[32] This presents fundamental democratic limitations of the decision-making practices: 'for law-making to become democratic, it cannot end up in intergovernmental ad hoc decisions that bypass an already established procedure whenever convenient.'[33] At the same time, it is difficult to think of any case where the implementation of a deal made in the European Council was hindered by the Court of Justice. In practice, the Court 'places considerable reliance on the emergency of the situation' and its pragmatic approach 'resonates the crisis language'.[34]

This collection examines these power dynamics in the EU through several combined and separate horizontal and vertical inquiries demonstrating how recent economic and political developments affect the EU's institutional framework. For this purpose, it analyses how the different branches of government, from different layers of governance, co-determine each other's powers in EU governance structures today. This edited collection examines three fields: the Economic and Monetary Union (EMU), migration, and trade through the lens of separation of powers. These fields are selected based on three criteria: (1) politically controversial; (2) rights-sensitive; and (3) having been in their own way subjected to crisis narratives. They are for these reasons particularly salient for unearthing de facto power shifts between the EU and the Member States, as well as between the EU institutions. These three examples enable the authors to explore how recent developments relate on the allocation and interaction of powers between the three branches of government within the EU.

[29] D Dyzenhaus, *The Constitution of Law: Legality in a Time of Emergency* (CUP, 2006) 42.

[30] P Leino-Sandberg, *The Politics of Legal Expertise in EU Policy Making* (CUP, 2021); AW Ghavanini, 'The CJEU's Give-and-Give Relationship with Executive Actors in Times of Crisis' (2023) *European Law Open* 284.

[31] See eg in the context of Case C-156/21 *Hungary v European Parliament v Council* ECLI:EU:C:2022:97 and C-157/21 *Poland v Parliament and Council* ECLI:EU:C:2022:98, which involve questions of the European Council's role in the rule of law framework and the general regime of conditionality for the protection of the EU budget.

[32] Leino-Sandberg and Ruffert (n 25).

[33] C Möllers, *The Three Branches: a comparative model of separation of powers* (OUP, 2013) 194.

[34] C Kombos, 'Constitutional review and the economic crisis: In the courts we trust?' (2019) 25 *European Public Law* 105, 126–127.

Our ambition has been to reach 'beyond law': to make the daily practices of institutions visible for a critical examination. This is why several of the chapters rely on empirical research methods. In chapter eleven, Ghavanini, Östlund and Waldenström base their analysis on hand-coded data from the SepaRope Judiciary Dataset that includes all Court cases decided between 1 January 2010 and 31 December 2020 in the selected policy fields EMU, trade and migration.[35] Krajewski's chapter builds on interviews conducted with EU officials, experts and stakeholders. In chapter four, Gnes and Sormunen combine legal and political science approaches through documentary analysis and interviews, as well as access to documents requests and a complaint to the European Ombudsman. In chapter nine, Ronkainen analyses a data set of Court pleadings received through access to documents requests but also engages in a multidisciplinary analysis of the economic merits of the legal argumentation presented by the institutions. The latter two chapters also make visible what is not visible: Ronkainen's requests were initially rejected and the documents later disclosed, but only in part, which makes some of the institutional arguments difficult to analyse. Much of the joint research project by Gnes and Sormunen evolved specifically around the attempt to shed light on the informal practices of migration control where access to documents requests were used systematically as a method for studying the informalisation of EU readmission policy arrangements. While most of the relevant documents were not disclosed, it contributed to uncovering secretive practices of the EU executive as the authors gained insights into the rationale driving readmission policy in general.[36]

II. Separation of Powers: Why does it Matter?

Separation of powers is the traditional and well-known concept referring in practice to a designation and delimitation (rather than separation) of powers with mutual control structures and constraints between the three branches: the legislative, executive and judicial. We distinguish between separation of powers as a *concept* that serves as a regulatory ideal that has an *identifiable purpose* but cannot be realised entirely, and the different *conceptions* of separation of powers, ie, realisations of that purpose in the different legal orders.

Separation of powers is primarily concerned with preventing the concentration of power in a single source through procedural rules and institutional boundaries, rather than with the substantive outcome of decision-making. It focuses on the procedural and institutional 'how' of law-making. The concept of separation of powers is open to change, including change that has consequences for the precise division of powers

[35] For a detailed description of research methods for compiling the SepaRope judiciary dataset for the analysis, see A Wallerman-Ghavanini et al, 'An Empirical Approach to Separation of Powers in the EU' (2022) 1 *CERGU Working Paper Series*.

[36] See D Gnes and M Sormunen, 'Learning through rejection: studying the informalisation of EU readmission policy with access to documents requests' in M Hillebrandt, P Leino-Sandberg and I Koivisto (eds), *(In)visible European government. Critical approaches to transparency as an ideal and a practice* (Routledge, 2023) 72.

between the branches, as a natural part of democratic processes. Therefore, separation of powers is not about substantial restrictions but about procedural guarantees.[37] We understand the non-concentration of power to serve the double objectives of ensuring collective will-formation and control of those in power.[38] Different conceptions of separation of powers are legally prescribed in the constitutions of various states and other political entities, but in reality the relations between the branches of government develop dynamically through practice.

In the EU context the concept of 'institutional balance' is more often used than separation of powers. Rather than actual balance, this doctrine refers to the prerogatives of each institution under the Treaties. Article 13(2) TEU stipulates that each institution 'shall act within the limits of the powers conferred on it in the Treaties, and in conformity with the procedures, conditions and objectives set out in them'. It links the principle of conferral to the institutional balance as 'a system for distributing powers among the different … institutions, assigning to each institution its own role in the institutional structure of the [Union] and the accomplishment of the tasks entrusted to the [Union]'.[39] This aim of this coupling seems to be to protect the rules governing will-formation within the Union from interference by the Member States or the EU institutions.[40] When assessing interinstitutional cases the Court mirrors the institutional practice against the relevant Treaty provisions. For the purposes of this collection, institutional balance represents a particular *conception* of power differentiation, as it is realised within the EU.[41] This EU conception can be evaluated in the light of the concept of separation of powers and its purpose. For this reason of conceptual distance, we find separation of powers a more useful lens for a normative examination of the empirical power shifts in the EU.

This edited collection is based on a *relational conception* of separation of powers, which emphasises interaction, collaboration and conflict between branches rather than a strict separation. Will-formation in a relational understanding of separation of powers *includes* control functions throughout the process. Repeated instances of mutual control between the three branches ensure that collective will is continuously formed and reformed by institutions guarding the prerogatives, interests and claims to legitimacy that they are mandated to defend.

The relational conception is different from both an institutional conception of separation of powers, under which institutions perform a distinct constitutional role as opposed to a clear function,[42] and a functionalist approach, which focusses on identifying the core tasks of the different branches.[43] Our conception may be seen as closer

[37] Möllers (n 33) 77–79.

[38] Möllers (n 33).

[39] Case C-70/88 *EP v Council* ECLI:EU:C:1990:217 [21].

[40] Case C-28/12 *Commission v Council (US Air Transport Agreement)* ECLI:EU:C:2015:282 [41] et seq.

[41] JP Jacqué, 'The Principle of Institutional Balance' (2004) 41 *Common Market Law Review* 383. R Schütze, 'Constitutionalism and the European Union' in C Barnard and S Peers (eds), *European Union Law*, 2nd edn (OUP, 2017) 87–88. Convincingly questioning the conceptual clarity of institutional balance: G Conway, 'Recovering a Separation of Powers in the European Union' (2011) 17 *European Law Journal* 304.

[42] PL Strauss, 'Formal and Functional Approaches to Separation of Powers Questions: A Foolish Inconsistency?' (1987) 72 *Cornell Law Review* 488, 493.

[43] J Waldron, 'Separation of Powers in Thought and Practice' (2013) 54 *Boston College Law Review* 441; MJC Vile, *Constitutionalism and the Separation of Powers* (OUP, 1967).

to a collaborative model;[44] however, it does not express a normative guideline that the branches 'should' strive to collaborate. On the contrary, we emphasise that conflict can have a distinct value in democratic will-formation. We also consider that the utility of institutional conflict to make disagreement procedurally productive is potentially even greater in the multilayered and polycentric construction of the EU. Thus, conflict is not a necessary evil, but a necessity in separation of powers that serves to enable democratic law-making. It is a feature rather than a bug in separation of powers.

In this focus on collaboration and conflict, we show how the interactions between the institutions and between the institutions and the Member States have evolved in the context of crisis, and how consensual decision-making has become the rule, sidelining those that could suggest, defend and develop alternatives, suppressing channels in which such alternatives could come up.

Separation of powers is the institutional setting that is amongst other things aimed to protect the rights of citizens and their place in the collective will-formation. However, while citizens are represented in, and benefit from, the democratic safeguards that result from separation of powers, they are not themselves actors in the institutional set-up. In the EU, citizens have weak legal and political links with the federal polity. Their EU citizenship, including the political rights that come with it, depends on their position as citizens of the Member States. The exercise of their political rights in the EU is structured along national fault lines. The public sphere, media coverage and judicial settings remain centred on national institutions. Trans-linguistic and trans-national engagements remain limited to the exchanges of selected groups and are often focused on selected topics. Our relational conception of separation of powers emphasises that the institutional set-up must allow citizens with very diverse views and partially irreconcilable convictions to see their perspectives taken up and represented in the institutional collaboration and the resolution of political conflict. Möllers pointedly argues that 'the democratic process depends on a consensus on the procedure, but also on dissident on the merits.'[45] Even if the institutions have broad agreement on the merits on certain topics, citizens may not share that conviction. Democratic society is characterised by the difference of opinions. This highlights why decision-making based on the idea that consensus is possible and desirable, including on deeply controversial political issues, by definition, cannot make all citizens see their views reflected.

Within the relational conception of separation of powers, interaction, collaboration and conflict between the three branches form part and parcel of the ideal of the separation of powers. Separation of powers both '*restrains* and *constitutes power*.'[46] Political power 'can be divided without decreasing it, and the interplay of powers with their checks and balances is even liable to generate more power, so long, at least, as the interplay is alive and has not resulted in a stalemate'.[47] In other words, separation of powers does not only serve confinement of the three branches, but also has a constructive constitutive function to enable law-making.

[44] A Kavanagh, 'The Constitutional Separation of Powers' in D Dyzenhaus and M Thorburn, *Philosophical Foundations of Constitutional Law* (OUP, 2016). A Kavanagh, *The Collaborative Constitution* (CUP, 2023).

[45] Möllers (n 33) 76.

[46] Möllers (n 33) 10.

[47] H Arendt, *The Human Condition*, 2nd edn (University of Chicago Press, 2018) 201.

As Leino-Sandberg and Minkkinen elaborate in chapter two, inter-institutional relations presume the potentiality of disagreements, where politics is an outcome of disagreement and contestation between actors with different and often incompatible interests that are played out in the exercise of public powers. The commitment in decision-making procedures to interaction between different actors is an institutional means of ensuring that different points of view are considered. This allows the channelling of conflict and disagreement in an increasingly heterogeneous and politicised, in certain respects even conflictualised environment.

In this edited collection, we analyse the emergence of new divisions of power in the EU against the traditional term referring to a designation and delimitation of public powers with mutual control structures and constraints between the three branches of government.[48] We also address in particular concerns relating to the increase of executive powers against the traditional tripartite institutional model, which requires clearly distinguishable legislative and executive branches. Each of the chapters reflects on the power shifts between the branches of government in one or several areas, over time, or in relation to the regulatory ideal. They consider whether collective will-formation is functioning effectively in the respective area and whether the three branches are able to fulfil their task of law-making adequately; whether constructive will-formation and control remain ensured; and whether all three branches are autonomously engaged in the process of law-making.

One focus throughout the collection is the question of whether and to what extent the idea of consensual decision-making that lacks the counterweight of a different perspective is or is not able to engage and resolve potential conflicts; whether alternatives to the mainstream position are brought in and considered in the respective area; and whether institutional conflict is visible. The different chapters identify instances where conflict has been channelled into EU decision-making and instances where one institution or part of one branch fills the vacuum of inaction left by another. A good example of the former is the 2022/23 process of attempted reform and then withdrawal from the ECT, which is a mixed agreement with an Investor State Dispute Settlement Mechanism over which the EU and the Member States need to decide jointly (Eckes). While the coordinated withdrawal of the EU and its Member States remains difficult at this point and the ECT can also serve as an example of political paralysis at the EU level, the growing controversy about the desirability of investment protection in light of the green transition has nonetheless brought national governments in action against the EU decision-making process that was – up to that point – dominated by the Commission. As an example of the latter, ie where one branch steps in for the other, one could look at the repeated willingness of the German Federal Constitutional Court (GFCC) in reviewing (the national ratification of) European law (de Boer). This willingness and the GFCC's express attempts to strengthen the German Parliament may be read as motivated by the realisation that (national) parliamentary control of European law is too weak and hence the intention to counterbalance this with judicial intervention.

[48] C Eckes, P Leino-Sandberg and W Ghavanini, 'Conceptual Framework for the Project Separation of Powers for 21st Century Europe (SepaRope)' (2021) Amsterdam Law School Research Paper.

Examining EU governance through the lens of separation of powers reveals that governance shifts from the tripartite model explained above to a model in which a strong executive represents a single source of public power (Leino-Sandberg and Minkkinen). Various chapters demonstrate how the power of the executive is not counterbalanced by a sufficiently strong legislature and is generally supported by the judiciary (Gnes and Sormunen; Ronkainen), resulting in a dual model in which the legislature and the executive effectually merge into one. This leaves the legislature unable to control the executive, while the Court does not take this as its cue to step in.

In addition, the judiciary seems unwilling to provide the interaction of autonomous branches that establishes the crucial mechanisms of will-formation and control as foreseen by separation of powers. Various authors demonstrate that the EU Courts do not bring in a distinct perspective or exercise true control that would be capable of channelling opposition and challenge into the law-making process (Krajewski; Gnes and Sormunen; Ghavanini et al; Westlund; Ronkainen; Eckes). The weakness of judicial review is sometimes explained with reference to the complexity of technocratic decision-making (Morvillo) or the complexity and plurality of actors involved (Coman-Kund). Various authors also demonstrate how the Court of Justice's vagueness and hesitancy to offer adequate channels of conflictual engagement pushes national courts to step in and exercise constitutional scrutiny (de Boer; Ronkainen; Fasone; Eckes). At the EU level, the result is a model of consensual decision-making that lacks both political and judicial channels for opposition or mechanisms for control (Ankersmit; Gnes and Sormunen) but tries to solve highly political issues through an administrative approach (Möllers; Ronkainen).

III. Detailed Synopsis

The book consists of four parts. Part I introduces the conception of separation of powers on which this collection is based. It focusses on the cooperative and conflictual interaction between the different actors. This conceptualisation provides the umbrella for the following parts that explore the exercise of public power in the EU in practice.

Parts II–IV each further pursue the relations and interactions between (at least) two of the three branches as they play out in the three policy fields of migration, EMU and trade. Part II explores the relation between the legislative and the executive power, zooming in on the Commission as the main Union executive institution and investigating its relations to both national parliaments and the European Parliament in the three policy fields. Part III contains three contributions examining the relations between the Court of Justice and relevant executive and legislative actors within the Union. This includes on the side of the executive the European Central Bank, and the Member States.

Part IV takes a step back and compares the different policy fields with a focus on issues of particular importance for the modern-day EU, such as decision-making in a globalised context, the role of expertise in these decisions, and the phenomenon of shared powers and composite procedures in the adoption of hybrid acts. It also shares the conclusions that highlight comparative aspects of the analyses of the substantive chapters and discusses how the conception of separation of powers should be understood in contemporary EU.

In Part I two chapters propose conceptual considerations that guide the inquiries in the remaining chapters. Päivi Leino-Sandberg and Panu Minkkinen point out in chapter two that the factual institutional relationships in the EU are closer to a dual model than a traditional tripartite separation. The legislature's position in the EU is relatively weak to begin with. This could lead the EU Courts to take up the task of protecting rights and counter-balancing the other branch(s). Instead, the ECJ has increasingly acted as a guarantor of the EU executive's positions in the service of the project of deeper integration. The missing control mechanisms between the institutions, the non-existent or weak parliamentary scrutiny of the executive, and the tendency of the judiciary to tacitly advance the executive's agenda all contribute towards what classical notions of the separation of powers specifically sought to avoid, namely, the undemocratic concentration of public power. In chapter three, Christoph Möllers discusses for the EU the relation between the political homogeneity of a democratic federation and its organisation in separated powers. To put it simply, his contribution asks: which branch of the EU should be in charge of addressing the rule of law and democracy crises in some of its Member States? What about the relationship between law and politics? And how does the rather unique structure of the EU react to this topic? Möllers argues that the problem of politically deviant Member States is not new and has no settled institutional solution. The distinction between legal, administrative and political solutions demonstrates that such a core political problem should only be addressed by organs with a solid political legitimacy of their own. He argues that the central separation of powers feature missing in the EU is a unitary governmental function, which explains the lack of convincing institutional answers to the problem of deviant member states in the EU.

Part II is dedicated to the relationship between the political branches: the legislative and the executive. Four chapters highlight different aspects of that relationship in the policy fields of migration and trade. In chapter four, Davide Gnes and Milka Sormunen examine how non-binding arrangements have proliferated in the external dimension of migration and asylum policy, especially in readmission policy. They posed two interrelated questions through the analytical lens of political conflict, namely how the European Parliament and European Ombudsman have responded to the scrutiny and control challenges posed by this informalisation; and why these institutions have been reluctant or unable to challenge the conduct by the executive – here represented by the Commission and the Council of the EU. Both have in practice refrained from engaging in an actual political confrontation with the EU executive over informalisation of readmission policy. From the perspective of separation of powers, this appears highly problematic. The authors argue that a focus on a multi-faceted conceptualisation of conflict may help us understand how and why certain executive actors gain powers.

Laurens Ankersmit argues in chapter five that, despite a strengthening of the powers of the European Parliament under the Lisbon Treaty, the EU process of treaty-making in the area of trade is still dominated by the Commission and the Council. The author traces how this executive dominance is caused by the autonomy of the Commission during negotiations, the lack of a mandate from the European Parliament, the limited legal requirements for public debate and deliberation, and the potential for binding the legislature through executive action. As a result of this dominance, collective will-formation in the making of trade agreements in the EU is hampered. Finally, the author proposes ways to improve will-formation in trade agreements: 'parliamentarisation', deconstitutionalising trade agreements, introducing transparency obligations, and limiting the autonomy of the Commission.

In chapter six, Piotr Krajewski submits that the Commission's relative advantage over other EU institutions in the negotiation and conclusion of trade agreements stems from the combination of formal powers and expertise. He demonstrates how the Commission draws on its expertise and framing powers to define the long-term trade policy programme of the EU, seeking synergies between unilateral, plurilateral and multilateral measures. The same applies to Sustainability Impact Assessments (SIAs) addressing trade and investment agreements under negotiation and position papers accompanying them. Therein, the Commission endorses specific policy recommendations of external consultants and can selectively put emphasis on some findings of SIAs, all the while defending the cohesion of its trade policy agenda.

In chapter seven, Merijn Chamon shows that the inclusion of regulatory cooperation chapters in EU trade agreements has been contested by civil society and academics primarily based on democracy and throughput legitimacy arguments. In contrast, from a separation of powers perspective regulatory cooperation is, at least at first sight, innocuous since it is does not alter the internal procedures for the adoption of regulation and does not prescribe any substantive outcomes. However, this conclusion changes when regulatory cooperation is not assessed from a binary perspective opposing legality and illegality, but when scope is created for *a-legality*. Relying on Margit Cohn's internal tension model, Chamon argues that regulatory cooperation chapters constitute fuzzy law since they leave unbounded discretion to the executive and, in addition, they leverage an internal executive-driven deregulatory agenda to the international plane, insulating it from domestic contestation.

Part III turns to the relationship between the judiciary on the one hand and the other two branches – not coincidentally most often the executive – on the other. In chapter eight, Martin Westlund concludes that in the external dimension of migration law, EU executive actors pursue political aims by circumventing EU institutional powers. They challenge the EU separation of powers by adopting agreements without the European Parliament's involvement, curtailing the European Court of Justice's jurisdiction, and acting beyond their competences. Human rights and constitutional principles theoretically constitute powerful tools for judicial scrutiny of executive action. However, Westlund argues that the ECJ has mainly opted for rulings upholding and strengthening the powers of the executive actors involved in developing this field of law: Member State governments, national authorities, and EU agencies and institutions. In most cases, the ECJ has expanded executive powers under the Treaties and granted discretion to the Member State governments.

Antti Ronkainen demonstrates in chapter nine how the European Central Bank's (ECB) unconventional monetary instruments have transformed the ECB as an institution. He argues that the ECJ's preliminary rulings regarding government bond purchases have not only allowed the ECB to determine its own competences but also provided it with legal arguments to further expand its powers over both the sovereign debt markets and Euro Member States' fiscal policies. The transformation of the ECB's mandate has taken place without associated political or constitutional processes in the legislative and executive branches. Presenting government bond purchase programmes only as a continuation of the Economic and Monetary Union's (EMU) economic constitution has been mainly legal hocus-pocus that has led to an incomplete understanding of the ECB's institutional transformation.

In chapter ten, Cristina Fasone critically assesses the constitutional case law on the Euro crisis reform of the economic governance and implementation of Next Generation EU in France, Italy, Portugal and Spain. She demonstrates that constitutional courts have not acted as guardians of the democratic process or parliaments as budgetary authorities. Problems of separation of powers between the legislative and the executive branch have not been addressed by these courts and the case law tends to develop in continuity with the past. Judicial deference in most cases runs in favour of governments, thus strengthening the long-standing path to executive dominance. Political tensions and conflicts stemming from economic governance reforms have seldom been used by constitutional courts as opportunities to correct and revise the malfunctioning of the separation of powers' relationship.

Anna Ghavanini, Allison Östlund and Anna Waldenström show in chapter eleven how migration as a politically controversial, crisis-ridden and rights-sensitive policy field poses particular challenges for the separation of the powers between the three branches. Focusing on the judicial control of the two political branches, they trace how the ECJ's choices contribute to defining the interactions between the political and judicial branches in the diagonal relationship between the Union level judiciary and Member State executive and legislative bodies. They argue that EU judicial control of decentralised executive and legislative power is functional, hampered neither by judicial overreach nor by undue docility, and at least to some extent resisting a trend of conflating the two political branches. They question whether the Court's comparatively more active role vis-à-vis the national legislative and executive branches may not in fact amplify the position of the Union political powers, reinforcing the authoritative effects of EU law in the Member States.

In chapter twelve, Christina Eckes analyses, through a separation of powers lens, how the ECJ tries to strike a balance between the political autonomy of the EU and of the Member States in the context of trade agreements, where the Council, the Commission and national governments act alongside each other as an externally strengthened top-level split-executive. Separation of powers requires that the law and case law allocate responsibilities reasonably clearly and that decision-making in the EU can ultimately be traced back to national and European citizens (two-pronged structure of legitimation). Eckes concludes that the Court's attempt to walk a tightrope between EU and Member States' political autonomy contributes to the complexity of the legal constructions that are necessary for the EU to participate in international treaty-making. This removes the EU further from the ideal of separation of powers.

Part IV collects three cross-cutting inquiries which bring together analyses of all three policy fields from a particular perspective. It also contains the editors' conclusions, drawing on the collection as a whole. In chapter thirteen, Marta Morvillo recalls that expertise is one of the ways in which the three branches exercise their power and control each other. She asks in what way(s) each of the three branches is empowered and/or disempowered by the availability and deployment of expertise. Her analysis starts from each of the three areas' most emblematic configuration of the expert-executive nexus: the ECB in EMU, the Commission and its expert groups in trade, and Frontex in migration. Her findings yield a concerning picture, whereby the executive tends to monopolise expertise, encountering a very limited and erratic counterbalance from the other two branches. When it comes to expertise, the EU is an example of separation of powers failure, which undermines expertise's potential to effectively contribute will-formation and control.

In chapter fourteen, Florin Coman-Kund discusses hybrid decision-making procedures within the executive branch, comparing instance of hybridity in the three policy fields examined in this edited collection. These procedures are characterised by complex decision-making and implementation processes that in increasingly intricate ways involve both Union and national actors, with the final decision requiring participation of both. This chapter demonstrates how these hybrid procedures stand in tension with separation of powers. Hybridity obscures responsibilities and creates blind spots in the common accountability and control structures. Coman-Kund suggests addressing these blind spots by: (1) enhancing transparency regarding the ways in which such powers are exercised; and (2) developing multilevel control mechanisms bringing together EU and national actors.

Nik de Boer assesses in chapter fifteen whether the review of European law by national constitutional courts could address the EU's separation of powers problems. Examining the German Federal Constitutional Court's (GFCC) case law on the EU, he argues that constitutional courts instead risk exceeding the limits of their proper role and end up deciding contested political issues on the EU that would be better left to legislative institutions. To avoid this dilemma, de Boer reasons that constitutional courts should concentrate on protecting the room for legislatures to decide on fundamental constitutional questions regarding the EU.

The collection builds on a three-year research consortium 'Separation of powers for 21st century Europe (SepaRope)' between the Universities of Amsterdam, Gothenburg and Helsinki financed through the programme 'NORFACE Democratic Governance in a Turbulent Age' funded by a group of European Academies of Science and the European Commission through the Horizon2020 Programme.

2

From Separated Powers to Consensual Executive Government in the EU

PÄIVI LEINO-SANDBERG AND PANU MINKKINEN

I. Introduction

As a principle, separation of powers is, no doubt, a constitutive element of democratic governance. Its democratic pedigree can be communicated in different ways. It can be seen as an essential element of democracy per se,[1] or it can be introduced as a logically necessary condition of other central principles, such as the rule of law.[2] The standard configuration of this separation involves three independent branches of government as in Immanuel Kant's 'political trinity'[3] where each 'person' of the trinity oversees the activities of the other two. The democratic aim of the oversight is, using the American vernacular, to provide 'checks and balances' that would prevent abuses of public power by one branch or another and pre-empt the concentration of public power into too few hands.[4] All such presentations of separation of powers are, of course, simplifications and idealisations. They overdetermine the ways in which public power supposedly operates and how the reciprocal checks and balances are meant to temper that power. In this liberal model, the inter-institutional oversight supposedly also produces a balance that allows the statist or transnational entity to go about its business in a way that is deemed democratic. In his influential article, Eric Barendt identifies four democratic values that a separation of powers can enhance: it protects from government tyranny; it sets limits to legislative supremacy; it reduces arbitrariness in government; and it promotes efficiency in government.[5] As Koen Lenaerts argued in 1991, the separation of powers

[1] As in, eg, United Nations General Assembly Resolution, *Enhancing the role of regional, subregional and other organizations and arrangements in promoting and consolidating democracy* A/RES/59/201 (20 December 2004) para 1.

[2] Such as the rule of law as in, eg, European Commission for Democracy through Law (Venice Commission), *Rule of Law Checklist* (Council of Europe, 18 March 2016) 35.

[3] I Kant, *The Metaphysics of Morals* (Mary Gregor tr, Cambridge University Press, 1991) 125.

[4] eg C Montesquieu, *The Spirit of the Laws* (Anne M Cohler tr, Cambridge University Press, 1989) 157.

[5] E Barendt, 'Separation of Powers and Constitutional Government' (1995) *Public Law* 599, 601–05. For a critical assessment, see NW Barber, *The Principles of Constitutionalism* (Oxford University Press, 2018) 51–84.

shields 'the subjects of law against any concentration of power in a single authority' and 'thus contributes in a very fundamental way to upholding the democratic character of a legal order'.[6] Therefore, he argued, the 'European Community cannot remain indifferent to the imperatives flowing from this principle in relation to the structuring of its own constitutional system of exercise of public authority'.[7] We agree, and like Conway, we find that separation of powers remains 'normatively attractive as a means of practically safeguarding the principles of democracy and the rule of law'.[8]

In this chapter, we investigate the way in which separation of powers has developed in current societal discourse more generally and as it applies to the institutional make-up of the EU more specifically. One could well argue that the EU does not include separation of powers at all. In both institutional and academic debates, its claimed *sui generis* character is often seen to justify not applying a classic separation of powers analysis to it. As the Court stressed in *Opinion 2/13*, the EU is 'precluded by its very nature from being considered a State'; instead, it is to be considered 'a new kind of legal order, the nature of which is peculiar to the EU, its own constitutional framework and founding principles, a particularly sophisticated institutional structure and a full set of legal rules to ensure its operation'.[9]

This does not need to be where the discussion ends. There is 'no particular proposition of political or legal morality can be automatically inferred or excluded from the attributed generic novelty of the EU relative to States'.[10] The academic literature addressing this question is rather dated. In the article by Lenaerts quoted above, he argues that 'an organic understanding of the separation of powers is not practicable' in the EU context as it 'simply appears impossible to characterise the several Community institutions as holders of one or the other power'. Instead, one should adopt a 'functional' understanding of the concept.[11] More often, the concept itself is avoided by using alternatives. The most dominant one is the Court-invented 'institutional balance',[12] which effectively places the monopoly of interpretation on the Court itself, and in practice 'conjoins the distribution of power between the member states and among Union organisations, the effect of which tends to strengthen the latter',[13] or is 'too vague and indeterminate to be a satisfactory alternative'.[14] Questions relating to the exercise of power can also be framed as a question of 'competences' instead of powers, or a 'horizontal division' instead of a separation.[15]

[6] K Lenaerts, 'Some Reflections on the Separation of Powers in the European Community' (1991) 28 *Common Market Law Review* 11, 12.

[7] ibid 35.

[8] G Conway, 'Recovering a Separation of Powers in the European Union' (2011) 17 *European Law Journal* 304, 304.

[9] *Opinion 2/13* ECLI:EU:C:2014:2454 [158].

[10] Conway (n 8) 304.

[11] Lenaerts (n 6) 12–13.

[12] See eg J-P Jacqué, 'The Principle of Institutional Balance' (2004) 41 *Common Market Law Review* 383; Conway (n 8).

[13] C Möllers, *The Three Branches: A Comparative Model of Separation of Powers* (Oxford University Press, 2013) 47.

[14] Conway (n 8) 304.

[15] eg T Konstadinides, *Division of Powers in European Union Law. The Delimitation of Internal Competence between the EU and the Member States* (Wolters Kluwer, 2009) esp at 51–80.

We argue in this chapter that the EU's institutional make-up was never designed to mirror the separation of powers in democratic nation-states at all. Instead, the EU relies on some of the language familiar from separation of powers frameworks to allude to its democratic pedigree. European democracy action plan (2020) emphasises how 'Democracy, the rule of law and fundamental rights are the foundations on which the European Union is based' and how 'Democracy allows citizens to shape laws and public policies at European, national, regional and local levels. It requires safeguards, checks and balances, and institutions that fulfil their roles and uphold the rules of pluralistic democratic debate.'[16]

Instead of forming the foundational principles that the EU institutional framework would mirror and be designed to uphold, these values seem to be primarily, and sometimes solely, applicable to the Member States. The Charter of Fundamental Rights, of course, applies to the EU institutions and the Member States when they apply EU law. However, its final provisions leave a great deal of discretion to the institutions to define how these rights affect individual situations and whether a matter is framed as a fundamental rights issue at all. Instead of checks and balances, we see the EU having a horizontal design that functions as a technocratic division of labour in service of a common cause, that is, the 'European project'.

In this chapter, we draw on an agonistic framework as a way for understanding the institutional conflicts that the separation of powers may also involve. We further argue that the relationships between EU institutions are closer to a bipartite or dualistic model than a traditional nation-state tripartite separation. A similar development toward bipartite models can be seen also in many nation-states, where the executive and the legislature have gradually merged into a single political super-institution in which the executive determines the political agenda with the support of a weak rubber-stamp legislature. This places the judiciary in an opportune position to ensure that the merged institutions of government use public power in legitimate and appropriate ways. In the EU, however, the executive-led dualistic design has less to do with any institutional merging per se, but is the result of constitutional design and a direct consequence of the relatively weak position of the legislature. The European Parliament is often reduced to merely symbolising democratic values that do not necessarily apply in practice. Instead of filling in the democratic vacuum that a weak legislature has left behind, we argue that the EU Courts have increasingly seen their role as a guarantor of the executive in the service of the project of deeper integration, and seldom intervene in the processes of will-formation.

We conclude that in the EU's institutional design, the missing 'checks and balances' between the three institutions, the factually weak or non-existent parliamentary scrutiny of the executive, and the tendency of the judiciary to tacitly advance the executive's agenda all contribute towards what classical notions of separation of powers specifically sought to avoid, namely the undemocratic concentration of public power in the hands of actors with no direct democratic mandate.

[16] Commission, 'On the Democracy action plan' COM(2020) 790 final.

II. Separation, Balance and Disagreement

Theories of democracy suggest that separation of powers achieves a balance between the institutions all fulfilling their specific tasks. The idea of 'balance' implies that none of the institutions is overpowering the others at the outset. While the balance may be somewhat dynamic, no one branch should be constantly weaker or stronger than the other two.

Powers are, in other words, not only 'separated', but reciprocally 'balanced' as well. Inter-institutional relations presume the potentiality of disagreements where politics is an outcome of disagreement and contestation between actors with different and often incompatible interests that are played out in the exercise of public power. The commitment in decision-making procedures to interaction between different actors is an institutional means of ensuring that different points of view are taken into account, which is a fundamental aspect of democratic governance. This allows channelling conflict and disagreement in an increasingly heterogeneous and politicised, in certain respects even conflictualised environment.

Inter-institutional disagreements need not always *actualise* into open disputes where the institutions would make their differences public, but the *potentiality* of disagreements is always there. When inter-institutional relations are potentially conflictual, they are also intrinsically *agonistic*.[17] The Greek word '*agon*' translates into competition, contestation, strife and conflict, and it was the competitive process through which the Greeks of antiquity identified their best individuals regardless of whether at issue is the mastery of military skills, sports, poetry recital or political oratory. In contemporary political theory, agonism which sees politics essentially as an outcome of disagreement and contestation between different actors is best known from the work of, for example, William E Connolly,[18] Bonnie Honig[19] and Chantal Mouffe.[20] Agonistic inter-institutional relations often involve incompatible interests and agendas that must then be played out in the exercise of public power. Consequently, inter-institutional relations always involve the use of factual power, an element that is usually bracketed out in liberal accounts of the same phenomena. Möllers argues that:

> The democratic process depends on a consensus on the procedure, but also on dissent on the merits. The significance of conflicts for a democracy is sometimes underestimated. But it is obvious that the whole democratic process would be useless under the condition of perpetual consensus.[21]

[17] See eg P Minkkinen, 'Agonism, Democracy, and Law' in M Del Mar, B Meyler and S Stern (eds), *The Oxford Handbook of Law and the Humanities* (Oxford University Press, 2020); M Wenman, *Agonistic Democracy. Constituent Power in the Era of Globalisation* (Cambridge University Press, 2013).

[18] WE Connolly, *Identity\Difference. Democratic Negotiations of Political Paradox*, expanded edn (University of Minnesota Press, 2002).

[19] B Honig, *Political Theory and the Displacement of Politics* (Cornell University Press, 1993).

[20] C Mouffe, *Agonistics. Thinking the World Politically* (Verso, 2013). With some reservations we can identify agonistic elements even in controversial constitutional theorist Carl Schmitt's friend/enemy distinction. See C Schmitt, *The Concept of the Political*, expanded edn (George Schwab tr, University of Chicago Press, 2007).

[21] Möllers (n 13) 76.

In other words, the potentiality of institutional conflict has a distinct value in democratic governance.

III. Separation of Powers in the EU

The EU has always had its own particular take on separation of powers. While the EU emulates the democratic features of its Member States, it does not de facto have the same democratic pedigree. The characteristics of the separation of powers in the EU are, to say the least, different compared to the nation-state models adopted in most Member States. In addition to functions being shared and overlapping between the institutions, we identify several reasons for this.

First, separation of powers in the EU never started off with the democratic objectives that are central in nation-state environments. It was not established on the principles of sovereignty and popular rule, but rather has always derived its powers from 'the Member States [who] confer competences to attain objectives they have in common'. Even if Article 10 TEU recognises that 'The functioning of the Union shall be founded on representative democracy', the Treaties include fairly little on how its democratic form of governance is realised through a representative and parliamentary form of government, or requiring that public power is exercised under the law.[22] The closest that the Treaties come to the latter principle is when defining that the 'limits of Union competences are governed by the principle of conferral' (Article 5(1) TEU) and in requiring that the institutions 'act within the limits of the powers conferred on it in the Treaties'. Instead of separating powers, the idea of respecting certain boundaries is framed as a question of institutional balance: the institutions are to act 'in conformity with the procedures, conditions and objectives set out in [the Treaties]'. The EU Courts are to 'ensure that in the interpretation and application of the Treaties the law is observed' (Article 19(1) TEU). We will discuss below how this principle is applied in the EU.

Instead of democratic principles and separation of powers, the EU Treaty starts with defining the mission: the 'process of creating an ever-closer union among the peoples of Europe' (Article 1 TEU). Following this, the Treaties define an institutional 'division of labour' providing optimal efficiency to the common objective of European integration rather than to enable cross-institutional democratic oversight as such. The Treaties provide several examples of this approach. Under Article 13(1) TEU, the function of the EU's institutional framework is specifically to 'promote its values, advance its objectives, serve its interests, those of its citizens, and those of the Member States, and ensure the consistency, effectiveness and continuity of its policies and actions.' In other words, the institutions exist to pursue the EU as a political project.

Second, the EU does not have a defined conception of separation of powers, even if some of the Treaty language may create such an illusion. Concealed within this language is a fundamentally different power structure where the three branches are

[22] See eg Constitution of Finland, ss 1–3; Instrument of Government of Sweden, ch 1; German Basic Law (with the Bill of Rights placed first), Art 20; The latter requires that 'the legislature shall be bound by the constitutional order, the executive and the judiciary by law and justice'.

far from 'balanced'. Deirdre Curtin has argued that, in creating an operational separation of powers, it tends to be easier to define and delimit 'judicial power' or 'legislative power', which often leads to a 'residual' approach on executive power; the latter becomes 'power that is not exercised by anyone else – what is 'left over'.[23] In contrast, in the EU constitutional structure executive power does not come last but first; it has always been the EU's most powerful branch, which the two other branches are struggling to control. As a polity, the EU is executive-led by design. The political engines of the Union (the European Council, the Council and the Commission) would all be primarily regarded as executive institutions in the nation-state analogy, as is the EU's new power-holder, the European Central Bank, and the growing range of EU agencies, many of which exercise significant powers. Whatever changes happen, they are unlikely to alter this starting-point. The Commission is the most dominant among the executives, and its 'power is ultimately justified by its mission as an independent, impartial and authoritative body'[24] whose legitimacy is based on knowledge and specialisation.[25] Unlike national executives, the Commission cannot be regarded as an 'elected branch' since its mandate does not come, directly or indirectly, from the European citizenry. The mere fact that the Commission's competences have been spelled out in the Treaties hardly justifies those competences as 'democratic'.

Third, the position of the European Parliament has traditionally been weak in the EU construction, and the principle of parliamentarism has been difficult to identify in the Treaties. As the Court has stated, in the system governing EU powers,

> the powers of the institutions and the conditions on their exercise derive from various specific provisions of the Treaty, and the differences between those provisions, particularly as regards the involvement of the European Parliament, are not always based on consistent criteria.[26]

The lead critic of the limitations of the EU's parliamentary democracy has no doubt been the German Federal Constitutional Court, which emphasises that citizens' democratic rights are best ensured by national parliaments, as the European Parliament cannot sufficiently fill the gap between the extent of the decision-making power of the EU institutions and the citizens' democratic rights in the Member States.[27] While the engagement of national parliaments remains important because they provide the second channel of legitimacy that the EU builds on,[28] their role in the Treaties is narrow: they merely 'contribute actively to the good functioning of the Union' (Article 12 TEU) and thus promote the EU as a political project.

[23] D Curtin, *Executive Power of the European Union. Law, Practices, and the Living Constitution* (Oxford University Press, 2009) 53.

[24] MJ Martınez Iglesias, 'The Accidental Democracy: A European Model' in S Garben, I Govaere and P Nemitz (eds), *Critical Reflections on Constitutional Democracy in the European* Union (Hart, 2019) 205.

[25] ibid 203–04.

[26] Case 242/87 *Commission v Council* ECLI:EU:C:1989:217 [13].

[27] eg Lisbon Urteil, BVerfG, Urteil des Zweiten Senats vom 30. Juni 2009 – 2 BvE 2/08 -, Rn. 1-421, paras 258–60.

[28] See eg J Habermas, 'Citizens and State Equality in a Supranational Political Community: Degressive Proportionality and the Pouvoir Constituant Mixte' (2017) 55 *Journal of Common Market Studies* 171; F Scharpf, 'Legitimacy in the multilevel European polity' (2009) *MPIfG Working Paper no 1*, at www.econstor.eu/bitstream/10419/41652/1/610149423.pdf.

Over time, much has been done to strengthen the institutional position of the European Parliament. Since the Single European Act especially, the European Parliament has gradually gained more powers through Treaty changes, Court jurisprudence and through practice,[29] to the point that today, it is not clear that formal powers are the limiting factor in its effective oversight of the Commission. The European Parliament is a co-legislator on an equal footing with the Council in almost all relevant policy fields, it approves the Commission President, co-decides on the annual budget, and grants discharge to the Commission on its implementation of the budget.

Still, it does not feel like power is with the people through the European Parliament. The capacity of the European Parliament to represent a European people, and its ability to translate the voice of the electorate into a political agenda for the Commission remains weak compared to national parliaments in parliamentary democracies. This is largely down to the weakness of political organisation at the European level.[30] The European Parliament's political groups are ideologically heterogenous collections of national parties, mainly organised on the basis of the traditional left–right political spectrum. Their political agendas have little relevance for an institution that has no say on social policies, no right to tax, and whose budget essentially defined by the Member States. On matters where the EU has powers to act, electoral agendas are vague and difficult to distinguish from one another.[31] In many important votes, national interests still trump EU-political considerations in determining parliamentarians' voting behaviour. As the result, EU citizens find it difficult to identify with the European political groups, which leads to low voter turnout in European elections and, ultimately, a weak political mandate from voters.[32] As a result, Hix and Hoyland argue, the EU is 'not a particularly democratic system'. While in procedural terms it

> ticks all the boxes for a state to be considered to be democratic … in substantive terms – where the substance of democratic politics is a competition between rival elites for political power which allows citizens to make educated choices about who should govern them and the direction of the policy agenda – the EU is far from democratic.[33]

Yet, even with its shortcomings, the European Parliament constitutes the only forum for broad EU-level political debate and is important as such, and we maintain hope that it will one day grow into an efficient conduit between the people and the Commission. This indeed was the broad aim behind the amendments introduced in the Treaty of Lisbon that tightened the links of the Commission with the European Parliament.[34]

[29] See P Leino-Sandberg, 'WANTED: A Creative Lawyer with Great Technical Skills for Demanding Work in the European Parliament' in E Korkea-aho and P Leino-Sandberg (eds), *Law, Legal Expertise and EU Policy-Making* (Cambridge University Press, 2022).

[30] For a classic account, see eg A Follesdal and S Hix, 'Why There is a Democratic Deficit in the EU: A Response to Majone and Moravcsik' (2006) 44 *Journal of Common Market Studies* 533.

[31] Lately, clearer distinctions have been visible on some environmental matters while the populist groups have been rather clear in their general opposition to increasing the EU's powers.

[32] See S Hix, *What's Wrong with the European Union and How to Fix it* (Polity, 2008).

[33] S Hix and B Hoyland, *The Political System of the European Union* (Bloomsbury, 2022) 172.

[34] For the close linkages between the Commission and the Parliament, see Art 17(7)–(8) TEU, and Framework Agreement on relations between the European Parliament and the Commission [2010] OJ L304/47, 47. See also J Weiler, 'Dispatch from the Euro Titanic: And the Orchestra Played On [EJIL Editorial]' (*EJIL:Talk!*, 2 February 2011), at www.ejiltalk.org/dispatch-from-the-euro-titanic-and-the-orchestraplayed- on-ejil-editorial.

They sought to move the EU political system closer to maturity by creating a parliamentary government more similar to those in Member States, with a 'more political, and politicised, Commission elected as the "EU Executive" by a majority in the European Parliament'.[35] When elected, President Ursula von der Leyen specifically emphasised her wish to 'strengthen the *partnership* between the European Commission and the European Parliament'. In her view,

> we should give a stronger role to the voice of the people, the European Parliament, in initiating legislation. I support a right of initiative for the European Parliament. When Parliament, acting by a majority of its members, adopts resolutions requesting that the Commission submit legislative proposals, I commit to responding with a legislative act, in full respect of the proportionality, subsidiarity and better law making principles. To make this process as effective as possible, I will ask my Commissioners to work hand-inhand with the European Parliament at every stage of designing and debating resolutions. To do this I will ensure my Commissioners brief the European Parliament at all stages of all international negotiations, following the mould set by the Brexit negotiations. I will also ensure more appearances in Committee meetings and Commissioner presence in trilogue discussions between the European Parliament and the Council. … I will also ensure a permanent dialogue between the Commission and the European Parliament as a matter of priority. I will be happy to revive the tradition of a Question Hour, a regular debate with the European Parliament.[36]

At the same time, these reforms, and the vision of 'partnership' with the European Parliament create a tension with requirement that 'In carrying out its responsibilities, the Commission shall be completely independent' (Article 17(3) TEU). In practice, the Commission balances between the requirement of independence and the wish to be seen as a democratically accountable executive. As Möllers writes in his chapter, 'strong indicators exist that the Commission has for quite a while weakened its stance as a politically neutral enforcer of EU law in order to remain politically influential and successful with its policy proposals'.[37]

The reality remains that the composition and substantive agenda of the Commission have little to do with the results of the European elections or the electoral platforms of the European Parliament political groups. Instead, and despite the Parliament's best efforts to insert itself in the heart of the process through the *Spizenkandidaten*-process, the Member States have kept the selection of the Commission President and Commissioners firmly in their own hands, leaving the European Parliament only the formal Treaty power to vote on the Commission as a whole at the end of the process. Formally, the Commission is responsible as a body to the Parliament, and the latter may ultimately force the Commission to resign (Article 17(8) TEU). But while in a parliamentary system, a parliament that votes out a government would be in the driver's seat in forming the next one, in the EU, the selection of new Commission and its President would again be a task for the Member States, with the European Parliament's role in the

[35] SB Hobolt, 'A Vote for the President? The role of Spitzenkandidaten in the 2014 European Parliament elections' (2014) 21 *Journal of European Public Policy* 1528, 1538.

[36] U von der Leyen, European Commission, 'Political guidelines for the next European Commission 2019–2024' (Publications Office of the European Union, 2020), at op.europa.eu/en/publication-detail/-/publication/62e534f4-62c1-11ea-b735-01aa75ed71a1+.

[37] Möllers, ch 3 in this volume.

process mostly as a bystander. For the Parliament, forcing the Commission to resign is a nuclear option with little upside, and thus a woefully ineffective way to control the political agenda. It has so far been used only once, and even then, in the context of a corruption scandal rather than political differences.[38]

With its limited powers, what the European Parliament can and does do is to produce 'havoc' – use its rights of information, question Commission members and officials in the plenary and in the Committees, and otherwise make noise and create reputational consequences for the Commission. Occasionally, as we will discuss below, this is effective in pressuring the Commission to change its position, but it is also unpredictable and sometimes disproportionate to the issue at hand.[39] While today often acting as co-legislature in most EU policy matters, Parliament actions also continue to suffer from a lack of expertise and make it vulnerable to high influence by interest representatives, which, in addition, remains largely invisible.[40]

The weak position of the European Parliament was a key factor fuelling the debate of a 'democratic deficit' at the heart of the Union in the 1990s and leading up to the Lisbon Treaty. Today, 17 years after the Lisbon Treaty, the link between European elections and the new Commission's agenda remains as remote as it was in the 1990s. Yet, concerns about the democratic deficit have abated, and rather than remedied, the thinness of the Union's democratic veneer has come to be accepted as the norm, an aspect of the *sui generis* nature of the Union, instead of a flaw that needs to be addressed. As Möllers writes in his chapter, in the fear of engaging in complete constitutional transformation, the current state of affairs is accepted as a 'second-best solution without giving it too much justificatory credit. To translate political problems into administrative ones may be, given the state of integration, less satisfying and less acceptable from a separation of powers perspective than ever before'.[41]

The EU may dress itself in democratic vocabulary that resembles national constitutions, but beneath such garb, instead of political contestation the direction for action is provided by a mixture of technocratic instincts, faith in the European idea, and secretive machinations typical of international diplomatic circles. Open democratic debates and disagreements are considered a complication that the institutions should be protected from.[42]

IV. From Tripartite to Dualistic Models

Arend Lijphart famously claimed that systems based on proportional representation and coalition governments are more capable of promoting democratic values than

[38] In some cases, the President has requested individual members of the Commission to resign.

[39] A good example is the recent Selmayer gate, which led to a riot in the European Parliament, but had no institutional or administrative consequences within the Commission: no mistakes were admitted, no one resigned. P Leino-Sandberg, *The Politics of Legal Expertise in EU Policy Making* (Cambridge University Press, 2021) ch 5.

[40] On this, see eg P Leino-Sandberg, 'Transparency and trialogues: real legislative work for grown ups?' (2022) 14 *European Journal of Risk Regulation* 271.

[41] Möllers, ch 3 in this volume.

[42] Leino-Sandberg (n 39) chs 4 and 8.

systems based on what is known as the majoritarian Westminster model. In the latter, a political party that wins the elections usually gains an absolute majority in the legislature after which the leader of the winning party – a prime minister or other – can with relative ease further her political agenda until the next elections.[43] We can, perhaps, assume that Lijphart's observation also applies at least to some extent to interinstitutional relations. Political scientists have, however, pointed out that recent developments, especially after the terrorist attacks of 2001, 2004 and 2005 and the subsequent prominence of security concerns, have shifted models of government closer to strategically motivated political leadership and the premises of the Westminster model. In consensual governance, a prime minister or other executive leader is not only the leader of her parliamentary party or a representative of a political group in the Parliament, but also a political CEO who secures an agenda with the help of a culture of discipline. The aim of the discipline is to strengthen the strategic power of the leadership – that is, the executive – in relation to individual parliamentarians.

Claims about the increase of executive powers are still inferred from a traditional notion of separation of powers and a tripartite institutional model that requires clearly distinguishable legislative and executive branches. But in many cases, we are factually dealing with a model where two institutional persons of the 'political trinity', namely the legislature and the executive, have merged into a single political super-institution that German political scientist Winfried Steffani has termed a *Regierungsmehrheit*: literally a 'governmental majority'.[44] Such a governmental majority refers to a single institutional entity, seldom explicitly mentioned in the constitutional framework, that includes a strong executive government pushing forward a political agenda with the support of its majority in an otherwise weakened legislature. In this sense, a *Regierungsmehrheit* resembles the English expression 'the elected branches' that also conflates two institutions into one. A governmental majority can successfully draw on its democratic mandate in so far as the electorate is understood to have given its blessing to the party's political agenda. The executive then orchestrates all legislative matters by putting this political agenda into effect with the help of a legislature bound by a rigid culture of party discipline.[45]

How does this discussion apply to the EU context? In addition to the formal constitutional design slightly amended through the Treaty of Lisbon and as described above, connections between the Commission and the European Parliament have grown closer in informal ways which, though difficult to measure, affect the potential emergence of interinstitutional conflict between the two. The work plan of the Commission is negotiated with the Parliament before the election of the Commission. In practice, the Commission prepares its legislative plan as part of its annual work programme, which is also negotiated with the Parliament.[46] This provides an opportunity for the

[43] A Lijphart, Patterns of Democracy. Government Forms and Performance in Thirty-Six Countries (Yale University Press, 1999).

[44] W Steffani, 'Regierungsmehrheit und Opposition' in W Steffani (ed), *Gewaltenteilung und Parteien im Wandel* (Springer Fachmedien, 1997).

[45] See eg M Flinders, 'Shifting the Balance? Parliament, the Executive and the British Constitution' (2002) 50 *Political Studies* 23.

[46] Leino-Sandberg (n 39).

Commission to anticipate what the Parliament expects. To the extent the Parliament's inputs reflected the political agendas settled in EU elections, the process would strengthen the EU's democratic qualities. Yet, in the absence of a clear political ideology to give direction to the Parliament's work, its interventions appear rather random and incidental, motivated more by tactical and tribal considerations rather than a true political intent.

The strengthening of the relationship between the Commission and the Parliament affects also the daily work of the Commission, from the level of Commissioners to individual officials.[47] The unpredictability of Parliament reactions creates uncertainty and makes it possible for the Parliament to exercise influence on the daily work in the Commission.[48] The Parliament's influence has also been boosted by the fact that political groups have started to operate within the Commission as well as the Parliament. These connections have grown stronger as regards both agenda setting and coordination,[49] and they continue all through the legislative process. There is a perception that, in the final drafting of legislation in trialogue negotiations, the Commission's approval of a solution tends to reflect the Parliament's position.[50]

While the EU may have received a closer executive-parliament relationship, it has not yet developed into an effective means for electoral will to shape and affect agenda-setting. At the same time, the new stronger Parliament–Commission 'partnership' has also affected the latter's self-identity from a technocratic executive actor into an openly political actor,[51] a 'hybrid between an independent executive agency and a political government'.[52] Invisibility of EU policy-making may also mask underlying tensions. We could, for example, understand institutional relationships in game-theoretical terms as a 'balance of power' in which one institution reluctantly stays within certain bounds due to a fear of reprisals from another. We can formulate a few hypothetical examples by building on the distinction often made between *potentiality* and *actuality*. We can ask, for instance, whether the executive has drafted its agenda already with the legislature's potential criticism in mind, or if the legislature tempers its legislation because it anticipates what the judiciary may potentially find unacceptable if the legislation in question was tested in review.

The relationship between the Parliament and the executive is a core element of separation of powers in normal times. However, the type of governance model where a legislature is factually subjected to an executive functioning as the political engine is both typical and particularly necessary in times that are deemed to be exceptional.[53]

[47] ibid ch 5.

[48] For Piris, the 2010 Framework Agreement did not constitute an impartial interpretation of the Treaty. Instead, it aimed to modify the balance established by the Treaties between the institutions, accord powers to the Parliament not conferred by the Treaties and limit the autonomy of the Commission and its President by broadening the role of the EP in various respects. JC Piris, *The Future of Europe: Towards a Two-Speed EU?* (Cambridge University Press, 2012) 30.

[49] Leino-Sandberg (n 39) ch 5.

[50] ibid.

[51] FW Scharpf, 'Political Legitimacy in a Non-optimal Currency Area' in O Cramme and S Binzar Hobolt (eds), *Democratic Politics in a European Union under Stress* (Oxford University Press, 2015) 23.

[52] European Fiscal Board, *Annual Report 2017* (2017) 63.

[53] See eg C Rossiter, Constitutional Dictatorship. Crisis Government in the Modern Democracies (Transaction Publishers, 2002).

From the perspective of Western liberal democracies, the era after the terrorist attacks of 2001, 2004 and 2005 has undoubtedly been exceptional. Think of the new anti-terrorism measures adopted in many countries. The financial crisis, as well as the risks of new widespread pandemics and geopolitical conflicts are likely to strengthen these features further. Developments during the last decade have also made the EU even less responsive to democratic objectives. In the EU, relations between the institutions have during the past decade been affected by the EU's polycrisis, which has – like crises in general – strengthened executive actors[54] and driven the EU towards a model of highly consensual policy-making led by the executive branch, as the polycrisis model of operation has further reduced political debates among different policy alternatives.

However, while there are signs of more permanent changes in the governmental inter-institutional relations of nation-states, the growing significance of the executive branch cannot be unambiguously attributed to the exceptional crisis circumstances. Although there is more or less unanimous agreement on the increase of executive powers, especially in relation to the powers of democratically elected legislatures, the reasons for this 'constitutional crisis management' are more varied.[55]

V. Independent or 'Political' Judiciary?

In terms of standard accounts of separation of powers, nation-state environments seem to be gradually moving from textbook tripartite institutional models to more dualistic models, comprising an executive-led institution and the judiciary. This development echoes the more general shift towards executive-led 'Westminsteresque' models of government mentioned earlier. In such a dualistic model, the relative position of the judiciary will also have to change. If the traditional starting point of the tripartite separation was that a deferent judiciary primarily applied laws passed by a legislature, its motivation for showing deference to an executive institution cannot be the same. Inter-institutional relations are always relative, meaning that changes in the position of one institution will always affect the others. So, we can at least hypothesise that, in such a dualistic model, the judiciary may eventually balance the scales by taking on democratic functions that a weakened rubber-stamp legislature has lost in the merge. From a liberal perspective, this shift in judicial power may seem worrying because it suggests a more 'activist' position into which unelected courts move in relation to the elected branches. And in such a juxtaposition of two institutional entities, disagreement is always at least potential.

Alexander Hamilton, one of the best-known 'Founding Fathers' of the United States, famously wrote, together with his colleagues James Madison and John Jay, 85 newspaper articles known as 'The Federalist Papers' to support the ratification

[54] On this, see eg J Grogan, 'States of Emergency: Analysing Global Use of Emergency Powers in Response to COVID-19' (2020) 22 *European Journal of Law Reform* 338.

[55] See eg JE Owens and R Pelizzo, *The 'War on Terror' and the Growth of Executive Power? A Comparative Analysis* (Routledge, 2010).

process of the country's draft Constitution. Hamilton claimed that the judiciary cannot be regarded as a threat if its powers are defined and delimited in a rigorous enough way. Judicial power did not extend to congressional law-making or to the President's executive powers, so the courts had no influence over 'either the sword or the purse'. This is why the judiciary is, in Hamilton's well-known expression, the 'least dangerous branch'.[56]

Hamilton's allusion to 'dangerousness' calls for at least two observations. As indicated earlier, traditional accounts of the separation usually refer to a concern about public power being concentrated into too few hands. The same concern was echoed by Hamilton's colleague James Madison, who elaborated on the reciprocal mechanisms with which government branches would oversee each other's activities. In terms of the judiciary, such mechanisms of 'checks and balances' referred primarily to the constitutional review of legislation and of executive orders. Reciprocity, on the other hand, was based on the idea that if the Constitution assigned all institutions equally ambitious tasks, no single institution would be in an inferior position in relation to the others.[57] As indicated above, powers are not only 'separated', but also reciprocally 'balanced'. The institution using judicial power is deemed to be the 'least dangerous' when it functions from a position of deference in relation to a democratically elected legislature. Judicial power implies a corresponding competence which, in turn, suggests limits and boundaries that the judiciary is expected to respect, and is usually limited to applying laws in individual cases. Overstepping the boundaries of judicial power would usually be expressed by claiming that the judiciary is meddling in 'political' affairs that do not belong to the legal realm. In what circumstances could judicial power be considered political? The word 'political' can, of course, take on several different meanings here[58] – the most obvious being of course the process of politicisation of the courts that is taking place in Poland. But here we focus on the less obvious examples.

First, the judiciary is an institutional actor in the general framework that makes up a statist or a transnational entity. So as one person of the 'political trinity', the judiciary performs tasks that are significant for the trinity as a unitary political whole. In this sense, judicial power is undoubtedly also political.[59] Second, the decisions that the judiciary makes will affect the rights and obligations of individuals and incorporated entities in profound ways that can with good reason be described as political. The courts make decisions on the allocation of resources and services, and they oversee the lawfulness of public authorities performing their functions.[60] Third, individual judges can be seen as social and political influencers. They network among each other, with

[56] A Hamilton, J Madison and J Jay, *The Federalist Papers* (Oxford University Press, 2008) 380. See also AM Bickel, *The Least Dangerous Branch. The Supreme Court at the Bar of Politics*, 2nd edn (Yale University Press, 1986).

[57] ibid 256–60.

[58] eg BW Joondeph, 'The Many Meanings of "Politics" in Judicial Decision Making' (2008) 77 *University of Missouri – Kansas City Law Review*, 347.

[59] See eg B Friedman, 'The Politics of Judicial Review' (2005) 84 *Texas Law Review* 257; J Ferejohn, 'Judicializing Politics, Politicizing Law' (2004) 65 *Law and Contemporary Problems* 41.

[60] eg E Palmer, 'Resource Allocation, Welfare Rights: Mapping the Boundaries of Judicial Control in Public Administrative Law' (2000) 20 *Oxford Journal of Legal Studies* 63.

politicians and with civil servants, and their views will factually influence the way in which political decisions are made. Even in this third sense, the judiciary is part of a larger political whole.[61] All three meanings are 'positive' in the sense that they do not necessarily imply a political bias in judicial decision-making.

The discussion about a political court in the EU context is of course well-established and well-known and focuses on the role of the Court as one of the key drivers of integration. Horsley's study demonstrates the Court as using its 'direct policymaking platform in order to override, adjust or step beyond the EU legislature's clearly articulated policy choices' in manners that remain at odds with the EU Treaty framework. The way the Court applies 'directly effective norms as tools to contest and/or reshape the EU legislature's clearly articulated policy choices is fundamentally at odds with the EU Treaty framework's increasingly strong normative commitment to the value of representative democracy'.[62] The Court, like the Commission, is institutionally biased towards promoting integration, no doubt for many noble reasons, but perhaps also because more integration leads to a greater role for the institution itself. In this regard, their institutional interests coincide. In various instances, the Court has also exercised its power to bridge over and eliminate political resistance. In this respect, it is certainly an example of 'political judiciary'.

From a separation of powers perspective, this finding may be problematic as the exercise of judicial power also requires the judiciary to be independent in relation to the elected branches:[63] 'A court that depends on other branches loses its institutional virtues and starts to resemble a subdivision of the administration'.[64] Historically speaking, judicial independence was first associated with the courts' impartiality in relation to the parties of the process. The association with the elected branches is of a later origin.[65] Independence also played an important role in the development of the rule of law because it enabled the courts to secure the rights of individuals and incorporated entities who were litigating against the state or government authorities.[66] How could the independence of the courts, in principle applying laws passed by the legislator with deference, be justified? Shouldn't judges merely be 'slaves to the law', as the French expressed it?[67]

[61] eg HP Lee, *Judiciaries in Comparative Perspective* (Cambridge University Press, 2011).

[62] T Horsley, *The Court of Justice of the European Union As an Institutional Actor: Judicial Lawmaking and Its Limits* (Cambridge University Press, 2018) 265–66.

[63] See J Ferejohn, 'Independent Judges, Dependent Judiciary: Explaining Judicial Independence' (1999) 72 *Southern California Law Review* 353; S Burbank and B Friedman, *Judicial Independence at the Crossroads. An Interdisciplinary Approach* (SAGE, 2002); G Gee, R Hazell, K Malleson, and P O'Brien, *The Politics of Judicial Independence in the UK's Changing Constitution* (Cambridge University Press, 2015). From a comparative perspective, see A Seibert-Fohr, *Judicial Independence in Transition* (Springer, 2012). In the EU context, see RD Kelemen, 'The Political Foundations of Judicial Independence in the European Union' (2012) 19 *Journal of European Public Policy* 43.

[64] Möllers (n 13) 45.

[65] See eg DC North and BR Weingast, 'Constitutions and Commitment: The Evolution of Institutions Governing Public Choice in Seventeenth-Century England' (1989) 49 *Journal of Economic History* 803.

[66] B Sordi, 'Révolution, Rechtsstaat and the Rule of Law: Historical Reflections on the Emergence of Administrative Law in Europe' in S Rose-Ackerman and PL Lindseth (eds), *Comparative Administrative Law* (Edward Elgar, 2010).

[67] MF Renoux-Zagamé, 'Le "Royaume de la loi": équité et rigueur du droit selon la doctrine des parlements de la monarchie' (1998) 9 *Justices: Revue générale de droit processual* 17.

The key argument was the paradoxical claim, usually attributed to Montesquieu, that judicial power is not 'power' at all. Montesquieu believed that if all judges were appointed from untrained laymen on an *ad hoc* basis – so without either a permanent judiciary or a professional legal elite – then a judicial power that is not associated with either the state or a profession would be 'invisible and null'.[68] If this were the case, then individuals who acted lawfully would do so out of respect for the law and not for fear of the authorities. Montesquieu's idea of lay *ad hoc* courts never gained support, but the idea of a judicial '*nul-pouvoir*' lingered on. Its echoes can still be heard in the persistent delusion that decisions in the courtroom somehow resemble a logical model of subsumption. Even though the factual basis of that logical model was easy enough to falsify – namely that this is not the way in which judges actually think – it had important social and political consequences. An automated logical machine cannot namely have a will. And by the same token, it cannot use power. In this way, the judiciary could be distanced from the political institutions as 'independent' and 'impartial'.[69] Any discussion about judicial activism begins at the point where we perceive the judiciary to have a 'will' of its own in relation to the elected branches.

In contemporary times, the clearest way for the judiciary to express its independent will is through judicial and constitutional review. As a critical reviewer of primary legislation, the judiciary departs from the narrow 'deferent' definition of an applier of laws that the separation of powers implies. The judiciary can, using Alec Stone Sweet's vocabulary, interfere with primary legislation in either direct or indirect ways.[70] The interference of a disagreeing judiciary is direct when it specifically refers to its competence to do so. If the court's decision has a 'legislative' basis comparable to positing legal norms as in the case of the German Federal Constitutional Court, the judiciary becomes a disagreeing 'negative legislator', as Hans Kelsen critically described the role of constitutional courts.[71] On the other hand, a court may express disagreement with a legislative agenda more indirectly in, for example, pre-legislative consultations that at the national level often include the judiciary.

The contribution of the European Court of Justice (ECJ) to the EU's integration process is well documented and well known. The empirical work conducted in this project adds another dimension to the ECJ as a 'political court'. The exercise of judicial power requires that the judiciary is independent in relation to the elected branches. In the EU, judicial review of the other branches is not geared towards ensuring a balance of powers but rather towards safeguarding interinstitutional balance from the point of view of the roles of institutions as established by the Treaties. This means that the ECJ seldom engages with matters from a broader point of constitutionality, with the exception of scrutinising institutional action in light of fundamental rights.

[68] Montesquieu (n 4) 158.

[69] P Pasquino, 'Prolegomena to a Theory of Judicial Power: The Concept of Judicial Independence in Theory and History' (2003) 2 *The Law & Practice of International Courts and Tribunals* 18–19.

[70] A Stone Sweet, 'The Politics of Constitutional Review in France and Europe' (2007) 5 *International Journal of Constitutional Law* 69. See also A Stone Sweet, *Governing with Judges. Constitutional Politics in Europe* (Oxford University Press, 2000).

[71] H Kelsen, *General Theory of Law and State* (A Wedberg tr, Harvard University Press, 1949) 268–69.

The ECJ is also deeply committed to the EU as a political project and sees furthering it as part of its mandate. The case studies conducted in this project demonstrate that the EU judicial system is also either unwilling or unable to properly scrutinise highly political measures, particularly those taken in crisis context, such as the Euro crisis or the migration crisis. These are the contexts where the executive acts under a broad mandate, and where judicial scrutiny of exceptional powers would be particularly important. If the executive can rely on the support of a court that is not expected to intervene, this is also a democratic problem. Excess consensus calls into question the democratic process and may also lead to de-democratisation, if political conflicts remain but are not openly debated.[72]

One can of course speculate that the passivity of the Court relates to how the institutions do no wrong. Yet, it is difficult to believe in the existence of stringent constitutional scrutiny if it exists only in theory but is not applied in practice. This also broadens the institutional margin of manoeuvre quite considerably. This pattern has also been noted in the national apex courts. In December 2022, the German Federal Constitutional Court observed that referring the interpretation of the EU's Own Resources Decision to the ECJ for a preliminary ruling was not worth pursuing:

> There is also no reason to assume that the Court of Justice of the European Union would interpret the competences in Art. 122 and Art. 311(2) TFEU more narrowly than the Federal Constitutional Court. Against this background, the constitutional complaints would remain unsuccessful even after a referral.[73]

This assumption is not without empirical basis, but appears problematic from a separation of powers perspective, which presumes at least the existence of a potential conflict between the branches. A functioning constitutional democracy requires a constitutional court that takes its agonistic role seriously, with authority and credibility in the eyes of its constituencies. This requires balancing between 'activism' and deference, and we wonder if the ECJ has always achieved the right balance. A court that intervenes in the will-formation of political or executive branches is, perhaps, too much of an activist court, but a court that never intervenes is no less of a problem, as it removes a key source of potential for conflict that acts as a check to the exercise of power by the elected branches. This should be a source for concern particularly where, as in the EU, not being a state and having a low degree of political integration, the power is largely in the hands non-elected executives.

VI. Conclusion

In analysing the concept of separation of powers, the conventional liberal notions tend to emphasise competences, which does not necessarily give a very nuanced account of what is happening in the background. Instead, we proposed an agonistic premise which, unlike standard liberal accounts, suggests that all inter-institutional relations

[72] Möllers (n 13) 4.

[73] BVerfG, Judgment of the Second Senate of 6 December 2022, para. 236. English translation available at https://www.bundesverfassungsgericht.de/SharedDocs/Entscheidungen/EN/2022/12/rs20221206_2bvr054721en.html.

are potentially conflictual even if disagreements do not necessarily actualise. The disagreements are there, albeit often dormant.

We discussed how powers are possibly separated among the main institutions in both statist and transnational environments. One way of looking at recent developments is to conjecture that all three institutional persons of the 'political trinity' have the same goal of fulfilling a liberal – or possibly neoliberal – political programme. This single programme, in turn, is executed through a 'division of labour' where 'separate institutions share powers', to borrow an expression from Richard Neustadt's well-known study of the American presidency.[74] So if all institutions strive to accomplish a single political agenda, no separation of powers actually exists making all claims of 'checks and balances' equally problematic. If there is no disagreement, the unitary 'trinity' will by necessity take on an authoritarian flavour.

Looking at recent developments at the nation-state level, one can observe a gradual shift from tripartite models of government towards factually dualistic models which conflate the executive and legislative branches into a single super-institution, where the executive, supported by a weak legislature, functions as the main political engine of government. If legislative and executive powers are merged, and if the function of the legislature seems to be reduced to simply symbolising democratic values that don't necessarily work in practice, the judiciary's role becomes critical. The judiciary finds itself in a new position from which it must rethink its political and democratic tasks.

Drawing on analogy, our diagnosis of the conception of separation of powers in the EU seems to point to the following elements. The basic structure of the institutional make-up of the Union resembles a bipartite or dualistic model rather than the standard tripartite separation. Unlike in nation-state environments, in the EU, the dualistic model is not really the outcome of any 'development' from a tripartite separation but, rather, the gradual solidification of a 'division of labour' where the EU judiciary is primarily the guarantor and legitimator of the Commission's political project of European integration. The concentration of power is motivated partly by crisis management and efficiency arguments, but partly also by the weak political organisation at the European level. The European Parliament, which in theory could have the capacity to oversee the activities of the executive and the judiciary, is unlikely to do so, due to its inherently weak position among the main EU institutions.

The EU can be understood either as a community of democratic Member States or as the institutional framework that governs that community. As far as the latter is concerned, there are good reasons to doubt whether that framework fulfils all the criteria of a constitutional democracy. While the EU flirts with elements commonly associated with the democratic governance of nation-states, it lacks the political structures and the functional channels for elections to shape politics that would be needed for it to truly qualify as a constitutional democracy. This also undermines its capacity for an effective separation of powers.

In nation-state environments like the EU Member States, the separation is considered one of the key elements of securing democracy and of avoiding the authoritarian

[74] See RE Neustadt, *Presidential Power and the Modern Presidents. The Politics of Leadership from Roosevelt to Reagan* (Free Press, 1990).

concentration of power into too few hands. The branches of government are assigned tasks that include the overseeing the other branches implied in the separation and ensuring that powers are not abused. In the Treaties, the EU alludes to such a separation and its democratic pedigree by mirroring a design with specific institutions for legislative, executive and judicial powers. And yet, it can hardly be seen as a 'separation' in the traditional sense. Rather, in the spirit of the enlightened absolutism of European monarchies, the EU has focused all its institutional power to advance the Commission-led political project of integration. In this project, what matters are the results, the delivery of the intended objectives, rather than the democratic credentials of the process on the way there. And this, of course, is the point at which the word 'technocracy' creeps in.

3

Political Authority, Separated Powers and the Problem of Deviant Member States

CHRISTOPH MÖLLERS

I. Introduction

Charles de Montesquieu is well-known as one of the founding thinkers of the doctrine of separated powers, but Montesquieu was also an early theorist of federalism. In his *De l'esprit des lois*, Montesquieu remarks that 'the federal constitution must be composed of states of the same nature, above all of republican states'.[1] A federation whose members have different political systems is, according to Montesquieu, more politically fragile than a homogenous one. Such a heterogenous federation could only (and not necessarily so) function, if it was governed by a strong executive, a monarch. The relationship between the two problems, the political homogeneity of a democratic federation, and its organisation in separated powers, with regard to the EU, will be the topic of this contribution. To put it simply: which branch of the EU should be in charge of addressing the rule of law and democracy crises in some of its Member States? What about the relationship between law and politics? And how does the rather unique structure of the EU react to this topic?

The argument will proceed in four steps. It will start with an introduction to the general problem of political homogeneity in federations and three possible models of a solution – political, legal and administrative – as an application of separation of powers (section II). It will then take a look at the way the EU has dealt with the problem of politically deviant Member States in the ongoing so-called rule of law crisis (section III) and connect this with the problem of separated powers and political authority in the EU (section IV). This may simultaneously explain a very specific and ultimately quite a typical reaction to the crisis, which deserves a closer analysis: the conditionality regulation (section V). Finally, the results shall be gathered into a conceptual framework (section VI).

[1] C Montesquieu, *De l'esprit des lois* (Gallimard, 1951) IX/II 371 (my translation).

II. The Problem of Political Homogeneity in the EU

A. A General Problem of Federal Structures

Montesquieu's observation is rarely quoted, but as a matter of constitutional reality many modern constitutions have accepted its wisdom. The founding documents of democratic federations commonly require that all members follow the same political form. A minimum of political and constitutional similarity is the basis for their functioning. Such regulations can be found, for example, in the Constitution of the United States, in the Basic Law of the Federal Republic of Germany, and in the Swiss Federal Constitution.[2]

What does this mean for the EU? The EU is not a federation in the sense of a federal state.[3] Do other rules apply than for genuine federal states like Germany, the USA or Switzerland? At least at first glance, similarities may be more striking than differences, even though we will later observe the very specific (lack of) political authority of the EU to be relevant.[4] In any case, it is not by chance that criteria comparable to those in the quoted federal constitutions can also be found in the European Treaties. The Treaty of Maastricht commits the Member States, through Article 2 TEU (formerly Article 6 TEU; formerly Article F TEU), to a particular set of values, including standards of democracy and the rule of law (interestingly enough not to a system of separated powers).[5] As in Montesquieu's observation these founding norms assume that the federation can only be constituted if all constituent members adhere to essentially similar criteria of political legitimacy. The plurality of members as well as the necessary political conflicts between them must rest on a fundamental consensus of political form. Therefore, it is no accident that most federations, accepting conflict, contestation and variation on such a basis, are democracies.[6]

The problem of federal homogeneity within the EU is urgent because of the intertwinement in its system of executive federalism.[7] All binding decisions taken within the EU require a double democratic legitimation through EU institutions and through the Member States: Article 10 TEU.[8] Thus, the lack of democratic legitimacy of one Member State produces a lack of legitimacy both in other Member States and on the EU level. This is also the case because of Member States' power to regulate the political process in the field of European Parliament elections, and because of the transnational recognition and enforcement of decisions of one Member State in

[2] Art IV(4) of the US Constitution; Art 51(1) of the Federal Constitution of the Swiss Confederation; Art 28(1) of the German Basic Law.

[3] See eg M Nettesheim, 'Art. 1 EUV' in E Grabitz, M Hilf and M Nettesheim (eds), *Das Recht der Europäischen Union: EUV/AEUV* (Beck, 2023) para 66 ff.

[4] See below at IV.B.

[5] Art 13 TEU mentions an 'institutional framework' that serves the values in Art 2 TEU, which seems to say that it is not a value in itself. More below at IV.A.

[6] C Möllers, 'Verwaltungsrecht und Politik' in A von Bogdandy, S Cassese and P Huber (eds), *Handbuch Ius Publicum Europaeum* (Müller, 2014) vol V sec 93.

[7] K Lenaerts, P van Nuffel and T Corthaut, *EU Constitutional Law* (Oxford University Press, 2021) 565 ff.

[8] On this duplication, see J von Achenbach, *Demokratische Gesetzgebung in der Europäischen Union* (Springer, 2014); C Franzius and UK Preuß, *Die Zukunft der europäischen Demokratie* (Nomos, 2012).

other Member States.[9] Therefore, democratic deficits in one Member State produce democratic deficits in the Council and in the European Parliament, which then produce democratic deficits in other Member States. In this respect, it does not matter whether the Union can or should continue to develop into a genuine democratic federal state. As long as the EU takes binding decisions that interfere with the rights of citizens, in which the Member States represented in the Council are significantly involved, and as long as the Union remains a system of mutual recognition of Member State decisions, the adoption of elementary standards of democratic legitimacy in one Member State affects the EU system at all levels.[10]

B. The Quest for Institutional Solutions

There is no easy institutional answer to the question of what should happen when members of a federation no longer respect the founding consensus of their political federation. What would happen in Germany, the USA or Switzerland if Hesse, Texas or Graubünden turned away from democratic principles? Although, as we shall see, there are institutional mechanisms that have been established to deal with such a question, the problem has never been generally solved by means of constitutional institutions – perhaps it cannot be solved. The problem expresses a fundamental dilemma, especially if democratic standards are in question: a Member State will regard its actions as the result of democratic self-determination and, in the very name of democracy, will not be inclined to make itself subject to a set of rules defined by the federation. This is even more the case if the democratic legitimacy of the superior structure is itself considered contested. Such doubts concerning the central level are common among federations.[11] Accordingly, US federal authorities are traditionally suspected of behaving in a bureaucratic and undemocratic manner; a similar political discourse exists in Switzerland – and of course – in assessments of the 'democratic deficit' of the EU.

Which institutional instruments (the term 'solution' is, as we will see, too demanding) are available? Before taking a closer look at different instruments, it is important to shortly reflect upon the technocratic bias that underpins the quest for 'instruments'. The problem we are dealing with is a core political conflict about the right form of government; today it is also a conflict between liberal and illiberal concepts of democracy.[12] Therefore, it is far from clear if such conflicts can be 'solved' or at least mitigated by institutional means. The basic assumption that this is possible seems to be typical for the EU whose original political project is the domestication of its Member States. The claim that this can be achieved by technical means, by technocratic 'instruments', seems particularly characteristic for the Commission. The old

[9] On this, see M Ruffert, 'Rechtsquellen und Rechtsschichten des Verwaltungsrechts' in W Hoffmann-Riem, E Schmidt-Aßmann and A Voßkuhle (eds), *Grundlagen des Verwaltungsrechts* (Beck, 2012) vol I sec 17.

[10] K Lenaerts, 'The Principle of Mutual Recognition in the EU's Area of Freedom, Security and Justice' (Sir Jeremy Lever Lecture, University of Oxford, 2015).

[11] C Möllers, 'Im Übergang. Institutionelle Bedingungen sogenannter EU-Skepsis' (2022) 31 *Mittelweg 36* 17.

[12] C Mudde, 'Populism in Europe: An Illiberal Democratic Response to Undemocratic Liberalism' (2021) 56 *Government and Opposition* 577.

debate about the 'White Paper on Governance'[13] is an example of a mindset that tries to substitute political conflicts with institutional engineering.[14] Overall, however, we should remember how unlikely it is to simply organise away a deep-seated political or social problem.

Furthermore, we should keep in mind the historical developments and experiences of democratic federations. The political integration of federations often drags on for centuries and has never taken place without dramatic political conflicts. On the other hand, the EU has experienced rapid institutional change since the Single European Act of 1986. One might think that, despite the currently widespread impression of slowness, its institutional development has picked up a speed with which the Member States' societies have not been able to cope. Therefore, to dwell on the political character of the conflict may not be sufficient either. Rather, it may help to distinguish between different types of institutional reactions. We can draw a distinction between political, administrative and legal instruments in order to better understand the options and their political and legal trade-offs. This distinction is a loose reception of the tripartite distinction between legislative, executive and judicial action in the doctrine of separation of powers, a concept we will explore later.

i. Legal Approaches

Many consolidated federations adopt legal solutions for conflicts between constituent states and the federal level, namely by introducing judicial review for conflicts of competencies. Historically, possible conflicts between federal levels were a central reason for the introduction of constitutional review.[15] There is something obviously attractive about such a solution. The conflict is settled by a neutral and independent institution based on norms that have been set in a legitimate political procedure. Still, there are problems with this kind of approach.

Firstly, the legalisation or judicialisation of political conflicts requires a high level of political consolidation to create legitimacy and acceptance of the central court. This legitimacy is not only needed for the court, but also for the whole federal level to which the court belongs. In other words: if there were consensus that the resolution of the conflict is a pure legal matter, the conflict would essentially be resolved. Therefore, judicial solutions may be desirable,[16] but are not necessarily available.

Secondly, historical experience from consolidated federations shows that courts are not always able to resolve such fundamental conflicts.[17] The relevant historical cases

[13] Commission, 'European Governance – A White Paper' COM(2001) 428 final; and the mostly critical contributions in C Joerges, Y Mény and JHH Weiler (eds), *Mountain or Molehill* (Robert Schuman Centre/Jean Monnet Center, 2002).

[14] Another example is the economic governance framework, which tries to define deeply political issues as technical ones: K Tuori and K Tuori, *The Eurozone Crisis: A Constitutional Analysis* (Cambridge University Press, 2014).

[15] O Beaud, 'De quelques particularités de la justice constitutionnelle dans un système federal' in O Jouanjan, E Maulin and P Wachsman (eds), *La notion de la 'justice constitutionnelle'* (Dalloz, 2005) 49 ff.

[16] We will not get into the highly contested question of the legitimacy of courts vis à vis political decisions.

[17] That such a conflict resolution is not always necessary is seen in the decision of general principle of the US Supreme Court in *Marbury v Madison* [1803] 5 US 137 and of the European Court of Justice/ECJ in Case 26/62 *Van Gend en Loos* ECLI:EU:C:1963:1, and Case 6/64 *Costa/E.N.E.L.* ECLI:EU:C:1964:66.

may not all correspond directly to undemocratic structures in democratic federations, but they do concern similar problems: namely the claim of a member to leave the federation in order to win democratic political autonomy. The examples of Catalonia and Quebec illustrate how different the consequences of judicial interventions in such a scenario can be. While the decisions of the Supreme Court of Canada have contained and restricted the conflict,[18] those of the Spanish *Tribunal Constitucional* are regarded as the cause of escalation.[19] In such cases the institutional performance of courts takes place in a politically sensitive area, and thus on the border between politics and law. This bears risks, as illustrated by the disastrous role of the US Supreme Court in the outbreak of the American Civil War.[20]

Finally, it is just remarkably difficult to develop clear legal criteria for the judicial review of political developments, like the loss of democratic and rule of law standards. The shift from democratic rule of law to authoritarianism is incremental and often works with the conscious attempt to bypass existing safeguards. This shift is a creeping, gradual process made up of small changes which regularly evade judicial review, which is mainly designed to respond to individual cases.

ii. *Functional-Administrative Approaches*

Functional-administrative approaches address the problem of safeguarding democracy through a strict, perhaps even quantifiable system of criteria.[21] The practical implementation of measures derived from these criteria is left to an independent, depoliticised administrative authority. In this context, implementation frequently means primarily offering support rather than overcoming political resistance. One example of the use of such technocratic tools is the rule of law-based support offered by the European Commission to the Member States. Here, the European Commission can independently decide to provide advice and other means to particular states, in order to combat corruption and strengthen an independent judiciary. These instruments are accompanied by formalised reporting in a manner typical of international organisations. Another example is the European Union Agency for Fundamental Rights.[22] This is an expert commission dealing with questions of fundamental rights in the EU and its Member States in the context of the implementation of EU law.[23] Its function is to provide both

[18] *Reference Re Secession of Quebec* [1998] 2 SCR 217; on this, see P Leslie, 'The Supreme Court Sets Rules for the Secession of Quebec' (1999) 29 *The Journal of Federalism* 35.

[19] Tribunal Constitucional de España, Case STC 31/2010, ECLI:ES:TC:2010:31. On this, see V Ferreres Comella, 'The Catalan Secessionist Movement and Europe – Remarks on the Venice Commission's Opinion 827/2015' (*Verfassungsblog*, 22 March 2017), at www.verfassungsblog.de/the-catalan-secessionist-movement-and-europe-remarks-on-the-venice-commissions-opinion-8272015.

[20] *Scott v Sandford* [1856] 60 US 19 How 393. On this, see B Ackerman, *We the People: Foundations* (HUP, 1991) 63 ff.

[21] For problems and biases in the quantification of rule of law standards: M Versteeg and T Ginsburg, 'Measuring the rule of law: A comparison of indicators' (2007) 42 *Law & Social Inquiry* 100.

[22] On its oversight of fundamental rights, see A von Bogdandy, 'Grundrechtsschutz durch die Europäische Grundrechteagentur' in D Merten and HJ Papier (eds), *Handbuch der Grundrechte in Deutschland und Europa, Volume VI/1, Europäische Grundrechte I* (Müller, 2010) 1241; A von Bogdandy and J von Bernstorff, 'Die Europäische Agentur für Grundrechte in der europäischen Menschenrechtsarchitektur und ihre Fortbildung durch den Vertrag von Lissabon' (2010) 45 *Europarecht* 141.

[23] Council Regulation (EC) No 168/2007 establishing a European Union Agency for Fundamental Rights [2007] OJ L53, Art 3(3).

the EU itself and its Member States with professional expertise, for example, through the production of advisory opinions and studies or the development of standards and methods of comparison to support their full compliance with fundamental rights when they introduce measures, or commit themselves to actions within their respective areas of authority.[24]

Apart from the question as to how successful these procedures have been, functional-administrative approaches are better suited to some scenarios than to others. They are applicable to situations where the presence of a systemic problem is recognised by the Member State involved. This is because only a consensus between the EU and the Member State permits the establishment of technical solutions and their transfer to administrative actors. If the very existence of a problem is controversial, and if the European level addresses a domestic deficiency while the Member State refers to its democratic mandate, the problem unavoidably turns into a political conflict. There are, however, no administrative bodies with an adequate political mandate to deal with such conflict. Thus, this type of solution rapidly reaches its limits. Consequently, at least in a supporting role, political solutions are indispensable.

iii. Political Approaches

We talk about a political instrument when the choice of countermeasures is made by political bodies. This approach may have the advantage of openly addressing the political background of the conflict. However, this does not alter the fact that it remains a political conflict which threatens to overstretch the existing institutional set-up and boundaries of the European community.

Such political procedures are well known in comparative constitutional law. Under the German Basic Law, for example, the enforcement of federal law by the federal Government against *a Land* (federated state) depends on the agreement of the *Bundesrat*, representing the *Länder*: Article 37(1) Basic Law.[25] The procedure in Article 7 TEU is, as we will see, also a political procedure. It requires the consensus of the other Member States and – as a last resort – provides for the suspension of all political rights of the Member State concerned. In other federal conflicts, even military measures have been used as political instruments such as in the 'German-Prussian' War before the founding of the North German Confederation,[26] or in the case of the American Civil War, which, in the view of the northern states, was necessary in order to uphold the supremacy of the federal Constitution.[27]

When assessing political solutions, it is, however, necessary to note the dialectic of these historical experiences. If we do not accept the military enforcement of political rules as a legitimate instrument – and there are many arguments in favour of this view,

[24] Council Regulation (EC) No 168/2007 (n 23) Arts 2 and 4.

[25] For an early work on federal execution, see H Criepel, *Die Reichsaufsicht: Untersuchungen zum Staatsrecht des Deutschen Reiches* (Springer, 1917) 665 ff. See also F Shirvani, 'Die Bundes- und Reichsexekution in der neueren Deutschen Verfassungsgeschichte' (2011) 50 *Der Staat* 102.

[26] For a concise summary of the judicial background, see H Boldt, *Deutsche Verfassungsgeschichte Volume II: Von 1806 bis zur Gegenwart* (dtv, 1990) 164 ff.

[27] AR Amar, *America's Constitution: a biography* (Random House, 2005) 355.

especially with regard to the peace project of European integration – then the enforcement of federal rules simply reaches certain limits that do not exist when law has to be enforced against individuals or groups of citizens. According to continental European understandings, the notion of 'rule of law' also includes the possibility of compulsory enforcement of legal norms.[28] If this option is not available, because the use of force would not be limited to the enforcement of individual decisions, but rather amount to a full military conflict, the last resort in a conflict of this nature either lies in the exclusion of the federated state in question, or in the toleration of its deviant political practice.

However, neither of these options is available in the case of the EU: unlike the Council of Europe, the EU does not have the right to exclude a state for serious violations of its common principles.[29] On the other hand, the toleration of a disregard for basic normative standards is – as we have seen – not an option, given the level of institutional intertwinement. Political developments in a Member State are no longer solely domestic affairs. It is highly problematic to tolerate political practices which deviate from the fundamental consensus of the Union and the other Member States. The loss of a member's democratic form of government is the expression of a political conflict for which no simple solution exists. There seems rather to be a trilemma: legal solutions have to be accepted; they cannot easily cope with the incremental backslide into authoritarianism; and they often have to apply very general norms like Article 2 TEU. Administrative solutions lack the legitimacy to cope with political problems. Political solutions are often unprincipled and opportunistic.

iv. Framing the Problem: Rule of Law or Democracy?

The distinction between these three forms of solutions draws on the distinction between law, administration and politics. It is important to recognise that this distinction is in itself also relevant in the way the problem is framed. When the Hungarian and later the Polish Government simultaneously started to curtail judicial independence and media freedom this was mostly framed by the EU as a 'rule of law crisis'. But the lack of independent media is clearly a democracy problem and from a political theory perspective it seems rather dubious if the connection between rule of law and democracy can be dismantled without giving up both.[30] Yet, the institutional development of the EU is not governed by political theory, but by more or less plausible claims for legitimacy

[28] E Schmidt-Aßmann, 'Der Rechtsstaat' in J Isensee and P Kirchhof (eds), *Handbuch des Staatsrechts der Bundesrepublik Deutschland, Volume II* (Müller, 2004) ref 71; L Heuschling, *État de droit, rule of law, Rechtsstaat* (Dalloz, 2002). See also the German Constitutional Court on the relationship between the state's monopoly of force and fundamental basic rights in a liberal democracy BVerfG, Beschluss vom 17 January 2017 – 2 BvB 1/13 – *NPD-Verbotsverfahren (Banning of the NPD)* [2017], ref 547.

[29] Art 8 of the Statute of the Council of Europe of 5 May 1949 states: 'Any member of the Council of Europe which has seriously violated Article 3 may be suspended from its rights of representation and requested by the Committee of Ministers to withdraw under Article 7. If such member does not comply with this request, the Committee may decide that it has ceased to be a member of the Council as from such date as the Committee may determine.'

[30] For a fundamental reasoning in this direction: J Habermas, 'On the Relation Between the Nation, The Rule of Law, and Democracy' in C Cronin and P de Greiff (eds), *The Inclusion of the Other: Studies in Political Theory* (MIT Press, 1998).

of its bodies. A reason for this framing was probably the lack of a genuine democratic political authority of the EU bodies and the absence of a pan-European public sphere. One might argue that norms like Article 2 and 10 TEU empower the EU bodies with the task to protect democracy in the Member States.[31] But as a matter of institutional politics, the Commission especially does not seem like a good candidate to remind Member States of their lack of democratic legitimacy. To translate a fight against rule of law and democracy into a mere rule of law problem meant to meet the conflict on a field on which the EU seems to be more within its institutional comfort zone: a political problem becomes a legal problem that can be addressed by expertise[32] and does not require genuine political authority.

III. The EU Meets Deviant Member States: Some Observations

Looking at the European Treaties from this background gives some remarkable insights.[33]

The first is that the Treaties themselves have an explicitly political solution to the problem. The introduction of Article 7 TEU after the misguided action against Austria[34] tried to formalise a political process, not to legalise or judicialise it. To the contrary, Article 269 TFEU which excludes the ECJ from any substantial review of the process underlined the assumption that the criteria in Article 2 TEU should be fundamentally treated as political ones developed and applied first and foremost by the Member State governments. The idea to make the Member States supreme judges of the domestic political processes of one of their peers according to European value standards accepted both: the precarious state of European political authority and the need to explicitly claim this authority beyond any artificial border between European and domestic affairs. From a theoretical point of view, this did not altogether look like a bad idea. It corresponded with the rise of the European Council to become one of the political centres of the EU since the Maastricht Treaty.

Still, the second observation is that this political approach flatly failed. While the normative evaluation of the political developments in Poland and Hungary became increasingly critical, the Council and the European Council remained unable or unwilling to act. This was less due to the majority rules in Article 7 TEU than to the fact that the members of the Council bodies seemed to be stuck in a diplomatic or international law mindset in which the domestic affairs of the Member States are not legitimate

[31] For such an argument: J Bast and A von Bogdandy (eds), *Unionsverfassungsrecht* (Beck, 2024) (forthcoming).

[32] For the quasi-constitutive understanding of law as an expertocratic instrument in the EU: P Leino-Sandberg, *The Politics of Legal Expertise in EU Policy-Making* (Cambridge University Press, 2021).

[33] There is now a lot of literature about the ongoing conflict: W Sadurski, *Poland's Constitutional Breakdown* (Oxford University Press, 2019); Möllers and Schneider, *Demokratiesicherung in der Europäischen Union* (Mohr Siebeck, 2018); A von Bogdandy et al (eds), *Defending Checks and Balances in EU Member States: Taking Stock of Europe's Actions* (Springer, 2021).

[34] For this: F Schorkopf, *Die Maßnahmen der XIV EU-Mitgliedsstaaten gegen Österreich: Möglichkeiten und Grenzen einer „streitbaren Demokratie" auf europäischer Ebene* (Springer, 2002).

issues to be addressed. Even today, the Council is hesitant to pick up the Article 7 TEU initiatives of Parliament and Commission and it is anecdotally well known that even at a point in which the political state of affairs in Hungary was seen extremely critical by most observers, it was not addressed in the Council bodies. The institutional consciousness of the Council members lagged behind the institutional duties Articles 2 and 7 TEU had obliged them to. The conditionality regulation can also be interpreted as the confession that the bodies were overwhelmed by this task given the fact that the Council never initiated any form of decisive action against Poland and Hungary.[35]

The third observation is that the ECJ reluctantly started to step in and to fill the void left by the political bodies. Not surprisingly, it did so with regard to rule of law issues, namely judicial independence, rather than with questions of democratic government. The success of these interventions is contestable. The Court was able to support single members of the judicial branch, namely in Poland, but it seems dubious that it will be able to reverse a more systemic political takeover of the judicial branch in the long run. The concentration of the ECJ upon judicial issues may also illustrate a certain form of self-referentiality: legal institutions protect legal procedures; courts protect courts. So, it remains an open question if a court that is ready to protect the institutional integrity of courts is equally ready to intervene into the merits of political rights and institutional politics.

Finally, while the European Parliament provided the most important European political forum to debate political developments in the Member States from the start, the European Commission was much slower and more hesitant in addressing the issues. Given its technocratic background, it is not surprising that the Commission tended to frame the issues mostly as problems of the rule of law. This corresponds to our assumption that non-political authorities stick to non-political criteria and non-political solutions. The Commission's course of action in the case of the *lex tusk* in which it sued Poland for breach of democratic principles during the electoral campaign in 2023[36] may be a remarkable development in this context. Of even greater significance thus far is the decision on the Conditionality Regulation, a common project of all bodies, Commission, Council, Parliament and the ECJ, which I will address at the end of this chapter.

IV. Separated Powers and Governmental Authority in the EU

A. The Contested Issue of EU Separation of Powers

The question of how models of separation of powers are applicable to the EU is widely contested. One reason for this fundamental uncertainty lies in the unique character

[35] For the history of this (non-)development: C Möllers and L Schneider, *Demokratiesicherung in der Europäischen Union* (Mohr Siebeck, 2018) sub II.

[36] Commission, 'Rule of Law: Commission launches infringement procedure against Poland for violating EU law with the new law establishing a special committee' (European Commission, 22 December 2021), at ec.europa.eu/commission/presscorner/detail/en/ip_23_3134.

of the EU with the always underlying issue of the applicability of notions like 'state' and 'federation' to it. Is the EU a federation, and if so, does it matter for any normative argument? The problem is even more intricate because the European Treaties avoid any principled approach to this question. While generally rather overgenerous with values and principles, Article 13 TEU is even more modest in its wording than the reference of the ECJ to 'institutional balance', which seems to work as an anti-principled reminder of a textual interpretation of the Treaties.[37]

Another problem lies in the doctrine itself, which is in many regards unclear and contested.[38] Even as a pure piece of theory it can be understood either as a descriptive tool or as a normative model. If this question is not clarified in advance, considerable confusion may be the consequence. In the following, I will use the distinction of the three branches as a theoretical tool with a normative background in political theory, not in positive EU law. To manage this complex landscape in a concise manner, I will distinguish three degrees of contestation with regard to the application of the idea of separated powers to the EU. This will make it easier to find common ground and not to get stuck in purely conceptual issues.

At the first level, there is a relatively strong consensus that it is plausible to identity the core functions of judicial, legislative and executive action within the EU.[39] This is nothing trivial as many international organisations do not have such functions. There is also a strong case to see the integrated court system as a legitimate institutional setup to carry out the judicial function and to identify the European Parliament as a legitimate co-legislator within a traditional framework of separated powers.

At the second level, it remains a more contested question whether the inter-governmental, inter-administrative or executive federal character of the EU constitutes a breach of a settled concept of separated powers, in which executive consensus serves as legislature, delegating and delegated instance,[40] or if this is part of a normal integrated federal system in which governments of the members have to be part of the legislative process. This is a question that addresses the identification of a legitimate legislator as well as the complex system of the EU executive in which the Commission, EU agencies and the Member States singularly and jointly within different forms of cooperation share the task of carrying out the executive function. Even if this is a contested question, the way in which it is contested seems fairly easy. It revolves around the question of how far the analogy to executive federalism has explanatory or even justificatory power for the EU. If we take executive federalism to be a legitimate political form, then the role of the Council as a legislative chamber particularly seems to be less problematic.

[37] B de Witte, 'The Role of the Court of Justice in Shaping the Institutional Balance in the EU' in J Mendes and I Venzke (eds), *Allocating Authority. Who Should Do What in European and International Law?* (Hart, 2018).

[38] My take: C Möllers, 'Epilogue: separation of powers – a short manual for the perplexed' in HM Ten Napel and W Voermans (eds), *The Powers that be* (Leiden University Press, 2016).

[39] J Ziller, 'Separation of Powers in the European Union's intertwined System of Government: A Treaty based Analysis for the Use of Political Scientists and Constitutional Lawyers' (2008) 73 *Il Politico* 133; K Lenaerts, 'Some Reflections on the Separation of Powers in the European Community' (1991) 28 *Common Market Law Review* 11; C Möllers, *The Three Branches – A Comparative Model of Separation of Powers* (Oxford University Press, 2013) 169.

[40] Leino-Sandberg and Minkkinen, ch 2 in this volume.

Finally, there is an even more open issue that goes to the core of the political authority of the EU: the still underrated question of where the governmental function in the EU lies and, behind this, whether a model of separated powers has to deal with a governmental function as a specific part of the executive. Here, the conflict between a rule of law-oriented reading that takes the executive as purely administrative and a rather political approach that endorses political actions reappears.[41] If we identify government with some specific tasks, namely political leadership through instigation of legislative acts, administrative leadership through action at the apex of the bureaucratic apparatus, external representation of the Union and federal oversight over its members, it is clear that in the EU these functions are dispersed between different institutions, mostly between the European Commission and the European Council, but sometimes also between powerful Member States or the ECJ. Not by accident, one of the central issues of the recent case law about Article 13 TEU concerns the difficult relationship between the European Commission and the European Council with regard to foreign affairs.[42] Interestingly enough, this lack of a unitary governmental body is rarely noted in our context, maybe because the crucial difference between administrative and governmental actions often vanishes behind a general notion of the executive that is blind for a distinction which also defines a border between the two poles of political action and the application of legal norms.

B. Political Authority in the EU and of the EU: A Double Bind

The lack of a unitary governmental responsibility is both a remarkable institutional expression of the kind of political authority the EU can claim at this point of the integration process, as well as a potential explanation for the strange paths the fight for the protection of democracy and rule of law took.

For at least a historical moment in the development of the European integration it seemed to be possible that the European Commission could occupy the place of a European government.[43] More interesting than the question of why this did not happen is the fact that the Commission acquired a governmental role in some policy areas procedures, but not in many others.[44] But while the idea that competencies, procedures and policies are differentiated is typical for the EU, it is virtually impossible for a political government which has to claim omnicompetent political leadership. To be

[41] For a careful sense of both elements that avoids strong juxtapositions between the executive as either administrative and law-abiding or political and unbound: H Heller, 'Genie und Funktionär in der Politik' in H Buchstein and D Jörke (eds), *Hermann Heller, Kämpfen für die Demokratie* (Europäische Verlagsanstalt, 2023); for an attempt to solve the relation between the two elements of the executive: Möllers (n 39).

[42] For instance: Case C-425/13 *Commission v Council* ECLI:EU:C:2015:483 [67] ff; Case C-73/14 *Council v Commission* ECLI:EU:C:2015:663 [61] ff; Case C-660/13 *Council v Commission* ECLI:EU:C:2016:616 [32] ff; and V Demedts and M Chamon, 'The Commission Back on the Leash. No Autonomy to Sign Non-binding Agreements on Behalf of the EU. Council v Commission' (2017) 54 *Common Market Law Review* 245.

[43] J Fischer, 'Rede des Bundesministers des Auswärtigen Joschka Fischer' (Speech, Humboldt-Universität Berlin, 12 May 2000), at www.bundesregierung.de/breg-de/service/bulletin/rede-des-bundesministers-des-auswaertigen-joschka-fischer-808150.

[44] For an assessment of the plurality of EU procedures: N Otto, *Die Vielfalt unionaler Rechtsetzungsverfahren* (Mohr, 2022).

sure, omnicompetence does not mean unlimited power; it means omnicompetence within a system of separated and federal powers. To be politically omnicompetent means to be the only governmental agent *within the limits of governmental power and federal competencies* like the US President or the German Chancellor. But even within this double constraint no institution in the EU can make this claim.

The fact that not only political authority *in* the EU itself is shared between EU bodies and Member States, but that political authority *of* the EU is fragmented between Member States and Union bodies, but also by the complicated internal structure of the latter, is something unique. It is best illustrated by the fact that the main candidate for governmental (even presidential) powers of the EU today is the European Council.[45] There are legitimate doubts as to why this should be a convincing allocation of powers: it seems dubious to understand a body whose members have received their political legitimacy only through Member State procedures as genuine political authority for the EU. It seems equally dubious to what extent a federally structured body can fulfil the unitary side of a governmental function. But even putting these conceptual doubts aside, we can just observe by looking at Article 7 TEU that the European Council was unable to act with the required authority. This is no wonder given the fact that it has to turn against its own members to do so. In Article 7 TEU the political sanction of the EU versus a Member State functions as the sanction of a body against the very units it is composed of. From a purely organisational perspective, it seems improbable to work, and it did not.

While the restricted wording of Article 13 TEU and the rather literalistic treaty-positivistic approach of the ECJ towards institutional balance cannot provide any remedies for our problem, it is at least easy to see the institutional double bind EU institutions find themselves in. The institutional intertwinement of the EU demands a core political homogeneity; this is Montesquieu's insight that we started the chapter with. It is difficult to execute this demand with purely administrative or judicial means, as we saw, in theory as well as in the institutional reality. Finally, a political authority is needed. This authority that in separation of powers terms is called a governmental function is lacking on an EU level, especially when we look at the failure of the European Council. Here is the bind: the EU creates a need for political authority it is unable to provide. It does not build an EU governmental function because the actors do not trust its political authority; it does not leave the Member States alone because it does not trust their democratic legitimacy. Both kinds of doubts seem plausible, but both defeat any solution of the problem.

C. Contestation and Cooperation

When we understand separation of powers as a system that has, at least under democratic conditions, to organise political contestation, and not only the executive

[45] L van Middelaar and U Pütter, 'The European Council: The Union's Supreme Decision-Maker' in D Hodson, U Pütter, S Saurugger and J Peterson (eds), *The Institutions of the European Union* (Oxford University Press, 2022).

consensus which has characterised much of the process of European integration,[46] we will gain a further perspective on our problem. For the time being, it is hard to think of the EU without a dominating need for executive consensus. The fact that Council and European Council are politically and institutionally close to the constituent treaty-making power of the EU may be the main reason for that. The room for the formalised contestation is limited to the European Parliament, but even the parliamentary procedure is characterised by consensus-building. EU-specific features like the legislative trilogue and the important form of the inter-institutional agreements illustrate this.[47]

Still, there is a need for contestation, but where is its institutional locus? To be sure, the European Parliament has been the locus of an open and contested debate addressing this issue for quite a while.[48] And this has not only been a debate between parliamentary groups but also between parliamentarians and Member State governments who regularly appear in the debates to make their (sometimes illiberal) case. Meanwhile, as we have seen, the Council bodies have not been able to live up to the political constitutional role Article 7 TEU has assigned to them, and this can also be read as a lack of political contestation. That does not mean that there are not enough political conflicts in the Council – there are – but that these conflicts are still framed as conflicts between Member States‘ interests, not as conflicts around the definition of European political identity or common good.

It is doubtful that this problem can be solved through institutional reforms. It seems that the Council is what it is, and that the Member States' governments are not ready to completely accept their functions as members of a political bodies. Experiences with federalism, the development of the German Bundesrat or the US Senate show that the self-understanding of bodies that represent the lower level in the federation depend on the political integration of the whole federation, especially on the existence of a public sphere that asks for unitary political responsibility. The deficit of the Council deliberation expresses the same problem as the lack of a politically responsible EU government structure. Therefore, it is by no means accidental that the most recent 'solution' the EU has developed is in my taxonomy, as we will see, not a political, but an administrative one.

V. The Curious Case of Conditionality

The most recent step to address the problem was the introduction of the 'Conditionality Regulation'[49] and its acceptance by the ECJ.[50] The rationale of the Regulation is

[46] For the enabling process Möllers (n 39) 51.

[47] F von Alemann, *Die Handlungsform der interinstitutionellen Vereinbarung: Eine Untersuchung des Interorganverhältnisses der europäischen Verfassung* (Springer, 2006).

[48] K Granat, 'The parliamentary politics of the rule of law crisis in the EU' (2023) 45 *Journal of European Integration* 1017.

[49] Regulation (EU, Euratom) 2020/2092 of the European Parliament and of the Council on a general regime of conditionality for the protection of the Union budget [2020] OJ L433I.

[50] Case C-157/21 *Poland v Parliament and Council* ECLI:EU:C:2022:98.

remarkable in many regards. By tying the problem of deviant Member States to the question of a correct use of EU funds and by founding it on the competence in Article 322 TEU, EU law gives a fundamentally depoliticised interpretation of the development. In this approach EU law does not address the problem of illiberal democracies but protects the independent review of its funding mechanisms. While the values of Article 2 TEU are often mentioned in the documents of the Regulation and in the decision of the Court of Justice, the central argument is purely instrumentalist:

> That sound financial management and those financial interests are liable to be seriously compromised by breaches of the principles of the rule of law committed in a Member State, since those breaches may result, inter alia, in there being no guarantee that expenditure covered by the Union budget satisfies all the financing conditions laid down by EU law and therefore meets the objectives pursued by the European Union when it finances such expenditure.
>
> In particular, compliance with those conditions and objectives, as elements of EU law, cannot be fully guaranteed in the absence of effective judicial review designed to ensure compliance with EU law; the existence of such review, both in the Member States and at EU level, by independent courts and tribunals, is of the essence of the rule of law (see, to that effect, judgment of 21 December 2021, Euro Box Promotion and Others, C-357/19, C-379/19, C-547/19, C-811/19 and C-840/19, EU:C:2021:1034, paragraphs 219 and 222).[51]

The relationship between practical means and normative ends in this argument is remarkable. The rule of law, in particular judicial independence, is not merely an end in itself, as it should be as a value (Article 2 TEU), but instead functions as an instrument that serves another ultimate end: 'the financing conditions laid down by EU law'.

This is a substantive inversion of a normative system that claims to be based on values and principles. Functionally, the creation does not implement a substantial normative hierarchy, but rather a reification of the supremacy of EU law. The conditionality protects the financing conditions of the entire EU legal order. A corresponding inversion of hierarchy appears on the procedural level. While the procedure in Article 7 TEU was a product of primary law in order to protect the basic values of Article 2 TEU,[52] it is now secondary legislation that defines the procedure. Finally, while the initiation of an Article 7 TEU procedure was in the hands of Council, Commission and Parliament, the new mechanism is controlled by the Commission who alone can initiate a procedure in which the Council seems to be obliged to follow the Commission's proposal. In the distinction developed earlier in this chapter we can observe a shift from a political to an administrative solution on three levels: its normative fundament (from a constitutional or Treaty to an administrative law regulation basis); the rationale of the procedure (from the protection of values to the use of value protection as an instrument to review the financial conditions of the whole legal order); and the responsible institutions (from Council and European Council to Commission).

[51] ibid [149]–[150].

[52] Or even super-primary values, for such an argument and the concept of a substantial hierarchy between Arts 1–3 TEU and other norms of the Treaties: L Spieker, *EU Values Before the Court of Justice* (Oxford University Press, 2023).

But the administrative form of the new mechanism is only one side. If the thesis that the control of deviant Member States is a genuine political and governmental function is correct, the political character of the task will have to be ventilated by a politicisation of the institutions. In other words: the political pressure that accompanies the task of discipling deviant Member States will not be contained in the framework of this Regulation. If the assumption is correct that neither a purely administrative nor a judicial framework regime can solve the problem, then the political side of it will finally reappear. This will be especially demanding for bodies with a deficient political legitimacy of their own, namely with regard to the European Commission. There are already indicators that the Commission has for quite a while weakened its stance as a politically neutral enforcer of EU law in order to remain politically influential and successful with its policy proposals.[53] There is no reason while this would change with regard to problems of rule of law and democracy, especially because they hint at the core legitimacy problem of the Commission itself. One possible (and not the first)[54] example are reports of the Commission compromising on sanctions against Hungary with regard to its vote on sanctions against Russia.[55] This corresponds to the classical problem of conditionality as an informal form of political intervention in international law.[56]

The absence of a genuine governmental authority, the need for an intervention that is political at its core, the implication of giving the intervention an administrative form and the observation that such an intervention cannot be immunised from repoliticisation all illustrate the core separation of power issue of the EU: the need of a minimum degree of systemic political homogeneity, the necessity to have government secure this minimum, and the impossibility of establishing such a government. Under these conditions, the combination of formalisation (through administrative legalism) and deformalisation (by including conditionality into general package deals) seems to be both unsatisfying and consequent, especially thinking of the rhetoric of EU bodies with regard to the hierarchy of norms and values.

VI. Outlook: Two Interpretations

Any integration of the EU into a more general framework of constitutional theory faces the dilemma that it either tends to ignore the EU's unique specificities or that it capitulates before them and treats the EU as an institutional individual without general

[53] RD Kelemen and T Pavone, 'Where Have the Guardians Gone? Law Enforcement and the Politics of Supranational Forbearance in the European Union' (2023) 75 *World Politics* 779.

[54] C Hillon, 'Compromising (on) the general conditionality mechanism and the rule of law' (2021) 58 *Common Market Law Review* 267.

[55] J Jaraczewski, 'Unexpected Complications: The impact of the Russian invasion of Ukraine on the rule of law crisis in the EU: An anti-rule of law alliance' (*Verfassungsblog*, 23 December 2022), at verfassungsblog.de/unexpected-complications-the-impact-of-the-russian-invasion-of-ukraine-on-the-rule-of-law-crisis-in-the-eu.

[56] If it is externally not effective, it may also be ineffective against Member States: KE Smith, 'The Use of Political Conditionality in the EU's Relations with Third Countries: How Effective?' (1998) 3 *European Foreign Affairs Review* 253.

features. This seems especially problematic with regard to the notoriously complex concept of separation of powers. In this contribution, two approaches were applied to mitigate this problem: the first one is a comparative look at federal systems which has always served as an intermediary between state-centred constitutionalism and international law.[57] The second approach looks at the concrete feature that makes the EU not fit a traditional scheme of separated powers.

The look at federalism provided some insights. The problem of politically deviant Member States is neither new nor is there a settled institutional solution to it. The distinction between legal, administrative and political solutions showed that such a core political problem should only be addressed by bodies with a solid political legitimacy of their own. The look at the EU specifics led us to the diagnosis that the central separation of powers feature missing in the EU is a unitary governmental function. Tying both aspects together explains the lack of convincing institutional answers to the problem of deviant Member States in the EU.

But this is not the whole story. With the conditionality regulation a new instrument was enacted that claims to address the problem, but also redefines it on the operational level as the technical question of a correct use of EU funding and its independent review. This reinterpretation of a political problem into an administrative one is nothing new, especially in the EU. Neither is it a novelty that political pressure still has to be ventilated, namely in the way the Commission understands its role as guardian of EU law. Still, the question remains of how to evaluate this process, and here our dilemma reappears. From a 'traditional' separation of powers perspective the solution would lie in the establishment of a fully fledged EU government. But an EU with a government would no longer be the EU; instead of institutional reform the solution would lie in a complete constitutional transformation. From a perspective that takes EU specifics seriously we may accept the current state of affairs as a second-best solution without giving it too much justificatory credit. To translate political problems into administrative ones may be, given the state of integration, less satisfying and less acceptable from a separation of powers perspective than ever before. It may also be the only answer the EU has to the problem of politically deviant Member States. From this point of view the idea of separated powers may not provide us with handy institutional solutions, but at least with critical arguments.

[57] K Nicolaidis and R Howse (eds), *The Federal Vision: Legitimacy and Levels of Governance in the United States and the European Union* (Oxford University Press, 2001); R Schütze, *From Dual To Cooperative Federalism: The Changing Structure Of European Law* (Oxford University Press, 2009).

PART II

The Relationship between the Legislature and the Executive

4

No Appetite for Conflict? Assessing how the European Parliament and the European Ombudsman Engage with Executive Discretion in Informalised EU Readmission Policy

DAVIDE GNES AND MILKA SORMUNEN[1]

I. Introduction

EU migration and asylum policies have been constitutionalised in recent years as the Lisbon Treaty strengthened democratic control, judicial scrutiny and fundamental rights in the policy field.[2] Among other changes, the European Parliament acquired new powers in the legislative process[3] in relation to migration and asylum, including in external relations. In the latter, based on Articles 79(3) and 218 TFEU, the European Commission and the Council of the EU are now required to obtain the Parliament's consent before an international agreement is concluded in an area to which the ordinary legislative procedure applies, such as visa facilitation or readmission.

Readmission agreements are formal international agreements concluded between the EU and a third country in accordance with Treaty procedures, and they aim to guarantee identification and return of unauthorised migrants by concretising the international law obligation to readmit own nationals.[4] Since the entry into force of the Lisbon Treaty, the EU has concluded seven readmission agreements with the

[1] Both authors equally contributed to this chapter. Names are presented in alphabetical order.

[2] S Carrera, J Santos Vara and T Strik, *Constitutionalising the External Dimensions of EU Migration Policies in Times of Crisis: Legality, Rule of Law and Fundamental Rights Reconsidered* (Edward Elgar Publishing, 2019).

[3] See eg B Rittberger, 'Institutionalizing Representative Democracy in the European Union: The Case of the European Parliament' (2012) 50 *Journal of Common Market Studies* 18.

[4] eg N Coleman, *European Readmission Policy. Third Country Interests and Refugee Rights* (Martinus Nijhoff, 2009).

formal involvement of the Parliament, including with countries such as Pakistan and Georgia.[5] Despite the existence of this formal process, the Commission and the Council have since 2016 begun to conclude non-binding, 'informal' readmission arrangements outside Treaty procedures and without the participation of the Parliament. Informal arrangements claim to be non-binding despite a strong resemblance to formal agreements. For example, the Joint Declaration on Migration Cooperation between Afghanistan and the EU states that it is 'not intended to create legal rights or obligations under international or domestic law'. In the arrangement, the parties agree to facilitate the return of Afghan nationals, and it contains provisions about matters such as travel documents, return flights as well as the EU's financial assistance to Afghanistan.[6] The legal basis of informal arrangements is unclear, and they are usually not made publicly available. From a separation of powers perspective, informalisation poses a challenge to Parliamentary prerogatives and to transparency and accountability of EU executive institutions more in general, particularly in an area of migration that can have important human rights implications.[7]

In many policy areas, the use of soft law by the EU executive is not controversial *per se* nor specifically prohibited by the Treaties.[8] The use of political, non-binding instruments to cooperate on migration is nothing new.[9] However, research has suggested that informal instruments in the external dimension of migration and asylum policy are used to replace formal instruments, therefore affecting the institutional balance of powers within the EU.[10] The reliance on informal instruments intensified in conjunction with the political crisis triggered by the EU Member States' inability to deal with an unusual surge in migrant arrivals in 2015/16.[11] Crises can create the opportunity for

[5] eg Agreement between the European Community and the Islamic Republic of Pakistan on the readmission of persons residing without authorization [2010] OJ L287/52; Agreement between the European Union and Georgia on the readmission of persons residing without authorization [2011] OJ L52/47.

[6] See Joint Declaration on Migration Cooperation between Afghanistan and the EU [2021], at www.eeas.europa.eu/sites/default/files/jmcd_-_english_version_signed_26apr2021.pdf. According to the CJEU, the bindingness of an instrument is determined based on its content and context as well as powers of the EU institution that adopted it, see Case C-911/19 *Fédération bancaire française (FBF)* v *Autorité de contrôle prudentiel et de résolution (ACPR)* ECLI:EU:C:2021:599 [36]–[38].

[7] See M Giuffré, 'Readmission Agreements and Refugee Rights: From a Critique to a Proposal' (2013) 32 *Refugee Survey Quarterly* 79, 85–88; N Coleman, *European Readmission Policy. Third Country Interests and Refugee Rights* (Leiden, Brill, 2009) 303, 310–16; F Trauner et al, 'Values versus security in the external dimension of EU migration policy: a case study on the readmission agreement with Russia' in G Noutcheva et al (eds), *The EU and its neighbours: values vs. security in European foreign policy* (Manchester University Press, 2013) 201–17; P Slominski and F Trauner, 'Reforming me softly – how soft law has changed EU return policy since the migration crisis' (2021) 44 *West European Politics* 93.

[8] See eg F Terpan, 'Soft Law in the European Union – The Changing Nature of EU Law' (2014) 21 *European Law Journal* 68.

[9] S Lavenex and L Stucky, 'Partnering for migration in EU external relations,' in R Kunz, S Lavenex and M Panizzon (eds), *Multilayered Migration Governance: The Promise of Partnership* (Routledge, 2011).

[10] A Ott, 'Informalization of EU Bilateral Instruments: Categorization, Contestation, and Challenges' (2020) 39 *Yearbook of European Law*; E Kassoti and N Idriz, 'The informalisation of the EU's External Action in the Field of Migration and Asylum' in E Kassoti and N Idriz (eds) *The Informalisation of the EU's External Action in the Field of Migration and Asylum* (Asser Press and Springer, 2022).

[11] Slominski and Trauner (n 7); S Smeets and D Beach, 'When success is an orphan: informal institutional governance and the EU–Turkey deal' (2019) 43 *West European Politics* 129; V Moreno-Lax, 'The "Crisification" of Migration Law: Insights from the EU External Border' (2023) Queen Mary Law Research Paper No 403/2023.

actors to legitimise power shifts, major institutional changes or policy interventions that previously appeared impossible.[12] Moreover, crises tend to favour the executive[13] as they create a public expectation of speedy political action.[14] In the area of migration, the increasing framing of (irregular) migration as a security threat – a trend also known as *securitisation* of migration[15] – has encouraged states to prioritise the fight against irregular migration and return and readmission of migrants. In parallel, the public perception of migration as an ever-lasting crisis has provided governments with a justification to bypass existing checks and balances, erode accountability requirements and establish a permanent state of 'crisis policy making'.[16]

In this chapter, we explore two interrelated questions: how the European Parliament and the European Ombudsman have responded to the scrutiny and control challenges posed by informalisation of readmission policy; and why those institutions have been reluctant to challenge the executive conduct. We argue that a multifaceted conceptualisation of political conflict can help us understand how and why certain actors may be able to tilt the balance of power in their favour. We demonstrate that both the Parliament and the Ombudsman have in practice refrained from engaging in an actual political confrontation with the EU executive over informalisation of readmission policy by, for example, refraining from challenging the policy procedure employed to bypass Parliamentary consent and transparency requirements. Lack of inter-institutional conflict over procedures may be explained by intra-institutional conflict on policy choices within the Parliament and the unwillingness to interfere in executive policies in the case of the Ombudsman. From the perspective of separation of powers, the lack of inter-institutional conflict appears problematic.

Previous research on EU readmission policy has explored how informalisation weakens the formal opportunities of the Parliament and Court to scrutinise the executive and influence this policy area. Besides the risks of human rights violations, increased reliance on informal readmission arrangements instead of formal agreements intensifies problems for separation of powers, as it erodes checks and balances in the EU inter-institutional structure as well as transparency and accountability of the executive.[17] While previous research has focused on the Parliament formal role, the Parliament's actions and the rationale for such behaviour remain understudied. Similarly, the role of the Ombudsman in readmission policy has not been examined in practice nor studied in previous research.

[12] KH Goetz and D Sindbjerg Martinsen, 'COVID-19: a dual challenge to European liberal democracy' (2021) 44 *West European Politics* 1003, 1007. See also Carrera, Santos Vara and Strik (n 2) 2.

[13] M Rhinard, 'The Crisisification of Policy-making in the European Union' (2019) 57 *Journal of Common Market Studies* 616, 627.

[14] J White, 'Emergency Europe' (2015) 63 *Political Studies* 300.

[15] Moreno-Lax (n 11).

[16] See also Rhinard (n 13); Moreno-Lax (n 11).

[17] See eg M Gatti, 'The Right to Transparency in the External Dimension of the EU Migration Policy: Past and Future Secrets' in E Kassoti and N Idriz (eds), *The Informalisation of the EU's External Action in the Field of Migration and Asylum* (Springer, 2022); P García Andrade, 'The role of the European Parliament in the adoption of non-legally binding agreements with third countries' in J Santos Vara and S Rodríguez Sánchez-Tabernero (eds), *The Democratisation of EU International Relations Through EU Law* (Routledge, 2018) 115; C Molinari, 'The EU and its Perilous journey through the migration crisis: Informalisation of the EU return policy and rule of law concerns' (2019) 44 *European Law Review* 824.

Our findings draw on examples from an empirical project on the roles of the Parliament and the Ombudsman in EU readmission policy. Legal scholars have called for greater attention to the role of institutional practices in shaping EU governance beyond formal rules.[18] As acknowledged in the introduction of this book, conceptions of separation of powers 'are legally prescribed' but 'develop dynamically through practice'. As executive action tends to be structurally invisible in the EU,[19] it is all the more important to identify if, what and on what basis counteractions are undertaken by affected institutional actors. Our empirical contribution aims to shed light on how internal and inter-institutional dynamics shape separation of powers in this field in practice. Our study combined legal and political science approaches and relied on qualitative empirical methods in studying readmission arrangements, such as documentary analysis and interviews, as well as access to documents requests and a complaint to the Ombudsman. The case studies of the Parliament and the Ombudsman do not lend themselves to a strict comparison but offer two interesting examples of how scrutiny and control actors in this policy field respond to growing executive dominance.

The structure of the chapter is as follows. We first introduce the separation of powers framework that we rely on, with a focus on the role of inter-institutional conflict in this framework. We then present the findings of our studies concerning the role of the Parliament and Ombudsman through this lens.

II. Separation of Powers in EU Readmission Policy: Formal Prerogatives and the Impact of Informalisation

In line with the framing of this book (see introduction), we rely on a relational understanding of separation of powers that focuses on relations and dynamics between the three branches rather than strict separation or clear-cut functional delimitations. We understand separation of powers as a 'regulatory ideal' of procedural checks and balances that serves 'the double objectives of ensuring collective will-formation and control of those in power',[20] but that nonetheless is declined differently across institutional systems and policy fields. In the context of the EU's *sui generis* institutional structure, we focus on its configuration in readmission policy. We then present our analytical framework on conflict to better understand how separation of powers develops through practice.

The competence to conclude readmission agreements enshrined in Article 79(3) TFEU is the only explicit competence of the EU in external migration policy. Readmission agreements are concluded in accordance with the procedure specified in Article 218 TFEU which assigns a specific role to each institution. The Council authorises the opening of negotiations, adopts negotiating directives, authorises the signing

[18] B De Witte, 'Legal Methods for the Study of EU Institutional Practice' (2022) 18 *European Constitutional Law Review* 637.

[19] D Curtin, *Executive Power of the European Union. Law, Practices, and the Living Constitution* (Oxford University Press, 2009) 3.

[20] ch 1 in this book.

of agreements and concludes them as well as nominates the negotiator, thus exercising executive powers together with the Commission who negotiates the agreements. The Parliament's consent is, however, necessary for the conclusion of an agreement, and the Parliament must be immediately and fully informed at all stages of the procedure. Moreover, the Parliament has the opportunity to obtain the CJEU's binding opinion as to whether an envisaged agreement is compatible with the Treaties. Although the Parliament does not have a similar role as in the internal dimension of migration and asylum policy as the co-legislator, it still retains several central control and scrutiny powers in concluding formal readmission agreements.

While the division of roles between institutions under Article 218 TFEU may appear clear, it is in practice much more contested, as EU institutions have repeatedly litigated their prerogatives in different policy areas.[21] From the perspective of the Parliament, such configuration begs the question of whether its involvement in readmission policy approximates more that of a watchdog exercising control or a legislator exercising will-formation. While legal scholarship tends to equate the right of consent and the Commission's reporting obligations as the formal justification for Parliament's scrutiny role, political scientists have shown that Parliament may also use its de facto veto power as a way to insert substantial preferences in international agreements, therefore de facto contributing to the legislative process and will formation.[22]

Informal arrangements dramatically reduce Parliament's formal role in the process regarding both scrutiny and control on the one side and will formation on the other.[23] Council and Commission negotiate them without the Parliament's participation and consent. The Parliament does not have a formal prerogative to be informed about the negotiations, neither can it ask for the CJEU's *ex ante* opinion. From the perspective of transparency, informal arrangements differ from formal agreements, which are published in the *Official Journal*, as informal arrangements are usually not publicly available (although often leaked).[24] In principle, informal arrangements can be reviewed afterwards by the CJEU pursuant to Article 263 TFEU, but the reviewability depends

[21] See eg Case C-263/14 *European Parliament v Council of the European Union* ('*Tanzania*') ECLI:EU:C:2016:435; Case C-28/12 *European Commission v Council of the European Union* ('*US Air Transport Agreement*') ECLI:EU:C:2015:282; AP van der Mei, 'EU External Relations and Internal Inter-Institutional Conflicts: The Battlefield of Article 218 TFEU' (2016) 23 *Maastricht Journal of European and Comparative Law* 1051.

[22] See eg A Héritier et al, *European Parliament Ascendant* (Palgrave MacMillan, 2019); M Frennhoff Larsén, 'Parliamentary Influence Ten Years After Lisbon: EU Trade Negotiations with Japan' (2020) 58 *Journal of Common Market Studies* 1540; L Van den Putte, F De Ville and J Orbie, 'The European Parliament as an international actor in trade' in S Stavridis and D Irrera (eds), *The European Parliament and its International Relation* (Routledge, 2015); AR Servent, 'The Role of the European Parliament in International Negotiations after Lisbon' (2014) 21 *Journal of European Public Policy* 568.

[23] D Gnes and M Sormunen, 'Controlling the executive in external migration policy? A preliminary assessment of the role of the European Parliament in scrutinising and influencing EU informal readmission arrangements' (2022) CLEER Working Paper.

[24] See M Sormunen and D Gnes, 'Learning through rejection: studying the informalisation of EU readmission policy with access to documents requests' in M Hillebrandt et al (eds), *(In)visible European government. Critical approaches to transparency as an ideal and a practice* (Routledge, 2023); M Gatti, 'The right to transparency in the external dimension of the EU migration policy: Past and future secrets' in E Kassoti and N Idriz (eds), *The informalisation of the EU's external action in the field of migration and asylum* (TMC Asser Press and Springer, 2022).

on whether the Court considers an arrangement to have binding effects.[25] From a legitimacy perspective, such sidelining of the Parliament is problematic as it is the only democratically elected EU institution.

As the informalisation of readmission policy moreover intensifies problems such as lack of transparency and absence of judicial remedies, it is worth asking whether other institutions, such as the European Ombudsman, may provide other forms of control on the conduct of EU executive actors. From the perspective of separation of powers, the Ombudsman is a quasi-judicial actor with control powers that escapes easy attempts of classification; indeed, some scholars have classified the Ombudsman as part of the 'fourth branch'.[26] The Ombudsman arguably complements the judiciary[27] with her broader mandate and provides non-judicial redress with non-binding decisions.[28] Both the Court and the Ombudsman share the objective of framing and constraining EU institutions' and bodies' discretionary powers.[29] As the Ombudsman is entitled to monitor 'instances of maladministration', the concept of maladministration is central to defining the Ombudsman's mandate, as we will see in the empirical sections of this chapter.[30]

III. Assessing Inter-institutional Relations and Separation of Powers Through the Lens of Conflict

Recent trends in external migration policy have challenged the core idea of separation of powers, the non-concentration of power in a single source not countered by a strong legislature and judiciary.[31] Such trends resonate with Minkkinen and Leino-Sandberg's

[25] For the cases concerning the EU–Turkey statement, see Case T-192/16 *NF v European Council* ECLI:EU:T:2017:12; Case T-193/16 *NG v European Council* ECLI:EU:T:2017:129; Case T-257/16 *NM v European Council* ECLI:EU:T:2017:130.

[26] C Eckes et al, 'Conceptual Framework for the Project Separation of Powers for 21st Century Europe (SepaRope)' (2021) Amsterdam Law School Research Paper No 2021-06, 10; BW Head, 'The contribution of integrity agencies to good governance' (2012) 33 *Policy Studies* 7.

[27] eg A Wille and M Bovens, 'Watching EU watchdogs assessing the accountability powers of the European Court of auditors and the European Ombudsman' (2022) 44 *Journal of European* Integration 183; M Eliantonio and N Vogiatzis, 'Judicial and Extra-Judicial Challenges in the EU Multi- and Cross-Level Administrative Framework' (2021) 22 *German Law* Journal 315.

[28] M Krajewski, *Relative Authority of Judicial and Extra-Judicial Review: EU Courts, Boards of Appeal, Ombudsman* (Hart Publishing, 2021).

[29] ibid 8.

[30] On maladministration, see eg HCH Hofmann, 'The developing role of the European ombudsman' in HCH Hofmann and J Ziller (eds), *Accountability in the EU* (Edward Elgar Publishing, 2017) 11–16; D Dragos and B Neamtu, 'Freedom of Information in the EU in the Midst of Legal Rules. Jurisprudence and Ombudsprudence: The European Ombudsman as Developer of Norms of Good Administration' (2017) 13 *European Constitutional Law Review* 641.

[31] J Santos Vara, 'Soft international agreements on migration cooperation with third countries: a challenge to democratic and judicial controls in the EU' in S Carrera, J Santos Vara and T Strik (eds), *Constitutionalising the External Dimensions of EU Migration Policies in Times of Crisis* (Edward Elgar Publishing, 2019); C Molinari, 'The EU and its Perilous Journey through the Migration Crisis: Informalisation of the EU Return Policy and Rule of Law Concerns' (2019) 44 *European Law Review* 824; PG Andrade, 'The role of the European Parliament in the adoption of non-legally binding agreements with third countries' in J Santos Vara and SR Sánchez-Tabernero (eds), *The Democratisation of EU International Relations Through EU Law* (Routledge, 2018).

analysis (in this book) that the EU is moving from three branches to consensual executive government characterised by a weak Parliament and weak Court, resulting in a dual instead of a tripartite model. The concept of crisis, as already discussed in the introduction, is key to understanding this development. At the same time, in the context of inter-institutional relations, Minkkinen and Leino-Sandberg also detect a lack of disagreement and contestation on executive conduct and choices at EU level. Accordingly, a central feature of recent developments underlying growing executive dominance is a lack of *conflict* between institutions: other branches may be not only unable but also unwilling to interfere, leaving a wide margin for discretion to the executive and displaying deference by not questioning its assessment.[32]

We suggest that conflict, or the lack thereof, is in fact key to understand changing inter-institutional relations in the context of separation of powers in the EU, including in EU readmission policy. We define conflict in this context as fundamental political disagreement within or between EU institutions resulting in a confrontation of varying intensity over policy choices and/or policy procedures. Conflict over policy procedures may be particularly salient in cases where certain institutional actors – for example, the executive – appropriate competences and/or prerogatives of other institutions. For the purpose of this chapter, and in line with the focus of the book, we are particularly interested in conflict over procedures. However, as we will see in our case study, conflict over policy choices and procedures are often deeply intertwined. In line with our definition, we further understand conflict as taking place *between* institutions (*inter-institutional conflict*) or within institutions (*intra-institutional* conflict).

A normative assessment of conflict in the EU from a perspective of separation of powers is a complex endeavour. To paraphrase Möllers, while the democratic process implies dissent on the merits – so that policy choices can truly be an expression of will-formation – it also depends on societal consensus on procedures in order to function.[33] Those considerations can be applied to the context of the EU as well. However, the EU's multilayered and polycentric construction, with an institutional configuration in flux, the existence of several decision-making procedures depending on the policy field and the absence of a unitary executive, call for a more fine-grained analysis of the implications of conflict, both regarding policy choices and policy procedures. This picture is further complicated by the fact that both the Parliament and the Council routinely experience conflict internally as well and that their political interests and constituencies are often at odds with each other.[34] From a democratic perspective, and particularly when competences and prerogatives are being challenged by a given actor, lack of conflict may over time hinder democratic will-formation altogether. In that sense, failing to use powers may therefore be as problematic to separation of powers as

[32] For a definition of deference, see eg J Zglinski, *Europe's Passive Virtues: Deference to National Authorities in EU Free Movement Law* (Oxford University Press, 2020).

[33] C Möllers, *The Three Branches. A Comparative Model of Separation of Powers* (Oxford University Press, 2013) 76.

[34] M Mühlböck and B Rittberger, 'The Council, the European Parliament, and the paradox of inter-institutional cooperation' (2015) 19 *European Integration online Papers*, Art 4, 1–20, at eiop.or.at/eiop/texte/2015-004a.htm; S Hix, 'Parliamentary Behavior with Two Principals: Preferences, Parties, and Voting in the European Parliament' (2002) 46 *American Journal of Political Science* 688.

seizing powers, as failing to use powers can eventually result in a collapse of separation of powers.[35]

Several factors may explain the lack of inter-institutional conflict over policy procedures. Starting from the Parliament, the content of policies is in fact the first factor: for example, if the views of the Parliament substantively align with those of the executive regarding the content of readmission policy, questioning the policy may not be in the Parliament's interest. Regarding the content of policies as a relevant factor is in line with theories of rational choice institutionalism in political science, according to which inter-institutional conflicts tend to originate from different preferences of actors as well as the different intra-institutional structures. MEPs represent the ideological preferences of both their national parties and their European party groups.[36] Along the same lines, a strong divergence in political preferences within the Parliament may trigger intra-institutional conflict that prevents political parties to form a unified Parliamentary to challenge the political behaviour of other actors, namely the EU executive, on procedural matters.

Second, Otjes and Van der Veer have demonstrated that, regarding the Parliament specifically, voting reflects not only substantive disagreements over policy outcomes but also views as to whether the Parliament should procedurally aspire to maximise its powers.[37] The traditional understanding that Parliament is a unitary actor always desiring more power is therefore misleading. Particularly in recent times, Parliamentary powers are instead debated in the Parliament alongside substantive questions. They are therefore 'not just part of the process of constitution-writing, but a continuous and intra-institutional conflict'. Political parties have different preferences on whether the Parliament should extend its powers, which results in intra-institutional conflicts.[38] Consequently, the lack of inter-institutional conflict does not mean there are no conflicts, rather that such conflicts are located on a different level.

Third, embedded factors such as institutional structures may have contributed to decreasing inter-institutional conflict. According to theories of sociological constructivism, actors' preferences are shaped by the institutional environment.[39] For example, the development of shared norms around inter-institutional cooperation and the need to act 'responsibly' by embracing compromise have influenced Parliamentary behaviour since its enhanced powers post-Lisbon.[40] Additionally, along these lines, the Parliament may view readmission policy (or any other given field) as belonging to the executive. Internal decision-making procedures may further contribute to explaining the existence or lack of conflict. For example, rapporteurs of particular files have a lot of power in parliamentary committees.[41] The Parliament

[35] A Wallerman Ghavanini, 'The CJEU's give-and-give relationship with executive actors in times of crisis' (2023) 2 *European Law Open* 284.

[36] Mühlböck and Rittberger (n 34); Hix (n 34).

[37] H Van der Veer and S Otjes, 'A House Divided against Itself. The Intra-institutional Conflict about the Powers of the European Parliament' (2021) 59 *Journal of Common Market Studies* 822.

[38] ibid.

[39] Mühlböck and Rittberger (n 34) 8.

[40] A Ripoll Servent, 'Playing the Co-Decision Game? Rules' Changes and Institutional Adaptation at the LIBE Committee' (2012) 34 *Journal of European Integration* 55.

[41] eg P Leino-Sandberg, *The Politics of Legal Expertise in EU Policy-Making* (Cambridge University Press, 2021).

is characterised by political disagreements, and not managing to solve these internal disagreements contributes to a lack of inter-institutional conflict. The relatively weak position of the Parliament in relation to other branches may also prevent the Parliament from creating inter-institutional conflict.

Some of these elements do not apply to the Ombudsman as the Ombudsman is not a political institution but a quasi-judicial redress mechanism. However, as the Ombudsman operates at the intersection of the legal and political spheres, she is afforded a certain degree of flexibility over whether to open an inquiry. Previous research has found that the current Ombudsman has taken a 'pragmatic' approach aiming at tackling systemic problems.[42] First, from a rational choice perspective, factors such as the general political consensus on the topic, the nature of the policy field as well as the public opinion may be weighed by the Ombudsman when considering the opening of an inquiry. This may be all the more salient in the field of migration, which has been deeply politicised over the last decade. The politicisation has affected the behaviour of courts; for example, Wallerman Ghavanini has demonstrated that the CJEU has been more deferential towards both EU and national executives in its migration law after the 2015-16 crisis.[43] The CJEU's approach in migration cases has been considered deferential in general.[44]

Second, the role of the institutional environment in shaping the actors' preferences[45] is a relevant factor regarding the Ombudsman, too. Like the Parliament, the Ombudsman may view the specific policy field as belonging to the executive. If the Ombudsman sees the decision to choose whether to conclude a formal or an informal instrument as a prerogative of the executive, she does not see any reason to intervene. Moreover, the Ombudsman's position suffers from the need to motivate institutions to cooperate, as the Ombudsman's decisions are not binding. Rational choice explanations emphasise strategic aspects that shape the decision to engage in conflict or not, such as the likelihood to win the dispute and obtain gains, potential damage to inter-institutional collaboration, as well as availability of internal resources. Potential explanations for the behaviour of the Parliament and the Ombudsman are further teased out in the context of our empirical analysis in the following sections.

IV. Political Control: The European Parliament

The Parliament has four central prerogatives in formal readmission agreements: accessing information; giving its consent; asking the CJEU's *ex ante* opinion; and challenging a readmission agreement under Article 263 TFEU. The prerogative to give its consent means that the Parliament possesses a veto power over executive action as it can decide not to approve an agreement. In principle, informal readmission arrangements weaken

[42] DM Curtin and P Leino, 'In search of transparency for EU law-making: Trilogues on the cusp of dawn' (2017) 54 *Common Market Law Review* 1673; M Krajewski, *Relative Authority of Judicial and Extra-Judicial Review: EU Courts, Boards of Appeal, Ombudsman* (Hart Publishing, 2021) 143.

[43] Wallerman Ghavanini (n 35).

[44] I Goldner Lang, 'Towards "Judicial Passivism" in EU Migration and Asylum Law?' in T Cárpeta et al (eds), *The Changing European Union: A Critical View on the Role of Law and Courts* (Hart Publishing, 2020).

[45] Mühlböck and Rittberger (n 34) 8.

all of these prerogatives and limit the Parliament's capacity to control the executive and to participate in will-formation. To analyse how informalisation of readmission practically impacted Parliament's behaviour in this policy field, we studied two aspects: Parliament's access to information concerning informal and formal readmission agreements; and Parliament's behaviour in influencing readmission policy. Methodologically, we conducted an analysis of Parliamentary and legislative documents and hearings from 2009 to 2022 as well as 25 semi-structured interviews with MEPs, Parliamentary advisors and other relevant actors.[46] For this chapter, we analysed our findings from the perspective of assessing whether, in both access to information and policy influence, Parliament engaged in a political confrontation – or conflict as we call it in this chapter – with EU executive institutions.

A. Access to Information (Scrutiny and Control)

Concerning access to information, we examined the extent to which the Parliament challenged its limited access to information on informal readmission arrangements provided by the European Commission. Access to information is generally considered a key precondition for effective Parliamentary scrutiny.[47] According to the CJEU, the obligation to inform the Parliament is broad and extends to all stages of the procedure when it comes to the conclusion of formal agreements.[48] Although such obligation does not exist for informal arrangements, the Commission did acknowledge the need to assess whether informing the European Parliament 'on a case-by-case level … is appropriate'.[49] On the content of the informal arrangements, our findings indicated that the EU executive did not systematically and proactively inform the Parliament.[50] Most readmission arrangements were made publicly available through leaks only, and MEPs usually learned about the arrangements through those leaks or via Commission press releases. Being barred from access to information, Parliament decided in this case to engage in an open conflict with the Commission: it actively fought what it saw as a breach of its prerogatives of control and scrutiny over EU readmission policy. It did so through the strategic use of political pressure on the Commission, by employing three main tools: non-legislative resolutions, adopted in plenary; written questions to the executive, especially the Commission; and committee hearings and written correspondence with the Commission.[51] In particular, committee hearings and written correspondence proved to be the most effective means to gain access to information which could not be obtained from publicly available press releases and reports prepared by the Commission.

[46] For further details on the methodology: D Gnes and M Sormunen (n 23), D Gnes and M Sormunen, 'From parliamentarization to informalization? Assessing the influence of the European Parliament in EU readmission policy in Post-Lisbon EU' (Paper presented at the conference of the European Consortium for Political Research (ECPR), Innsbruck, 24 August 2022).

[47] GJ Brandsma, 'The effect of information on oversight: the European Parliament's response to increasing information on comitology decision-making' (2012) 78 *International Review of Administrative Sciences* 74.

[48] Case C-263/14 *European Parliament v Council of the European Union* ECLI:EU:C:2016:435 [76].

[49] Commission, 'Vademecum on the external action of the European Union' [2011] SEC(2011)881/3, 53.

[50] Gnes and Sormunen (n 23).

[51] For an overview of the actions, see Gnes and Sormunen (n 23).

Committee hearings form the basis for exchange of information between the Commission and LIBE. The practice of including readmission arrangements in select hearings on readmission policy first developed as a result of the political pressure coming from several political groups within the LIBE committee.[52] Importantly, there was a general consensus amongst the majority of political parties across the ideological spectrum that Parliament's right to be informed and involved in scrutinising readmission policy should be protected and publicly asserted.[53] Besides the drafting of questions to the Commission (and sometimes the Council) in plenary and committee sessions,[54] such pressure translated in plenary resolutions touching upon Parliament's sidelining in informalisation[55] and, more importantly, in the organisation of committee events on documents such as the Joint Way Forward with Afghanistan (JWF), the first readmission arrangement concluded by the EU in October 2016. In particular, in December 2016, taking advantage of a pre-established exchange venue for regular Parliamentary hearings on readmission agreements – as well as a pre-existing working relationship with DG HOME officials – LIBE members were able to include the JWF on the agenda of the hearing on readmission agreements.[56] While the Commission is not under the legal obligation of doing so, it has since accepted the practice and regularly stresses that it 'regularly provides updates on readmission agreements and *arrangements* [emphasis added]' to the LIBE Committee.'[57]

Following explicit requests by former LIBE Chair Claude Moraes, DG HOME in parallel began to inform the Parliament on readmission arrangements, inaugurating the practice of sending LIBE members a letter ahead of a scheduled hearing providing the 'state of play' on readmission cooperation with third countries (including arrangements).[58] Such information did not cover the texts of the arrangements per se, but rather focused on the broader context of their conclusion and implementation vis-à-vis specific third countries.[59] The quality of information provided by the Commission has often been criticised by MEPs. The Commission has indeed

[52] European Parliament, '"EU–Afghanistan Joint Way Forward on migration issues": Role and consultation of the European Parliament' [13 October 2016] Parliamentary Question O-000123/2016.

[53] Maintaining right of scrutiny and access to information has been a concern repeatedly expressed by (almost) all of the main political groups since the post-Lisbon reform in this policy field. This was expressed in several ways: resolutions voted in EP plenary on several occasions, most recently in European Parliament resolution of 19 May 2021 on human rights protection and the EU external migration policy (2020/2116(INI)) P9_TA(2021)0242; reference in several reports on the conclusion of formal readmission agreements by rapporteurs of various political groups; expressed in several interventions during exchange of views with the Commission, particularly between late 2016 and late 2018 when many of the current readmission arrangements were concluded. For more details, see Gnes and Sormunen (n 23).

[54] European Parliament (n 52).

[55] eg European Parliament Resolution of 5 April 2017 on addressing refugee and migrant movements: the role of EU External Action (2015/2342(INI)) [2017] P8_TA(2017)0124, paras 69–70; European Parliament Resolution of 19 May 2021 on human rights protection and the EU external migration policy (2020/2116(INI)) [2021] P9_TA(2021)0242.

[56] European Parliament, 'Meeting of LIBE of Monday, 5 December 2016' [2016] LIBE_PV(2016)12-05-1, Comment by MEP and LIBE Chair, Claude Moraes.

[57] European Parliament, 'Answer given by Mr Avramopoulos on behalf of the Commission' [31 May 2018] Parliamentary Question E-000956/2018(ASW).

[58] European Parliament (n 56).

[59] An example of this type of letter, which remains confidential, is available at www.statewatch.org/news/2017/november/statewatch-news-online-returns-and-readmissions-highlight-reluctance-of-african-states-to-comply-with-eu-demands.

responded evasively especially to questions concerning Parliamentary prerogatives and the decision to adopt soft law,[60] and it has still refused to grant direct access to the arrangements themselves.[61] Nevertheless, when compared with what the Commission disclosed regarding formal agreements, particularly regarding implementation, the differences did not appear significant. This analysis therefore demonstrates that the Parliament was willing to engage in a certain level of confrontation with the Commission to assert its right to information. Importantly, to such inter-institutional conflict corresponded a lack of intra-institutional conflict, as all major political groups supported such goal. This state of affairs allowed the Parliament as a collective entity to exercise sufficient political pressure for the Commission to offer procedural concessions.

B. Influence on the Substance of EU Readmission Policy and Informalisation (Will Formation)

Concerning Parliament's behaviour, we analysed the extent to which the Parliament was willing to engage in a political confrontation with the Commission (and/or the Council) regarding the latter's decision to bypass Parliamentary consent. In this case, Parliament initially engaged in a certain degree of political conflict over the issue. Individual MEPs criticised both procedural and substantive issues related to informal arrangements, including diminished democratic oversight and potential problems related to human rights, monitoring and increased conditionality, including using development aid to pressure third countries to cooperate.[62] A central strategy was to raise readmission policy in areas where the Parliament's prerogatives are stronger than in readmission, for example, through budget-related legislation. MEPs have since used a variety of measures to criticise informalisation of readmission policy, including legislative and non-legislative resolutions in related policy fields, non-legislative motions, and request for a legal opinion to inquire about the legal status of informal arrangements.[63] Despite such variety of actions, Parliament has refused to escalate the dispute into a full-blown conflict. It did not block or stall legislation in other areas, including in migration and asylum or on budget matters. Even more consequentially, it refused to use one of the strongest actions at its disposal, that is challenging informal readmission arrangements before the CJEU. Such an action would not have been so far-fetched in light of the Parliament's history as an active litigator concerned with defending its institutional prerogatives.[64] As a result, we may conclude that, while Parliament made its discontent known to the Commission on several occasions, it was unwilling to escalate the

[60] European Parliament, 'Minutes, Meeting of LIBE from Monday, 22 March 2021 to Tuesday, 23 March 2021' [2021] LIBE_PV(2021)0322_1; European Parliament, 'Minutes, Meeting of LIBE from Monday 31 January 2022, to Tuesday 1 February 2022' [2022] LIBE_PV(2022)0131_1.

[61] European Parliament, 'Readmission arrangements' [16 April 2019] Parliamentary Question E-001881/2019, Question for written answer E-001881/19 to the Commission by MEP Lamberts (Verts/ALE); European Parliament, 'Answer given by Mr Avramopoulos on behalf of the European Commission' [8 July 2019] Parliamentary Question E-001881/2019(ASW).

[62] European Parliament Resolution of 5 April 2017 (n 55) para 59.

[63] Following our access to documents request, the legal advice on readmission cooperation is available at www.asktheeu.org/en/request/legal_advice_on_readmission_coop.

[64] eg Leino-Sandberg (n 41).

dispute to defend its formal prerogatives, both to gain formal access to the text of the arrangements and to grant its consent upon their conclusion.

The low level of inter-institutional conflict we observed between the Parliament and the Commission then begs the question of why that was the case. As we argued elsewhere,[65] intra-institutional conflict is in fact a key element to explain the Parliament's acquiescence in external migration policy. Up until the early 2010s, relatively few intra-institutional conflicts took place on migration issues within relevant Parliamentary committees. Until then, a pro-human rights position was shared by the majority of members of committees such as AFET and LIBE. Since such a position was usually in contrast with positions held by the Commission and especially the Council, it was also perfectly compatible with a power-maximising stance calling for increased Parliamentary powers and influence in this field. As a result, Parliamentary conflict was primarily projected externally in relation to other institutions, as the institution was able to project a unified and arguably much more influential front vis-à-vis the Council and the Commission.

In our research, we have suggested that Parliamentary behaviour aiming at maximising the Parliament's powers began to change in the mid-2010s, in parallel with the growing political salience of migration as a security threat.[66] The politicisation of migration has since strengthened the front of Parliament's political groups that is in favour of restrictive migration control policies, including a more aggressive stance on readmission cooperation with third countries. The views of this front – including the European People's Party (EPP) Group, the European Conservatives and Reformists (ECR) Group, the far-right and part of Alliance of Liberals and Democrats for Europe (ALDE)/Renew Group – have aligned with emerging positions inside the Council, the Commission and, most consequentially, the European Council. When the EU executive actors launched informal readmission arrangements as a way to make readmission 'more effective',[67] in the context of increased emphasis on migration control and combating irregular migration, a majority of political actors inside Parliament supported or at least did not openly question this policy turn. In practice, while pro-migration control Parliamentarians in the LIBE and AFET committees did mildly criticise informalisation of readmission on grounds of breach of Parliamentary prerogatives, they also endorsed the content of readmission arrangements since they believed the arrangements addressed major demands from their constituents to manage irregular migration. Moreover, while pro-human rights Parliamentarians challenged informalisation both on procedural and substantive grounds, especially human rights concerns, they were unable to muster a majority to escalate the conflict towards the other institutions. Political pressure from the Council and the European Council, limited available resources and the relatively small expected gain prompted the critical political groups – mainly the European United Left/Nordic Green Left (GUE/NGL)/The Left, the Greens European Free Alliance (EFA), the Progressive Alliance of Socialists and Democrats (S&D) and a minority of ALDE/Renew – to resort to actions

[65] D Gnes and M Sormunen 'Solving the problem or protecting its turf? Explaining the European Parliament's reluctance to counter informalization of EU readmission policy' (unpublished).

[66] ibid.

[67] Commission, 'Communication on establishing a new Partnership Framework with third countries under the European Agenda on Migration' [2016] COM(2016) 0385 final.

that can be characterised as political grandstanding. As a result, conflict remained primarily intra-institutional and could not escalate at inter-institutional level.

Our study therefore raises interesting questions regarding the relationship between internal and external conflict dynamics in EU institutions. On the one side, as long as it does not lead to a paralysis of internal deliberation and decision-making procedures, internal conflict within the Parliament may signal positive deliberation and a healthy democratic institution. On the other, because of the specific institutional configuration of the EU, internal conflict may neutralise external conflict when Parliamentary actors are unable to muster a unitary front against other institutions, either because they perceive a benefit on the substance of the policy pursued or perceive the costs of action as too high.

V. Remedial Control: The European Ombudsman

In addition to the weak Parliament, informalised readmission policy is characterised by a lack of remedial mechanisms for control. The unwillingness of the CJEU to intervene in informalised readmission policy was demonstrated in the EU–Turkey statement cases by the General Court. As both the European Parliament and the Court appear to be incapable of or reluctant to scrutinise readmission policy, the question remains as to whether other EU bodies may be willing or able to fill this vacuum and create inter-institutional conflict in migration.

From the perspective of controlling readmission policy, its non-transparency is a major factor in preventing the Parliament but also the public from controlling readmission policy. Because of the EU's complex governance structures, transparency has been viewed as a particularly important element to control the EU executive.[68] In our study, we wanted to empirically test institutional transparency practices and the European Ombudsman's control powers in external migration policy. We were interested especially in whether the Ombudsman could have a role in overseeing the informalisation of EU readmission policy. We anticipated that the Ombudsman's mandate would be broad enough to allow her to do this; according to the Ombudsman's own definition of maladministration that is at the core of her mandate,

> Maladministration occurs if an institution or body fails to act in accordance with the law or the principles of good administration, or violates human rights. Maladministration can include administrative irregularities, unfairness, discrimination or the abuse of power, for example in the managing of EU funds, procurement or recruitment policies. It also includes the failure to reply, or the refusal or unnecessary delay in granting access to information in the public interest.[69]

The definition is thus broad and covers also misconduct that would be difficult to raise before courts.[70]

[68] D Curtin, *Executive Power of the European Union. Law, Practices, and the Living Constitution* (Oxford University Press, 2009).

[69] European Ombudsman, 'Make a Complaint to the European Ombudsman' (no date), at www.ombudsman.europa.eu/en/make-a-complaint; for earlier definitions, see Hofmann (n 30) 12.

[70] Hofmann (n 30) 13–14.

Our analysis is based on empirical data consisting of access to documents requests submitted to the Council of the EU under Regulation 1049/2001 concerning existing readmission arrangements – Afghanistan, Mali, Guinea, Bangladesh, Ethiopia, The Gambia, and Ivory Coast – and of a consequent complaint we made to the Ombudsman in 2022 concerning the Council's non-disclosure practice. We systematically requested access from the Council to informal readmission arrangements and related documents, namely early drafts of the arrangements or cover documents detailing the procedures for approval or the classification of documents, and pursued the applications to the confirmatory stage.[71] As the Parliament does not have privileged access to informal readmission arrangements, the method also allowed us to test the extent to which the Parliament or individual MEPs may be able to obtain information about them as EU citizens, by invoking the right of public access. This is a relevant dimension to discuss as individual MEPs have used this avenue in relation to other agreements, such as SWIFT and ACTA agreements.[72] Our study was inspired by action research[73] and strategic litigation:[74] we actively participated in creating the materials studied by submitting access to documents requests, appealing the negative replies, and complaining to the Ombudsman about the Council's systematic non-disclosure policy as one of the elements of maladministration related to informal arrangements.

The Council refused access to most documents on the ground of the public interest exception of Article 4(1)(a) of the Transparency Regulation (Regulation 1049/2001), arguing that disclosure would harm international relations by revealing to other negotiating partners key strategic considerations, which could then compromise further negotiations. EU institutions often rely on this exception, and it has been argued that a wide interpretation of exceptions to the right to access documents held by EU institutions negatively affects transparency and public participation.[75] In our complaint to the Ombudsman, we identified five problematic elements in the Council's restrictive policy on access to documents:

- an expansive application of the public interest exception as regards international relations;

[71] M Sormunen and D Gnes, 'Learning through rejection: studying the informalisation of EU readmission policy with access to documents requests' in M Hillebrandt et al (eds), *(In)visible European government. Critical approaches to transparency as an ideal and a practice* (Routledge, 2023).

[72] See Case C-350/12 P *Council of the European Union v Sophie in' t Veld* ECLI:EU:C:2014:2039, concerning the SWIFT agreement; Case T-301/10 *In 't Veld v Commission* ECLI:EU:T:2013:135, concerning the ACTA agreement.

[73] R McTaggart, 'Participatory Action Research: issues in theory and practice' (1994) 2 *Educational Action Research* 313; P Leino-Sandberg, 'Transparency as a critical research agenda: Engaging with the EU institutions on access to documents' in M Hillebrandt, P Leino-Sandberg and I Koivisto (eds), *(In)visible European government. Critical approaches to transparency as an ideal and a practice* (Routledge, 2023) (forthcoming).

[74] eg H Duffy, *Strategic Human Rights Litigation: Understanding and Maximising Impact* (Bloomsbury Publishing, 2018) 3; A Pijnenburg and K van der Pas, 'Strategic Litigation against European Migration Control Policies: The Legal Battleground of the Central Mediterranean Migration Route' (2022) 24 *European Journal of Migration and Law* 401.

[75] L Ankersmit and J Peters, 'Public Access to Documents in EU External Relations' (2022) Amsterdam Law School Research Paper No 2022-08; P Leino, 'The Principle of Transparency in EU External Relations Law: Does Diplomatic Secrecy Stand a Chance of Surviving the Age of Twitter?' in M Cremona (ed), *Structural Principles in EU External Relations Law* (Hart Publishing, 2018).

- a restrictive understanding of legislative activities, as the requested documents arguably have legislative implications;
- a restrictive partial access policy of granting access to irrelevant parts of the documents;
- an expansive application of EU document classifications; and
- an unwillingness to release documents already available through leaks.

The purpose of this distinction was to show how interpreting some of the elements restrictively and some expansively results in a restrictive access to documents policy. In handling the case, the Ombudsman sided with the Council and accepted that the non-disclosure of documents did not constitute maladministration while claiming that the broader practice of informal readmission arrangements as carried out by the Commission with the support of the Council falls outside her mandate.[76]

By analysing the Ombudsman's argumentation during the correspondence related to our case and in her decision, we found that perceiving the choice of instrument – soft law or hard law – as falling completely within executive discretion displays deference towards the executive. The executive currently exercises broad discretion when deciding whether informal arrangements should be disclosed. In our case, the Ombudsman did not seem willing to engage in inter-institutional conflict by reducing this margin; rather, she interpreted her mandate restrictively by claiming that the decision to choose between formal and informal instruments in readmission policy is part of the institutions' political work. Firstly, the decision constructs deference by framing the case in line with the Council's arguments and understanding some central concepts, such as public interest, in a way that justifies the Council's restrictive access to documents policy. While the Ombudsman's argumentation can be criticised, it is also true that previous cases show that her predominant approach is to endorse the institution's assessment of the harm to international relations,[77] however conducting a stricter review in some cases.[78]

Secondly, the decision constructs deference by leaving some aspects of the case outside by merging the claims and refusing to address the broader maladministration claim. The Ombudsman distinguished two separate claims in our complaint – one concerning the Council's refusal to grant access to the requested documents and another concerning the Council's practice of making informal readmission arrangements instead of formal ones – and held that the second claim falls outside her mandate and also that we should have first tried to resolve the matter with the Council. However,

[76] European Ombudsman, Case 815/2022/MIG, Decision on the refusal by the Council of the EU to grant public access to documents concerning informal arrangements with non-EU countries about returning migrants (readmission agreements) [1 September 2022].

[77] eg the ACTA case: European Ombudsman, Case 90/2009/(JD)OV, Decision of the European Ombudsman closing his inquiry into complaint 90/2009/(JD)OV against the Council of the European Union [23 July 2010].

[78] eg European Ombudsman, Case 1703/2021/AMF, Decision on the Council of the EU's refusal to give public access to documents concerning the ongoing negotiations on the taxation of digital services [30 May 2022] para 25; European Ombudsman, Case 1499/2021/SF, Decision on the Council of the European Union's refusal to give full public access to a legal opinion related to the EU trade agreement with the United Kingdom [24 February 2022] para 19.

while this choice was communicated to us during the correspondence, the decision does not clearly express that we did not only complain about access to documents but also raised a broader claim. Consequently, our central finding was that while the Ombudsman's mandate would arguably allow her to actively oversee the various instruments of readmission policy, our case demonstrates her reluctancy to take this role.

From the perspective of the idea that conflicts are vital for separation of powers, it is important to assess whether an actor is unable or unwilling to engage in inter-institutional conflicts. The Ombudsman's view that the decision to use soft law is not part of the institutions' administrative activity and therefore falls outside her mandate can be questioned. Firstly, political work and maladministration are not synonymous; the Ombudsman's own definition of maladministration is wide, therefore covering various types of misconduct.[79] Administrative activity and maladministration are also not synonymous.[80] Secondly, distinguishing between the political and administrative spheres is difficult, which has also been acknowledged by the Ombudsman in previous cases.[81] Previously, the Ombudsman has excluded the Parliament's political work from her mandate[82] and otherwise shown willingness to review actions that institutions themselves have characterised as political.[83] The Ombudsman has not handled many cases related to informal migration arrangements, but in the existing cases she has focused on human rights impact assessments – that is, substantive questions – instead of procedural shortcomings such as the Parliament's exclusion.[84] However, the Ombudsman has handled several complaints and conducted own-initiative inquiries in the activities of Frontex, recommending that Frontex increase transparency and monitoring[85] and improve accessibility of the complaints mechanism.[86]

[79] For the current definition, see European Ombudsman (n 69); for earlier definitions, see Hofmann (n 30) 12.

[80] I Harden, 'The European Ombudsman's role in promoting good governance' in HCH Hofmann and J Ziller (eds), *Accountability in the EU. The Role of the European Ombudsman* (Edward Elgar Publishing 2017) 202–03.

[81] European Ombudsman, Cases 506-509-674-784-927-1381/2016/MHZ, Decision of the European Ombudsman in the joint inquiry into complaints 506-509-674-784-927-1381/2016/MHZ against the European Commission concerning a human rights impact assessment in the context of the EU-Turkey Agreement [18 January 2017] para 26; Curtin and Leino (n 42) 1686–88.

[82] European Ombudsman, Case 417/2015/NF, Decision in case 417/2015/NF against the European Commission regarding delegated and implementing acts in the area of the Common Agricultural Policy [21 September 2016] para 12.

[83] eg European Ombudsman, Case OI/2015/JAS, Decision of the European Ombudsman setting out proposals following her strategic inquiry OI/8/2015/JAS concerning the transparency of Trilogues [12 July 2016].

[84] European Ombudsman, Cases 506-509-674-784-927-1381/2016/MHZ [2017] (n 81) para 25; European Ombudsman, Case SI/5/2023/MHZ, Strategic initiative SI/5/2023/MHZ on how the European Commission intends to guarantee respect for human rights in the context of the EU-Tunisia Memorandum of Understanding [13 September 2023].

[85] European Ombudsman, Case OI/4/2021/MHZ, Decision in OI/4/2021/MHZ on how the European Border and Coast Guard Agency (Frontex) complies with its fundamental rights obligations and ensures accountability in relation to its enhanced responsibilities [17 January 2022].

[86] European Ombudsman, Case OI/5/2020/MHZ, Decision in OI/5/2020/MHZ on the functioning of the European Border and Coast Guard Agency's (Frontex) complaints mechanism for alleged breaches of fundamental rights and the role of the Fundamental Rights Officer (no maladministration) [15 June 2021].

From the perspective of the public, our method was useful since it enabled us to push institutions to justify their choice to deviate from the general presumption of transparency, a central value of the EU expressed in Article 15(1) TFEU. Moreover, Article 15(3) TFEU guarantees any EU citizen a right of access to documents of EU institutions, formulated as an individual right. The obligation of the administration to give reasons for its decisions is guaranteed by Article 41(2) of the Charter of Fundamental Rights of the EU. According to Eckes, the public has the right to ask justifications from the political branches especially for choices that interfere with fundamental rights. The judiciary has a central role in enabling the public to make such claims.[87] In our Ombudsman case, the Ombudsman did not explain in the decision why she regarded the broader maladministration claim as falling outside her mandate. From the perspective of the right to receive reasoned decisions, it can be considered problematic that the grounds for not examining a complaint and not creating inter-institutional conflict are not included and cannot be assessed by the public.

We did not study the Ombudsman's reasons for not interfering with executive action and creating inter-institutional conflict, but it is interesting to reflect on the reasons behind such a choice in light of the factors that may explain the lack of conflict. It is possible, of course, that the Ombudsman considered the Council's decisions to be substantively correct and therefore chose to solve the case accordingly. The Ombudsman may also have viewed the decision to choose between formal and informal instruments in readmission policy as a prerogative of the executive. However, we may speculate that other considerations might have affected the outcome, too, because of the several deferential choices that the Ombudsman arguably made during the process. In terms of strategic considerations, the Ombudsman exercises soft power and needs to persuade EU institutions and bodies to cooperate. Courts are affected by similar considerations, too. The Ombudsman might therefore be unwilling to interfere in the relations between the institutions. It is important to keep in mind the Ombudsman's role as a quasi-judicial body and not place unrealistic expectations on how much conflict she would be able to create without possessing the means to motivate other institutions to cooperate. In our complaint, we explained that we find problematic the Parliament's exclusion from the decision-making process for informal readmission arrangements. When indicating her interpretation that the broader maladministration claim falls outside her mandate, the Ombudsman suggested that we bring the matter to the attention of the Parliament itself, which does not seem like an effective channel to address the Parliament's exclusion. Finally, we may speculate that another possible factor explaining the Ombudsman's conduct is related to the polarised nature of migration policy. It is possible that the Ombudsman, in line with similar actions by the CJEU, decided to steer clear from a field that is too politicised and touches upon the sensitivities of Member States. More research is needed to better understand the motivations and reasoning behind the Ombudsman's actions in this and other policy fields.

[87] C Eckes, 'Tackling the Climate Crisis with Counter-majoritarian Instruments: Judges Between Political Paralysis, Science, and International Law' (2021) 6 *European Papers* 1307, 1321–22.

VI. Conclusions: Lack of Inter-institutional Conflict in Informalised Readmission Policy

The empirical studies discussed in this chapter show how the informalisation turn in EU readmission policy raises concerns about effective control of the EU executive. By focusing on the importance of conflict for separation of powers, we demonstrated that informalised readmission policy has not triggered a significant inter-institutional conflict between institutions on the procedural aspects of informalisation of readmission policy; both the European Parliament and the Ombudsman leave a wide margin to the executive, avoiding challenging its conduct in fundamental terms. While the Parliament has acted to assert its right to information, it has also been unable (but also unwilling) to intervene in informalisation. Through the lens of political conflict, we argue that intra-institutional conflicts around migration policy choices have prevented the Parliament from developing a robust inter-institutional conflict with the Commission beyond the one meant to secure (limited) access to information. The Ombudsman also seems reluctant to intervene in matters she characterises as political, thus leaving a wide discretion to the executive to steer readmission policy with informal instruments.

With this chapter, we attempted to show how conflict is an important aspect of separation of powers on the ground and, consequently, how different types of conflict (inter-institutional or intra-institutional) may challenge or buttress changing institutional configurations of power. From a relational perspective, formal prerogatives and competences written on the books are enacted, expanded, protected and contested by institutional actors in everyday political practice. Along these lines, we also suggested that a focus on a multifaceted conceptualisation of conflict can help us understand how and why certain actors may be able to upset the balance of power in the EU's institutional setting. In our specific case, we argued that lack of inter-institutional conflict over policy *procedures* may be explained by intra-institutional conflict on policy *choices* (within Parliament), and the Ombudsman's unwillingness to endanger working relationships with the executive by granting deference in a politicised field. In particular, in the case of the Parliament, we witness the paradox that what is usually seen as a healthy feature of a democratic institution – the existence of diverging views on political choices, and a corresponding internal conflict amongst political factions on such choices – may actually neutralise the Parliament's ability to counter executive overreach and defend those very democratic prerogatives. This is all the more relevant in the EU, where checks and balances have evolved over the years and are not as sedimented as in national contexts. Our conflict framework may be applicable to other policy fields as well, particularly in areas where we witness executive overreach but, at the same time, the political stakes over the policy content of the measure are high.

Our findings thus question the assumption of Parliament as an institution always committed to defending its institutional prerogatives and using all means at its disposal to maximise its power and influence, which has been documented in previous research.[88] The cost of low-level inter-institutional conflict may well be Parliament's

[88] eg A Héritier et al, *The European Parliament as a Driving Force of Constitutionalisation* (Technical Report, European University Institute, 2015); B Rittberger, *Building Europe's Parliament. Democratic Representation beyond the Nation-State* (Oxford University Press, 2005); Leino-Sandberg (n 41).

abdication of its formal prerogatives and influence and an erosion of checks and balances on the executive in this policy field. These questions may become even more relevant depending on the degree of change in Parliament's ideological composition in future elections, especially should a further tilt to the right of the political spectrum take place; based on our findings, it seems unlikely that the Parliament would be willing to challenge informalisation as long as the latter continues to align with its political preferences. As the configuration of political groups continues to change, for example by preventing the creation of variable but overall stable voting majorities, we may also witness the beginning of an era where internal Parliamentary politics prevail over its concerns for its powers and prerogatives vis-à-vis other institutions. Concerning the Ombudsman, our case illustrates the various dynamics at play when the Ombudsman defines the scope of her mandate in a specific case. It seems that in the context of informal migration arrangements, the Ombudsman sees her role as including criticism of possible human rights violations but not relations between EU institutions, even when the division of powers is used to create situations in which human rights violations take place. By distancing herself from inter-institutional relations, the Ombudsman might secure a working relationship with the executive, but contributes to the low level of inter-institutional conflict in readmission policy.

5

Separation of Powers in the Making of the EU's Twenty-first-century Trade Agreements

LAURENS ANKERSMIT

I. Introduction

The negotiations for the Transatlantic Trade and Investment Partnership (TTIP) between the EU and the United States, and the Comprehensive Economic and Trade Agreement (CETA) between Canada and the EU saw protests of an unprecedented scale in Europe. In the autumn of 2015 hundreds of thousands of citizens took to the streets in protest rallies across Europe.[1] The STOP TTIP campaign collected over three million signatures of citizens against TTIP in 2015.[2] Civil society opposed these flagship initiatives of the Juncker Commission because of their potential threat to democracy and democratic decision-making. This threat identified by civil society is two-fold.

On the one hand, the contents of these agreements are feared to have a negative impact on the ability of democracies to regulate and protect public interests or to fund or maintain public services. For instance, environmental and consumer groups opposed the introduction of investment chapters containing forms of investor–state dispute settlement (ISDS), because of fears of 'regulatory chill'.[3] Claims, threats of claims by transnational investors, and awards by investment tribunals over public interest decision-making, such as phasing out the use of coal, would expand the stifling of such democratic decision-making out of fear to have to pay large amounts of damages.[4]

[1] C Johnston, 'Berlin anti-TTIP trade deal protest attracts hundreds of thousands' *The Guardian* (10 October 2015), at www.theguardian.com/world/2015/oct/10/berlin-anti-ttip-trade-deal-rally-hundreds-thousands-protesters.

[2] S Morgan, 'Anti-TTIP petition signed by 3 million people' *Euractiv* (9 November 2015), at www.euractiv.com/section/agriculture-food/news/anti-ttip-petition-signed-by-3-million-people.

[3] P Eberhardt, 'The zombie ISDS: Rebranded as ICS, rights for corporations to sue states refuse to die' *Corporate Europe Observatory* (March 2016), at corporateeurope.org/sites/default/files/attachments/the_zombie_isds_0.pdf.

[4] J Kelsey, 'Regulatory Chill: Learnings from New Zealand's Plain Packaging Tobacco Law' (2017) 17 *QUT Law Review* 21; K Tienhaara, 'Regulatory Chill in a Warming World: The Threat to Climate Policy Posed by Investor-State Dispute Settlement' (2018) 7 *Transnational Environmental Law* 229; L Ankersmit, 'Regulatory autonomy and regulatory chill in Opinion 1/17' (2022) 4 *Europe and the World: A law review* 1.

On the other, the *process* of negotiation and conclusion of TTIP and CETA *itself* was considered a threat to democracy. Negotiations were initially conducted on the European side by the European Commission in almost complete secrecy while, for instance, ExxonMobil was given privileged access to documents drafted for the negotiations.[5] Members of European Parliament and national parliaments were only given access to some negotiation documents incrementally as protests surged in so-called 'reading rooms'.[6] Moreover, despite the magnitude of these deals and their potential impact on public life and decision-making, parliamentarians were only able to approve or reject the deals as a whole, putting them in a 'take it or leave it' situation. This meant that they had very little control over the actual content of the agreements, and were faced with the complicated task of scrutinising an elaborate, complicated and technical end-result over which they had little control. CETA, for instance, takes up 1,057 pages in the EU's *Official Journal* and is full of legal and technical jargon that requires significant expertise to properly comprehend.[7] Lastly, even after the Commission sought clarity over the division of powers in trade matters in *Opinion 2/15*, parliamentarians were still unsure whether and to what extent national parliaments or the European Parliament would be involved in scrutinising these agreements.[8]

This criticism might be surprising in light of the democratisation efforts undertaken by EU Member States with the Lisbon Treaty. That treaty-amendment, after all, sought to enlarge the role of the European Parliament in the decision-making of the Union, including trade. Article 207 TFEU saw the introduction of the ordinary legislative procedure for autonomous trade measures, making the European Parliament co-legislator.[9] Moreover, the European Parliament's consent was needed for any Council decision concluding international agreements in the field of trade. The European Parliament also had to be 'immediately and fully informed at all stages of the procedure' of negotiating and concluding such agreements.[10] This meant an increase in the powers of the European Parliament in this area that was before fully dominated by the Commission and the Council.

To be sure, this constitutional shift *has* led to more parliamentary involvement at the European level. The European Parliament has been able to contest the Commission, for instance by pushing for more transparency during negotiations, and by adopting

[5] G Lübbe-Wolff, 'Democracy, Separation of Powers, and International Treaty-making The example of TTIP' (2016) 69 *Current Legal Problems* 175; A Nelsen, 'TTIP Talks: EU Alleged to Have Given ExxonMobil Access to Confidential Strategies' *The Guardian* (26 November 2015), at www.theguardian.com/environment/2015/nov/26/ttip-talks-eu-alleged-to-have-given-exxonmobil-access-to-confidential-papers.

[6] Lübbe-Wolff (n 5) 187.

[7] Comprehensive Economic and Trade Agreement (CETA) between Canada, of the one part, and the European Union and its Member States, of the other part [2017] OJ L 11/23.

[8] L Ankersmit, 'The EU's Powers to Green International Investment Law' in X Groussot, M-L Öberg and G Butler (eds), *The EU Law of Investment: Past, Present, and Future* (Bloomsbury, 2024, forthcoming). See for the importance of the role of the judiciary and particularities of the Opinion procedure that require the Court to take decisions such as *Opinion 2/15* with significant separation of powers implications, Eckes, ch 12 in this volume.

[9] AM Krajewski, 'The Reform of the Common Commercial Policy' in A Biondi et al (eds), *EU Law After Lisbon* (Oxford University Press, 2011) 292–311.

[10] Art 218(10) TFEU; Art 207(3) TFEU furthermore states: 'The Commission shall report regularly to the special committee and to the European Parliament on the progress of negotiations.'

resolutions calling for reform of ISDS (the so-called Investment Court System).[11] This contestation has certainly been at least partially successful. The Commission is adopting a policy of more transparency during negotiations and refers to European Parliament resolutions when making policy shifts. Most notably, the Commission proposed a new system of ISDS in response to the European Parliament's TTIP resolution of 8 July 2015.[12] One can certainly argue therefore that the constitutional shift brought about with Lisbon has enabled the European Parliament to raise a distinct and noticeable voice in the EU decision-making surrounding these trade deals. To an extent this has furthered collective will-formation at EU level, as the Commission and Council had to respond to the views of European Parliament. Greater access to information has also allowed for a greater ability for those MEPs and civil society opposing these deals to debate the merits more effectively.

This chapter will nonetheless argue that, despite these reforms, the current EU decision-making process for the formation of trade agreements hampers collective will formation.[13] The separation of powers in the EU for the formation of such agreements largely follows a rationale that sees this power as a prerogative of the Executive. Not collective will-formation, but practical considerations such as the need for secrecy (that are often diametrically opposed to collective will-formation) and a trust in a process led by technical expertise have led to the attribution of powers to the executive in the formation of trade agreements. This is problematic given the nature and content of current twenty-first-century trade agreements. Far from simply reducing customs duties, these agreements seek convergence of regulatory standards and removal of other 'barriers to trade' that occur 'behind the border' and introduce a system of protection of foreign investments that can have significant impacts on environmental, health, and other public interest rules.[14]

In addition to this general rationale for executive dominance, this chapter will argue that there are four reasons particular to the EU why that collective will-formation in the creation of trade agreements does not function particularly well. First, in the EU context, the Commission does not receive a mandate from the European Parliament but from the Council. Second, even though the Commission has recently adopted a stronger transparency policy during negotiations, EU law offers only limited possibilities for deliberation and open debate before and during the negotiations, impacting final outcomes. Third, under EU law, the Commission can operate almost entirely autonomously from the Council and European Parliament during the negotiating phase of trade agreements. Finally, EU law gives such constitutional weight to trade agreements that they have almost constitutional status, potentially creating a dynamic where the legislature must execute or is bound by these acts dominated by the executive rather than the other way around.

[11] European Parliament resolution of 8 July 2015 containing the European Parliament's recommendations to the European Commission on the negotiations for the Transatlantic Trade and Investment Partnership (TTIP) (2014/2228(INI)), at www.europarl.europa.eu/doceo/document/TA-8-2015-0252_EN.html.

[12] European Commission, 'Commission proposes new Investment Court System for TTIP and other EU trade and investment negotiations' IP/15/5651 (16 September 2015), at ec.europa.eu/commission/presscorner/detail/en/IP_15_5651.

[13] See for a different line of argument that also emphasises and elaborates on the autonomy of the Commission in the formation of trade agreements, Krajewski, ch 6 in this volume.

[14] See section II.B and sources cited there.

This contribution proceeds as follows. In section II, it outlines the rationales for executive dominance in the making of trade agreements. It evaluates in particular the rationale for dominance of the executive out of a need for expertise for the formation of trade agreements. In the section III, this contribution discusses the four reasons outlined above specific to EU law that hampers collective will-formation in the making of trade agreements. Section IV concludes.

II. The Rationales for Executive Dominance in the Making of Trade Agreements

A. Traditional Rationales

Writing on separation of powers has traditionally placed the formation of trade agreements within the powers of the executive. The reason for executive dominance appears to be overwhelmingly practical, rather than inspired by a desire to ensure will-formation or democratic (let alone deliberative) decision-making.[15] In fact, foreign affairs in separation of powers frameworks seem to be much of an afterthought, as they were designed for domestic policy.[16] Agreements needed to be negotiated in secret and often the practicalities of negotiating with a foreign power meant that some form of unitary representation was required that would be able to bind the Government of a state.

The legislature was deemed to be ill-equipped for this task. In a time where it took several weeks to even convene a parliament, as members often travelled long distances by horse and cart, it was considered unfeasible to allow such a body to conduct negotiations and conclude such agreements. It would simply take too long and have too much of an impact on the activities of the legislature to send the entire body on ships or horses to meet with foreign representatives and to conduct negotiations (the argument based on *physical difficulties*). Gertrude Lübbe-Wolff explains the spirit of the time:

> It is anything but amazing that in an age when parliaments were sitting only in intervals upon convocation and needed weeks to convene, when horses were the fastest means of transport and communication, and when declaring war, making peace, sending or receiving embassies, and providing against invasion were the only objects of the foreign relations power that eminent philosophers found worth mentioning in a description of that power, all of these were found to be best placed in the monarch alone.[17]

As parliaments generally consisted of many individuals and represented a cacophony of voices and interests, they were not able to easily speak with one voice with the negotiating partner (the argument based on *the inability to speak with one voice*). This would hamper the general interest of the state as negotiations led by parliamentarians might be prone to be captured to special interests or simply result in ineffective negotiations.

[15] See R Schütze, 'The Treaty Power' and Parliamentary Democracy: Comparative Perspectives' in *Foreign Affairs and the EU Constitution: Selected Essays* (Cambridge University Press, 2014) 359; C Möllers, *The Three Branches: A Comparative Model of Separation of Powers* (Oxford University Press, 2013) 160–61.

[16] Möllers (n 15) 160.

[17] Lübbe-Wolff (n 5) 195.

A single representative of the Government would be in a better position to protect the interest of the state by offering more effective and clearer representation at the negotiating table.[18]

Lastly, involving such a large body of people would also undermine the effectiveness of negotiations, because it would be much more difficult to ensure *secrecy of the negotiations*. Secrecy was at the time considered a virtue, not a vice, because it would allow for more effective decision-making.[19]

These views on treating treaty-making as the prerogative of the state were absolute for most of these thinkers.[20] In the later nineteenth century, with constitutional reforms in Europe centred around strengthening democracy and the powers of parliaments, more opposition began to emerge to this unchecked power of the Executive, in particular where such powers threatened internal prerogatives of the legislature.[21] This opposition led to the gradual emergence of granting parliaments the right of political control. In several European states, therefore, a constitutional system emerged whereby the executive would be in the lead and in control over the negotiating process. The legislature would be given tools to control this process, most often by giving the legislature the power to approve or vote down the negotiated result.

Modern-day thinking on separation of powers still reflects this early thinking on the relationship between the Executive and the legislature. Christoph Möllers, a proponent of using the separation of powers framework to generate general will-formation, argues that 'foreign policy power has to be centralized, and this centralization comes at the expense of parliamentary and judicial accountability'.[22] He also emphasises that governments find themselves in a position of negotiation with foreign governments in the formation of international agreements. This feature calls for a more restrictive position of the legislature, also because in his view, 'parliaments cannot or do not want to be involved too intimately in a negotiating process: majorities tend to back their own government; minorities cannot claim decision-making powers'.[23] Nonetheless, Möllers recognises that the dominance of the executive deficient from the perspective of will-formation. He suggests therefore that 'parliamentarization' of foreign affairs can mitigate this problem (albeit not offer a complete solution).

Parliamentarization, in this view, consists of three key features. First, government must represent more closely a parliamentary system where the parliament has political control over the executive. Second, to facilitate contestation and deliberation, parliaments would need to have 'the right to complete information' in particular to allow (the minority) in parliament to exercise parliamentary control. Third, Möllers argues for parliaments to have the power 'to clearly define the governmental mandate in international negotiations from the outset'.[24] This would give more democratic legitimacy to international agreements and allow for better democratic deliberation before discussions move on to the international sphere.

[18] ibid 193–94.
[19] See the argument of Hamilton presented in Schütze (n 15) 366–67.
[20] Cited from Schütze (n 15) 359.
[21] ibid, 359–63.
[22] Möllers (n 15) 160.
[23] ibid 161.
[24] ibid 161.

B. Expertise and Politics in the EU's Twenty-first-century Trade Agreements

An important rationale in the EU context for executive dominance, distinct for trade agreements as opposed to international agreements more generally, is that trade negotiations should be run by technocratic experts because they are in a better position to ensure that the general interest is protected in negotiations. The Executive has access to a larger body of administrative officials with legal, economic and other technical expertise. These experts, in turn, should be put in the position of independence and be able to work in secret freed from parliamentary or political oversight. Through this process led by independent expertise, special interests can be better constrained in favour of the general interest during the negotiations. That general interest is generally understood as reaching an agreement that would result in economic growth. As political scientists Ferdi De Ville and Gabriel Siles-Brügge explain of the era leading up to TTIP:

> The starting point here has generally been the view that trade liberalization is desirable, but that it faces important political obstacles for realization. Given the high costs of organizing politically (the 'logic of collective action'...), the interest in trade protection, being concentrated in those sectors negatively affected by trade liberalization, would thus usually trump the more diffuse, general interest in a liberal trade policy, as represented, for example, by consumers. One way of overcoming this was said to be the delegation of trade policy-making from political figures to more technical bodies, such as by the EU's member states to the supranational European Commission in the Treaty of Rome. Through such 'collusive delegation' states were said to be insulating themselves from protectionist pressures to deliver the 'public good' of trade liberalization ... A second way of altering the balance of interests was to introduce 'reciprocity' to trade talks, which helped to 'concentrate' the benefits of trade liberalization on certain exporters ... Given this dominant understanding of trade policy-making, it is not surprising that, in the case of TTIP, negotiators began by arguing that secrecy was a necessary 'rule of the game'. Given the need to craft 'reciprocal' agreements, the argument was that it made sense to keep provisional agreements with negative distributive effects for certain domestic groups secret until a package deal was reached, which might swing a sufficient majority in favour of ratifying the agreement.[25]

It is worth unpacking and critically reflecting this rationale for executive dominance through technocratic expertise in three ways. This rationale assumes that:

(1) in the context of trade such a process of executive dominance by technocratic experts avoids regulatory capture of special interests;
(2) the purpose and nature of trade agreements (contributing to economic growth) is politically not contestable;
(3) given their technical nature, trade agreements do not impact public interest decision-making.

First, this rationale suggests that a process led by experts that can operate in an autonomous and secretive manner from parliament would best avoid regulatory

[25] F De Ville and G Siles-Brügge, 'Why TTIP is a game-changer and its critics have a point' (2017) 24 *Journal of European Public Policy* 1500.

capture by special interests. This rationale assumes that the most powerful political actors in trade are those that represent import-competing interests. These are businesses that would suffer from competition resulting from free trade and accordingly would be willing and able to influence decision-making for protectionist policies that would harm the general interest (so called 'beggar-thy-neighbour' policies). However, this political economy perspective is not necessarily true in today's globalised economy. An alternative political economy perspective put forward by Dani Rodrik is that current trade policy (largely resulting from the independence and expert-driven model) is itself captured by special interests. Under this perspective,

> trade agreements are shaped largely by rent-seeking, self-interested behavior on the *export side*. Rather than reigning in protectionists, trade agreements empower another set of special interests and politically well-connected firms, such as international banks, pharmaceutical companies, and multinational corporations. Such agreements may result in freer, mutually beneficial trade, through exchange of market access. But they are as likely to produce welfare-reducing, or purely redistributive outcomes under the guise of free trade.[26]

Second, this rationale for executive dominance through independent expertise presumes that the purpose and nature of trade agreements is not politically contestable. It assumes that trade agreements can be left outside the political process of will-formation and allocated to a technocratic executive because trade agreements result in economic growth. This position has long been seen as self-evident, especially in Europe. For the EU, it has been the essence of its own making. Proponents of trade agreements, such as the Commission, often point out the economic benefits trade agreements entail (growth and jobs!). Trade agreements spur economic growth and the positive economic effects of free trade outweigh the negative effects. This argument finds its roots in economic theory and has almost universal support under economists. As Rodrik has put it, the theory of comparative advantage developed by David Ricardo in the eighteenth century, is still seen as one of the 'profession's most significant intellectual achievements'.[27] Trade liberalisation (understood mainly as cutting tariffs on goods rather than anything else) is *always* a good thing because it generates economic growth for *all* trading countries measured in terms of goods produced. Free trade results in comparative advantage, which leads to specialisation; specialisation leads to economies of scale; which will lead to an increase in consumer welfare.[28] Ricardo's theory holds that free trade is even beneficial for those countries that are less efficient in the production of any goods and services, as long as the country focusses on what it does most efficient. Free trade under economists is therefore uncontroversial, as its efficiency-inducing effects allow the size of the pie to grow.

However, economists do recognise that free trade has distributional consequences. In other words, there are winners and losers from free trade. Some domestic industries lose out because of foreign competition and jobs may be lost. For economists this is not a problem if a country compensates the losers with the rewards that come from trade

[26] D Rodrik, 'What Do Trade Agreements Really Do?' (2018) 32 *Journal of Economic Perspectives* 73, 75–76.
[27] ibid 80.
[28] GATT, Trade Policies for a Better Future: Proposals for action (1985); M Friedman, 'The Case for Free Trade' (1997) 4 *Hoover Digest*; see critically for a more elaborate discussion and references Rodrik (n 26).

liberalisation. However, redistribution is politically and practically extremely difficult to realise. In fact, it is so difficult, it is simply not done in the first place, leaving losers worse off.

As Rodrik has argued,

> Free trade advocates will often grant that some people may get hurt in the short run, but will continue to argue that in the long run everyone (or at least most people) will be better off. In fact there is nothing in economics that guarantees this, and much that suggests otherwise. A famous result due to Wolfgang Stolper and Paul Samuelson states that some groups will necessarily suffer long-term losses in income from free trade … In a wealthy country such as the United States, these are likely to be unskilled workers such as high school drop-outs. This renders the whole notion of 'gains from trade' suspect, since it is not at all clear how we can decide whether a country as a whole is better off when some people gain and others lose.[29]

Another factor that complicates the possibilities of offsetting or compensating those that 'lose out' from free trade, is that these redistributive effects can be very large compared to the modest gains in economic growth. This 'redistribution-to-efficiency-gains ratio' is particularly large in a scenario where a country like the United States already has low tariffs and decides to remove them altogether.[30] All in all, even within the economic paradigm, and under the understanding that economic growth is a good outcome, the political choice for free trade has distributional consequences with difficult political consequences attached to it.

What is more, the fact that mainstream economists see free trade as beneficial because of economic growth does not imply that the goal of economic growth is politically uncontested. The theory of comparative advantage is based on economic growth measured in an increase of goods produced through free trade. However, from an ecological perspective, the increase in the production of goods puts pressure on the environment. More goods produced means more materials extracted and used for the production of such goods. As the Earth is already reaching the limits of its carrying capacity, further increase of production of goods is not necessarily a good thing. A growing body of ecological economists make the argument that it is implausible to decouple growth from increased extraction and use of materials and therefore argue for policies that support *degrowth.*[31]

Degrowth means organising the economy by means of policies that scale down economic activity by decreasing the use and extraction of materials. This position therefore no longer sees free trade beneficial for the sole reason that it promotes economic growth. It is no surprise, then, that environmental groups and green political parties in particular take issue with free trade agreements for the very reason that they may result in economic growth. What is more, where trade agreements do realise economic growth through an increase in goods produced, they may undercut the realisation of

[29] D Rodrik, *Globalization Paradox: Why Global Markets, States, and Democracy Can't Coexist* (Oxford University Press, 2011) 56.

[30] ibid 57–59.

[31] J Vogel and J Hickel, 'Is green growth happening? An empirical analysis of achieved versus Paris-compliant CO2–GDP decoupling in high-income countries' (2023) *Lancet Planet Health* 759; J Hickel and G Kallis, 'Is Green Growth Possible?' (2020) 25 *New Political Economy* 469.

other political objectives valuable to society, such as reducing economic incentives for deforestation.[32]

There is a third reason why relying on executive dominance in the formation of trade agreements is contestable: the contents of these agreements are no longer merely 'technical' in nature (with a focus on reducing customs duties); they have a much more profound impact on public interest decision-making. Agreements such as CETA and TTIP contain provisions that concern an entire democratic community: they impact how and when legislation is made. They do not merely slash tariffs and quantitative restrictions on goods, but predominantly seek to impact the regulatory environment of the parties to the benefit of transnational businesses. While agreements such as TTIP and CETA indeed also cut (already very low) tariffs and quantitative restrictions on goods, they do a lot more as well. They are therefore much broader in scope. As Rodrik points out,

> Contemporary trade agreements go much beyond traditional trade restrictions at the border. They cover regulatory standards, health and safety rules, investment, banking and finance, intellectual property, labor, the environment, and many other subjects. They reach well beyond national borders and seek deep integration among nations rather than shallow integration.[33]

As a result, these agreements are much more complex and much larger than in the past. By way of example, it is worth comparing the stark differences between the first free trade agreement negotiated by the Union (with Spain) with CETA in 1970. This agreement consists of roughly 172 pages in the *Official Journal* (four pages concern the agreement itself; the rest are annexes and declarations).[34] It progressively eliminates quantitative restrictions and customs duties (elimination of border measures) for a variety of imported goods and introduces national treatment obligations for those imported goods. Tariff rates were relatively high at the time and quantitative restrictions significant. It is a traditional trade agreement, based on the elimination of instruments designed to protect domestic industry at the time. CETA, on the other hand, consists of 1,080 pages in the *Official Journal* (of which 195 pages concern the main text without the annexes, declarations and other texts).[35] While it also liberalises trade in goods, it does so where tariff rates are already at historically low levels and quantitative restrictions much less prevalent than in the 1970s. On the other hand, the most significant additions in CETA are those aspects that seek to protect foreign investors and investment, intellectual property, liberalise trade in services and regulate the regulatory environment in the context of and with the objective of trade liberalisation.

Fundamentally, two issues contained in these agreements are important to discuss here as they have an impact on domestic politics of democratic communities. The first is that these agreements address so-called non-tariff barriers that are the result of divergences in regulation of goods and services between the parties through 'regulatory

[32] R Abman and C Lundberg, 'Does Free Trade Increase Deforestation? The Effects of Regional Trade Agreements' (2020) 7 *Journal of the Association of Environmental and Resource Economists* 35.

[33] Rodrik (n 25) 75.

[34] Overeenkomst tussen de Europese Economische Gemeenschap en Spanje [1970] OJ L 182/2.

[35] Brede Economische en Handelsovereenkomst (CETA) tussen Canada, enerzijds, en de Europese Unie en haar lidstaten, anderzijds [2017] OJ L 11/23.

cooperation'. The second is the protection of foreign investment through investment chapters that allow foreign investors to sue governments for damages for any act or omission that violates their rights contained in the agreement before special investment tribunals.

From a trade perspective, divergences in regulatory approaches between different trading partners create obstacles to trade for transnational businesses. Harmonising or bringing regulations in, for instance, food safety standards, chemicals, toys, vehicles or data protection closer together can reduce the costs for those transnational businesses. Producing economic growth by harmonising approaches to regulation and reducing technical barriers to trade, is in fact, the most important reason to generate economic growth. According to the impact assessment on which the Commission bases the economic benefits of TTIP:

> Reducing non-tariff barriers will be a key part of transatlantic liberalisation. As much as 80% of the total potential gains come from cutting costs imposed by bureaucracy and regulations, as well as from liberalising trade in services and public procurement.[36]

The EU's recent trade agreements seek to address these 'non-tariff' measures by introducing instruments of consultation and collaboration on the regulatory processes of each party as well as underline the value of avoiding trade barriers when regulating.[37] As De Ville and Siles-Brügge point out in the context of TTIP, this 'is problematic because it subtly promotes the (socially constructed) interests of those who merely see regulation as inefficient 'red tape' [and] restrict alternatives in the democratic process.'[38] The promotion of the interests of transnational businesses through regulatory cooperation happens in two ways. First, these instruments introduce a constitutional obligation (a matter returned to below)[39] for the parties to consider trade interests when regulating in the public interests. This creates a regulatory context in which the making of regulation is seen as a problem, a potential obstacle to trade, rather than a solution. It introduces the protection of a particular interest in the regulatory process. Second, through the various forms of consultation introduced under regulatory cooperation, these interests are specifically empowered to advocate their interests in the regulatory process. Regulatory cooperation usually introduces these consultation obligations at an early (and therefore crucial and important) stage of the regulatory process, even before the legislature is involved.[40] This means that an agreement such as TTIP 'could inhibit regulators, primarily by exposing them to subtle pressures within a policy-making environment that increasingly privileges the elimination of trade barriers over other policy objectives. This is the central function of the provisions rendering TTIP a "living agreement"'.[41]

[36] J Francois, 'Reducing Transatlantic Barriers to Trade and Investment: An economic assessment' *Centre for Economic Policy research* (March 2013), at www.italaw.com/sites/default/files/archive/Reducing%20Trans-Atlantic%20Barriers%20to%20Trade%20and%20Investment.pdf.

[37] See on regulatory cooperation Chamon, ch 7 in this volume.

[38] De Ville and Siles-Brügge (n 25) 1492.

[39] Section III.D.

[40] M Bartl, 'Making transnational markets: the institutional politics behind the TTIP' (2017) 1 *Europe and the World: A Law Review* 1.

[41] De Ville and Siles-Brügge (n 25) 1497.

The second aspect is investment protection. Agreements such as CETA and TTIP contain a chapter of investment protection that makes profound political choices. These chapters give foreign investors, and to the exclusion of everyone else, several rights that parties to the agreement need to respect. When foreign investors consider that these rights have been violated and they have suffered damages as a result, the agreement envisages giving them direct access to investment tribunals where they can claim compensation (so-called systems of investor–state dispute settlement such as the EU's 'Investment Court System'). These chapters effectively empower certain groups in a democratic community over others. They also ensure that these groups have access to a judicial system that is placed entirely outside and operates independent of the constitutional legal system of the parties. As they 'remove disputes from the courts' of the parties to the agreement, they also ensure that disputes are not decided in accordance with the constitutional framework of a party, including whatever other rights or interests are protected by that constitutional framework. Lastly, the potential for significant damages awarded to foreign investors by these tribunals over public interest decision-making that negatively affects investments can have a so-called chilling effect ('regulatory chill') on the decision-making within a democratic community.[42]

III. Reasons why this Executive Dominance in the EU is Problematic from the Perspective of Generating Collective Will-formation

EU law follows the model outlined above of executive dominance in the formation of trade agreements. While the reforms brought under the Treaty of Lisbon have ensured a greater role for the European Parliament, this chapter outlines why the EU's particular model of executive dominance in this field is problematic from the perspective of generating collective will-formation.

A. The Lack of a Parliamentary Mandate to Conduct Negotiations

First, even where the European Parliament has new veto powers during the ratification phase of EU trade agreements under Lisbon, it does not have the power to authorise negotiations or to issue negotiating directives. Even if we follow Möllers' more modest argument for 'parliamentarization' of foreign policy, the EU's current system falls short. The European Parliament does not have the power 'to clearly define the governmental mandate in international negotiations from the outset' and thereby allow for better democratic deliberation *ex ante* rather than ex post when the text of the agreement has already been formulated and a third state or international organisation

[42] Kelsey (n 4); Tienhaara (n 4); Ankersmit (n 4).

has already been engaged.[43] This is particularly important given that the EU does not have a parliamentary system: the elections for European Parliament are not the decisive political event in the EU that decides the composition of the executive, nor is there a coalition-based system whereby the European Parliament effectively controls the Commission.[44]

Instead, the Commission's mandate comes from the Council, an institution that cannot offer the same degree of democratic legitimacy as the European Parliament would be able to as the space for deliberation and contestation is significantly reduced within the Council. First, the Council formation responsible for the mandate are normally trade ministers from the governments of the Member States. In other words, the mandate is given by ministers that are responsible for a particular policy area and trade, and not responsible for issues and interests that may be linked or affected by trade policy, such as energy policy or environmental protection.

A telling example of how a different Council formation can impact decision-making is the controversy surrounding the Energy Charter Treaty, a trade and investment agreement for the energy sector.[45] This agreement was renegotiated by the Commission to bring it in line with the approach taken to investment protection in CETA, but the Commission did not obtain support within the Council to approve the negotiated text within the ECT's Energy Charter Conference. While the formation of trade and investment agreements fall under the responsibility of trade ministers meeting in the foreign affairs formation of the Council, the Energy Charter Treaty due to its sectoral focus, fell within the responsibilities of Transport, Telecommunications and Energy Council. Those ministers were responsible for climate policies and energy transition and therefore had a different perspective on the consequences of the 'modernised' Energy Charter Treaty for their ministerial portfolio. Instead of endorsing the negotiated results, Member States started pulling out of the ECT. Spain, as one of the first EU Member States, decided to withdraw from the ECT rather than to endorse the modernised text over climate change concerns in October 2022.[46] Its intention to withdraw was announced by the Spanish minister for ecological transition, Teresa Ribera. A week later, Dutch minister for climate and energy, Rob Jetten, took the same decision for the Netherlands, stating that the modernised text was not in line with the goals of the Paris Agreement.[47] By November it was clear that the Commission had no support for its negotiated text. Ultimately the Commission had to resort to a proposal for 'coordinated withdrawal' from the ECT by the EU and its Member States.[48]

The more technocratic (rather than parliamentary) nature of the mandate given to the Commission by the Council is reinforced by the fact that the Commission

[43] Möllers (n 15) 161.

[44] Editorial, 'Spitzenkandidaten and the European Union's system of government' (2019) 15 *European Constitutional Law Review* 609.

[45] L Ankersmit, 'The EU's Strategy for More 'Rules-Based Trade' and the EU's Withdrawal from the Energy Charter Treaty' (2023) 50 *Legal Issues of Economic Integration* 117.

[46] K Mathiesen, 'Spain pulls out of energy treaty over climate concerns' *Politico* (12 October 2022), at www.politico.eu/article/spain-pulls-out-of-energy-treaty-over-climate-concerns.

[47] A Meesterburrie, 'Nederland stapt uit omstreden energieverdrag ECT' *NRC* (18 October 2022), at www.nrc.nl/nieuws/2022/10/18/nederland-stapt-uit-omstreden-energieverdrag-ect-a4145575?t=1680518393.

[48] Commission, 'Proposal for a Council Decision on the withdrawal of the Union from the Energy Charter Treaty' COM(2023) 447 final.

is 'assisted' by a technocratic body appointed by the Council – the Trade Policy Committee – for the negotiations. This body consists of trade experts from the various governments of the Member States and is most closely involved in the discussions surrounding the mandate and the negotiations themselves. Similar to Commission officials, these are government officials with a specific expertise in trade and investment matters, rather than members of parliament.

A related issue is that the Council consists of government representatives and therefore of politicians that generally favour more centrist political positions.[49] The degree of contestation, possible in parliament by representatives not part of a government supporting coalition, is therefore lacking within the Council.

Lastly, EU law offers only limited possibilities for public deliberation and scrutiny of the mandate given by the Council through national parliaments. As trade agreements are not legislative acts,[50] the process of negotiating and concluding trade agreements is constitutionally less transparent. In contrast to draft legislative acts, the EU Treaties do not require the Commission to send preparatory acts, such as the draft authorisation and negotiating directives, to national parliaments.[51] Nor do the EU Treaties require discussions in the Council over the negotiations to be in public or the discussions as well as the vote in the Council on the decision to conclude the agreement to be public.[52] The Council Rules of Procedure, equally, restrict the ability for members of national parliament, whether in opposition or not, to scrutinise their minister before or after deliberations in the Council. Council meetings discussing non-legislative acts concerning 'international relations' (such as recommendations to open trade negotiations or adoption of negotiating directives) are not public.[53] Votes will not be made public in relation to preparatory acts, such as negotiating directives and authorisations to negotiate, and votes will only be made public in relation to Council decisions to conclude, sign or provisionally apply a negotiated international trade agreement where one of the Council members so requests.[54]

Current policy and practice by the Commission mitigates to a degree the issue that national parliaments have limited insight in the Council's power to give a negotiating mandate to the Commission. The Commission has committed to making its draft negotiating directives public (as well as a number of other documents, further discussed below). According to the Commission, this practice allows the public 'to have a better informed view and to discuss issues of interest and concern right from

[49] P Manow and H Döring 'Electoral and Mechanical Causes of Divided Government in the European Union' (2007) 41 *Comparative Political Studies* 1349–70.

[50] The Joined Cases C-643/15 and C-647/15, *Slovak Republic and Hungary v Council (Reallocation quota)* EU:C:2017:631 make clear in [62] that 'a legal act can be classified as a legislative act of the European Union only if it has been adopted on the basis of a provision of the Treaties which expressly refers either to the ordinary legislative procedure or the special legislative procedure.' Art 207(3) TFEU does not make such an express reference. Rather it makes clear that the procedure of Art 218 TFEU is to be followed subject to the specifics of Art 207 TFEU.

[51] ibid [59].

[52] ibid.

[53] Art 8(1) of the Consolidated version of Council Decision 2009/937/EU of 1 December 2009 adopting the Council's Rules of Procedure [2009] OJ L 325/35.

[54] Art 9(2)(b) and 9(3) Rules of Procedure.

the start of preparations for a negotiation'.[55] This commitment to transparency benefits national parliamentary oversight over Council ministers, yet, the Commission is not legally required to do so, and this degree of transparency is at the discretion of the Commission.

The European Parliament's role during the definition of the negotiating mandate for the Commission is under EU law reduced to the more passive and reactionary role of being kept informed. This right to information outlined in Article 218(10) TFEU and Article 207(3) TFEU is laid out in more detail in the 2010 Framework Agreement on relations between the European Parliament and the European Commission.[56] The agreement makes clear that members of European Parliament have access to information that is comparable to the information the Council and the trade policy committee receives. This includes draft negotiating directives. Yet, the Framework Agreement also specifies that public debate and disclosure of this information can be restricted.[57] And while the European Parliament is able on its own initiative to debate the issue of negotiating mandates and issue resolutions expressing the views of the European Parliament, the Framework Agreement makes clear that the Commission's only obligation towards the European Parliament's views on the negotiations is that it 'shall take due account of Parliament's comments throughout the negotiations'.[58]

B. Limited Possibilities for Public Deliberation and Open Debate During Negotiations under EU Law

A second feature of the formation of trade and investment agreements in the EU context that negatively affects collective will-formation is the more limited possibilities for deliberation and open debate during the negotiating phase under EU law.[59] From the outset, this is to a degree inherent in international negotiations where EU negotiators need to find common ground with a third party over a text and thus are dependent on the willingness of that third party to commit to a transparent process that allows for meaningful public scrutiny of negotiations. Moreover, the Commission has made significant commitments in its transparency policy during the negotiations of trade agreements in response to criticism of the opaque nature of these negotiations, by among others, the European Ombudsman.[60] Its current disclosure policy of negotiating documents undoubtedly allows for more public contestation and deliberation of trade

[55] European Commission, 'Transparency Policy in DG Trade', at circabc.europa.eu/ui/group/7fc51410-46a1-4871-8979-20cce8df0896/library/ebae888d-6243-48a2-a766-e21923793a71/details.

[56] Consolidated version of the Framework Agreement on relations between the European Parliament and the European Commission [2010] OJ L 304/47.

[57] ibid point 24 and Annex II. See also below section III.B.

[58] Point 3 Annex III of the Framework Agreement (n 56), see also point 24.

[59] The argument presented here is more about public deliberation of the contents of these agreements during the negotiating phase and the Court's interpretation of EU access to documents law. For a detailed discussion about the Court's role in allowing contestation through national parliaments through the Opinion procedure, see Eckes, ch 12 in this volume.

[60] Ombudsman Decision of the European Ombudsman closing her own-initiative inquiry OI/10/2014/RA concerning the European Commission [2015].

agreements during their negotiations. In addition to the draft negotiating directives, the Commission is committed to publishing all its initial proposals, explanatory documents, and reports of negotiating rounds, but not texts that have been amended as a result of discussions with a trade partner.

As mentioned above in the context of the negotiating mandate of the Commission, these transparency commitments are nonetheless not legal obligations for the Commission. The EU legal framework on public access to documents, as well as access to documents for members of European Parliament and national parliaments, still underlines the need for secrecy during negotiations of international agreements more than in the context of deliberations for legislative acts.[61]

Several features of the EU transparency law highlight the stronger commitment to secrecy during the negotiations of international agreements. First, public access to documents relating to international trade negotiations is placed under the *mandatory* (as opposed to a discretionary) exception to the EU's general right to access to documents held by the EU institutions under Regulation 1049/2001 (the EU's Access to Documents Regulation). In other words, the EU institutions are obliged to refuse access to documents where this interest would be undermined through disclosure. Second, this exception has been interpreted by the EU courts in a manner that allows the EU institutions *significant discretion* as to when this exception applies.[62] For the EU Courts, all that is required for an EU institution to withhold access is providing a convincing rationale why disclosure of a document undermines the public interest as regards international relations, and it needs to do so in a concrete manner for the document in question. The EU Courts do not tend to second-guess justifications put forward and only rarely do not accept justifications under the international relations exception.[63]

Parliamentary ability to openly deliberate during the negotiating phase is also legally more constrained than during the formation of legislative acts. Again, similar to the rules on access to the mandate for the Commission, national parliaments cannot benefit from increased EU transparency and involvement that applies for legislative acts.[64]

The European Parliament, however, benefits from the constitutional right to information under Article 218(10) TFEU and Article 207(3) TFEU, laid out in more detail in the 2010 Framework Agreement on relations between the European Parliament and the European Commission.[65] The agreement makes clear that members of European Parliament have access to information that is comparable to the information the Council and the trade policy committee receives. This includes draft negotiating directives, the negotiating texts as well as agreed texts. Disclosure of this information is, however, subject to limitations based on the need to maintain confidentiality during the

[61] See L Ankersmit and J Peters, 'Public Access to Documents in EU External Relations' (2022) *Maastricht Journal of European and Comparative Law*; Case C-350/12 *Council v in 't Veld* ECLI:EU:C:2014:203 [76].

[62] Art 4(1) a third indent of Regulation 1049/2001 of the European Parliament and of the Council of 30 May 2001 regarding public access to European Parliament, Council and Commission documents [2001] OJ L 145/43.

[63] Ankersmit and Peters (n 61).

[64] See above section III.A.

[65] Consolidated version of the Framework Agreement on relations between the European Parliament and the European Commission [2010] OJ L 304/47.

negotiations. Not all MEPs will have unrestricted access to this information. Usually, only members of the European Parliament's committee on international trade (INTA) will receive such clearance. Moreover, MEPs only have access to confidential information in a restricted 'reading room' where MEPs are not allowed to access their phones or make copies, for instance.[66] MEPs are not in a position to disclose such information or publicly debate it. Furthermore, discussions of the state of play of negotiations or of the confidential information happens often 'in camera' and is thus not open to the public.

C. The Autonomy and Central Role of the Commission During the Negotiation Phase

Third, the EU's system of formation of trade agreements gives the Commission so much autonomy over the negotiations that there is no meaningful possibility for even the Council (let alone the European Parliament) to exercise control over of the text of the agreement. The Commission is the only institution that has direct control over the negotiated text, whereas the Council's and the European Parliament's roles under EU law are reduced to reactionary forces. This significantly reduces the space for contestation by other institutions endowed with greater democratic legitimacy during this crucial phase of the formation of trade agreements. This also means that the making of the text is dominated by the executive that can operate with a great deal of autonomy from the legislature, and reduces the legislature to a subordinate role. As the Court of Justice has maintained, 'initiating and conducting negotiations in order to conclude an international agreement fall, in principle, within the domain of the executive'.[67]

The considerable degree of autonomy is the result of the Court of Justice's interpretation of the respective roles of the EU institutions during the negotiating phase of international agreements in the EU Treaties.[68] Articles 207(3) and 218(2)–(3) TFEU determine that the Commission negotiates a text based on a mandate received from the Council. Moreover, the Commission reports to the European Parliament and the Trade Policy Committee (TPC), the latter having the role to 'assist' the Commission in the negotiations. At least for the Council, both the mandate and reporting obligations could allow it to exercise direct control over the text, through detailed directives and by regularly issuing instructions to the Commission. However, for the Court, the Council (and committees similar to the TPC), should not be in the position to bind the Commission.

In *Commission v Council (ETS with Australia)* the Court significantly circumscribed the ability for the Council to exercise meaningful control over the Commission during the negotiating phase of international agreements.[69] The Commission had sought to partially annul the Council decision to open negotiations with Australia over an

[66] See Annex II of the Framework Agreement (n 56); see also Lübbe-Wolff (n 5) 185.

[67] Case C-350/12 *Council v in 't Veld* ECLI:EU:C:2014:2039 [76].

[68] See for a separate but related view that also highlights the autonomy granted by the Court to the Council vis-à-vis the Member States, Eckes, ch 12 in this volume.

[69] Case C-425/13 *Commission v Council (ETS with Australia)* ECLI:EU:C:2015:483 esp [62]–[67], [78], [85]–[89].

international agreement that would link Australia's greenhouse gas emissions trading system to that of the Union. The negotiating directives provided that the special committee designated by the Council could issue 'negotiating positions' to the Commission during the negotiations, in addition to reporting obligations for the Commission to the special committee. Ruling in favour of the Commission, the Court took the position that the Council merely had the ability to ensure that it was properly informed and consulted during the negotiating phase with a view of ensuring that the Council is adequately prepared for any future decision on the conclusion of an international agreement. However, the Council was not empowered to 'bind' the Commission during this phase. Neither the Council nor any special committee reporting to the Council can adopt negotiating positions that 'bind the negotiator'.[70] According to the Court, committees set up for the monitoring of the negotiations have merely a 'consultative function' and allowing them to instruct the Commission would go beyond this task.[71] Moreover, whilst the Treaties authorise 'the Council to draw up negotiating directives, it does not, on the other hand, … invest that institution with the power to impose 'detailed negotiating positions' on the negotiator.'[72]

The judgment makes clear that the Commission has considerable autonomy during the negotiating phase of international agreements. The Court reads in the power of the Commission to represent the EU externally the power to autonomously decide what the EU's position is on matters falling within the scope of the mandate that has been issued to it. Negotiating directives, then, cannot be detailed and can only set out in a general manner the scope and content of an envisaged agreement. Negotiating directives, in other words, do not enable the Council to determine the actual content of the agreement. Practice shows that those negotiating directives released to the public (for TTIP and CETA) only contain generally worded instructions on the scope and direction of the agreement. Negotiating directives only consist of a handful of pages, in contrast to the hundreds of pages of negotiated text. The role of the Council and its committees is reduced to merely assisting in the preparation of any future decision concluding the agreement as a whole. This means that the Council cannot take meaningful control over the actual text of any envisaged agreement. The tools it has at its disposal during the negotiating phase of the agreement only serve as tools of preparation for a decision over the entirety of the agreement. This type of decision-making, where the Council only has consultative powers in the shaping of the text, can therefore not properly be understood as a legislative task, but merely a task of political control over the Commission's negotiated end-result.

The Court's views on the degree of autonomy for the Commission during negotiations could not be further from Alain Juppé's famous characterisation of the role of the Commission. Furious about the outcome of the so-called 'Blair House agreement', a US–EU agreement on trade concessions in agriculture in 1992, Juppé told the Commissioner for trade Ian Brittan: 'You want to know whether we trust you Mr Brittan? Well, we do not trust you: *your role is to be the servant of the Council*.'[73]

[70] ibid [86].
[71] ibid [89].
[72] ibid [90].
[73] As reported by S Meunier and K Ncolaïdis, 'Who Speaks for Europe? The Delegation of Trade authority in the EU' (1999) 37 *Journal of Common Market Studies* 483.

The autonomy of the Commission exists a fortiori in relation to the European Parliament. The latter does not have a power under the Treaties to authorise the opening of negotiations, issue negotiating directives (and thereby determine the scope and nature of the agreement), or instruct the Commission to take negotiating positions. The powers of the European Parliament are limited to the earlier discussed right to information.[74] The European Parliament's role is therefore even less strong, as it is in a position of being informed, rather than consulted. The Framework Agreement between the European Parliament and the Commission reflects this position. While delegations of the European Parliament may be granted observer status during the negotiations where possible, the Framework Agreement underlines that it is the Commission that represents the EU externally and that 'Members of the European Parliament may not participate directly in these negotiations'.

Following the rationale of *Commission v Council (ETS with Australia)* the function of this right to information is merely to allow the European Parliament to prepare itself for any potential consent it might need to give to a future decision of the Council to conclude the agreement. The right to information does not, therefore, allow the European Parliament to take control over the text under negotiation.

Instead, the European Parliament's ability to influence the negotiations is indirect and informal. It is based on the later need to obtain the Parliament's consent for a potential future Council decision concluding a trade agreement. Through the shadow of this 'nuclear option' the European Parliament is able to contest the overall direction or the direction of key elements of an international agreement and persuade the Commission to change course. During the negotiations for the TTIP, the European Parliament adopted a resolution that called for reform of ISDS based on several general points (calling for a 'new system' with more transparency, independent judges and an appeal mechanism).[75] A few months later, the Commission proposed the so-called Investment Court System that responded to these Parliamentary demands.[76] Yet, this is one of the few examples in which the European Parliament seems to have been able to influence the Commission during the negotiations. Yet, one might wonder whether the Commission had not already envisaged these reforms, as they were already present in its concept paper 'Investment in TTIP and beyond – the path for reform. Enhancing the right to regulate and moving from current ad hoc arbitration towards an Investment Court' from two months before the resolution of the European Parliament.[77] The concept paper was a response to a public consultation that showed massive opposition to including ISDS in TTIP. Inclusion of ISDS was therefore likely to be a key issue

[74] AP Van der Mei, 'EU External Relations and Internal Inter-Institutional Conflicts: The Battlefield of Article 218 TFEU' (2016) 23 *Maastricht Journal of European and Comparative Law* 1051, 1064–68.

[75] European Parliament resolution of 8 July 2015 containing the European Parliament's recommendations to the European Commission on the negotiations for the Transatlantic Trade and Investment Partnership (TTIP) (*n*) fe 10, at XV.

[76] Commission, 'Commission proposes new Investment Court System for TTIP and other EU trade and investment negotiations' (16 September 2015), at ec.europa.eu/commission/presscorner/detail/en/IP_15_5651.

[77] Commission, 'Investment in TTIP and beyond – the path for reform. Enhancing the right to regulate and moving from current ad hoc arbitration towards an Investment Court', concept paper published on the 5 May 2015.

that could result in bringing down the entire agreement. The Parliament's influence was therefore more exceptional as it was linked to the survival of the agreement. It was not an example of the ease by which the Parliament could influence, let alone control, the text of international trade agreements under negotiation.

D. The Significance of International Trade Agreements in the EU's Hierarchy of Norms

A final point that underlines why the EU's model of executive dominance in the formation of trade agreements is problematic from the perspective of generating collective will-formation is the constitutional status of this type of executive law-making and its hierarchical superiority over parliamentary law-making. EU law, in other words, allows the executive to exercise control over the legislature through international agreements, rather than the other way around. It is considered completely normal, for instance, that President of the Commission, Ursula von der Leyen, would caveat her idea for legislative proposal for carbon border adjustment mechanism with compliance with WTO rules. To an extent this is inherent to how international law sees its relationship with domestic law of states.[78] Yet, the approach taken by the EU towards international law reinforces the power of the executive over the legislature.

The starting point of this argument starts with the Court's judgment in *Haegeman*. The case concerned who had the power to interpret the Association Agreement with Greece that was annexed to the Council decision concluding it. If the agreement itself was EU law, following a more monist approach to international law, it would be the Court of Justice. The EU Treaties did not clarify this point. However, even where the Council decision concluding the agreement and the agreement itself were two separate acts, the Court considered international agreements concluded by the Council 'an integral part' of EU law.[79]

By making EU international agreements part of EU law, the Court not only ensured that it had the power to interpret those agreements, but also that such international agreements could be given the unique characteristics of EU law itself: supremacy over all Member State law and direct effect. This has two significant consequences for legislatures of Member States. First, as Mendez points out, for those Member States that have a dualist approach to international law, 'it is no longer the domestic legislature which determines the role of domestic courts in treaty enforcement. Rather it is a role that the ECJ has assumed for itself.'[80] Second, for all Member States it meant that regardless of the status of domestic law, be it constitutional, legislative of merely administrative, the doctrine of supremacy of EU law meant that Member State law would have to give way to these international agreements.

[78] Art 27 VCLT.

[79] Case 181/73 *R & V Haegeman v Belgian State* EU:C:1974:41. The Court later clarified that this principle even extended to decisions of bodies set up under international agreements in Case C-192/89 *SZ Sevince v Staatssecretaris van Justitie* EU:C:1990:322.

[80] M Mendez, 'The Legal Effect of Community Agreements: Maximalist Treaty Enforcement and Judicial Avoidance Techniques' (2010) 21 *European Journal of International Law* 88.

A second related point is implications of this type of executive law-making for the EU's own legislature. In a consistent line of cases, the Court has maintained that 'international agreements concluded by the European Union bind its institutions and consequently prevail over the acts laid down by those institutions'.[81] Trade agreements concluded by the EU, therefore, are hierarchically superior to any EU act that has a much greater degree of parliamentary involvement. Legislative acts adopted under the ordinary legislative procedure, for instance, need to conform to such agreements.

Certainly, Article 207(3) TFEU provides that 'the Council and the Commission shall be responsible for ensuring that the agreements negotiated are compatible with internal Union policies and rules.' That provision has not been interpreted by the Court of Justice. The provision is formulated as an obligation addressed to the Commission and the Council, rather than setting out that internal Union policies and rules prevail over international agreements concluded under the CCP. It seems therefore that the provision most likely introduces a procedural obligation on these institutions to verify whether the negotiated agreement complies with existing policies and rules. Such a formal obligation would not allow for substantive judicial review of the compatibility of the agreement with EU law (including secondary law), but would nonetheless somewhat shield existing internal legislation through a procedural check. The provision could, however, also entail a procedural obligation of the part of the Commission and Council to ensure that future internal rules and policies are compatible with already existing international trade agreements. Although such an interpretation would neglect the fact that the rule is part of a set of rules on the procedure for the formation of trade agreements, this would be a specific additional obligation of the part of these two institutions that would reinforce the rule that international agreements prevail over acts of EU institutions.

It is true that the effects of *Haegeman* are mitigated by the fact that the EU in the latest generation of trade agreements explicitly excludes direct effect. This is an institutional choice made possible through the Court's approach to direct effect of international agreements.[82] However, the EU's constitutional system ensures that this choice essentially needs to be made in a process dominated by the Executive, not the legislature.

The constitutional importance of this executive form of law-making is underlined by the difficulty in changing international commitments themselves, even where the legislature would like to see these international commitments changed or terminated. Given that trade agreements are part of EU law itself, the EU would need to renegotiate or seek to terminate these international agreements. Already under international law this is by no means an easy process.[83] Where international agreements do allow for termination or withdrawal, the internal EU process is again dominated by the Executive, not the legislature. While the EU Treaties do not provide for an explicit procedure, current institutional practice suggests that the same procedure is followed as for the conclusion

[81] Joined Cases C 401/12 P to C 403/12 P *Vereniging Milieudefensie* EU:C:2015:4 [52].

[82] Case 104/81 *Kupferberg* EU:C:1982:362 [17]–[22].

[83] J Harrison, 'The Life and Death of BITs: Legal Issues Concerning Survival Clauses and the Termination of Investment Treaties' (2012) 13 *Journal of World Investment & Trade* 928.

of an international agreement. The numbers for termination present a clear picture in this sense. Of the 2,935 international agreements that the EU has listed, only five agreements have so far been terminated (trade agreements with Russia and Syria remain in effect, for instance).[84]

Again, the power of the legislature in initiating the termination of international agreements lies with an informal signaling function to the Commission. In the Commission's proposal for a 'coordinated withdrawal' from the Energy Charter Treaty, for instance, the Commission states that its proposal is based on the fact that the European Parliament 'does not support the reform of the Treaty and calls on the EU and Member States to organize a coordinated withdrawal from the ECT'.[85] Even so, such withdrawal would still need support from a qualified majority in the Council.

IV. Conclusion

Strengthening the powers of the European Parliament under the Lisbon Treaty in the formation of trade agreements was no doubt intended to ensure greater democratic legitimacy of EU trade policy. As the previous process had been entirely dominated by the Commission and the Council, this change brought about an increased ability of the European Parliament to contest the Executive in the formation of trade agreements. However, it did not fundamentally change the initial choice for executive dominance in the formation of trade agreements. The autonomy of the Commission during negotiations, the lack of a mandate from the European Parliament, the limited legal requirements for public debate and deliberation, and the potential for binding the legislature through executive action, all hamper collective will-formation in the making of trade agreements in the EU.

Yet, the need for a proper process that induces collective will-formation for trade agreements is greater than it has ever been. Both the intellectual foundations for free trade agreements (economic growth) and their contents (investment protection, regulatory cooperation) are under such public scrutiny that the old model of relying on technocratic expertise no longer suffices. 'Parliamentarization' in the EU of the process would certainly be a step forward from the perspective of general will-formation, especially given the fact that the European Parliament is the only institution that consists of representatives of Union citizens. Other possibilities would be deconstitutionalising trade agreements, introducing transparency obligations, and limiting the autonomy of the Commission. Most of these options would require further changes to the EU Treaties.

[84] PJ Kuijper et al, *The Law of EU External Relations*, 2nd edn (Oxford University Press, 2015) 88–92; Agreement on partnership and cooperation establishing a partnership between the European Communities and their Member States, of one part, and the Russian Federation, of the other part [1997] OJ L 327/3.

[85] Commission, 'Proposal for a Council Decision on the withdrawal of the Union from the Energy Charter Treaty' COM(2023) 447 final, 2; European Parliament resolution of 24 November 2022 on the outcome of the modernisation of the Energy Charter Treaty (2022/2934(RSP)) [2023] OJ C 167/68.

6

The European Commission as a Driver of EU Trade Policy: Executive Leadership by Technocratic Means

PIOTR KRAJEWSKI

I. Introduction

Who speaks on behalf of a political community in international relations? Who takes the lead when representing this community vis-à-vis third-country partners, for instance during treaty negotiations?

The traditional reply to these questions would be: the Executive branch. It would seem that managing foreign affairs requires a certain degree of secrecy and space for discretionary judgement unconstrained by the pressure of partisan politics associated with the legislative branch.[1] At the same time, defining the core of executive power in the foreign policy domain is not straightforward. In this context, it is difficult to locate a 'transmission belt' whereby the executive organs merely implement and apply general provisions of law adopted in a legitimate legislative procedure. Margit Cohn argued that the Executive epitomises 'irresolvable tension between its role as executor of the law, under the separation of powers ideal, and its function as a manager, or dominant decision-maker in the political sphere, in which it acts above and beyond the law.'[2] Cohn's definition acknowledges the ambiguity inherent in activities undertaken by modern executives – the executive branch, on one hand, needs support and authorisation from the legislature, but, at the same time, tends to assume (and often usurp) political leadership in a way that often escapes democratic control. Risks associated with executive dominance seem to be especially prominent in the foreign policy domain.[3]

[1] A Hamilton et al *The Federalist* (Hackett Pub Co, 2005) 345–46; RF Turner, 'Separation of Powers in Foreign Policy: The Theoretical Underpinnings' (1988) 11 *George Mason University Law Review* 97, 98–99; J Locke, *Two Treatises of Government* (Cambridge University Press, 1988) 365–66. For a critical take on the dominant role of the executive in foreign affairs see Ankersmit, ch 5 in this volume.

[2] M Cohn, 'Tension and Legality: Towards a Theory of the Executive Branch' (2016) 29 *Canadian Journal of Law & Jurisprudence* 321, 322.

[3] M Cohn, *A Theory of the Executive Branch: Tension and Legality* (Oxford University Press, 2021) 47–52.

The emergence of "imperial executives" has been diagnosed in various institutional contexts, especially with respect to the US presidency.[4] This term can be traced back to the study authored by Arthur Schlesinger[5] and can be associated with executive power that aims to actively steer the social and economic spheres by political decisions, often escaping constitutional mechanisms of legislative authorisation and control.[6] Imperial executives tend to dominate other branches of government and address emerging policymaking challenges in a discretional manner.[7]

In the EU context, pinpointing the locus of executive power in the broadly understood foreign policy field is not straightforward either.[8] On one hand, pursuant to Article 17(1) TEU, the European Commission is explicitly tasked with discharging executive functions and ensuring the EU's external representation (except for the Common Foreign and Security Policy – CFSP). This constitutional mandate is concretised, inter alia, by the Commission's responsibility to negotiate international agreements falling under the EU's exclusive and shared competences[9] and managing litigation on the EU's behalf before international dispute resolution bodies.[10] On the other hand, the Council wields several functions that can be plausibly described as external representation of the EU and hence could fall in the executive domain as well. The Council adopts the decisions that formally open the negotiation of an international agreement on the EU's side (Article 218(3) TFEU). It likewise adopts the decisions on provisional application, authorises the signing (Article 218(5) TFEU) and concludes international agreements (Article 218(6) TFEU). The EU legal order does not recognise 'executive agreements' that could be concluded by the Commission alone.[11] Finally, the Council adopts decisions establishing the positions to be adopted on the Union's behalf in bodies set up by an international agreement (Article 218(9) TFEU). The Council formally discharges legislative as well policy-making and coordinating functions (Article 16(1) TEU) which hints at the Council's potential for broader political leadership. In this context, the Foreign Affairs Council is also tasked with elaborating the EU's external action on the basis of strategic guidelines laid down by heads of state in the European Council (Article 16(6) TEU). Thus, the Council also seems to exercise executive power in EU external relations, especially with respect to functions that enable it to coordinate foreign policy, assume rights and obligations on the EU's behalf or present the EU's position to third-country partners.[12] The European Parliament's role in this context is perhaps most straightforward: the Parliament exercises the function of political control

[4] EA Posner and A Vermeule, *The Executive Unbound: After the Madisonian Republic* (Oxford University Press, 2010).

[5] AM Schlesinger, *The Imperial Presidency* (Mariner Books, 2004).

[6] Cohn (n 2) 334–42.

[7] ibid.

[8] See the discussion in Chamon, ch 7 in this volume, section III.

[9] See the discussion in section II.B below.

[10] See Art 335 TFEU and Case C-73/14 *ITLOS* ECLI:EU:C:2015:663 [58].

[11] Case C-327/91 *France v Commission* ECLI:EU:C:1994:305 [41]–[42].

[12] M Cremona, 'Making Treaties and Other International Agreements: The European Union' in CA Bradley (ed) and M Cremona, *The Oxford Handbook of Comparative Foreign Relations Law* (Oxford University Press 2019) 246.

which is a crucial tool of legislative actors that allows them to hold accountable.[13] This mandate is concretised by the Parliament's information rights in treaty negotiations (Article 218(10) TFEU)[14] and the power of consent needed for the conclusion of an international agreement (Article 218(6) TFEU).

Against this backdrop, it is submitted that there is a degree of tension between the Council's and Commission's constitutional functions.[15] The Commission was once described as a 'technocratic executive'; the Council a 'political executive'.[16] This chapter sheds some light on this relationship by examining the relative strength of the Commission in specific institutional contexts and compares it to the institutional powers of the Council and the Parliament. The analysis presented in this chapter focusses on the field of Common Commercial Policy (CCP) and explains the nature of executive power exercised by the European Commission, reflecting on how its powers are shaped and constrained by other actors, especially the Council and the Parliament. In this context, it also illustrates the relational nature of the separation of powers.

The main claim advanced in the present chapter is as follows: the Commission should be considered a primary actor in EU trade policy, substantively shaping the CCP and exercising a significant degree of *political* leadership in this domain. The Commission's unique constitutional position enables it to harness expertise in order to reinforce its political power in EU trade policy. This claim goes against the view that is occasionally voiced in legal and political science scholarship, namely that the Commission is an apolitical technocratic actor, a sort of an agent acting on behalf of more powerful principals, especially the Council.[17] Against this view, it is submitted that the Council and the Parliament do not instruct the Commission but *moderate* its political leadership, drawing political red lines and leveraging its veto powers to steer the Commission in a desired direction. Notwithstanding this, the Commission enjoys the potential to shape EU trade policy over time, even if this is likely to happen in an evolutionary fashion promoting centrist political outcomes.[18] This claim combined with the fact that the CCP is the only EU exclusive competence within the broadly understood foreign policy field indicates that in the CCP the EU has the potential to define strategic objectives and pursue them in a coherent manner.

The political dimension of executive power wielded by the Commission is illustrated by an analysis of several practices and decision-making processes where the

[13] C Möllers, *The Three Branches: A Comparative Model of Separation of Powers* (Oxford University Press, 2013) 121.

[14] The Parliament's information rights are to be understood broadly – see to that effect Case C-263/14 *Tanzania* ECLI:EU:C:2016:435 [75]–[76].

[15] In this context, Eckes refers to the 'top-down split executive' comprising the Commission, the Council and the Member States – see Eckes, ch 12 in this volume, section II.A.

[16] The distinction between technocratic and political executive as applied to the Commission and the Council was made by D Curtin in her lecture 'Seeing Power: EU Executive Technocracy in Crisis' available at: www.youtube.com/watch?v=uF5LlDtw8WI.

[17] K Lenaerts and A Verhoeven, 'Institutional Balance as a Guarantee for Democracy in EU Governance' in C Joerges and R Dehousse (eds), *Good Governance in Europe's Integrated Market* (Oxford University Press, 2002) 51–55; E Da Conceição-Heldt, 'Multiple Principals' Preferences, Types of Control Mechanisms and Agent's Discretion in Trade Negotiations' in T Delreux and J Adriaensen (eds), *The Principal Agent Model and the European Union* (Springer International Publishing, 2017).

[18] *cf* S Hix, *What's Wrong with the European Union and How to Fix It* (Polity Press, 2008) 48.

Commission wields the decision-making initiative as well as framing powers, substantively determining the scope and content of the subsequent policy debate. The proposed argument is developed as follows. First, it is demonstrated how formal powers of initiative and Treaty-based autonomy vis-à-vis other institutions enable the Commission to set the policy-making agenda. To this end, this chapter examines the Commission's power of initiative in unilateral and bilateral decision-making processes and discusses the scope of this power as it is interpreted by the case law of the Court of Justice (section II.A). In addition to that, it scrutinises the Commission's role as a negotiator of trade, investment and association agreements and implications thereof, examining the Commission's institutional autonomy and political control exercised by the Parliament and the Council (section II.B).

In the section III, it is discussed how expertise reinforces the Commission's relative power vis-à-vis the Council and the Parliament. To this end, it analyses the role of comprehensive trade policy programmes, examining how the Commission can outline strategic objectives and advocate for the adoption of an array of different trade policy instruments (section III.A). It is also discussed how some practices enshrined in the Commission's Better Regulation Agenda allow it to harness expertise and frame factual complexity, compelling other institutions to either endorse or counter the Commission's political position (section III.B). In this context, the chapter focuses specifically on Sustainability Impact Assessments (SIAs) and their role in strengthening the political rationale for the conclusion of trade and investment agreements. Section IV concludes.[19]

This chapter does not present a comprehensive study focussing on the effectiveness of the Commission's agenda-setting powers;[20] however, it combines the analysis of the legal powers of the Commission with empirical examination of policy documents, illustrating how expertise and framing factual complexity complement formal powers of policy initiative. Thus, apart from 'traditional' legal sources, the section II of this chapter examines policy communications of the Commission and studies published by external consultants within the framework of SIAs as well as position papers in which the Commission presents its political stance towards different forecasts of possible impact of agreements under negotiation. These sources are public but seldom become the subject of interest of legal scholars even though they play a crucial role in how the

[19] By combining doctrinal analysis of the EU trade policy competence framework with reflections on the role of policy communications and expertise, this chapter will hopefully contribute to the rich body of scholarship dealing with such issues as the role of expertise and soft law in the EU context. On the effects of soft law in the EU legal order see chapters authored by M Dawson and S Garben in: S Garben and I Govaere (eds), *The Division of Competences between the EU and the Member States: Reflections on the Past, the Present and the Future* (Hart Publishing, 2017). On the expert–executive nexus in the context of risk regulation and EU policies see: M Weimer and A de Ruijter (eds), *Regulating risks in the European Union: the co-production of expert and executive power* (Hart Publishing, 2017). On the role of legal expertise in EU policy-making see: E Korkea-aho and P Leino-Sandberg (eds), *Law, Legal Expertise and EU Policy-Making* (Cambridge University Press 2022).

[20] A Kreppel and B Oztas conducted an empirical analysis of the Commission's agenda setting powers between 2000 and 2011, examining the life cycle of Commission's proposals outlined in yearly Work Programmes and verifying their adoption rate and the extent to which they reflect the Commission's institutional priorities. However, recommendations for trade and investment agreements are not included in the Commission's Work Programmes – A Kreppel and B Oztas, 'Leading the Band or Just Playing the Tune? Reassessing the Agenda-Setting Powers of the European Commission' (2017) 50 *Comparative Political Studies* 1118.

Commission operationalises its constitutional mandate and legitimises compliance of EU trade policy with constitutional objectives of EU external action (Article 21 TEU). The chapter also incorporates findings from some of the 20 interviews conducted with EU officials, experts, and stakeholders for the purposes of the PhD research conducted within NORFACE-funded SepaRope project.

II. The Commission's Formal Powers of Policy Initiative and External Representation

A. Commission's Decision-making Initiative in the Field of CCP

This section reviews the Commission's right of initiative in unilateral and plurilateral decision-making procedures relevant to the CCP. It examines the scope of this power as it has been interpreted by the Court of Justice. It will be demonstrated that a broad understanding of the Commission's formal power of initiative can, in combination with the Commission's framing powers, translate into broader political leadership in the field of CCP and consequently shape the nature of executive power exercised by the Commission.

Unilateral measures in EU trade policy are adopted in the Ordinary Legislative Procedure which gives the Commission the power to take the lead in the legislative process and initiate the debate over policy substance by submitting a legislative proposal (Article 17(2) TEU; Article 207(2) TFEU; Article 294 TFEU). The legal basis of Article 207(2) TFEU has been relied upon to put forward a variety of instruments, especially in recent years. This corresponds with the current trade policy paradigm of the Commission which acknowledges, much more forcefully than in the past, the role of unilateral instruments in the pursuit of EU trade policy objectives.[21] Some notable examples here include the proposed Anti-Coercion Instrument[22] that seems to acknowledge the increasingly geoeconomic character of the present-day trade policy, the Foreign Subsidies Regulation[23] that essentially aims to apply EU state aid regime extraterritorially or the proposed Forced Labour Regulation[24] that has the potential to curb imports from countries that do not prevent forced labour.

An important qualification to the Commission's power of initiative is laid out in Article 293 TFEU. On one hand, when the Council acts on a proposal from the Commission, it can amend the proposal as long as there is unanimity in the Council

[21] Commission, 'Trade Policy Review – An Open, Sustainable and Assertive Trade Policy' COM(2021) 10.

[22] Regulation (EU) 2023/2675 of the European Parliament and of the Council of 22 November 2023 on the protection of the Union and its Member States from economic coercion by third countries [2023] OJ L 2023/2675.

[23] Regulation (EU) 2022/2560 of the European Parliament and of the Council of 14 December 2022 on foreign subsidies distorting the internal market [2022] OJ L 330, 1–45; the Regulation is also based on Art 114 TFEU.

[24] Proposal for a Regulation of the European Parliament and of the Council on prohibiting products made with forced labour on the Union market (2022), COM(2022) 453 final; the proposal is also based on Art 114 TFEU.

(Article 293(1) TFEU). On the other hand, the Commission may alter its proposal at any time during the decision-making procedure (Article 293(2) TFEU). This clearly illustrates that in procedural terms the Council has a high threshold to overcome in order to modify the Commission's proposal. Furthermore, the case law of the Court formulated several limitations to the Council's power of amendment. As highlighted by Merijn Chamon, there are three important cases to mention in this context:[25] in the *Commission v Council* case of 1989, the Court argued that the Council is free to amend a Commission's proposal as long as it does not 'depart from [its] subject matter' or 'alter its objective'.[26] In the *Eurotunnel* case, the Court claimed that the Council must not exceed in its amendment the scope of the legal act originally proposed by the Commission.[27] Finally, in the most recent *Macro-financial assistance* case, the Court explicitly said that the Commission's power of initiative translates into a power to withdraw its proposal in the event when an amendment 'distorts the proposal for a legislative act in a manner which prevents achievement of the objectives pursued by the proposal and which, therefore, deprives it of its raison d'être'.[28]

In my view, it is possible to establish parallels between the architecture of the internal and external decision-making processes; this likewise applies to the Commission's role and its power of initiative.[29] At first sight, the most important dimension of this parallelism is the Commission's competence to submit recommendations to the Council for opening negotiations of a trade or investment agreement (Article 207(3) TFEU). The word 'recommendations' is perhaps slightly misleading here because these are essentially draft negotiating directives outlining the scope and negotiating objectives of the proposed agreement.[30] In other words, they contain the substance of the proposed negotiating directives that can be modified by the Council. For instance, the Commission's recommendation for a Council decision authorising the opening of negotiations for an FTA with New Zealand outlines in an Annex all the elements of the proposed negotiating directives, discussing the scope and objectives thereof and specific trade disciplines, such as trade in goods, trade in services, public procurement, trade and sustainable development, etc.[31] Admittedly, the content of the Commission's recommendations usually reflects the outcome of the scoping exercise involving representatives of a third-country partner; they often also contain some inputs from Member States.[32] At the same time, the Commission's initiative forces the Council to either endorse the proposed negotiating directives or modify them. The mechanism whereby the Commission proposes, and the Council decides, is reiterated in other stages of the negotiations, namely with

[25] M Chamon, 'Reinforcing the Community Method – the Commission as a veto player in EU external relations' *EU Law Live*, 30 November 2022, at eulawlive.com/op-ed-reinforcing-the-community-method-the-commission-as-a-veto-player-in-eu-external-relations-by-merijn-chamon.

[26] Case 355/87 *Commission v Council* ECLI: EU:C:1989:220 [44].

[27] Case C-408/95 *Eurotunnel* ECLI: EU:C:1997:532 [39].

[28] Case C-409/13 *Council v Commission* ECLI: EU:C:2015:217 [83].

[29] The Court itself has alluded to possible symmetries between the legislative and treaty-making procedures: Case C-244/17 *Kazakhstan* ECLI:EU:C:2018:662,[21]–[22].

[30] See for instance ANNEX to the Recommendation for a Council Decision authorising the opening of negotiations for a Free Trade Agreement with New Zealand, COM(2017) 469 final.

[31] ibid.

[32] M Frennhoff Larsén, 'Parliamentary Influence Ten Years after Lisbon: EU Trade Negotiations with Japan' (2020) 58 *JCMS: Journal of Common Market Studies* 1540, 1544.

regard to decisions on signing as well as provisionally applying (Article 218(5) TFEU) and concluding a trade or investment agreement (Article 218(6) TFEU).

What distinguishes Commission recommendations for a Council decision opening the negotiations (Article 218(3) TFEU) from proposals of the Commission that trigger the Council to adopt decisions on signing, provisional application and conclusion (Article 218(5) and Article 218(6) TFEU) is the majority threshold in the Council needed to modify the Commission's draft decisions. Whereas amending the Commission's proposals requires unanimity in the Council (Article 293(1), this does not apply to Commission's recommendations, which means that the Council enjoys more leeway if it wishes to introduce changes to draft negotiating directives prepared by the Commission.

Relying on the pronouncements of the Court in the recent *Geneva Act* judgment, it is demonstrated below that the Commission's power of initiative in trade negotiations translates into a broader political leadership informed by the Commission's constitutional mandate to represent the EU externally and safeguard the general interest of the Union (Article 17 TEU).

In the judgment at hand, the Commission sought to annul the Council's decision on the accession of the EU to the Geneva Act of the Lisbon Agreement on Appellations of Origin and Geographical Indications.[33] The decision was adopted on the basis of Article 218(6) TFEU on the proposal of the Commission. Importantly, the subject matter of the international agreement at hand fell under the scope of the CCP ('commercial aspects of intellectual property' as laid out in Article 207 TFEU). The Council's decision modified the Commission's proposal in a specific way: against the Commission's wishes, it added to the said decision provisions that authorised Member States to accede to the Geneva Act alongside the EU.[34] *Ceci n'est pas un amendement* – AG Szpunar summarised the Commission's argumentation in the dispute at hand.[35] Indeed, the Commission argued, inter alia, that modifying a proposal in a field of the CCP in a way that adds an authorisation for individual Member States to accede to the agreement at hand goes beyond the scope of the Council's discretion, even though the unanimity threshold was met. Given that the CCP constitutes an exclusive competence of the EU, Member States can only act in this policy field if authorised by EU institutions (Article 2(1) TFEU).[36] The Council's amendments were argued to exceed the Council's discretion as interpreted in the light of the exclusive character of the EU competence in the field.[37]

The Court sided with the Commission. It linked the Commission's power to submit a proposal for a decision concluding an international agreement in the domain of the CCP to its constitutional mandate to act in the general interest of the Union and represent it externally (Article 17(1) TEU).[38] In the specific context of the *Geneva Act* case, this meant that a part of the Commission's assessment linked to considerations of the

[33] Case C-24/20 Judgment of 22 November 2022, *Geneva Act* ECLI: EU:C:2022:911 [1].
[34] ibid [16]–[27].
[35] Opinion of AG Szpunar in the Case C-24/20 *Geneva Act* ECLI: EU:C:2022:404 [2].
[36] See also to that effect: Case 41/76 *Donckerwolcke and Schou* ECLI: EU:C:1976:182 [32]; Case C-70/94 *Werner* ECLI:EU:C:1995:328 [12]; Case C-83/94 *Leifer and Others* ECLI:EU:C:1995:329 [12].
[37] Case C-24/20 *Geneva Act*, ECLI: EU:C:2022:911 [60]–[61].
[38] ibid [102]–[105].

general interest of the Union was whether or not to include an authorisation for Member States to act in a field of exclusive competence of the EU.[39]

In more general terms, although the Court only addressed the procedure related to the decision on the conclusion of a trade agreement, it is argued that its reasoning can be applied to other institutional mechanisms laid out in Article 218 TFEU, where the Commission submits a substantive proposal for a decision, and the Council adopts it. The Commission's initiative and power to shape the substance of a proposal (of a decision) express a considerable amount of discretion in its exercise of executive functions in EU trade policy. This discretion is linked to the Commission's constitutional mandate to promote the general interest of the Union and safeguarded by its power to withdraw the proposal, both in internal and external decision-making processes. Thus, there is a certain universal, systemic rationale behind the Commission's power of initiative: in principle, it applies in relation to the adoption of all EU legal acts[40] and constitutes a crucial element of the constitutional balance of powers between institutions relying on supranational legitimacy on one hand and national democratic communities, on the other hand.[41] With respect to the CCP specifically, the Commission's powers are further reinforced by the exclusive character of the competence which makes Member States' actions depend on an authorisation by the EU institutions which can only be initiated by the Commission.

B. Commission's Autonomy as a Negotiator of Trade, Investment and Association Agreements

This section examines the Commission's role as a negotiator of trade, investment and association agreements.[42] First, it discusses the fact that the Commission often negotiates trade agreements whose scope exceeds the confines of the CCP. It is also demonstrated that the Commission's role in this respect is not merely technical and cannot be reduced to that of an agent of the Council or the Parliament. The Commission enjoys some space for political leadership in the context of managing negotiations of trade agreements even if this space is ultimately narrowed down by political red lines expressed by the Council and the Parliament.

Agreements that fall squarely within the scope of the CCP are always negotiated by the European Commission – this is clear from the wording of Article 207, which sets out that the Commission conducts agreements within the CCP framework, acting in consultation with a special committee appointed by the Council (Article 207(3) TFEU). However, provisions related to trade liberalisation or market access for investors are often accompanied by commitments falling beyond the scope of the CCP. In *Opinion 2/15*, the Court of Justice clarified that portfolio investment and investor–state dispute

[39] Chamon (n 25).

[40] Opinion of AG Szpunar in the Case C-24/20, *Geneva Act*, ECLI: EU:C:2022:404 [68].

[41] ibid [71].

[42] Also on the Commission's constitutional autonomy and relative advantage over other institutions, see Ankersmit, ch 5 in this volume, section II.C.

settlement which are often found in comprehensive trade agreements fall outside of the scope of the CCP.[43]

Furthermore, trade and investment liberalisation commitments are often negotiated within a framework of a further-reaching political partnership enshrined in an association agreement. These agreements tend to combine trade liberalisation provisions with commitments related to political and sectoral cooperation, the latter usually falling outside of the scope of the CCP. As per the Treaties, these agreements can involve reciprocal rights and obligations, common action and special procedure (Article 217 TFEU). In practice, association agreements aim to establish special, privileged links with a block of countries, going beyond purely economic considerations.[44] Even though the wording of Article 217 TFEU suggests that association agreements could be concluded by the EU alone (with the unanimity requirement in the Council (Article 218(8) TFEU) and after obtaining the consent of the Parliament (Article 218(6)(a)(i)), in practice association agreements are almost always mixed.[45] Notable examples to this rule include the EU–Kosovo Stabilisation and Association Agreement and the EU–UK Trade and Cooperation Agreement, both of which were concluded as EU-only agreements.[46]

In this connection, one should ask: who negotiates a trade or investment agreement including provisions that fall outside of the scope of the CCP? Article 218(3) TFEU speaks of the Council nominating the Union negotiator without further specifying who that would be.[47] Mauro Gatti and Pietro Manzini argued that a systematic interpretation of the Treaties supports the claim that the task of treaty negotiation should be linked to the constitutional power to represent the EU externally.[48] The latter is divided into two institutions: The High Representative of the Union for Foreign Affairs and Security Policy for CFSP matters (Article 27 TEU) and the European Commission for all other matters (Article 17 TEU). This would suggest that the Commission should be responsible for negotiating agreements that combine trade-related commitments with provisions falling under shared EU competences, for instance pertaining to environmental protection. According to Gatti and Manzini, a natural conclusion to be drawn from this claim is to locate the source of the Commission's authority directly in the Treaties, and not in the Council's decision to nominate a negotiator.[49]

In the past, the Commission has been also tasked with negotiating trade-related agreements that include provisions falling under exclusive competences of Member States, ie agreements that would fall under the category of obligatory mixity upon conclusion.[50] The Council, as a Union institution, has no authority to nominate the Commission as a negotiator of such agreements, hence, the Commission is tasked to

[43] Opinion 2/15 ECLI:EU:C:2017:376, [225]–[256], [285]–[304].

[44] *cf* Case 12/86 *Demirel* ECLI:EU:C:1987:400 [9].

[45] M Chamon and P van Elsuwege, 'The Meaning of 'association' under EU Law: A Study on the Law and Practices of EU Association Agreements' (Publications Office, 2019) 18–19.

[46] See C Eckes and P Leino-Sandberg, 'The EU–UK Trade and Cooperation Agreement – Exceptional Circumstances or a New Paradigm for EU External Relations?' (2022) 85 *The Modern Law Review* 164.

[47] See also: M Gatti and P Manzini, 'External Representation of the European Union in the Conclusion of International Agreements' (2012) 49 *Common Market Law Review* 1703, 1708.

[48] ibid 1709.

[49] ibid 1707–11.

[50] A Rosas, 'Mixity Past, Present and Future: Some Observations' in M Chamon and I Govaere (eds), *EU External Relations Post-Lisbon: The Law and Practice of Facultative Mixity* (Brill Nijhoff, 2020) 13–14.

negotiate them by virtue of a decision of the Member States.[51] During the negotiation process, Member States might want to exercise tighter control over the conduct of Commission negotiators; this does not change the fact that the Commission ends up managing the negotiations and speaking on behalf of the EU and Member States to third-country partners.

Testimonies of interviewed EU officials reveal that Member States acting in the Council or outside of it are comfortable with nominating the Commission to negotiate trade agreements whose content might exceed the scope of the CCP.[52] The first reason for that is pragmatic – the Commission's expertise and experience argue in favour of making it responsible for the entirety of topics laid out in negotiation directives even if some of them, like investment protection, are not covered by the CCP. In addition, nominating other negotiators for the non-CCP part would unduly complicate the process and coordination of the EU's negotiating tactics.[53] Furthermore, the nomination of a negotiator is constitutionally much less significant than the question related to who will become a party to an agreement when it comes to signing and conclusion. The appointment of a negotiator does not establish a precedent, nor is it covered by the principle of pre-emption (*cf* Article 2(2) TFEU). Thus, as long as Member States trust the Commission's negotiators and feel that they can exercise a sufficient amount of political control over its negotiating decisions, they seem willing to accept the Commission's responsibility for tackling negotiation topics that are not covered by the exclusive competence of the EU. The question of mixity, if it materialises, can be then addressed at the end of the negotiation process.[54]

The Commission negotiators are subject to political control exercised by a special committee appointed by the Council (Article 207(3) TFEU; see also Article 218(4) TFEU). With respect to trade agreements, the role of the special committee is most often exercised by the Trade Policy Committee (TPC), which is one of the preparatory bodies of the Council. In the institutional structure, the TPC is situated below the level of COREPER and should facilitate the formal dialogue between the Commission and the Council.[55] It operates under the supervision of the Foreign Affairs Council and has one representative per Member State.[56] The TPC has the following subgroups: Full Members, Deputies, Experts Services, and Investment and Generalised System of Preferences.[57] In this context, depending on the subject matter of negotiations, the role of the special committee can be exercised by different compositions of the TPC.[58]

[51] See to that effect: Decision of the representatives of the governments of the Member States, meeting within the Council, authorising the European Commission to negotiate, on behalf of the Member States, the provisions of a Framework Agreement between the European Union and its Member States, of the one part, and Japan, of the other part, that fall within the competences of the Member States (2012), 16445/12.

[52] Interview 1, Interview 2.

[53] Gatti and Manzini (n 47) 1714.

[54] Interview 1, Interview 3.

[55] See the discussion in: E Coremans and B Kerremans, 'Agents as Information Asymmetry Managers in EU Trade Policy-Making' in T Delreux and J Adriaensen (eds), *The Principal Agent Model and the European Union* (Springer International Publishing, 2017) 235.

[56] Council, Mandates of Council preparatory bodies. Approval 8728/21, [2021] 3–5; S Boelaert, 'Mixity versus Unity: A View from the Other Side of the Rue de La Loi' in M Chamon and I Govaere (eds), *EU External Relations Post-Lisbon: The Law and Practice of Facultative Mixity* (Brill Nijhoff, 2020) 253.

[57] Council, Mandates of Council preparatory bodies. Approval 8728/21, [2021] 3–5.

[58] Interview 10, Interview 14.

The relationship between the special committee and the Commission and the degree of constitutional autonomy enjoyed by the latter during the negotiation process were discussed by the Court in the seminal *ETS* judgment.[59] The judgment was analysed extensively in legal scholarship;[60] here, I briefly recall its crucial implications and demonstrate its relevance for the main argument of this chapter.

The Court declared that the Council (or one of its special committees) may impose detailed procedural obligations on the Commission throughout the negotiation process. In practice, this means that the Commission can be obliged to report regularly to the special committee of the Council and consult with it. These procedural obligations are meant to allow the Council to formulate opinions and advice relating to the positions that the Commission would adopt in the negotiations. Nonetheless, *substantively*, the Commission enjoys a Treaty-based power to conduct the negotiations independently on behalf of the Union. Detailed negotiating positions established by the Council or by the special committee must not be imposed on the Commission to the extent that the latter has no flexibility in conducting the negotiation process.[61] It seems that the Commission cannot be bound to deliver a specific result (the Council itself rejected such a view[62]). On the contrary, the Commission should at best strive to achieve the broad objectives outlined by the Council.[63]

It is of paramount importance that the Commission's autonomy in conducting negotiations derives from the Treaties, and not from negotiation directives adopted by the Council. The Court thus declined to consider the Commission a technocratic agent of the political principal in the form of the Council and the TPC. The source of the Commission's autonomy was primarily located in provisions of Article 218 TFEU,[64] 'an autonomous and general provision of constitutional scope'.[65] Equally importantly, the Court linked the autonomy enjoyed by the negotiators to Article 17 TEU,[66] thus implicitly associating the autonomy and discretion enjoyed by the Commission negotiating international agreements with its task of ensuring the external representation of the EU in non-CFSP matters. This confirms the general argument advanced in this chapter whereby the Commission enjoys the political initiative across various instances of the exercise of power in the CCP domain, even if its initiative is constrained by veto powers and procedural obligations vis-à-vis the Council and the Parliament. It is important to note that the Court stated that the attempt to constrain the Commission in the negotiation process resulted in a breach of the principle of the institutional balance, a well-established constitutional benchmark in EU law.[67] According to the Court, the institutional balance is as 'a system for distributing powers among the different Community

[59] Case C-425/13 *Commission v Council (ETS)* ECLI:EU:C:2015:483.

[60] See for instance: J Heliskoski, 'The Procedural Law of International Agreements: A Thematic Journey through Article 218 TFEU' [2020] *Common Market Law Review* 79; PJ Kuijper, 'Litigation on External Relations Powers after Lisbon: The Member States Reject Their Own Treaty' (2016) *Legal Issues of Economic Integration* 1 as well as Ankersmit, ch 5 in this volume.

[61] *Commission v Council (ETS)* (n 59) [85]–[92]. See also: Kuijper (n 60) 9.

[62] ibid [87].

[63] *cf* Opinion of AG Wathelet in *Commission v Council (ETS)* ECLI:EU:C:2015:174 [71].

[64] *Commission v Council (ETS)* (n 59) [85]–[91].

[65] ibid [62].

[66] ibid [79].

[67] ibid [92].

[Union] institutions, assigning to each institution its own role in the institutional structure of the Community [Union] and the accomplishment of the tasks entrusted to the Community [Union].'[68] Thus, what from the perspective of constitutional theory can be described as the rivalry within a split executive (the Council and the Commission), is, from the EU-law perspective, an expression of the institutional balance informed by functional logic.

The European Parliament, exercising the legislative power and focusing on the function of control over the conduct of executive actors, does not formally participate in the negotiation process.[69] However, pursuant to Article 218(10) TFEU it enjoys the right to be informed and consulted throughout the negotiations. The Court of Justice has confirmed in the *Tanzania* case that the scope of this right is to be interpreted broadly.[70] The Parliament attempts to translate its right to be consulted into more tangible mechanisms of pressure over the EU Executive. It always tries to adopt a resolution before the approval of negotiating directives by the Council, establishing a political position on the draft negotiating directives shared by the Commission services.[71] Otherwise, the Parliament relies on the Committee on International Trade (INTA), standing and shadow rapporteurs and monitoring groups dedicated to specific geographical regions in order to scrutinise ongoing negotiations.[72] The intensity of the scrutiny depends on the Parliament's political priorities and the initiative of the INTA itself.[73] The INTA Committee and the rapporteurs can request a hearing with Commission officials as well as *in camera* meetings – these allow them to be debriefed about the progress of negotiations and exchange views with Commission negotiators.[74]

As a final note, a recent case before the Court of Justice might add another dimension to the Commission's executive power of representing the EU externally as understood in Article 17 TFEU. Case C-551/21 *Commission v Council* pertains to the interpretation of Article 218(5) TFEU and addresses the question of who should sign an international agreement on the EU's behalf. At the time of writing, the Court has not delivered its judgment. However, AG Kokott in her Opinion argued that the Commission's constitutional powers to represent the EU externally as per Article 17 TEU should also encompass the signing of an international agreement.[75] In doing so, AG Kokott chose to disregard an institutional practice whereby the Council not only authorises the signing of an agreement but also designates an EU representative who would do it, often choosing the Permanent Representative of the Member State holding the Council Presidency.[76] It remains to be seen if the Court upholds the AG's position; if it does, it will further broaden the scope of the Commission's powers of representation and, consequently, strengthen its executive powers in the foreign policy domain. These executive powers

[68] Case C-70/88 *Chernobyl* ECLI: EU:C:1990:217 [21].

[69] On structural limits of the European Parliament's role in trade negotiations see Ankersmit, ch 5 in this volume, section II.A.

[70] Case C-263/14 *Tanzania* ECLI:EU:C:2016:435 [76].

[71] Interview 15, Interview 16.

[72] ibid.

[73] Interview 11, Interview 15, Interview 16.

[74] Interview 20, Interview 15.

[75] Opinion of AG Kokott in Case C-551/21 *Commission v Council* ECLI:EU:C:2023:579 [82]–[84].

[76] ibid [57].

amount to a significant degree of autonomy vis-à-vis the Council and the Parliament and allow the Commission to initiate and, to a large extent, shape the policymaking process in the CCP.

III. Expertise and Commission's Framing Powers

This section discusses how expertise reinforces and connects with the Commission's formal powers of initiative. First, examining the question of the long-term EU trade policy agenda, I demonstrate that the Commission can steer the course of trade policy by proposing new instruments and framing the significance of specific initiatives in accordance with its preferences. By putting discursive emphasis on some instruments and downplaying the significance of others as well as by creative references to non-trade values, the Commission can pre-empt political opposition to the EU trade policy programme.[77] Furthermore, some elements of the Better Regulation agenda, notably Regulatory and Sustainability Impact Assessments, strengthen the expert–Executive nexus within the Commission and once again allow it to frame analytical complexity and draw on its expertise to defend its political stance. This does not imply that the Commission can disregard the preferences of other institutions such as the Council and the Parliament; however, in many cases, it can shift the burden of proof with respect to specific policy decisions.[78]

A. The Commission and the EU Trade Policy Programme

The common commercial policy is one of the oldest exclusive competences of the EU, dating back to the 1970s.[79] It was preceded by earlier measures aimed at deepening economic integration between Members of the EEC: these consisted of the tariff removal between the Members of the EEC and the gradual establishment of a common external tariff for EEC Members.[80] On balance, this means that the leading role of the Commission in EU trade policy has been consolidated and become less contested over time.[81] The Member States no longer try to impose their vision of the CCP on the Commission but are willing to accept its policy initiative and respond in a constructive fashion.[82] Considering the long time over which the EU has enjoyed an exclusive competence in the field of trade, the Commission has also been able to accumulate experience

[77] T Jacobs et al 'The Hegemonic Politics of "Strategic Autonomy" and "Resilience": COVID-19 and the Dislocation of EU Trade Policy' (2023) 61 *Journal of Common Market Studies* 3, 15.

[78] *cf* A de Ruijter and M Weimer, 'Regulating Risks in the European Union: The Co-Production of Expert and Executive Power' in M Weimer and A de Ruijter (eds), *Regulating risks in the European Union: the co-production of expert and executive power* (Hart Publishing 2017) 13.

[79] See *Opinion 1/75* ECLI:EU:C:1975:145.

[80] D De Bièvre, 'Directorate-General for Trade of the European Commission' in KE Jørgensen et al (eds), *The SAGE handbook of European foreign policy* (SAGE Publications Ltd, 2015) 4–5.

[81] Interview 3.

[82] ibid.

and foster institutional expertise.[83] This applies especially to DG Trade whose powers have grown with successive reforms of the Treaties and have been further reinforced by the expanding understanding of international trade regulation.[84] The latter now incorporates capital movements, intellectual property rights, regulatory cooperation and investment as well as trade and labour, and trade and sustainable development. Against this backdrop, several interviewees confirmed the strong capabilities of DG Trade in such areas as negotiating trade deals or litigating trade disputes in WTO.[85] In this connection, the increasingly technical nature of modern trade policy further strengthens the position of the Commission vis-à-vis other EU institutions whose resources and expertise cannot match that of the Commission.[86]

Trade policy communications can be considered an expression of the evolving priorities of the EU in trade policy, setting out legislative initiatives and forward-looking proposals.[87] These communications are adopted by virtue of a decision of the College of Commissioners.[88] It is not clear whether these communications are always subject to intense deliberation – the Commission Rules of Procedure allow for several modes of decision-making. The written procedure sets out a mechanism whereby a proposal is circulated among the Members of the Commission; if no Member makes a reservation, the proposal is adopted without a discussion.[89]

At the same time, EU officials pointed out that these communications are consulted upon with Member States, the Parliament and stakeholders.[90] Thus, it is fair to say that they will reflect a balanced view of the trade priorities of the EU formulated in an evolutionary, sometimes reactive way.[91] It is noteworthy that trade policy communications are sometimes adopted at the beginning of a new mandate of the Commission, marking political shifts and changing priorities of different Trade Commissioners and Commission presidents.[92] Often, they also reflect a broader political consensus among the EU institutions and Member States that current trade policy priorities are becoming obsolete in the light of a changing global environment, as was the case with the most recent 'Trade Policy Review' from 2021.[93] This communication marks a cautious departure from the liberal paradigm and puts more emphasis on protectionism and geoeconomic dimension of EU trade policy under the guise of 'Open Strategic Autonomy'.[94]

[83] Interview 1, Interview 2, Interview 3, Interview 11.

[84] De Bièvre (n 80) 6.

[85] Interview 2, Interview 3.

[86] Interview 3, Interview 11. On the expert–executive nexus in the context of the Commission and EU trade policy see also Ankersmit, ch 5 in this volume, section I.B.

[87] G Berends, 'The New European Parliament and Its Role in EU Trade Policy: Reset or Repeat?' in M Bungenberg et al (eds), *European Yearbook of International Economic Law 2020*, vol 11 (Springer International Publishing, 2020) 297.

[88] ibid.

[89] Rules of Procedure of the Commission [C(2000) 3614], OJ L 308, 08/12/2000 P. 0026 0034, Art 12.

[90] Interview 1, Interview 9.

[91] Interview 2, Interview 9.

[92] Interview 8.

[93] Interview 11.

[94] Commission (n 21); L Schmitz and T Seidl, 'As Open as Possible, as Autonomous as Necessary: Understanding the Rise of Open Strategic Autonomy in EU Trade Policy' (2022) *Journal of Common Market Studies*.

Outlining comprehensive policy programmes by the Commission is not unique to trade policy. What does make it unique, however, is the Commission's ability to define strategic objectives and present an array of multilateral, bilateral and unilateral instruments designed to meet these objectives in a policy field covered by an exclusive competence where the principle of pre-emption does not apply (Article 2(1) TFEU). In this context, the Commission's room for manoeuvre is reinforced by the possibility of initiating legislation addressing novel topics, without having to consider the scope of the Member State's existing legislation. The broad scope of the Commission's power of initiative was discussed in the previous section of this chapter. In this context, unilateral, bilateral and multilateral initiatives can be designed to complement and reinforce each other's impact.

'Trade Policy Review' (2021) illustrates the power of the Commission in this respect. The policy programme outlined therein constitutes a major revision of the strategy developed in 'Trade for all' (2015). Conducted against the background of the COVID-19 pandemic, accelerating climate crisis, disruptions of supply chains, the paralysis of the WTO appellate mechanism, and the exacerbating Sino-American rivalry, the review set out the framework for a more assertive and geopolitical EU trade policy. In this connection, the Review adapted for the purposes of trade policy the concept of strategic autonomy. The latter refers to the EU's capacity to act autonomously on the international plane and the EU's ability to shape the world through its leadership and engagement, reflecting its strategic interests and values.[95] The concept is highly relevant for trade policy where its crucial implication is the need to combine openness and assertiveness, and better integrate trade with other areas of EU external action. In this vein, the three crucial adjectives defining the geopolitical trade policy of the EU are 'open', 'sustainable', and 'assertive'.[96]

What is notable about trade policy programmes and what is illustrated by the 'Trade Policy Review' is the Commission's ability to present synergies and complementary effects of various instruments within the CCP. This gives the Commission strong arguments to defend its trade policy agenda against various types of criticism and argue that one type of instrument can compensate weakness of other types of instruments. The Commission, enjoying the monopoly on legislative initiative and being able to initiate trade negotiations, also controls the timing when it comes to implementing its agenda which ultimately strengthens its bargaining position.

For instance, in the context of discussions about the Comprehensive Agreement on Investment (CAI) between the EU and China, the Commission argued that its trade policy towards China needs to be based on the combination of active engagement (which is provided by the CAI) and strong unilateral measures aiming to safeguard defensive trade interests.[97] The latter include the Investment Screening Mechanism,[98]

[95] J Borrell, 'Why European Strategic Autonomy Matters', HR/VP Blog, 3 December 2020, at www.eeas.europa.eu/eeas/why-european-strategic-autonomy-matters_en.

[96] Commission (n 21) 1–3.

[97] ibid 9.

[98] Regulation (EU) 2019/452 of the European Parliament and of the Council of 19 March 2019 establishing a framework for the screening of foreign direct investments into the Union OJ L 79I, 1–14.

the regulation of foreign subsidies distorting the internal market,[99] or the anti-coercion instrument[100] combining trade defence logic with mechanisms resembling sanctions. The ideal of Open Strategic Autonomy provides a fitting conceptual framework for the Commission to argue that implementing its holistic perspective requires a continuation of bilateral negotiations on one hand and an adoption of several novel unilateral instruments on the other hand. The unilateral turn in EU trade policy can also be associated with the geoeconomic turn in EU external action. The ownership of agenda-setting powers in EU trade policy thus allows the Commission to advocate for a more assertive trade policy that would also concentrate more powers in the Commission's hands.

A somewhat similar type of argumentation was employed by the Commission with respect to criticism levelled towards the EU–Mercosur Association Agreement on the grounds that it can encourage deforestation of the Amazon rainforest and contradict the EU's climate policy ambitions.[101] The Commission emphasised that environmental risks related to the Agreement would be alleviated by several unilateral instruments designed to address concerns related to sustainability and labour standards beyond the EU borders, notably the Deforestation Regulation,[102] Carbon Border Adjustment Mechanism[103] and proposal on sustainable corporate governance.[104] These would allow the EU to apply extraterritorially its regulatory standards in a more effective way than through Trade and Sustainable Development chapters included in Free Trade Agreements. The adoption of such measures is partially a response to the growing pressure on the Commission from the European Parliament and civil society, who advocate the mainstreaming of climate policy objectives in EU trade policy.[105] What remains problematic is the broader legitimacy of such measures, especially vis-à-vis third-country partners. Even if their legality under WTO law can be defended on the grounds of regulating for legitimate objectives (Article XX GATT) in compliance with criteria developed in the *US-Shrimp* case,[106] it is incontestable that these measures disproportionally put the financial burden on the countries in the Global South.[107]

On balance, having control over the long-term trade policy agenda allows the Commission to manage normative conflicts over trade policy, shape the policy discourse

[99] Regulation (EU) 2022/2560 of the European Parliament and of the Council of 14 December 2022 on foreign subsidies distorting the internal market OJ L 330, 1–45.

[100] Regulation (EU) 2023/2675 of the European Parliament and of the Council of 22 November 2023 on the protection of the Union and its Member States from economic coercion by third countries OJ L 2023/2675.

[101] Commission (n 21) 13.

[102] Regulation (EU) 2023/1115 of the European Parliament and of the Council of 31 May 2023 on the making available on the Union market and the export from the Union of certain commodities and products associated with deforestation and forest degradation and repealing Regulation (EU) No 995/2010 OJ L 150, 206–47.

[103] Regulation (EU) 2023/956 of the European Parliament and of the Council of 10 May 2023 establishing a carbon border adjustment mechanism OJ L 130, 52–104.

[104] Commission (n 21) 13; Proposal for a Directive of the European Parliament and of the Council on Corporate Sustainability Due Diligence and amending Directive (EU) 2019/1937, COM/2022/71 final. See also: European Commission Services' Position Paper addressing Sustainability Impact Assessment for the EU–Mercosur Association Agreement, 14.

[105] Interview 11, Interview 18, Interview 20.

[106] United States – Import Prohibition of Certain Shrimp and Shrimp Products [1998] – AB-1998-4 – Report of the Appellate Body, paras 115–84.

[107] G Vidigal, 'The Unilateralization of Trade Governance: Constructive, Reconstructive, and Deconstructive Unilateralism' (2023) *Legal Issues of Economic Integration* 1, 4–6.

and defuse political criticism towards its decisions. Political scientists who have conducted discourse analysis of the Commission's trade communications have demonstrated that the Commission tends to acknowledge the arguments of its critics and often incorporates their ideas.[108] In this connection, the 'Trade for all' Communication published in 2015 at the height of the controversy over the TTIP and CETA framed EU trade policy as one guided by values, especially high consumer standards, transparency and labour rights.[109] In a similar vein, the 'Trade Policy Review' elevated sustainability to a defining feature of the updated EU trade policy, proclaiming the Commission's commitment to mainstream climate policy measures across different areas of trade policy.[110] The discursive focus on sustainability makes it possible to defuse criticism as to the environmental impact of some agreements, such as the EU–Mercosur Association Agreement. Thus, the skilful use of agenda-setting in EU trade policy ultimately allows the Commission to defend the coherence of its trade policy programme even if not all proposals ultimately come to fruition.[111]

B. Better Regulation Agenda, Sustainability Impact Assessments, and the Commission's Framing Powers

This section reflects on the role of impact assessments in trade policy-making, especially as regards trade and investment agreements. It is demonstrated that the complexity of these assessments combined with the Commission's framing powers further reinforce the latter's position vis-à-vis other institutional actors, allowing the Commission to draw on expert findings to defend its political priorities related to the entire trade policy agenda.

Regulatory and Sustainability Impact Assessments constitute a crucial piece of the Commission's Better Regulation Agenda. The latter emerged in the early 2000s within the framework of the Lisbon Strategy and should be seen as a part of the EU's efforts to adopt regulatory standards that would incentivise investment, innovation and economic growth.[112] To this end, impact assessments are meant to promote transparent and evidence-based policy-making.[113] According to the Commission, 'an impact assessment is required for Commission initiatives that are likely to have significant economic, environmental or social impacts or which entail significant spending, and where the Commission has a choice of policy options.'[114] Findings from a regulatory impact assessment are incorporated in explanatory memoranda included in the Commission's

[108] Jacobs et al (n 77) 15.

[109] Commission, 'Trade for all – Towards a more responsible trade and investment policy' COM(2015) 497, 14–20.

[110] Commission (n 21) 2–14.

[111] Kreppel and Oztas (n 20).

[112] A Alemanno, 'How Much Better Is Better Regulation? Assessing the Impact of the Better Regulation Package on the European Union – A Research Agenda' (2015) 6 *European journal of risk regulation* 344, 344–45; Ruijter and Weimer (n 69) 6.

[113] Commission Staff Working Document, Better Regulation Guidelines SWD(2021) 305 final, 10.

[114] ibid 30.

legislative proposals. They can also be found in the Commission's recommendations for Council decisions authorising the opening of trade negotiations.[115]

SIAs are a specific type of impact assessment study conducted during trade and investment negotiations with a view to providing policy considerations for EU negotiators.[116] As the name suggests, these studies are supposed to assess the sustainability of an agreement under negotiation in a broad sense, measuring its impact in economic, environmental and social terms.[117] This means that SIAs discuss, among other issues, the potential of an agreement to spur economic growth as well as its impact on labour and human rights and potential conflicts and synergies with climate policy objectives. It is important to note that SIAs are not conducted by the Commission alone, but are outsourced to external consultants. The Commission discusses the findings of an SIA in a separate position paper where it outlines its political stance vis-à-vis the findings of an SIA and policy recommendations put forward by consultants.[118]

As the Commission itself points out,

> trade SIAs consist of two complementary components of equal importance: (i) a robust analysis of economic, social, human rights and environmental impacts, using, among other methods, modelling techniques and causal chain analysis …; (ii) a wide consultation process involving stakeholders both in the EU and in the partner country, which provides opportunities for information-gathering and dissemination of results.[119]

The above description already indicates that SIAs entail conducting a hugely complex analysis incorporating various hypothetical scenarios and unpredictable variables. The question of hypothetical scenarios comes into play when an external consultant needs to assume what kind of trade liberalisation and regulatory changes would be brought about by a trade agreement under negotiation. In turn, the hypothetical and qualified nature of these findings gives the Commission more space to frame them in accordance with its institutional preferences.

SIAs are supposed to operationalise the constitutional principle of sustainable development as enshrined in the EU Treaties.[120] In addition to that, they also serve to gather inputs from interested stakeholders in civil society and the private sector alike.[121] The Commission has committed to treat these studies as an integral part of developing its trade policy agenda.[122] The complexity and uncertainty of analysis conducted within the framework of SIAs combined with the framing power of the Commission reinforces the latter's potential to promote its trade policy agenda. To illustrate this, I refer to an SIA conducted in relation to the EU–Mercosur Association Agreement and to one pertaining to the EU–Japan Economic Partnership Agreement. The EU–Mercosur Association

[115] Recommendation for a Council Decision authorising the opening of negotiations on a Free Trade Agreement between the European Union and Japan COM(2012) 390 final.

[116] Commission. Directorate General for Trade, Handbook for Trade Sustainability Impact Assessment (Publications Office, 2016) 7.

[117] ibid 5.

[118] Commission (n 116) 13.

[119] Commission (n 21) 8.

[120] ibid.

[121] ibid 8.

[122] Commission, 'Trade for all – Towards a more responsible trade and investment policy' COM(2015) 497 final, 12.

Agreement has proved to be much more controversial than the Agreement in Japan. In this context, it will be demonstrated that the Commission's framing of the possible impact and risks associated with the deal with Mercosur was more strategic and selective than with respect to the deal with Japan, which was not predicted to bring difficult trade-offs between economic growth and environmental protection.

The first SIA dealing with the EU–Mercosur Association Agreement was conducted between 2003 and 2007 and compared two contrasting scenarios: keeping the status quo with respect to trade and investment framework between the EU and Mercosur and a full liberalisation scenario assuming the removal of tariff and non-tariff barriers to trade. The second SIA conducted between 2017 and 2020 and addressing the same agreement also contemplated two contrasting scenarios.[123] It is important to note that the new SIA report was only published in December 2020 whereas the negotiations of the trade part of the Association Agreement were finalised in 2019. This delay has led to the proceedings before the European Ombudsman initiated by five civil society organisations.[124] The Ombudsman concluded that the Commission's failure to finalise the SIA before the conclusion of trade negotiations constituted maladministration.[125] The Ombudsman pointed out, relying on Commission's own assertions, that SIA can only serve its purpose if its findings are available beforehand and can thus inform the decision-making process.[126]

The conservative scenario in the second SIA assumed the elimination of tariffs in 90 per cent of the industrial products and 80 per cent in agricultural products for the Mercosur bloc; the ambitious scenario assumed the elimination of tariffs in 100 per cent of products for the Mercosur bloc.[127] The EU would eliminate tariffs on all industrial products in both scenarios, and apply partial tariff cuts of 15 per cent in the conservative scenario and 30 per cent in the ambitious scenario in rice, sugar, ruminant meat, and other meat sectors.[128]

The hypothetical scenarios never fully correspond to the negotiated outcome and only approximately reflect the potential impact of an agreement, assuming the accuracy of the forecasting methods. Given the nature of bilateral trade agreements, the SIAs tend to predict increased economic growth even if some sectors of the economy or groups of the population might be worse off as a result. Economic benefits can be seen in absolute terms and are usually presented as such: for instance, the second SIA for the EU–Mercosur AA predicted a 0.1 per cent increase in GDP by 2032 for the EU in the ambitious scenario; this corresponds to a GDP increase in roughly 15 billion euros in nominal terms.[129] In turn, environmental or societal risks are usually more qualified: for

[123] LSE Consulting, Sustainability Impact Assessment in Support of the Association Agreement Negotiations between the European Union and Mercosur [2020] 12.

[124] These organisations were: ClientEarth, Fern, Veblen Institute, La Fondation Nicolas Hulot pour la Nature et l'Homme and International Federation for Human Rights.

[125] European Ombudsman, 'Decision in case 1026/2020/MAS concerning the failure by the European Commission to finalise an updated 'sustainability impact assessment' before concluding the EU–Mercosur trade negotiations' (17 March 2021), www.ombudsman.europa.eu/en/decision/en/139418.

[126] ibid para 33.

[127] LSE Consulting, Sustainability Impact Assessment in Support of the Association Agreement Negotiations between the European Union and Mercosur [2020] 12.

[128] ibid.

[129] ibid. 29–30.

instance, the same SIA speaks of moderate risk of the Agreement incentivising deforestation in Mercosur countries in order to reclaim land needed for increased agricultural production.[130] Assessment of economic, environmental and societal impact is accompanied by policy recommendations. In the case at hand, some of them fall within the scope of competence of the EU (eg strengthening the enforcement of TSD chapters, establishing stronger regulatory cooperation with respect to the development and transfer of green technology); still others are entirely dependent on domestic regulation and enforcement in Mercosur countries, such as improvement of anti-deforestation laws in Brazil or promotion of more sustainable agricultural models in Mercosur countries.[131] Inevitably, the EU institutions have more limited influence over policy measures that lie at the discretion of third-country partners and their governments.

The complexity of SIAs, the hypothetical nature of their findings and the difficulty in comparing economic indicators with societal and environmental considerations increase the power of the Commission that presents policy papers addressing findings from the SIAs. In this connection, the Commission is able to put emphasis on selected findings that might be politically convenient and, conversely, omit those that are unfavourable to its broader trade policy agenda. Commission's position papers make it possible to put negotiated agreements in a wider trade policy context and demonstrate how unilateral and multilateral efforts complement bilateral trade agreements. This was also the case with regard to the Commission's position paper related to the SIA dedicated to the EU–Mercosur Association Agreement.

Responding to concerns related to potential impact of trade on deforestation, the Commission emphasised the importance of several unilateral instruments designed to export ambitious sustainability and labour standards beyond the EU borders.[132] It also evaded the criticism related to weak enforcement mechanism dedicated to TSD provisions and instead underlined that the TSD chapter enshrines the right to regulate and the non-regression principle that prohibits lowering regulatory standards in order to attract trade and investment.[133] The Commission hailed the reference to the Paris Climate Agreement enshrined in the TSD chapter, claiming that 'a breach of [the Paris Agreement] commitments would be also in breach of the EU-Mercosur agreement'.[134] It did not however discuss the question of how difficult it would be to ascertain the existence of such a breach and trigger effective enforcement under the TSD chapter in question.[135]

The SIA pertaining to the EU–Japan EPA stands in contrast to the EU–Mercosur AA. This stems from the fact that the Agreement with Japan, despite its scope and ambition, attracted surprisingly little public attention or controversy.[136] The lack of significant

[130] ibid 3–104.
[131] ibid 104–05.
[132] European Commission Services' Position Paper addressing Sustainability Impact Assessment for the EU–Mercosur Association Agreement [2021] 14.
[133] ibid 11.
[134] ibid 14.
[135] M Bronckers and G Gruni, 'Retooling the Sustainability Standards in EU Free Trade Agreements' (2021) 24 *Journal of International Economic Law* 25, 29.
[136] H Suzuki, 'The New Politics of Trade: EU–Japan' (2017) 39 *Journal of European Integration* 875; I Mancini, 'The European Parliament and Civil Society in EU Trade Negotiations: The Untold Story of an Erratic Engagement' (2022) *European Foreign Affairs Review* 241.

opposition to the Agreement can be attributed to a coincidence of several factors, notably a strong economic rationale for both sides to the Agreement, few redistributive threats to crucial constituencies such as farmers, and virtually no conflict between the EU and Japan over salient non-trade values such as climate policy or human rights. The SIA reinforced the economic case for the Agreement and did not identify major concerns related to labour and human rights and climate policy and environment.[137]

In light of the findings of the SIA, the Commission did not have a difficult job making a political case for the conclusion of the EPA with Japan. In this vein, the position paper picked up on major arguments in favour of the Agreement, reinforced the political case behind it, and promised that the Commission would follow up on crucial policy recommendations made by the consultants.[138] For instance, the consultants recommended taking action specifically targeted at European Small and Medium Enterprises (SMEs), aiming to help them mitigate the adverse impact of the Trans-Pacific Partnership Agreement[139] and, conversely, benefit from the opportunities resulting from the conclusion of the EU–Japan EPA. This translated into a first-ever chapter dedicated to SMEs in a trade agreement negotiated by the EU which was the result of targeted efforts of Commission negotiators.[140] The Commission also claimed that most of the recommendations related to social issues would be addressed by provisions of the TSD chapter, notably by enshrining the right to regulate and the non-regression principle.[141] It also invoked the importance of other trade policy instruments, such as the European Globalisation Adjustment Fund that helps mitigate the redistributive impact of trade liberalisation and help vulnerable groups.[142] The Commission concluded by claiming that the proposed Agreement combined economic benefits with positive social and environmental impact, thus integrating trade and non-trade values in a comprehensive agreement with symmetrical levels of trade liberalisation.[143]

The contrast between the EU–Mercosur Association Agreement and the EU–Japan Economic Partnership Agreement illustrates the shifting character of the Commission's framing powers in trade policy. Whereas the Commission's role in the process of negotiating an uncontroversial agreement such as the one in Japan remained fairly technocratic, with the Commission reiterating its support for policy considerations outlined by external consultants, the selective approach to concerns related to the EU–Mercosur Agreement reveals a blurred line between expert assessment and political commitment.[144] Engaging critically with the Commission's political stance towards the findings of the SIAs requires comprehensive knowledge of EU trade law and policy.

[137] Commission, Trade Sustainability Impact Assessment of the Free Trade Agreement between the European Union and Japan (2016) 194–233.

[138] European Commission Services, Position Paper on the Trade Sustainability Impact Assessment in support of negotiations of a Free Trade Agreement between the European Union and Japan (2017) 12–14.

[139] After the withdrawal of the United States from the TPP, the Agreement was concluded as the Comprehensive and Progressive Agreement for Trans-Pacific Partnership by the remaining parties in 2018.

[140] Interview 13; EU–Japan EPA Position Paper (n 138) 23.

[141] ibid 13–14.

[142] ibid 12–13.

[143] ibid 23–24.

[144] Å Gornitzka and C Holst, 'The Expert–Executive Nexus in the EU: An Introduction' (2015) 3 *Politics and Governance* 1, 2.

The limits of trade policy instruments (such as TSD provisions or unilateral instruments aiming to extraterritorially apply EU regulatory standards) are not always spelled out by the Commission. This reinforces the significance of political control exercised by the Council and the Parliament as well as their role in making the debate about EU trade policy more transparent and accessible to the broader public. As a final note, one should underline that impact assessments are a tool to achieve sound policy-making, not an end in itself. The latter point was reinforced by the Court of Justice in *Afton* where the Court emphasised that findings from impact assessments are not binding on the EU's legislative institutions, namely the Parliament and the Council.[145] In doing so, the Court expressed its support for preserving a clear separation between an expert assessment and a political commitment, the former always having a subservient role in the democratic legislative process.

IV. Conclusion

This contribution demonstrated that the European Commission enjoys the potential to shape EU trade policy in the long run and should be considered a primary actor in this policy domain. The Commission can initiate legislative processes and has significant autonomy as a negotiator of trade and investment agreements, also when their scope exceeds the confines of the CCP defined by the Court of Justice. Furthermore, the Commission draws on its expertise and framing powers to define the long-term trade policy programme, seeking synergies between unilateral, plurilateral and multilateral measures. The same applies to SIAs and position papers accompanying them where the Commission endorses specific policy recommendations of external consultants and can selectively put emphasis on some findings of SIAs, all the while defending the cohesion of its trade policy agenda. The combination of these powers amounts to a significant degree of executive leadership on the part of the Commission underpinned by the advantage of expertise. At the same time, the Commission's room for manoeuvre is limited by the Council and the Parliament.

The Commission's relationship with the Council in EU trade policy can be cautiously described as simultaneous rivalry and cooperation between two executives, one more technocratic (the Commission) and one more political in character (the Council). From the perspective of EU law, splitting the executive functions is an expression of the principle of institutional balance prescribing a functional division of powers in the EU constitutional setup. The analysis of case law of the Court, especially the *ETS* judgment, demonstrated that under the principle of institutional balance, the Commission and the Council enjoy their autonomous powers conferred in the Treaties.[146] In this context, the Commission cannot be seen as a technocratic agent of the Council. At the same time, the two institutions are forced to closely collaborate at different stages of policy-making (especially in the process of negotiation of trade and investment agreements). This is

[145] Case C-343/09 *Afton* ECLI:EU:C:2010:419 [30].
[146] See also: Cremona (n 12) 254–55.

also compatible with the interinstitutional (horizontal) duty of mutual sincere cooperation codified in the Treaties (Article 13(2) TEU, the last sentence).

The relationship between the Commission and the Parliament is more clear-cut. Unlike the Council, the Parliament's prerogatives are confined to the legislative sphere. It does not actively participate in the treaty-making processes, instead exercising functions of control and granting legislative consent over the final agreement. The Parliament disposes of tools of political control, being able to obtain information, express its political priorities and scrutinise the Commission's conduct as a negotiator of trade and investment agreements.

In the end, the Commission finds itself in a position where it can chart the course of EU trade policy in the long run; the other institutions in turn wield the tools to moderate the course chosen by the Commission. The helicopter view of the division of powers in EU trade policy-making evokes not an ideal of separation, but rather that of confusion of powers.[147] This stems from the fact that executive powers are divided between the Commission and the Council, and decision-making processes, either within the framework of the Ordinary Legislative Procedure or in the treaty-making procedure, require ongoing coordination between the crucial institutions. This results in a cooperative and consensus-oriented (not agonistic) policy-making set-up where preferences of the participating institutions are not always easy to discern.[148] Notwithstanding, the Commission remains a crucial player in the field of EU trade policy. Even if the Commission's executive powers are limited by prerogatives of the Council, and to a lesser extent, the Parliament, it enjoys a significant advantage vis-à-vis other institutions. This does not result from open-ended constitutional provisions or emergency powers, as has been often the case with national executives, but from the decision-making initiative complemented with expertise and framing powers.

[147] *cf* N Walker, 'The European Union's Unresolved Constitution' in M Rosenfeld and A Sajó, *The Oxford Handbook of Comparative Constitutional Law* (Oxford University Press, 2012) 1199–201.

[148] *cf* M Hinterleitner and F Sager, 'Anticipatory and Reactive Forms of Blame Avoidance: Of Foxes and Lions' (2017) 9 *European Political Science Review* 587, 598–99.

7

Regulatory Cooperation Chapters as Fuzzy Law

MERIJN CHAMON

I. Introduction

This chapter will focus on one relatively novel feature of the deep and comprehensive free trade agreements (DCFTAs) which the EU has been concluding over the past decade. These DCFTAs will now typically contain dedicated chapters on regulatory cooperation between the two parties. Such chapters have given rise to some contestation from civil society and academics. However, their effect remains relatively understudied. In addition, in so far as the critique levelled against these chapters makes the claim that regulatory cooperation chapter undermine democracy or, in separation of powers terms, the position of legislative branch, the typical features of regulatory cooperation chapters do not seem to raise many legitimacy problems. After all, regulatory cooperation chapters prescribe a voluntary and non-binding cooperation between the parties' regulators, leaving the parties' regulatory autonomy intact. This begs the question whether and how this trend in EU trade law could still be seen as an example of an executive branch that is structurally overreaching.

Before unpacking that question, this chapter will commence with a concrete example of 'regulatory cooperation in practice'. Presenting this example first may help the reader to understand what 'regulatory cooperation' (may) concretely boil(s) down to. To subsequently unpack the chapter's main question, the separation of powers and its specific expression in the area of EU trade will be recalled. While the chapters by Piotr Krajewski, Laurens Ankersmit and Christina Eckes rightly highlight that the Parliament's role in trade policy is limited, this is foremost so when compared to its role in the internal legislative process. However, if the European Parliament is compared to parliaments of other polities, it enjoys a relatively strong position. The chapter will then present the basic features of the regulatory cooperation chapters, allowing us to assess the critiques that have been developed in relation to regulatory cooperation, showing how these typically invoke certain potential risks (which so far do not seem to have materialised), which do not appear to directly affect the separation of powers.

The chapter's assessment thus suggests that the separation of powers is not really affected by regulatory cooperation and that the controversy surrounding it is 'much ado about nothing'. In a final section, however, it raises the possibility that no tension between 'regulatory cooperation' and the separation of powers was found because of a blind spot in the perspective which traditional constitutional scholarship takes, focussing on the binary question of legal/illegal, valid/invalid and constitutional/unconstitutional. To transcend that binarity and address that blind spot, the chapter will rely on and develop the internal tension model of the executive branch as proposed by Margit Cohn. Assessed against this model, regulatory cooperation chapters appear to be a perfect example of the internal tension model's central notion of 'fuzzy law'. The latter is understood as law that presents a façade of legality deriving from its binding formal status, while its content or application offer broad options for action (and possible abuse), concealing a reality of alegality.[1] If regulatory cooperation chapters in DCFTAs are indeed conceptualised as instances of fuzzy law, we can expose how they hide a reality of alegality in which the Commission (as an executive actor) can roam almost entirely freely. In addition, we can see a dynamic in which regulatory cooperation chapters leverage the internal executive-driven better regulation agenda on the international plane, discursively limiting the scope left for political contestation by the legislative branch and reinforcing the framing powers of the executive.

II. International Regulatory Cooperation Concretised

Before giving an illustration of regulatory cooperation pursuant to CETA, it is useful to look into the rules governing the functioning of the Regulatory Cooperation Forum (RCF). The RCF is a specialised committee pursuant to Article 26.2(1)(h) CETA, operating under the auspices of the CETA Joint Committee. It is required to meet at least once a year,[2] which it has also done since the provisional application of CETA. The RCF decided not to adopt separate rules of procedure but to apply those of the Joint Committee *mutatis mutandis*.[3] In the RCF, the EU delegation is led by the Commission, specifically by representatives of DG GROW and DG TRADE, while the Canadian delegation is led by the Treasury Board of Canada Secretariat and Global Affairs Canada. The work of the RCF is guided by a work plan which is continuously updated and which lists the items that both sides agree to cooperate on. Formally, there is no privileged industry access to the RCF: (i) RCF meetings themselves are strictly reserved to government officials; (ii) any stakeholder can make suggestions for regulatory cooperation through portals set up by both parties;[4] and (iii) any stakeholder can register to attend the debriefings of the RCF. Following each meeting, a report of the ongoing work of the RCF is also published.[5] However, the information provided therein is rather general and limited. When Foodwatch eV, an NGO, asked for access to

[1] M Cohn, *A Theory of the Executive Branch: Tension and Legality* (Oxford University Press, 2021) 59.

[2] Comprehensive Economic and Trade Agreement (CETA) between Canada, of the one part, and the European Union and its Member States, of the other part [2017] OJ L11/23, Art 21.6(4)(b).

[3] See Government of Canada, '1st Meeting of the CETA Regulatory Cooperation Forum – Summary Report' (December 2018) 2.

[4] For the EU this is at policy.trade.ec.europa.eu/consultations_en.

[5] These can be accessed through the EU's CIRCABC platform, see circabc.europa.eu/ui/explore.

a series of Commission documents preparing the second RCF meeting (of 2020), the Commission only provided partial access. It invoked Article 4(1)(a) of the transparency regulation,[6] requiring the EU institutions to refuse access if disclosure of the documents would undermine the EU's external relations. When Foodwatch eV contested this refusal before the General Court, the latter agreed with the Commission that the implementation of the CETA still came within the exception of the EU's external relations.[7] In addition, it rejected Foodwatch eV's further argument that the exception can only be invoked where bodies responsible for the implementation of international agreements are tasked to adopt binding acts.[8] By accepting the Commission's reasoning that Article 4(1)(a) applied, the level of transparency compared to internal Better Regulation is thus effectively lowered, since those access to documents requests would come under Article 4(2)–(3) where the institution concerned need not only show that disclosure would undermine the public interest, but also that there is no overriding public interest in favour of disclosure.

One of the first achievements of the international regulatory cooperation under CETA has been the reduction of barriers to marketing of a number of cosmetic like products in Canada. Under EU law,[9] sunscreen products are qualified as cosmetic products and the UV filters approved for use in sunscreen are listed in one of the annexes of the relevant secondary regulation.[10] In contrast, in Canada, sunscreen products are qualified as non-prescription drugs or natural health products. This means that sunscreen products may not be covered by the CETA Protocol on the mutual recognition of the compliance and enforcement programme regarding good manufacturing practices for pharmaceutical products.[11] In addition, cosmetic products are not listed in the covered products listed in Annex I of the CETA Protocol on the mutual acceptance of the results of conformity assessment. In light of this, the RCF, following its first meeting in December 2018, noted that the '[c]onfirmatory re-testing requirements for "cosmetic-like" low risk products can be duplicative and result in additional cost and delay in market access.'[12] The issue of the import of EU sunscreen products into Canada was taken up as one of the work plan topics for regulatory cooperation and at its third meeting, in 2021, the RCF reported that following a pilot project 'the exemption/quarantine of EU sunscreen products … have been implemented through regulation and this initiative is completed.'[13] This regulatory cooperation activity has thus resulted in tangible results for EU exporters of sunscreen, facilitating their access to the Canadian market.

While the added value or efficacy of regulatory cooperation is not the focus of this chapter, it is still worth pointing out that the facilitation of the exports of sunscreen

[6] See Regulation 1049/2001 regarding public access to European Parliament, Council and Commission documents [2001] OJ L145/43.

[7] Case T-643/21 *Foodwatch eV v Commission* ECLI:EU:T:2023:519 [56]–[60].

[8] ibid [61]–[67].

[9] Regulation 1223/2009 of the European Parliament and of the Council on cosmetic products [2009] OJ L342/59.

[10] ibid annex VI.

[11] As Art 3 of the Protocol provides, it only 'applies to all medicinal products or drugs to which GMP requirements apply in both Parties.'

[12] Government of Canada (n 3) 3.

[13] Government of Canada, '3rd Meeting of the CETA Regulatory Cooperation Forum – Joint Report' (February 2021) 2.

products may have been particularly low-hanging fruit. In 2017, Canada had already set up a pilot to facilitate the import of sunscreen products from the US pursuant to the US–Canada regulatory cooperation under the umbrella of the Canada–US Regulatory Cooperation Council.[14] That initiative itself resulted from pressure from industry, which links to the question of the agenda setting in regulatory cooperation (see section V). Returning to this chapter's main perspective, and from a Canadian point of view, it should be noted that EU–Canada regulatory cooperation had no direct separation of powers implications. Under the relevant constitutional framework, the Canadian executive was acting entirely within the scope of its powers allowed under the (legislative) Food and Drugs Act,[15] section 30 of which enables the executive to 'make regulations for carrying the purposes and provisions of this Act into effect.' The facilitation of sunscreen products was then concretely realised by adding subsection C.02.019(5) to the Food and Drug Regulations.[16] That subsection creates a new exemption on the testing requirement for those products on the List of Non-prescription Drugs that is already tested in a country or region appearing on the List of Foreign Countries or Regions and Their Regulatory Authorities for the Application of Subsection C.02.019(5). The Canadian Government publishes and updates both lists on its Health Canada website.[17] In a nutshell, the regulatory cooperation activities with the EU (and US) merely led the Canadian regulator to change its approach towards the regulation of certain cosmetic products while staying within the bounds of its regulatory power defined by the Canadian legislator.

Under Canadian constitutional law, that legislative authority (to delegate) is extremely broad,[18] and in and of itself 'international regulatory cooperation' does not diminish or extend the authority conferred on the executive. While there is a scholarly debate criticising the permissible standard of the Canadian Supreme Court and arguing, inter alia based on the separation of powers, for a more restrictive standard,[19] that discussion would appear to be an endogenous one unaffected by the international context in which the Canadian executive exercises its powers. This one example of the actual implementation of a horizontal regulatory cooperation chapter clearly focuses the problem statement that is central to this chapter. If regulatory cooperation does not seem to diminish or expand the executive's reach as defined in domestic law, can it then still raise independent legitimacy challenges under the separation of powers? This question will be explored in section V.

[14] See the Regulatory Impact Analysis Statement accompanying Regulations Amending the Food and Drug Regulations (Finished Product Testing): SOR/2020-73, *Canada Gazette*, Pt II, Vol 154, No 9.

[15] Food and Drugs Act, RSC, 1985, c F-27.

[16] See Food and Drug Regulations, CRC, c 870.

[17] For the lists, see www.canada.ca/en/health-canada/services/drugs-health-products/compliance-enforcement/legislation-regulatory-amendments/incorporation-by-reference/list-foreign-countries.html and www.canada.ca/en/health-canada/services/drugs-health-products/compliance-enforcement/legislation-regulatory-amendments/incorporation-by-reference/list-non-prescription-drugs.html.

[18] The main obstacle to delegation in Canadian constitutional law relates to delegation *between* different levels of government (federal vs provincial) rather than between branches within one level of government. For a recent reconfirmation, see Canadian Supreme Court, Reference re Pan-Canadian Securities Regulation [2018] 3 SCR 189 [72] ff.

[19] See eg AJ Johnson, 'The Case for a Canadian Nondelegation Doctrine' (2019) 52 *UBC Law Review* 817; L Neudorf, 'Reassessing the Constitutional Foundation of Delegated Legislation in Canada' (2018) 41 *Dalhousie Law Journal* 519.

III. Separation of Powers and Trade

This section will further set the scene for the present chapter by briefly commenting on the concept of separation of powers before turning to the conception of separation of powers at EU level and specifically for the conclusion of trade agreements. To provide this discussion with more context, the European Parliament's role in the conclusion of trade agreements will be briefly compared to that of other polities' legislative branches. The discussion will help in better understanding how precisely the three powers interrelate at EU level in the area of the EU's trade policy.

A. Separation of Powers

As the introductory chapter suggests, the concept of separation of powers is essentially contested or essentially contestable,[20] which perhaps explains its enduring appeal. However, the present chapter largely understands the concept as set out by Eckes, Leino-Sandberg and Ghavanini. Separation of powers assumes that public authority may be dissected into three different functions, which it requires to be coupled with an institutional (or organic) and personal separation of powers.[21] Since a pure separation of powers would be unworkable,[22] and because the principle is a means to an end and not the end in itself, such a pure separation should be rejected in favour of a partial one which results in a system characterised by checks and balances.[23] Differently from the introductory chapter, this chapter views the *telos* of those checks and balances as protecting against abuse of power (or arbitrary rule), or controlling those in power. Whether it allows for collective will-formation would be a secondary question. However, this slightly different conceptualisation of the separation of powers does not mean it is not regarded here as a collaborative model. In protecting against arbitrary rule, separation of powers should be balanced against the democratic requirement, meaning the polity's direction is ultimately in the hands of the people. This effectively also constitutes the reason why a pure separation of powers should not be pursued: it might result in the paralysis of a polity, preventing meaningful democratic decision-making.

B. Separation of Powers in EU Trade Policy

Understood in such a way, this means that the idea of checks and balances was only limitedly reflected in the making of international agreements in pre-Lisbon times. At least formally, the EU's trade policy was dominated by two executive bodies: the European

[20] See B Clarke, 'Eccentrically Contested Concepts' (1979) 9 *British Journal of Political Science* 122.

[21] AW Heringa and P Kliver, *Constitutions compared: an introduction to comparative constitutional law* (Intersentia, 2007) 7.

[22] R Pierce, 'Separation of Powers and the Limits of Independence' (1989) 30 *William & Mary Law Review* 365.

[23] E Carolan, *The New Separation of Powers: A Theory of the Modern State* (Oxford University Press, 2009) 18.

Commission negotiated and proposed trade agreements, while the Council approved and concluded them. Pursuant to Article 133(3) TEC *iuncto* Article 300(3) TEC, the European Parliament need not even be consulted before the conclusion of trade agreements. This constellation was a prime example of what has been termed 'executive federalism' which characterised (and characterises) EU governance. Generally, and outside an EU context, Richard Simeon referred to it to describe a federal system 'in which the relations between governments are conducted primarily through the negotiations of political executives.'[24] Acquiring a negative connotation in the EU context, Habermas and Oeter have drawn attention to how sensitive political files are drawn away from the national parliaments and entrusted to the national executives meeting at the EU level (in the (European) Council).[25] The dominant decision-making method in these executive settings is consensus, which undermines the possibilities for democratic contestation and deliberation,[26] or will-formation in accordance with democratic requirements. As Laurens Ankersmit explains more fully in chapter five, the Lisbon Treaty fundamentally altered this equation by upgrading the role of the European Parliament. Focusing again purely on the conclusion of international trade agreements through the common commercial policy (CCP), the European Parliament now has to consent to the conclusion of trade agreements pursuant to Article 218(6)(a)(v) TFEU *iuncto* Article 207(2) TFEU. In addition, Article 218(10) TFEU provides that the 'European Parliament shall be immediately and fully informed at all stages of the procedure' whereas pre-Lisbon this right, pursuant to Article 133(2) TEC, only applied to decisions on the provisional application or suspension of agreements or the establishment of EU positions in treaty bodies. In separation of powers terms, and specifically for the executive–legislative relations, the Lisbon Treaty constituted a watershed moment by introducing the European Parliament as a legitimate actor in the conduct of the EU's CCP through the conclusion of trade agreements.

From a comparative perspective, the formal position of the European Parliament is then relatively strong.[27] Its position also contrasts sharply with that of eg the UK Parliament which supposedly 'took back control' post-Brexit. The main relevant statutory piece here is the 2010 Constitutional Reform and Governance Act, which in its section 20 merely provides that the UK Government can only conclude agreements after having given the Parliament a 21-day period to scrutinise the agreement, allowing Parliament to reject it.[28] Further scrutiny powers of the UK Parliament essentially depend on voluntary commitments made by the Government.[29] The European Parliament occupying a decisive role in the EU's trade policy provides some necessary

[24] R Simeon, 'Criteria for Choice in Federal Systems' (1982–83) 8 *Queen's Law Journal* 152.

[25] J Habermas, *The crisis of the European Union: a response* (Polity, 2012) viii; S Oeter, 'Föderalismus und Demokratie', in A von Bogdandy and J Bast (eds), *Europäisches Verfassungsrecht: Theoretische und dogmatische Grundzüge* (Springer, 2010) 104.

[26] C Franzius, 'Demokratisierung der Europäischen Union' (2013) 48 *Europarecht* 655, 666–67.

[27] See B Kerremans et al, 'Parliamentary scrutiny of trade policies across the western world' (European Parliament, DG for External Policies, 2019) 48–49.

[28] See Constitutional Reform and Governance Act 2010, s 20.

[29] See for instance the Exchange of letters between Lord Grimstone and Baroness Hayter (19 May 2022). On the process of scrutiny of trade agreements in the UK, see House of Commons International Trade Committee, UK trade negotiations: Parliamentary scrutiny of free trade agreements, Fourth Report of Session 2022–23, HC 815, 27 O16-21.

perspective, but leaves the main question central to the present chapter still to be addressed: what is the precise formal role of the European Parliament when it comes to regulatory cooperation in the framework of free trade agreements and how should this role be assessed from a separation of powers perspective?

IV. Regulatory Cooperation: What's in a Name?

The regulatory cooperation chapters in the EU's DCFTAs can be seen as a feature of what Joseph Weiler has identified as the regulatory layer in the geology of international law, which presents different normative, democratic and legitimacy challenges compared to previous layers.[30] Still, the regulatory cooperation chapters look like a rather weak manifestation of the regulatory turn in the development of international law. Contrary to how Weiler describes this turn, and as we will see, the chapters do not create direct or indirect regulatory obligations, no norms are established at international level, no governance incentives are created and neither do the chapters establish an international civil service.[31] Instead, the regulatory cooperation chapters provide for a weak form of international proceduralisation and international insistence on domestic proceduralisation. They are 'weak' in the sense that they typically lack the effective enforcement regime, which according to Weiler, characterises regulatory governance.[32]

Zooming in on the EU, the origin of the regulatory cooperation chapters can at least be retraced to 2006, when the European Commission launched the Global Europe strategy[33] as the external complement to the internal Lisbon strategy which had aimed to turn the EU into the most competitive and dynamic knowledge-based economy in the world.[34] The timing of the former was no coincidence, since by 2006 it had become clear that the negotiations of the Doha round in the framework of the WTO would fail to produce results in the short term. The EU had pinned its hopes on the Doha round to secure further and deeper trade liberalisation, eg by including the four Singapore issues (investment, public procurement, competition and trade facilitation) in a new multilateral agreement. When the prospects of doing so diminished, the EU changed its approach as set out in the Global Europe strategy. To achieve its policy objectives of securing further trade liberalisation after most tariffs had been abolished or reduced, the EU started to aim at 'non-tariff barriers, such as unnecessarily trade-restricting regulations and procedures [which had] become the main obstacles.'[35]

In general terms, the costs flowing from regulatory heterogeneity are three-fold: firms are faced with information costs, since they need to know which are the regulatory requirements in a foreign market; specification costs, since production processes need to be adapted to different requirements; and conformity assessment costs since

[30] J Weiler, 'The Geology of International Law – Governance, Democracy and Legitimacy' (2004) 64 *Zeitschrift für ausländisches öffentliches Recht und Völkerrecht* 552.
[31] ibid 559.
[32] ibid 560.
[33] Commission, 'Global Europe: Competing in the World' COM(2006) 567 final.
[34] See European Parliament, 'Lisbon European Council 23 and 24 March 2000. Presidency Conclusions' (European Parliament, 2000), at www.europarl.europa.eu/summits/lis1_en.htm.
[35] Commission (n 33) 5.

firms need to demonstrate regulatory conformity to different authorities.[36] Addressing these non-tariff barriers requires a 'deep' trade agenda, for which the EU envisaged to follow a bilateral approach without, however, abandoning the multilateral (WTO) route altogether:

> Europe remains committed to the WTO [but] ... Free Trade Agreements (FTAs), if approached with care, can build on WTO and other international rules by going further and faster in promoting openness and integration, by tackling issues which are not ready for multilateral discussion and by preparing the ground for the next level of multilateral liberalisation.[37]

The 'going further and faster' then refers to the WTO+ (building on existing WTO commitments) and WTO-x (breaking new ground) areas of cooperation. The next level of multilateral liberalisation which the European Commission still hoped for in 2006 has remained forthcoming, however, meaning the EU's deep free trade agenda now rests entirely on the bilateral agreements it has been concluding in the past decade, starting with the 2010 FTA with Korea.

One area which the EU has devoted specific attention to in its deep free trade agenda is that of regulatory cooperation, with the CETA constituting the first FTA containing a dedicated chapter to the topic. As Elizabeth Golberg notes, regulatory cooperation is a broad notion that covers a plethora of very different activities.[38] From the least to the most intense form of cooperation, these could be ranked as follows:

Figure 7.1 Intensity of regulatory cooperation

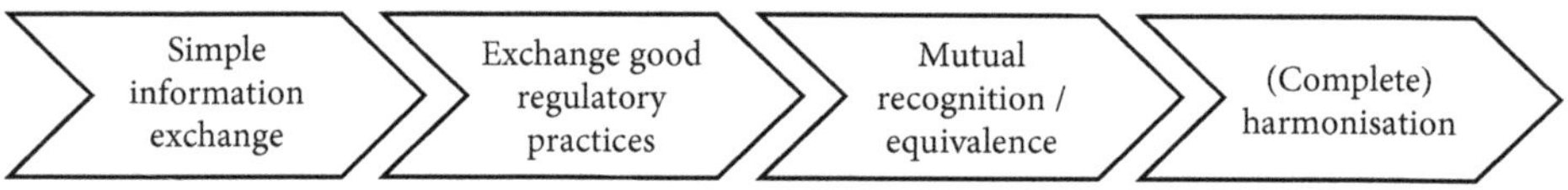

Cooperation between regulators is then needed, because the current (main) source of trade costs and inefficiencies is the difference in regulatory requirements between the trading parties.[39] As Bernard Hoekman notes, the challenge here is that (national) regulators act based on a specific regulatory mandate (typically defined by national legislators) and therefore do not have many incentives as such to consider the implications which regulation has for trade. To create those incentives, formalised rules and institutional mechanisms established in FTAs are then useful to integrate these concerns in regulatory decision-making.[40] By first establishing modest forms of cooperation, the necessary trust is built to (subsequently) move to higher forms of cooperation, such as regulatory convergence through equivalence and mutual recognition[41] of each other's

[36] See OECD, *International Regulatory Cooperation and Trade – Understanding the Trade Costs of Regulatory Divergence and the Remedies* (OECD Publishing, 2017) 16–18.

[37] Commission (n 33) 8.

[38] E Golberg, 'Regulatory Cooperation – a Reality Check' (2019) *M-RCBG Associate Working Paper Series*, April 2019, No 115, 3.

[39] B Hoekman, 'Trade Agreements and International Regulatory Cooperation in a Supply Chain World' (2015) *Robert Schuman Centre for Advanced Studies Research Paper* RSCAS 2015/04, 2.

[40] ibid 3.

[41] On the three models of mutual recognition, see I Van Damme, 'Technical Barriers to Trade in the New Generation of EU Trade Agreements' in M Hahn and G Van der Loo (eds), *Law and Practice of the Common Commercial Policy* (Brill, 2021) 210–13.

regulatory frameworks. The assumption in increased regulatory cooperation seems to be that it (should) focus(ses) on the rather benign task of tackling *unnecessary* differences in standards without aiming as such for domestic regulatory reform.[42] Whether that assumption holds is unclear, however, as regulatory cooperation enshrined in FTAs can also be seen as enshrining or cementing a (deregulatory) Better Regulation agenda (see section V).

A. WTO Insufficiency

Before zooming in on the regulatory cooperation foreseen in the EU's new generation of free trade agreements in the next section, it is useful to dwell on the point of the insufficiency of the WTO framework in tackling 'behind the border' trade impediments. After all, the WTO agreements effectively also target regulatory divergence. Why then are they insufficient? This point is best explained by contrasting the WTO disciplines with the general principles in the law of the EU internal market. In the EU, non-tariff barriers are, in principle, dispensed with easily since the logic of EU internal market law has been one of market access rather than (indirect) discrimination ever since *Cassis de Dijon*.[43] In the EU, the requirement of mutual recognition is coupled with the possibility for legislative harmonisation (now mainly pursuant to Article 114 TFEU) which constitute the most advanced form of regulatory cooperation (see above). In contrast, the WTO disciplines, the main relevant ones related to goods being contained in the Technical Barriers to Trade (TBT) and Sanitary and Phytosanitary (SPS) agreements, are not aimed at market access. Instead, they are limited to requiring regulations not to discriminate based on nationality, not to be more trade-restrictive than necessary (what would roughly equate with proportionality in EU law), to be based on international standards were possible, to have a scientific basis, and to be adopted transparently.[44] National regulations meeting these requirements are WTO-compliant and can therefore be imposed on importers.

Under EU law however, meeting these requirements would not be sufficient. In principle, an importing state would have to accept the commercialisation of goods and services not complying with national regulations as long as these goods and services are lawfully marketed in the exporting state. The TBT and SPS agreements also create institutional machinery allowing for international cooperation between the parties. This cooperation falls apart in three main categories: exchange information and experiences on envisaged regulation; addressing specific trade concerns of parties; and adopting guidance on the implementation of the TBT and SPS agreements.[45] In short, compared

[42] Hoekman (n 39) 3.

[43] See Case 120/78 *Cassis de Dijon* ECLI:EU:C:1979:42. The principle equally applies to the free movement of services which requires 'the abolition of any restriction, even if it applies without distinction to national providers of services and to those of other Member States, when it is liable to prohibit or otherwise impede the activities of a provider of services established in another Member State where he lawfully provides similar services.' See Case C-76/90 *Säger* ECLI:EU:C:1991:331 [12].

[44] See Agreement on Technical Barriers to Trade (TBT) (1995), Art 2; Agreement on the Application of Sanitary and Phytosanitary Measures (SPS) (1995), Arts 2 and 3.

[45] See OECD/WTO, *Facilitating trade through regulatory cooperation – The case of the WTO's TBT/SPS Agreements and Committees* (OECD Publishing, 2019) 50–62.

to the EU internal market, the WTO agreements are less ambitious both as regards negative and positive integration: there is no market access requirement but rather a non-discrimination requirement and the harmonisation of regulatory requirements is practically unfeasible.

In addition to limiting itself to 'weaker' forms of regulatory cooperation, the WTO disciplines are also sector-specific and not generalised. Ching-Fu Lin and Han-Wei Liu offer a further perspective by emphasising how WTO disciplines focus (mainly) on regulatory outputs (eg are they non-discriminatory, based on scientific evidence, etc) whereas the WTO+ and WTO-x provisions in DCFTAs further shift the focus to regulatory inputs[46] (or perhaps more correctly throughputs): *how* are regulatory measures conceived and adopted domestically?

B. The Regulatory Cooperation Chapters in the EU's FTAs

This section will focus specifically on some of those FTAs signed or concluded by the EU that contain chapters devoted to regulatory cooperation. CETA was the first such FTA and since then, other FTAs have followed, such as the FTA with Japan and the Trade and Cooperation Agreement (TCA) with the UK. The choice to focus on those FTAs with dedicated horizontal provisions on regulatory cooperation is informed by the alarming critique levelled against those provisions (see section V), but it should be pointed out that *all* FTAs concluded by the EU contain at least some (sector-specific) provisions on regulatory cooperation[47] and that in those FTAs dealt with below, the horizontal provisions were included *in addition* to the typical sector specific provisions on regulatory cooperation.

As to why horizontal provisions on regulatory cooperation are included, the official narrative from the European Commission's side is that making domestic regulation of two (or more) parties more compatible, allows companies to avoid a series of 'unnecessary' costs and gives the parties concerned more leverage on regulatory issues at the global level. These benefits seem to come at no cost since none of the parties relinquishes its right to regulate the way it sees fit and the level of protection offered to citizens and consumers is therefore not forcefully lowered.[48] This stands in contrast with the assessment of a part of civil society, which dubbed the regulatory cooperation envisaged in the EU's deep FTAs as 'a threat to democracy'.[49] In a nutshell, that critique argues that regulatory cooperation allows the EU's counterparty to influence the decision-making process even before the EU's own democratically legitimised actors (Parliament and Council) are involved, because it gives industry privileged access to the decision-making process and because (at the EU side) it keeps regulatory cooperation in the

[46] C-F Lin and H-W Liu, 'Regulatory Rationalisation Clauses in FTAs: A Complete Survey of The US, EU and China' (2018) 19 *Melbourne Journal of International Law* 150.

[47] ibid 173–74.

[48] See Commission, 'TTIP and Regulation: An Overview' [2015] 4–5.

[49] See Corporate Europe Observatory, 'TTIP: "Regulatory Cooperation" a threat to democracy – Statement from 45 organisations on the new EU proposal on Regulatory Cooperation' (Corporate Europe, 21 March 2016), at corporateeurope.org/en/international-trade/2016/03/ttip-regulatory-cooperation-threat-democracy.

hands of the European Commission. While this critique is framed in democratic terms, the implications for the separation of powers seems clear: regulatory cooperation would upset the checks and balances by concentrating powers in the hand of (part of) the EU executive (the Commission) without there being sufficient means for the legislative to counter this concentration of powers, frustrating collective will-formation. This critique is of course a world apart from the narrative that sees regulatory cooperation as nothing more than a tidying up exercise, preventing unnecessary trade impediments from arising. To evaluate these strongly divergent assessments of (international) regulatory cooperation, the starting point is the actual text of the FTAs.

The horizontal provisions dedicated to regulatory cooperation in the FTAs with Canada, Japan and the UK can be found in Chapters 21 (CETA), 18 (EPA) and Title 10 of Part II (TCA).[50] Before looking into the different agreements more in detail, it is important to point out that the TCA and EPA are for a great part identical, although the TCA is less extensive on regulatory cooperation. While this might be surprising, it may have to be understood as part of a clear objective of the UK Government to distance itself as much as possible from the EU's regulatory orbit (taking back control), resulting in a 'minimalistic' Title on regulatory cooperation.[51]

While the CETA chapter differs from the other two (see below), all three agreements emphasise that the regulatory cooperation envisaged is voluntarily and does not limit the parties' freedom to regulate as they see fit.[52] For the CETA this is superfluously emphasised again in the Joint Interpretative Instrument.[53] The risk that the capacity of the Union to operate autonomously within its unique constitutional framework is undermined, which the Court flagged as impermissible in *Opinion 1/17*,[54] therefore never poses itself. All three agreements also establish an institutional arrangement to facilitate and promote regulatory cooperation. This, however, is one of the issues on which the TCA is much more succinct than the other two agreements,[55] since it limits itself to setting up the Trade Specialised Committee on Regulatory Cooperation and by describing its three main functions (of promoting good regulatory practices and regulatory cooperation, exchanging of views and encouraging regulatory cooperation in international fora).[56] The Regulatory Cooperation Forum under the CETA and

[50] See Comprehensive Economic and Trade Agreement (CETA) (n 2); Agreement between the European Union and Japan for an Economic Partnership (EPA) [2018] OJ L330/3; Trade and Cooperation Agreement between the European Union and the European Atomic Energy Community, of the one part, and the United Kingdom of Great Britain and Northern Ireland, of the other part (TCA) [2021] OJ L149/10.

[51] Purely quantitatively, it may be noted that the Chapter in the EPA comprises 19 Articles where the relevant Title of the TCA only contains 14. In terms of word count, Chapter 18 of the EPA is 38% more elaborate than the equivalent Title in the TCA.

[52] See CETA (n 2) Art 21.2(4) and (6); EPA (n 50) Arts 18.1(2) and 18.12(6); TCA (n 50) Arts 340(3) and 351(1).

[53] See Joint Interpretative Instrument on the Comprehensive Economic and Trade Agreement (CETA) between Canada and the European Union and its Member States (2017) OJ L11/3, paras 2–3.

[54] See *Opinion 1/17* ECLI:EU:C:2019:341 [150].

[55] The ambitions might have also been modest from the start judging from the two meetings which the Trade Specialized Committee on Regulatory Cooperation had so far. The minutes of the meetings show that the EU and UK so far have limited themselves to explaining to each other how they adopt legislation and how they perceive 'better regulation'. As an exchange of views between the EU and a former EU Member State, that seems rather futile.

[56] See TCA (n 50), Art 352.

the Committee on Regulatory Cooperation of the EPA also fulfil those functions, but those agreements are much more detailed and specific on what concrete activities these committees will pursue. Importantly for all three, however, is that they have not been granted the power, unlike some other committees established by these FTAs, to amend the agreements or to adopt further binding decisions. The critique levelled against the new generation of FTAs by authors like Wolfgang Weiß and René Repasi (see below section V) therefore does not apply to the general regulatory cooperation chapters (although it may apply to the sectoral regulatory cooperation chapters; see above).

Turning to the further differences between these three agreements, it must be recalled that the TCA seems to be a (redacted) copy-paste of the EPA, making both stand apart from the CETA. The latter contains an extensive Article setting out the objectives of cooperation between the EU and Canada,[57] and further details the concrete activities which the EU and Canada will pursue to realise 'regulatory cooperation'.[58] In contrast, the focus of the EPA and TCA is on the internal procedures applicable in the parties internal decision-making. Both agreements essentially boil down to requiring the parties to pursue a 'Better Regulation' agenda internally. Thus, parties must clarify how their regulatory processes work (and how interested parties can influence them);[59] they must provide early information on 'major' regulatory measures which they plan;[60] parties commit to holding public consultations on such measures whereby anyone is offered the possibility to comment through electronic means, those comments are taken into account and the regulator adopts a report on how it took into account the comments;[61] parties commit to conducting impact assessments for major regulatory measures which should inter alia explicitly consider the option not to regulate;[62] and they commit to perform retrospective evaluations of regulation that has been already adopted.[63] These provisions with an internal focus make up the bulk of Chapter 18 of the EPA and Title 10 of Part II of the TCA. Their provisions on the actual international regulatory *cooperation* are limited to providing that the parties can invite each other to set up a concrete regulatory cooperation activity, but do not spell out as detailed as CETA what these concrete activities are and does not further specify the objectives of cooperation (beyond the general objectives).[64] Finally, the EPA and TCA exclude the regulatory cooperation chapter from the scope of the dispute settlement mechanism.[65]

The brief presentation of the horizontal regulatory chapters/titles in CETA, the EPA and the TCA seems to indicate that there are two features of these provisions with potential implication for the separation of powers. First, even when these provisions have not conferred binding powers on the bodies which they establish, the question in how far an international regulatory cooperation activity can empty the internal decision-making of its meaning can legitimately be raised. Second, at a more structural

[57] See CETA (n 2), Art 21.3.
[58] ibid Art 21.4.
[59] EPA, Art 18.5; TCA, Art 344 (n 50).
[60] EPA, Art 18.6; TCA, Art 345.
[61] EPA, Art 18.7; TCA, Art 346.
[62] EPA, Art 18.8; TCA, Art 347.
[63] EPA, Art 18.9; TCA, Art 348.
[64] See EPA, Arts 18.12 and 18.13; TCA, Art 351.
[65] EPA, Art 19.19; TCA, Art 354.

level, where deep FTAs prescribe a better regulation agenda, the dynamics of the latter in the internal sphere are fundamentally altered: 'Better regulation' does not remain an autonomous choice pursued by the EU but it becomes an obligation under international law assumed by the EU. The deregulatory (see section V) Better Regulation agenda is then being cemented. While substantively 'regulatory cooperation' remains voluntary and no regulatory outcomes are prescribed, the procedural prescriptions of regulatory cooperation are far from non-committal. Whether this could also be problematic from a separation of powers perspective then first of all depends on an assessment of the (original) 'endogeneous' Better Regulation paradigm. These aspects will be assessed in the subsequent sections.

V. Regulatory Cooperation in DCFTAs – A Critique and Counter-critique

From a separation of powers perspective, the DCFTAs have mainly been criticised because they create institutional arrangements to which the power to adopt supplementing or amending rules is conferred. Repasi noted that the legitimacy conferred on an international agreement through its internal ratification is undermined increasingly, the more that agreement is limited to setting a framework which the bodies established by the agreement are empowered to elaborate.[66] Even more critical, Weiß notes that since DCFTAs like CETA target 'behind the border' issues (rather than 'at the border' issues like tariffs), the traditional institutional set-up used for FTAs is insufficient. Since the newest generation of FTAs allow treaty bodies to deal with 'behind the border' issues, they allow the executive to impinge on internal policies which are to be regulated (internally) by the legislative branch. To uphold the EU institutional balance and the democratic principle, Weiß concludes that the European Parliament should be involved much more when DCFTAs like CETA are implemented.[67]

As section IV.B has shown, however, the provisions on 'regulatory cooperation' in the DCFTAs which the EU has so far negotiated do not delegate further decision-making powers to the treaty bodies set up under the chapters devoted to 'regulatory cooperation'. The more acute threat to an undermining of the separation of powers between the legislative and executive by these deep FTAs, of which Repasi and Weiß warn, does not seem to pose itself. Any implications which regulatory cooperation chapters might have would therefore need to be more subtle. This also hightens the threshold for any argument that would claim that these chapters affect or undermine the separation of powers.

While the critique of regulatory cooperation chapters by civil society organisations is typically rather alarmist,[68] serious academics have also questioned the legitimacy of

[66] R Repasi, 'Dynamisation of international trade cooperation – Powers and limits of Joint Committees in CETA' (2017) *Question of International Law* 87.

[67] W Weiß, 'Umsetzung von CETA in der EU: Herausforderungen für Demokratie und institutionelles Gleichgewicht' (2020) 55 *Europarecht* 407.

[68] Corporate Europe for instance noted that 'standards will, to a large extent, be set behind closed doors by a limited group of actors: big business and trade experts [and] unelected officials are ready to further sacrifice our democratic rules, and reduce our social and environmental protections, such as healthy working

pursuing regulatory cooperation within the framework of DCFTAs. However, one typical caveat here has been the preliminary nature of any analysis since the regulatory cooperation foreseen by the DCFTAs had not been put into effect yet (or the DCFTAs themselves were still being negotiated).

Marija Bartl noted that the institutional mechanisms set up under regulatory cooperation chapters are dominated by trade experts who share a specific cognitive framing of the world as a market.[69] The regulatory dialogue which these chapters set up may, according to Bartl, undermine the EU's precautionary approach in regulation because it is part of a trade facilitation agreement, it reinforces the deregulatory internal 'Better Regulation' agenda, and it gives privileged access to certain well-resourced stakeholders.[70] Bartl surmised that this would impact the institutional balance both within the Commission (to the benefit of the General Secretariat and DG Trade) and at the expense of the legislator, who will be more constrained, since even the non-binding work under regulatory cooperation 'changes the rules of the regulatory game by crucially altering, who must justify their policies to whom, when is a justification owed and, most importantly, what exactly is to be justified.'[71]

Joana Mendes for her part notes that it follows from CJEU case law that even non-binding acts adopted by international bodies established by agreements to which the EU is party, are part of EU law.[72] Although they are non-binding, they would have to be taken into account when interpreting the (binding) provisions of the agreement that they aim to implement.[73] According to Mendes, they will therefore have the potential of influencing EU law for a number of reasons. First, (binding) secondary legislation may contain dynamic references to those international decisions.[74] Second, the Court has not shied away from relying on such international 'expert' opinions/decisions to confirm the validity of EU law,[75] although Mendes notes that this does not imply that the CJEU could also find secondary EU legislation invalid in light of such non-binding decisions.[76] The reason for this is that a defining feature of the EU's DCFTAs is that they explicitly rule out the direct effect of the agreement,[77] and that

conditions and product safety, on the altar of trade.' See Corporate Europe, '"Regulatory cooperation": big business' wishes come true in TTIP and CETA' (Corporate Europe, February 2017), at corporateeurope.org/sites/default/files/attachments/ceo_regulatory_cooperation_06.1.pdf.

[69] M Bartl, 'Regulatory Convergence through the Backdoor: TTIP's Regulatory Cooperation and the Future of Precaution in Europe' (2017) 18 *German Law Journal* 987.

[70] ibid 985.

[71] ibid 991.

[72] J Mendes, 'The External Administrative Layer of EU Law-Making: International Decisions in EU Law and the Case of CETA' (2017) 2 *European Papers* 489, 495–98. This follows from Case C-188/91 *Deutsche Shell AG* ECLI:EU:C:1993:24.

[73] *Deutsche Shell AG* (ibid) [18]. This is of course no different from internal soft law which also needs to be taken into account by national judges. See Case C-322/88 *Grimaldi* ECLI:EU:C:1989:646.

[74] Mendes (n 72) 498. As exemplified in the *OIV* case. See Case C-399/12 *Germany v Council* ECLI:EU:C:2014:2258. However, there are no dynamic references to regulatory cooperation measures in EU secondary legislation to the present author's knowledge.

[75] Mendes (n 72) 499–500. Mendes points out this was the case in Case C-547/14 *Philip Morris Brands SARL* ECLI:EU:C:2016:325 and Case C-190/16 *Werner Fries* ECLI:EU:C:2017:513.

[76] Mendes (n 72) 503–07.

[77] See A Semertzi, 'The preclusion of direct effect in the recently concluded EU free trade agreements' (2014) 51 *Common Market Law Review* 1125.

under established case law of the Court, direct effect of a provision of an international agreement is a prerequisite for invalidating EU (secondary) legislation in light of such a provision.[78] Mendes' main critique then seems to point to the significant requirements it imposes on the domestic regulatory processes of the parties while at the same time showing a 'procedural disconnect', since the procedural framework for engaging in regulatory cooperation *within* the framework of the DCFTA is typically undeveloped.[79]

Finally, Charell van Rooy has argued that regulatory cooperation faces a four-fold legitimacy deficit. This would be so because of the transformation of the role of the executive in the setting of regulatory standards; the opening the regulatory process to the influence of foreign governments; the focus on facilitating trade, providing a privileged position to business influence; and the lack of parliamentary oversight and weak participatory rights in the EU's DCFTAs.[80]

While these critiques are shrouded in constitutional terms, they generally seem develop a *de lege ferenda* critique. That is to say, they aim to show that the current constitutional framework governing international cooperation and executive rule-making lacks legitimacy, going beyond (mere) legality. This is especially clear in the critiques of Mendes and Van Rooy who argue that the throughput legitimacy of regulatory cooperation should be improved through proceduralisation and participation.

Whether and how the legitimacy (exogenously understood) of regulatory decision-making can be improved is of course a different conversation from the question of whether and how regulatory cooperation affects or even undermines the separation of powers. Assessing the regulatory cooperation from an internal perspective, and given its features (see section IV.B) and the example of a specific case of regulatory cooperation under the CETA (see section II), the counterargument to the critique against regulatory cooperation appears straightforward. What would need to be shown is how regulatory cooperation chapters (de facto if not *de iure*) *alter* the legal framework for regulatory policy-making, altering the rules on collective will-formation or creating areas where control over governments actors is impossible, even though the chapters explicitly leave intact the regulatory autonomy of the parties and are voluntary. Neither in terms of substance (what can be done) or procedure (how is regulation adopted) does regulatory cooperation under DCFTAs allow the parties to dispense with internal constitutionally mandated procedures for adopting regulation. Given that the domestic legal framework is *de iure* left intact, the argument would have to be made how that legal framework is being eluded by regulatory cooperation. This is something also Anne Meuwese points out when observing that 'constitutional law should aim to regulate the risk that voluntary convergence de facto turns into circumvention of the properly competent legislative or regulatory bodies.'[81]

[78] See Joined Cases C-404/12 P & C-405/12 P *Council & Commission v. Stichting Natuur en Milieu* ECLI:EU:C:2015:5 [46].

[79] C van Rooy, 'Expertise and Legitimacy in Models of Regulatory Cooperation' (PhD Thesis, Cardiff University, 2022) 508–13.

[80] ibid 143.

[81] A Meuwese, 'Constitutional Aspects of Regulatory Coherence in TTIP: An EU Perspective' (2015) 78 *Law and Contemporary Problems* 153, 172.

Yet the existence of such a risk cannot be assumed and instead should be demonstrated. Absent an argument to that effect, it is unclear how legitimacy challenges could arise.[82]

The above discussion suggests that constitutional scholars struggle in 'capturing' the problematic structural implications of regulatory cooperation which they intuitively feel are 'out there'. The next section will therefore look into the potential of the internal tension model, recently proposed by Cohn, in helping us determine whether regulatory cooperation indeed has pertinent implications for the separation of powers. As noted above, and as also pointed to by Bartl, regulatory cooperation may thereby be conceptualised as the external dimension of the EU's internal Better Regulation agenda, requiring the latter to be integrated in the argument.

A. The Internal Tension Model – A Lens to Identify Constitutional Mutations?

In her internal tension model of the executive, Cohn provides a novel account of the contemporary executive branch in which she puts forward that contemporary executives are characterised by 'ingrained tensions' between the two opposing *Idealtypes* of executive power. These are, on the one hand, the idea (still relatively dominant in official discourse in parliamentary systems) that the executive is subservient to the legislative branch and, on the other hand, the idea that the executive effectively is an unchecked branch dominating the polity. Her model instead transcends these conflicting *Idealtypes* by proposing that 'both subservience and dominance of the executive prosper in reality just as much as they are backed by the basic ideals of modern Western democracy.'[83]

How both can simultaneously characterise a polity is explained by recourse to the notion of 'fuzzy law'. As noted in the introduction, such law is understood as a legal framework where an authorizing rule may present a façade of legality that derives from its binding formal status, while its content or application offer broad options for action (and possible abuse) which conceals a reality of a-legality.'[84] According to Cohn, the fuzzy law which creates a potential for the executive branch to aggrandise can be generated at three levels: constitutional (eg unclear constitutional provisions or judge-made constitutional doctrines); legislative (eg delegation of legislative powers and wide discretion left to the executive); or by the executive itself.[85] The usefulness of the internal tension model then lies in its potential to move beyond a binary assessment of practices as either lawful or unlawful, but instead reflect on how certain arrangements or

[82] Van Rooy aims to address this counter-critique by arguing that even if regulatory cooperation is voluntary, it involves the exercise of power, even if only a power of persuasion, thus requiring democratic control being exercised over it. On the argument that regulatory cooperation feeds into the agenda setting but does not alter the domestic decision-making procedures, she puts forward that 'the regulatory discourse [is] being affected at the start of the regulatory process in cooperation with a foreign government without parliamentary oversight and sufficiently balanced participatory rights.' See van Rooy (n 79) 157–58. However, these arguments (again) seem to belong to the different conversation of the legitimacy of regulatory cooperation.

[83] Cohn (n 1) 55.

[84] ibid 59.

[85] ibid 69.

practices are examples of fuzzy law or may contribute to the fuzziness in law. Its notion of alegality is interesting for the present chapter since it allows for the identification of subtle yet structural alterations to the separation of powers without implying there is any violation of the separation of powers.

The internal tension model thus offers potential to break through the above-noted apparent deadlock: regulatory cooperation chapters are viewed sceptically by commentators, but the argument remains stuck at identifying *potential* risks (that have so far not materialised) and at *de lege ferenda* pleas for improvements to the decision-making process, rather than showing a structural shift in the separation of powers. As will be shown below, the internal tension model helps to overcome the main counter-argument that regulatory cooperation does not affect the separation of powers since it is voluntary and non-binding, leaving internal (binding) decision-making intact. While the internal tension model accepts that law is necessarily indeterminate (to a degree), Cohn aims to show that *excessive* open-endedness (ie fuzziness) undermines proper (or good) governance by frustrating participatory democracy and by denying law to fulfil its function.[86] Fuzzy law then allows the executive to maintain its political dominance over law without, as such, moving into the zone of illegality.[87]

Before trying to transpose Cohn's internal tension model to the EU, one important caveat must be mentioned. The original model is based on experiences in two Anglo-Saxon national polities, meaning a transposition should be pursued with caution. In light of the subject of this chapter, two adaptations to the original internal tension model seem necessary in any event. First, in Cohn's original model, fuzzy law is repudiated for its negative implications to both the value of participatory democracy and the value of the rule of law. For the purposes of this chapter and given the subject of this edited collection, the main focus will lie only on the latter value.[88] While participatory democracy is not alien to the EU's constitutional set up,[89] the Union is founded on representative democracy.[90] As a result, where participatory democracy is affected, this will not go to the core of the EU's constitutional foundation (without arguing that it would be constitutionally irrelevant). In addition, arguing against the fuzziness of regulatory cooperation chapters because of its impact on participatory democracy would risk falling into the same pitfalls as the critiques discussed in section V, ie this chapter would develop a *de lege feranda* argument. Given this volume's focus on the separation of powers it is instead more appropriate to focus on the fuzziness of law that fails to fulfil law's function (under the rule of law) of ensuring that government is ruled by the law and subject to it,[91] ie the separation of powers' controlling function.

A second adaptation may be a further refinement of the internal tension model itself. As noted above, Cohn surmised that fuzziness can originate from three sources (constitutional text, legislative action and executive action). The case of the EU's DCFTAs'

[86] ibid 257–65.

[87] ibid 286.

[88] Focusing on only one of these values does not seem problematic from the perspective of the original model, since even in the original model both values constituted parallel (but not interdependent) normative foundations for critiquing fuzzy law. See Cohn (n 1) 256–57.

[89] Unlike in the Constitutional Treaty however (see Art I-47), the TEU and TFEU do not explicitly refer to the principle of participatory democracy.

[90] See Art 10(3) TEU.

[91] See J Raz, *The authority of law: Essays on law and morality* (Oxford University Press, 1979) 212.

chapters on regulatory cooperation may also indicate a fourth source of fuzziness that can be integrated in the internal tension model. This, in so far as these chapters are not simply cases of legislative delegation and neither are they the product of autonomous executive action. Instead, they suggest that fuzziness in a polity can also originate from international law to which that polity binds itself. The discussion by Ankersmit in chapter five makes clear how the negotiation and conclusion of EU trade agreements may be a process dominated by executive actors (Commission and Council) but since Lisbon, it always requires consent by the legislator (Parliament). Similar to constitutional text, (trade) agreements concluded by the EU rank above secondary legislation.[92] Conceptually, it then becomes possible for an international agreement to create a façade of legality for unregulated executive power.

If we take as a hypothesis that the regulatory cooperation chapters in EU DCFTAs may indeed constitute instances of fuzzy law that find their origin in a fourth source (ie, that of international law), what are the 'fuzzy' dynamics at play here? Part of the dynamic arguably aligns with the one that plays in internal regulation. That regulation *de iure* typically depends on a legislative mandate which in theory should structure and govern the exercise of regulatory power (by the executive) but in practice may not.[93] A regulatory mandate may be lopsided, empowering the executive without substantively restraining it; allow (arbitrary) selective enforcement by the executive; or simply remain unenforced.[94] Adding the source of the fuzziness to the equation (ie, the fact that the regulatory mandate is laid down in an international agreement) and the way the chapters are worded, shows how the fuzziness would be reinforced. Thus, the fact that regulatory cooperation is voluntary and non-binding, a typical counterargument for dispelling any legitimacy challenges (see section IV), becomes, from the perspective of the internal tension model, an aggravating factor. Indeed, regulatory cooperation leaves the executives unfettered discretion in terms of substance, outcome and priorities. Not enforcing it at all is equally legally valid as relying on it to pursue a full regulatory overhaul of multiple policies. This alegality undermines the function of law. Put differently and in separation of powers terms, if separation of powers both 'restrains and constitutes power',[95] the 'law' of regulatory cooperation is anathema to it, since it does not constitute power and neither does it restrain it.

Further, the source containing the fuzzy norm also contributes to the fuzziness. As observed by Bartl (section IV), regulatory cooperation chapters are imbued with the very same logic underpinning the internal Better Regulation agenda. That internal agenda is foremost an executive-driven agenda, promoted internationally by the Organisation for Economic Cooperation and Development (OECD)[96] and picked up, internally in the EU, by the European Commission. Even within the Commission it exercises centripetal forces, by reinforcing the role played by the Secretariat-General.[97]

[92] See Case C-344/04 *Air Transport Association* ECLI:EU:C:2006:10 [35].

[93] Cohn (n 1) 67.

[94] ibid 68.

[95] C Möllers, *The Three Branches: A Comparative Model of Separation of Powers* (Oxford University Press, 2013) 10.

[96] See S Garben, 'A taste of its own medicine: Assessing the impact of the EU Better Regulation Agenda' (2020) 26 *European Law Journal* 83.

[97] M Dawson, 'Better Regulation and the Future of EU Regulatory Law and Politics' (2016) 53 *Common Market Law Review* 1209, 1222.

The Commission later managed to convince the EU legislator (Parliament and Council) to accept and coopt it, as set out in the inter-institutional agreements (IIA) on Better Law-making.[98] As Mark Dawson noted, by (internally) pushing its Better Regulation agenda, the Commission has managed to have the legislative actors (within the EU) adopts its regulatory paradigm, thus fully domesticating its regulatory approach.[99] When the Parliament and Council, through the IIA, then accept that 'better regulation' should be pursued throughout the policy cycle and not just at the policy initiation phase, they accept a regulatory logic[100] (originally promoted by the Commission) that effectively reduces the scope for political choices made by more democratically legitimate actors,[101] even if the IIA prescribes that impact assessments are 'not a substitute for political decisions within the democratic decision-making process'.[102] By subsequently including this agenda in the DCFTAs which the EU concludes, Better Regulation is additionally enshrined in the EU's international commitments, entrenching it against possible modification or repeal internally. While leaving the formal rules governing collective will-formation intact, it can be argued that the entrenched deregulatory logic does effectively alter how and even which collective will-formation comes about.

To summarise, regulatory cooperation chapters arguably would have negative implications from a separation of powers perspective. This is so firstly *because* (and not despite) those chapters constituting non-binding and voluntary commitments and thereby constitute 'fuzzy' law which sets up a regime of alegality in which the Commission (as an executive actor) can act almost unbound. Secondly, regulatory cooperation chapters leverage the executive-driven better regulation agenda on the international plane, discursively limiting the scope left for political contestation by the legislative branch and reinforcing the framing powers of the executive. If this diagnosis is correct, it carries in it important implications for any reform agenda. Indeed, while calls for greater proceduralisation to ensure better (stakeholder) participation (see above) may be laudable from the perspective of throughput legitimacy, they would arguably not address the core problem identified here and would not address the concerns related to the separation of powers.

Further, while a reinforced participatory democracy might counterbalance the executive-driven deregulatory logic of Better Regulation, no amount of 'participation' will alter the fuzzy nature of the regulation cooperation chapters and it is this fuzziness that means that the legal rules in question cannot fulfil law's function. This is not to say that looking into the actual participatory democratic merits of the mechanisms

[98] Interinstitutional Agreement between the European Parliament, the Council of the European Union and the European Commission on Better Law-Making [2016] OJ L123/1.

[99] Dawson (n 97) 1214.

[100] Note that the original proposal for an IIA by the Commission was more far-reaching in terms of the Commission's interference in the legislative procedure. The Commission's proposal was criticised on this ground by Alemanno. See A Alemanno, 'How Much Better is Better Regulation?' (2015) 6 *European Journal of Risk Regulation* 344, 351–55. While the most intrusive interferences did not make it to the final IIA, the overall logic remained unchanged.

[101] Noting this also motivates the Commission in pursuing its Better Regulation agenda, see F Lafarge, 'The impact of the Better Regulation policy on EU delegated and implementing acts rule-making' in E Tauschinsky and W Weiß (eds), *The Legislative Choice Between Delegated and Implementing Acts in EU Law* (Edward Elgar, 2018) 79.

[102] Interinstitutional Agreement on Better Law-Making (n 98) para 12. As Dawson notes, this creates a tension with a non-technocratic (or political) understanding of Better Regulation. See Dawson (n 97) 1216.

under regulatory cooperation is pointless. From a separation of powers perspective, this would still be useful to determine whether the fuzziness (which is in any event problematic in itself) is effectively being used by the executive to aggrandise its domain. Where research on participatory democracy will be interested both in the actors that have access to the system and how their input results in regulatory output, research on the separation of powers will be interested mainly in the latter question. Identifying patterns linking input to output may indicate the degree of discretion which the executive has and to which extent it is used, indicating in how far the executive's regulatory mandate is effectively (un)regulated by law.

VI. Conclusion

This chapter addresses the question of whether and how the horizontal regulatory cooperation chapters, which are now being included in the FTAs concluded by the EU, could have an impact on the separation of powers. From the latter perspective, the EU post-Lisbon system is already relatively robust, since any trade agreement must be approved by the European Parliament and cannot simply be concluded by (autonomous) executive action. Differently from other chapters in the EU's DCFTAs, regulatory cooperation chapters do not establish treaty bodies with binding decision-making powers and instead they simply allow for voluntary cooperation without affecting the regulatory autonomy of the parties. In that light, those chapters at first sight seem unproblematic in separation of powers terms. One of the first concrete implementations of regulatory cooperation under the relevant chapter of the CETA, the modification to the Canadian regulatory framework governing sunscreen products, further reinforced this impression.

On a first reading of the regulatory cooperation chapters this chapter could not readily subscribe to the critique levelled against these chapters at least from a traditional perspective of separation of powers. At the same time, this chapter has not simply dismissed the possibility of the separation of powers being affected by horizontal regulatory cooperation chapters. Instead, it has proposed to change the frame of reference. To this end, the chapter borrowed the conceptual framework of the internal tension model developed by Cohn. Under this model, the focus is on so-called fuzzy, ie excessively indeterminate, law which creates a realm of alegality allowing the executive branch to (potentially) aggrandise. Looking at regulatory cooperation chapters from this perspective, they indeed constitute fuzzy law, combining the typical fuzziness of regulation with a new source of fuzziness, ie fuzziness generated under international law. Specifically for the EU, then, regulatory cooperation chapters essentially also leverage an internal executive-driven regulatory agenda to the international plane, cementing it and insulating it from possible (future) domestic contestation.

Importantly, the finding that the regulatory cooperation chapters constitute fuzzy law in itself raises problems under the separation of powers, regardless of the actual implementation of these chapters. This is the case because the fuzziness results in an alegal realm where executive power is largely unregulated, ie where power is neither restrained nor constituted.

PART III

The Relationship between the Judiciary and the Executive

8

Law as the Executive Likes it: How the European Court of Justice Accommodates the Executive in Migration's External Dimension

MARTIN WESTLUND

I. Introduction

The separation of powers within EU migration law reaches a critical point in the external dimension. EU executive actors have developed cooperative relationships with third countries to strengthen border controls and limit migration. They pursue such political aims by externalising migration control to third countries, often using informal arrangements.[1] This makes it possible for EU Member State governments to escape legal constraints.[2] The process of externalisation appears to weaken the judicial branch and strengthen the executive.[3] Davide Gnes and Milka Sormunen (chapter four) have demonstrated that informal arrangements sideline key institutions such as the European Parliament and the European Court of Justice (ECJ) while empowering the executive branch of the EU.[4] Other researchers share this view in their respective analyses of cases on the external dimension of immigration law.[5] These power shifts and lack of accountability are all the more concerning as human rights are at stake.[6]

[1] C Boswell, 'The "external dimension" of EU immigration and asylum policy' (2003) 79 *International affairs* 620.

[2] M Fink and N Idriz, 'Effective Judicial Protection in the External Dimension of the EU's Migration and Asylum Policies?' in E Kassoti and N Idriz (eds), *The Informalisation of the EU's External Action in the Field of Migration and Asylum* (TMC Asser Press and Springer, 2022) 118.

[3] AP García, 'The Distribution of Powers Between EU Institutions for Conducting External Affairs through Non-Binding Instruments' (2016) 1 *European Papers* 116.

[4] See Gnes and Sormunen, ch 4 in this volume.

[5] See eg N Idriz and M Fink, 'Effective Judicial Protection in the External Dimension of the EU's Migration and Asylum Policies?' (2021) *TMC Asser Institute for International & European Law Asser Research Paper Series*; T Spijkerboer, 'Bifurcation of people, bifurcation of law: Externalization of migration policy before the EU Court of Justice,' (2018) 31 *Journal of refugee studies* 2.

[6] While international law scholars often refer to 'human rights', the term 'fundamental rights' may be preferred by scholars of constitutional law. I use these terms interchangeably, mirroring the different expressions of the EU Treaties, the ECHR, and the Charter.

The political sensitivity of migration law and policy leads to a strong emphasis on national sovereignty and power. It weakens the weight of EU institutions and hardens governmental positions.[7] This can make the ECJ more willing to uphold the powers of the executive actors involved in developing this field of law, that is, Member State governments, national authorities, and EU agencies and institutions. Nevertheless, executive aims of controlling and managing migration flows come into tension with human rights, such as the right to seek asylum and the principle of *non-refoulement*. As these human rights are enshrined in international law and EU primary law, they in principle constitute powerful tools for judicial scrutiny of executive action, and their prominent position in the field ought to strengthen the judiciary's role. The ECJ could also apply constitutional principles and values such as the principles of conferral, sincere cooperation and the rule of law to temper executive action.

This chapter aims to show how the ECJ shapes the separation of powers in the external dimension of migration law and policy. Focus is on how the Court of Justice affects the executive branch, at both the EU and national levels. This is relevant since political interests of control tend to override migrants' rights.[8] Thus, the questions are what control powers apply to this area of law and how the Court of Justice uses these to ensure compliance with constitutional principles and rights. The argument I make in this chapter is that the Court is accommodating the concerns, interests and interpretations made by the executive. It is loyal to decisions made in secondary law and recognises the discretion of political actors to determine the migration law. Rather than channelling conflict and exercising substantive control, the Court is reluctant to oppose the Executive. The result is a consensual form of decision-making in migration's external dimension that lacks effective control mechanisms.

This argument is structured as follows. Section II explains the judicial powers and limitations in migration's external dimension. I discuss the role of the Court of Justice within the separation of powers framework of the EU and demonstrate that while the Court can review and strike down legal acts and measures, it is being challenged by trends of externalisation and informality. Section III presents case analyses on central issues of externalisation that the Court has ruled on in recent years. These judgments signal a reluctance of the Court to pronounce itself on political choices, which weakens the level of scrutiny, even in cases involving essential issues on human rights. Section IV delves deeper into possible explanations for judicial restraint and argues that the Court has a cautious understanding of its own role.

II. Judicial Powers and Limitations in Migration's External Dimension

In this section, I explain how externalisation challenges the powers of the Court of Justice. Within the separation of powers framework, I see it as important that the judiciary matches the ambitions of the executive. No power should be trusted without being

[7] D Thym, *European Migration Law* (Oxford University Press, 2023) 47.
[8] Spijkerboer (n 5).

checked, as John Adams wrote.[9] The Court is vested with a wide range of judicial review powers, which means that in theory it holds the potential to uphold a separation of powers in the EU and guard against abuse of power, competence creeps and human rights violations. The externalisation of migration law and informal arrangements may, however, make it possible for executive actors to evade such judicial control.

EU policies on migration have both an internal and external dimension. While the internal dimension can be understood as comprising the internal legal instruments on migration, with directives and regulations on, for instance, visa policies and the asylum procedure, the external concerns the EU's relations with third countries.[10] It is an intricate mix of both external instruments of cooperation with third countries and internal instruments given an externalisation purpose.[11] The external dimension is an important part of the EU migration policy. Increasing migration flows have led to a stronger emphasis on border security. To this end, there has been a shift in migration policies. Migration control has shifted from mainly reactive control focusing on individuals to migration management, which is more proactive and oriented on populations and stemming migration flows.[12]

New modes of governance characterise the external dimension. Against the background of the perceived limits and constraints of EU legal instruments, governance of migration has shifted towards measures which look and behave like law, but do not entail the same level of institutional scrutiny or the possibility of legal challenges.[13] There is a growing trend in using soft law and informal procedures to enhance the discretionary powers of Member States, especially in the externalisation of border and immigration control.[14] This is illustrated by the number of agreements, strategies, reports and programmes that are issued. Recent examples include the EU–Turkey Statement on the cooperation between EU states and Turkey. Other common measures are mobility partnerships, which provide an overarching framework for cooperation with third countries, readmission agreements and readmission clauses in other EU agreements, such as development projects, as well as the use of Frontex to manage external border controls. Case analyses in section III demonstrate how the Court has reacted to these measures.

Measures like these are motivated by different factors. Scholarship on the matter tends to emphasise effective problem-solving. Third-party cooperation is viewed as faster, cheaper and requiring fewer resource commitments than creating genuine EU capacities within the ordinary legislative process.[15] Informality and externalisation are

[9] T Jefferson and J J Looney, *The papers of Thomas Jefferson, retirement series, volume 9: 1 September 1815 to 30 April 1816* (Princeton University Press, 2018).

[10] B Parusel, 'The external dimension of EU migration policy – new proposals, possibilities, and risks', *Sieps* (February 2023), at www.sieps.se/globalassets/publikationer/2023/perpsective_the_external_dime-nsion_of_eu_migration_policy.pdf.

[11] PG Andrade, 'The External Dimension of the EU Immigration and Asylum Policies Before the Court of Justice' (2022) 7 *European Papers* 111.

[12] Spijkerboer (n 5).

[13] PJ Cardwell, 'New Modes of Governance in the External Dimension of EU Migration Policy' (2013) 51 *International migration* 62.

[14] F Terpan and S Saurugger, 'Soft and hard law in times of crisis: budget monitoring, migration and cybersecurity' (2021) 44 *West European Politics* 23.

[15] P Genschel and M Jachtenfuchs, 'From Market Integration to Core State Powers: The Eurozone Crisis, the Refugee Crisis and Integration Theory' (2018) 56 *Journal of Common Market Studies* 190.

also seen as strategies to escape legal constraints. This is visible in the EU's cooperation with third countries to stem migration flows. In the case of *Hirsi-Jamaa*, the European Court of Human Rights (ECtHR) imposed legal responsibility on Italy for asylum-seekers intercepted in the Mediterranean.[16] As Hirsi Jamaa and the other asylum-seekers had been taken onboard an Italian military vessel and had been under continuous and exclusive Italian control, their asylum applications fell under Italian jurisdiction, thus making the European Convention on Human Rights (ECHR) applicable.[17] To be able to continue with its push-back policy in line with this ruling, EU Member States worked to move the jurisdiction over asylum-seekers to Libya. Member States started providing funding and support for Libyan coast guards to intercept asylum-seekers at sea, which transferred jurisdiction from EU states to Libya.[18] Seen this way, the function of externalisation is to increase discretionary powers that are limited by legal standards.

While this makes Member State policies more effective, it has negative effects on democratic governance. Informal procedures and soft law create an intergovernmental form of decision-making, which empowers the Member States. There are several concerns with this form of decision-making. One concern is about transparency. As demonstrated by Davide Gnes and Milka Sormunen, informalisation diminishes transparency.[19] Informal agreements are usually not publicly available and as the European Parliament is not involved, there is less information and debate on ongoing negotiations. A related concern is the reduced possibility of accountability. The executive benefits from increasing discretionary powers that the judiciary may lack jurisdiction over. The lack of binding legal mechanisms means that the initiatives cannot be legally challenged by the migrants who are affected by them.[20]

The concept of separation of powers is relevant in addressing these concerns. Madison's expression that '*ambition must be made to counteract ambition*'[21] is informative in the context of migration governance. This is also acknowledged in the introduction of this book, namely that conflicts 'can have a distinct value in democratic will-formation'. For instance, Panu Minkkinen speaks of 'agonistic separation' that allows actors to oppose and counteract political aims through rights.[22] It creates the 'potentiality' of judicial intervention.[23] While EU Member States adopt creative ways to circumvent the legislature and the judiciary to reach their policy objectives, the ECJ can therefore provide a much-needed counterbalance not only through its actual intervention but also through the restraining force that goes beyond the actual intervention to potentially turn antagonism into agonism.[24]

[16] See *Hirsi Jamaa and Others v Italy*, App no 27765/09 (ECtHR, 23 February 2012).

[17] ibid [112]–[114].

[18] P Müller and P Slominski, 'Breaking the legal link but not the law? The externalization of EU migration control through orchestration in the Central Mediterranean,' (2021) 28 *Journal of European public policy* 802.

[19] See Gnes and Sormunen, ch 4 in this volume.

[20] Cardwell (n 13) 63.

[21] J Madison, 'Essay 51' in R Beeman (ed), *The Federalist Papers* (Penguin Group, 1788).

[22] P Minkkinen, 'Enemies of the People? The Judiciary and Claude Lefort's 'Savage Democracy'' in L Brännström M Arvidsson and P Minkkinen (eds), *Constituent Power – Law, Popular Rule and Politics* (Edinburgh University Press, 2020) 38.

[23] ibid 41. See also C Eckes, 'How Radical is the Understanding of Democracy in Justifying Contract in Europe?' (2022) 51 *Netherlands Journal of Legal Philosophy* 13.

[24] Eckes (n 23) 13.

The ECJ is confronted with the following dilemma in migration's external dimension. Externalisation and informality can be seen as developments motivated by a desire of Member States to retain decision-making powers. The political salience of migration makes restrictive national executives protect their national sovereignty over immigration to maximise political capital, by blocking supranational harmonisation.[25] This leads, in turn, to pressure on the Court of Justice to remain loyal to the choices made by the Member States.

At the same time, the ECJ may be asked to have human rights prevail over the decisions taken by the majority. Bearing in mind its mission of ensuring that EU law complies with the Treaties,[26] the ECJ needs to ensure that the choices made by the legislature or the executive are not in violation of fundamental values and principles. The EU institutions and the Member States are required to comply with human rights in all spheres governed by EU law, according to Articles 2 and 6 TEU and Article 51 Charter of Fundamental Rights. In the migration context, Article 78 TFEU states that the migration policy shall be developed in line with the Refugee Convention and ensure compliance with the right to seek asylum and the principle of *non-refoulement*. Thus, human rights that are covered by the EU Treaties empower the Court to counterbalance majority decision-making. Altogether this puts the Court in a difficult position, as it needs to choose between staying loyal to the choices made by the Member States or confronting them based on human rights.

Essentially, informality and externalisation represent a departure from the ordinary decision-making process and substantive laws on migration to increase the leeway of the Member State governments. Complex and constraining formal decision-making structures have been bypassed, so that Member States can focus on getting things done informally.[27] It leads to less transparency and weakens judicial and legislative mechanisms for accountability. Yet, while the executive actors seek to avoid the constraints of law, the ECJ can provide a counterbalance by emphasising such limits. It can provide 'a corrective to some of the energies which animate normal politics, such as those of political interest and power' by exercising substantive judicial review and in so doing foster democratic will-formation.[28] Thus, the question that drives the case analyses in the next subsection is how the ECJ responds to externalisation and informalisation. How does the Court exercise control and constrain the executive branch?

III. Cases on the External and Informal Aspects of Migration

This section examines how the ECJ exercises control in the external dimension of migration. Notably, only a very limited number of cases within this field have reached the ECJ

[25] T Givens and A Luedtke, 'The Politics of European Union Immigration Policy: Institutions, Salience, and Harmonization' (2004) 32 *Policy studies journal* 148.

[26] Art 19 TEU.

[27] M Vink and C Engelmann, 'Informal European Asylum Governance in an International Context' in T Christiansen and C Neuhold (eds), *International Handbook on Informal Governance* (Edward Elgar, 2012) 544.

[28] A Kavanagh, 'Participation and Judicial Review: A Reply to Jeremy Waldron,' (2003) 22 *Law and Philosophy* 451.

in recent years. Based on a quantitative study of migration's external dimension, Paula García Andrade has found that no ruling was delivered by the ECJ between the years 2018 and 2020.[29] Before that, the Court ruled on the scope of implementing powers concerning the surveillance of external sea borders,[30] the delimitation between readmission and development policies in EU external action,[31] the use of international soft law tools for migration cooperation purposes,[32] and the issuance of humanitarian visas by Member States.[33] These are the central cases that are often discussed by researchers working on the external dimension of migration law and are therefore selected for my analysis.[34] Researchers may also include association agreements,[35] or a wider range of cases on internal instruments,[36] but these are excluded from this study since I focus on the core practice of externalisation, namely when Member States seek to move jurisdiction and migration control to third countries and external territories.[37]

A. Fundamental Rights Limits to Delegated Powers: Frontex and External Sea Borders

The case *Parliament v Council* illustrates the relevance and use of fundamental rights as limits to executive decision-making.[38] This ruling is important since a central part of the external dimension of migration is to strengthen border controls. At the heart of this endeavour lies the sea border controls operated by Frontex. In 2010, the Council of the EU adopted a decision laying down rules and guidelines for Frontex maritime operations. Wide implementing powers may ensure effective law-making but leave certain decisions without the deliberation and transparency the legislature provides. The European Parliament therefore sought the annulment of the Council Decision because it exceeded the scope of implementing powers in Article 12(5) of the Schengen Borders Code (SBC). The rule is that delegated acts can only deal with non-essential elements, which the contested decision went beyond as it introduced rules on 'interception', 'search and rescue' and 'disembarkation' of persons intercepted at sea.

Initially, the Court stated that the adoption of rules essential to the subject matter is reserved to the legislature of the EU (at [64]). It further held that provisions requiring political choices falling within the responsibilities of the EU legislature cannot

[29] Andrade (n 11) 111.

[30] Case C-355/10 *European Parliament v Council* ECLI:EU:C:2012:516.

[31] Case C-377/12 *Commission v Council (PCA with the Philippines)* ECLI:EU:C:2014:1903.

[32] Case T-192/16 *NF v European Council* ECLI:EU:T:2017:128; Case T-193/16 *NG v European Council* ECLI:EU:T:2017:129; and Case T-257/16 *NM v European Council* ECLI:EU:T:2017:130.

[33] Case C-638/16 PPU *X and X v Belgium* ECLI:EU:C:2017:173.

[34] See eg Fink and Idriz (n 5); E Brouwer, *Challenges to EU Legality in the Field of Asylum and Migration Law* (Oxford University Press, 2021).

[35] Andrade (n 11) 110.

[36] See T Strik, 'Migration deals and responsibility sharing: can the two go together?' in JS Vara and T Strik and S Carrera (eds), *Constitutionalising the External Dimensions of EU Migration Policies in Times of Crisis: Legality, Rule of Law and Fundamental Rights Reconsidered* (Edward Elgar Publishing, 2019) 12.

[37] On 6 September 2023, the General Court delivered a judgment on the liability of Frontex for return operations. This case mostly concerned liability rules and is therefore not directly linked to externalisation. See Case T-600/21 *WS v European Border and Coast Guard Agency* ECLI:EU:T:2023:492.

[38] *European Parliament v Council of the European Union* (n 30).

be delegated (at [65]). The Court then observed that the categorisation of 'essential elements' is not for the assessment of the EU legislature alone but must be based on objective factors amenable to judicial review (at [67]). This is an important statement of the ECJ as it asserts its authority to review legislative and executive competences.

What constitutes essential elements of legislation, which is only within the legislature's powers, is open for interpretation and the ECJ determined in this case the boundaries between legislative and executive powers. In previous case law, the Court had remained rather vague on the concept, only defining essential elements as 'provisions which are intended to give concrete shape to the fundamental guidelines of Community policy'.[39] Now, in the current case, the Court made a key contribution to external migration by developing the meaning of essential elements.

The ruling demonstrates how fundamental rights can provide a distinct perspective for reviewing and limiting executive powers. The ECJ found that paragraph 2.4 of Part 1 to the Annex of the Council Decision and paragraph 1.1 of Part II regulated enforcement measures and obligations of the units participating in sea external border operations which the Schengen Borders Code did not contain (at [74]–[75]). The Court ruled that, because the conferral of such powers on border guards amends essential elements of external sea border surveillance, the decisions must be regarded as requiring political choices (at [76]). The Court stressed that the provisions in the Council decision, including stopping persons apprehended, seizing vessels, and conducting persons apprehended to a specific location, mean that the 'fundamental rights of the persons concerned may be interfered with to such an extent that the involvement of the European Union legislature is required' (at [77]). The mere fact that the title of Part II to the Annex of the contested decision contains the word 'guidelines' and that it states that they are 'non-binding' does not affect their classification as essential rules (at [80]). The Court argued that since these 'guidelines' form part of the operational plan for Frontex which conditions need to be complied with, the rules are intended to produce binding legal effects (at [82]). Hence, the Court decided to annul Council Decision 2010/252 supplementing the Schengen Borders Code concerning the surveillance of sea external borders.

The ruling has been praised for introducing a '*de minimis* rule, where the degree or severity of the human rights interference is decisive for considering a measure to constitute an essential element'.[40] Thus, a key finding of this case is that the Court uses fundamental rights to limit the exercise of executive powers and empower the legislature. The ECJ asserts its authority to decide on what constitutes essential elements and does so by reviewing the effects that the Council Decision has on fundamental rights. This approach limits the leeway for adopting non-legislative acts in the area of border security. It ensures that EU values and principles play a decisive role in evaluating specific provisions as essential elements, thereby protecting the authority of the European Parliament, and placing limitations on executive powers under the system of delegated powers.

[39] Case C-240/90 *Federal Republic of Germany v Commission of the European Communities* ECLI:EU:C:1992:408 [37].

[40] M den Heijer and E Tauschinsky, 'Where Human Rights Meet Administrative Law: Essential Elements and Limits to Delegation: European Court of Justice, Grand Chamber C-355/10: European Parliament v. Council of the European Union' (2013) 9 *European constitutional law review* 525.

B. Accommodating the Executive in Cases of Readmission Agreements

While a human rights-based approach has thus been visible on occasion in the external dimension, the overarching picture is that there is an underused potential of rights and principles in the ECJ's reasoning. The ECJ is in more recent cases accommodating the executive in its interpretation of EU migration law. This is demonstrated in two cases on the EU's relations with third countries in migration law. Cases on development cooperation and readmission agreements display a willingness of the ECJ to grant discretion to executive actors by giving weight to their views on the law. In contrast to the case of *Parliament v Council*, these cases demonstrate a weakening of judicial control, even in rights-sensitive issues.

First, case law shows a favourable attitude from the ECJ towards the use of development cooperation instruments for the readmission of asylum-seekers which extends the competence of the Commission, a central executive institution in EU external relations. In the *Partnership and Cooperation Agreement with the Philippines* case,[41] the Court of Justice was asked by the Commission to annul a Council decision on development cooperation for being based on the wrong legal bases. The Commission argued that the PCA should have been signed on the legal basis of Articles 207 and 209 TFEU concerning development, and not include Article 79(3) TFEU for readmission.

The principle of conferral holds that the EU can act only within the limits of the competences conferred upon it by the Member States in the Treaties to attain the objectives set out therein.[42] The Court could have either followed the argument of the Commission that development cooperation is broad and multifaceted and covers readmission, which would make EU development cooperation policy more effective and broaden the Commission's competence (at [18]), or it could have followed the Council's argument that a specific commitment to readmission requires the addition of a corresponding legal basis, which ties the executive to the restrains set up in the Treaty for adopting agreements with third countries (at [25]).

Recalling its prior ruling in *Portugal v Council*,[43] the Court stated that 'even if a measure contributes to the economic and social development of developing countries, it does not fall within development cooperation policy if it has as its main purpose the implementation of another policy' (at [38]). For this assessment, the Court recognised that EU development policy has evolved and is linked to security issues and migration. Referring to the European Consensus, a policy document, the ECJ observed that the aim of eradicating poverty has several aspects which broaden the scope of development activities (at [42]). For instance, the European Consensus saw migration as a positive factor for development and development was viewed as an effective response to forced migration (at [47]). The Court accepted that the readmission clause contained 'specific obligations' as the parties agreed to readmit their nationals and to conclude a readmission agreement as soon as possible. Nonetheless, the Court considered that

[41] *Commission v Council* (*PCA with the Philippines*) (n 31).
[42] Art 5(2) TEU.
[43] See Case C-268/94 *Portuguese Republic v Council of the European Union* ECLI:EU:1996:461.

the provision did not prescribe, as a fully fledged readmission agreement would do, the specific manner in which the commitments were to be implemented (at [58]), and readmission could thus be adopted within the legal basis for development cooperation (at [59]).

The Court's reasoning frames the Commission's development cooperation competence broadly. The extensive interpretation of the legal basis of development allows for expanding executive competences. Illustrative of this reading is how the ECJ pays heed to secondary law. The benchmark for determining the scope of Article 209 TFEU is derived from the European Consensus, a joint declaration by the Council, the Parliament and the Commission. As the interpretation of Treaty law is informed by policy developments led by the executive, the Court creates a broad construction of development cooperation that accommodates the views of the executive. This interpretation will benefit the Commission, which may wish to take a holistic approach to cooperation.[44] It strengthens the ability of the Commission to pursue multifaceted types of cooperation.

The practical effects of the Court's extensive interpretation of development might still be limited as the readmission clause did not contain any clear obligations on readmission. The reason why it was covered by the agreement was to incentivise the Philippines to enter into a readmission agreement at a later stage. This is, however, part of a general pattern of making readmission agreements, even those not fully fledged, by informal venues or adding them to other agreements. The conclusion of a readmission agreement is perhaps not an integral part of a development project, but due to the Court's interpretation, instrumental considerations based on the need for leverage in negotiations on a readmission agreement are accepted as grounds for the choice of legal basis. The support by the Court to executive aims of migration control creates a larger room for manoeuvre for executive actors, in this case, the Commission, that coopt readmission agreements to development cooperations. This may be contrary to the principle of conferral, which provides for an independent legal basis for readmission.

A second example of an accommodating reading of EU migration law is visible in the case of the EU–Turkey Statement.[45] In this case, the General Court had the opportunity to rule on an agreement with a third party, which is one of the core examples of informal and external law-making in recent years. The Statement outlined the cooperation with Turkey to manage the inflow of irregular migrants and refugees to Greece. It was adopted without a formal decision to authorise the opening of negotiations with Turkey according to Article 218(2) TFEU, and the text had not been submitted to the European Parliament for approval (Article 294(2) and 218(6) TFEU. For some the Statement simply reflects a political arrangement with no binding force.[46] Yet, others have considered it as an international agreement which requires judicial scrutiny.[47] The

[44] R Holdgaard and M Broberg, 'Demarcating the Union's Development Cooperation Policy after Lisbon: Commission v. Council (Philippines PCFA)" (2015) 51 *Common Market Law Review* 564.

[45] See *NF v European Council* (n 32); *NG v European Council* (n 32); and *NM v European Council* (n 32).

[46] See S Peers, 'The draft EU/Turkey deal on migration and refugees: is it legal?' EU Law Analysis (2016), at eulawanalysis.blogspot.com/2016/03/the-draft-euturkey-deal-on-migration.html; AG Fernández, 'The EU–Turkey Agreement: A Controversial Attempt at Patching up a Major Problem,' (2016) 1 *European Papers* 3.

[47] See eg M Den Heijer and T Spijkerboer, ' Is the EU–Turkey refugee and migration deal a treaty?' EU Law Analysis (2016), at eulawanalysis.blogspot.com/2016/04/is-eu-turkeyrefugee-and-migration-deal.html.

General Court's view in this regard is decisive for the scope of review of the Statement's compatibility with EU law.

The General Court first stated that whether or not an act is a European act is governed by European and not domestic law. The characterisation of the act in the act itself is not decisive (at [45]). Yet, when deciding on the authorship of the Statement, which determines whether it is an act of the EU or not, the General Court remained close to the views of the Council. The General Court found the terms 'Members of the European Council' and 'EU' in the Statement ambivalent, which implied that the Statement was concluded outside the procedures according to Article 218 TFEU (at [56]). These references could however also imply that the Statement did involve the EU. Yet, the General Court gave weight to the views of the EU institutions by referring to the Council's argument that the terms 'European Council' and 'EU' in the Statement amounted to simplified wording intended for the general public in the context of a press release and could not be taken literally (at [57]–[61]). When interpreting related documents, notes and press releases to the meetings with Turkey, the General Court treated them as carefully worded establishing that the Member States only met in their capacity as Heads of State or Government and not as the European Council (at [66]). The General Court thus concluded that the Statement was not an act of the EU. It therefore lacked jurisdiction and dismissed the case.

In addition to this accommodating interpretation of the views of the Council, the General Court did not consider the legal effects of the Statement. An act is reviewable by the General Court if it is 'intended to produce legal effects vis-á-vis third parties'.[48] This is the case even though an act might be worded as non-binding.[49] The Statement carries legal effect on the EU asylum system as there is an agreement on responsibility for asylum applications. This is important to consider in relation to the *ERTA* doctrine,[50] which is codified in Article 3(2) TFEU. It holds that once the EU implements a common policy in a certain field, the EU Member States no longer have the right 'to undertake obligations with third countries which affect those rules or alter their scope'.[51] Had the General Court attached more weight to the content of the Statement and its legal effects, it could have ruled that the Statement constitutes an EU international agreement that is within its jurisdiction. This would have allowed a much-needed review of the compatibility of the Statement with EU constitutional law and to ensure democratic will-formation in the adoption of external agreements.

Thus, I argue that the accommodating approach and lack of consideration of the legal effects of the arrangement show a reluctance of the ECJ to overrule Member States' actions, giving them considerable leeway in making EU law. Without engaging more with the substantive issues at hand, the Court is unable to provide effective judicial control of acts of externalisation. Judicial control can foster democratic will-formation

[48] Art 263(1) TFEU.

[49] *European Parliament v Council* (n 30) [80]–[82].

[50] See Case C-22/70 *Commission v Council* (ERTA) ECLI:EU:C:1971:32 [3]–[5].

[51] Joined cases C-181/91 and C-248/91 *European Parliament v. Council and Commission* ECLI:EU:C:1993:271 [17].

by guarding the prerogatives and procedural rules governing the area. As a result of the ECJ's reasoning, possible violations of the principle of *non-refoulement* are overlooked and EU rules on treaty-making are not applied. However, on the substantive issue of the compatibility of the Statement with EU constitutional law and human rights, the Court faced two difficult alternatives. Declaring incompatibility with human rights could lead to an 'explosive political situation' for the Court. Narrowly interpreting refugee law would be harmful to refugee protection and undermine the Court's authority from a human rights perspective.[52] Yet, by avoiding a ruling on substantive grounds, the Court decreases the legitimacy of externalisation instruments, as legitimacy also comes with judicial supervision. This weakens the EU separation of powers as the executive benefits from almost unconstrained powers when creating informal arrangements like the EU–Turkey Statement.

C. Doctrinal Reasoning and the Absence of Human Rights Considerations

The case analyses have so far demonstrated that while cases with an external dimension centrally concern human rights, such perspectives are not always visible in the judicial review of executive measures. This section will further show the lack of human rights considerations when the ECJ interprets secondary law provisions. This is demonstrated by the Court's textual interpretation of the scope of the Visa Code in the case of *X and X* concerning the possibility of humanitarian visas for asylum-seekers.[53] This case is relevant in the context of externalisation since the EU Visa Policy is increasingly used as a component of migration control. Visa facilitation and visa waiver agreements are important instruments of cooperation with third countries.[54] Internal instruments are thereby part of the process of externalisation. The Court's interpretation of such legal acts informs the scope of powers and obligations of executive actors implementing the rules.

In the case of *X and X*, the Court ruled that the option of applying for humanitarian visas for asylum-seekers at embassies does not fall within the scope of the Visa Code.[55] As the applicants intended to stay in Belgium when their short-term visa expired, the Court viewed their application as an application for a long-term visa (at [43]). The Court held that the EU has not adopted any measures on the issuance by Member States of long-term visas and residence permits to third-country nationals on humanitarian grounds (at [44]). It also held that establishing a right to humanitarian visas for asylum-seekers would be contrary to the aims of the Visa Code and the general structure of EU asylum law (at [41]). It was therefore not competent to rule on the substantive issue and dismissed the case. This formal and doctrinal reasoning limits the scope of judicial review and benefits national executive authorities.

[52] Spijkerboer (n 5) 224.
[53] *X and X v Belgium* (n 33).
[54] Andrade (n 11) 116.
[55] *X and X v Belgium* (n 33).

Advocate General Mengozzi proposed a different ruling that would have established positive obligations under the Visa Code for national authorities handling visa applications. The Advocate General argued that the applicants had applied for a short-term visa as they would only stay in Belgium for three months based on the visa and after that would remain based on their status as asylum-seekers.[56] By viewing their application as an application for a short-stay visa, the EU Visa Code and the Charter of Fundamental Rights were applicable and thereby made the ECJ competent to rule on the substantive issues. Had the ECJ followed this line of reasoning it could have explored the role of human rights in this context and possibly established positive obligations to issue humanitarian visas for asylum-seekers. For instance, the ECJ reaffirmed a few months after *X and X* that the EU Charter is applicable when Member States apply the provisions of the Visa Code.[57] Fundamental rights are highly relevant in the context of visa applications; yet they did not have any effect in this case as the Court focused on the scope of secondary law.

The Court found that the possibility of applying for a humanitarian visa to apply for asylum has not been created in EU law. Proposals to do so have been discussed but only remain at the stage of discussion.[58] The Court could construct this possibility by interpreting EU law along the lines proposed by the Advocate General. This would have empowered the Court and established positive obligations for Member States that limit their room for manoeuvre. By refusing to create such obligations, the Court recognised the discretion of the legislature to decide on the scope of permissible actions within the confines of EU law, including human rights. This limited review empowers executive actors whose competences flow from the interpretation of secondary law.

The level of judicial scrutiny is determined by the Court's willingness to engage in the development of substantive law. While the Court could have established the possibility of humanitarian visas for asylum-seekers, it remained close to the wording of the law and left a possible reformation of the asylum system to the legislature. This view is shared by the ECtHR, which has also ruled on the issue of humanitarian visas for asylum-seekers.[59] There is an element of choice in the use of human rights law. The case of *X and X* demonstrates that the Court is sometimes unwilling to explore such perspectives as it seeks to avoid expanding its powers into making policy choices. This line of reasoning is confirmed in the recent case of Frontex's liability in return operations.[60] While this case concerned rules on liability for damages of EU institutions, commentators argued that the ECJ should have pronounced itself on the legality of return operations and the mandate of Frontex by considering human rights issues.[61] A key takeaway is thus that formal interpretations of law that entail limited assessments of legal acts ensure greater discretionary powers of the executive.

[56] ibid Opinion of AG Mengozzi [53].

[57] Case C-403/16 *Soufiane El Hassani v Minister Spraw Zagranicznych* ECLI:EU:C:2017:960.

[58] Spijkerboer (n 5) 12.

[59] See *MN and Others v Belgium*, App no 3599/18, 5 March 2020 [119].

[60] See *WS v European Border and Coast Guard Agency* (n 37).

[61] M Fink and J Rijpma, 'Responsibility in Joint Returns after WS and Others v Frontex: Letting the Active By-Stander Off the Hook,' EU Law Analysis (2023), at eulawanalysis.-blogspot.com/2023/09/responsibility-in-joint-returns-after.html.

IV. The Court's Limited Role in Tempering the Executive

This section aims to delve deeper into the ECJ's approach and normatively assess its impact on the separation of powers. The examined cases demonstrate that while the legislation leaves plenty of room for manoeuvre for the Court to elaborate on human rights and constitutional principles, it appears unwilling to review executive actors in their development of migration law on such a basis. This leads to greater political autonomy of the EU Member States and almost unchecked executive powers. The objective of this section is to further weave in the principle of separation of powers into the Court's reluctance to meddle with controversial policies within migration by analysing how the ECJ's choices reflect a cautious view of its role relative to the political actors.

In recent times, the Court of Justice has paid special attention to the protection and enforcement of the rule of law, as a value enshrined in Article 2 TEU. It has said that EU values, such as the rule of law, 'define the very identity of the European Union as a legal order' and that 'compliance with those values cannot be reduced to an obligation which a candidate state must meet in order to accede to the European Union and which it may disregard after accession'.[62] It is, moreover, held that the rule of law requires that all public powers act within the constraints set out by law, which cover the values of democracy and the respect for human rights.[63] The rule of law can be distinguished into a 'formal' conception stressing 'the formal or instrumental aspects' of the theory and 'substantive' conceptions incorporating elements of political morality and human rights.[64] As the EU system of judicial review includes both procedural and substantive elements, the Court may in theory exercise a review based on a 'substantive' version of the rule of law.[65]

Threats posed to the rights of asylum -seekers are one of the many faces of the rule of law backsliding in the EU.[66] Human rights obligations have been deflected, with the institutionalising containment and externalisation in the EU's relations with third countries.[67] Within the separation of powers framework, it is the task of the Court to ensure that rights and rule of law guarantees are upheld. It seems, however, reluctant to exercise this power. While the ECJ has demonstrated that human rights can be used to constrain executive powers, its dominant approach seems to be judicial restraint. This is manifested in two ways.

First, by adopting the views of the executive, it is limiting its own powers while empowering the executive. This is illustrated when the Court accepted a deviation of EU development policy from its objectives in primary law by considering the policy developments and declared a lack of jurisdiction to rule on the EU–Turkey Statement by giving weight to the views of the Member States. Second, by focusing on the contents

[62] C-156/21 *Hungary v European Parliament, Council of the European Union* ECLI:EU:C:2022:97 [126].

[63] ibid [3].

[64] P Craig, 'Formal and Substantive Conceptions of the Rule of Law: An Analytical Framework' (1997) 3 *Public Law* 467.

[65] T Konstadinides, *The Rule of Law in the European Union: The Internal Dimension* (Hart Publishing, 2017) 58.

[66] E Tsourdi, 'Asylum in the EU: One of the Many Faces of Rule of Law Backsliding?' (2021) 17 *European Constitutional Law Review* 472.

[67] ibid 473.

of secondary law without considering relevant constitutional rights and principles, the ECJ limits the substantive review. The wish not to interfere in sensitive policy options, by providing political discretion to EU institutions and Member States and endorsing a security-oriented approach to migration, are central features of the ECJ case law on external aspects of migration policies.[68] These forms of judicial restraint show that the ECJ is not always using its full potential for conceptualisation and scrutiny of migration law.

There are numerous concerns associated with this limited approach. With its judgment on the EU–Turkey Statement, the General Court displayed less rigorous scrutiny at the cost of general principles of EU law. By declaring the annulment actions inadmissible, the General Court prevented itself from ruling on the compatibility of the Statement with EU asylum and human rights law, verifying its compliance with the rule of law, and upholding the separation of powers in the EU's external action. The lenient approach effectively amounts to a withdrawal from the judicial control function and enables an expansion of executive power. When the General Court established in *NF v Council* that statements outlining a system for sending asylum-seekers back to third countries can be outside of its jurisdiction, it confirmed the view that 'a transformation from hard to soft international arrangements runs the risk that key EU principles and constitutional guarantees are by-passed'.[69] The General Court acknowledged the executive discretion coming from externalisation and informality, rather than placing the necessary limitations on them. In the long term, this individual ruling can have disproportionate consequences. By framing the Statement as a non-EU act, it allows a situation in which EU Member States can create agreements with third countries with less transparency, circumventing the European Parliament, and without formal venues of accountability.

The effects of such legal reasoning are also visible in the case of development projects. Expansive readings of development are made to align with the policy developments on readmission and development. This extends executive competences and poses risks to human rights protections. This concern becomes apparent when considering similar EU practices of coopting development to migration control. It is relevant, for instance, in the EU Border Assistance Mission in Libya, a mission aimed at supporting Libya's security capacity while also managing and limiting migration flows to the EU.[70] As the ECJ has emphasised the aim of an act over its content when applying its traditional 'centre of gravity' test, a mission like the one in Libya would likely be accepted on an AFSJ legal basis, which expands the executive powers in a rights-sensitive field of law.[71] Thus, there are several concerns associated with these wide and almost unchecked executive powers in EU migration law.

A related question is whether this approach is aligned to, or differs from, the role played by the ECJ within the internal dimension of migration or in EU external relations law more generally. Paula García Andrade has argued that the Court has exercised more

[68] Andrade (n 11) 126.

[69] RA Wessel, 'Normative transformations in EU external relations: the phenomenon of "soft" international agreements' (2021) 44 *West European Politics* 85.

[70] Established by Council Decision 2013/233/CFSP of 22 May 2013 on the European Union Integrated Border Management Assistance Mission in Libya (EUBAM Libya), OJ L 138/15.

[71] PG Andrade, 'EU external competences in the field of migration: How to act externally when thinking internally,' (2018) 55 *Common market law review* 182.

self-restraint in the external dimension of migration compared to its earlier contribution to external relations law.[72] In cases on environmental, economic and trade issues, the ECJ has framed the EU's external actions through the definition of competencies and the delimitation of the contours of institutional balance.[73] This framing power is weaker in the external dimension of migration law. In this field of law, the ECJ displays a non-interventionist approach to the policy choices made by EU institutions as it gives weight to the views of EU political institutions.

In migration law, judicial self-restraint can be observed in the external dimension but could even be a defining feature of the whole legal field. In the internal dimension of migration, that is, the internal legal instruments, the ECJ has restricted executive and legislative actors by interpreting central concepts such as 'detention',[74] 'risk to public policy',[75] 'Member State responsible'[76] and 'safe third country'.[77,78] Rulings on return proceedings and the principle of safe third countries are particularly important examples of when the Court has read migration law in light of human rights.[79] Such reasoning extends the powers of the ECJ to structure and constrain executive power. Nonetheless, despite some examples of expansiveness in the case law, the Court's reasoning is mostly formal, focusing on the most immediate questions before it rather than exploring bigger issues of human rights.[80]

A central question is why the ECJ does not seek to assert its power by engaging more with substantive issues. There is room for more rights-based considerations by the ECJ. It is not for lack of opportunity that it remains silent on human rights or constitutional principles. The open-endedness of migration law opens the door for potentially agonistic separation, but in the current political climate, this remains difficult. The effectiveness of EU migration law relies on the ability to achieve consensus among the EU governments. This is illustrated by the current deadlock on the reformation of the EU asylum system.[81] To go further in terms of control, the Court would need to explore

[72] Andrade (n 11) 126.

[73] See eg Case C-399/12 *Federal Republic of Germany v Council of the European Union (OIV)* ECLI:EU:C:2014:2258; Case C-425/13 *European Commission v Council of the European Union ('Australian Greenhouse Gas Emissions')* ECLI:EU:C:2015:483; Case C-263/14, *European Parliament v Council of the European Union* ECLI:EU:C:2016:435.

[74] Cases C-924/19 PPU and C-925/19 PPU *FMS and Others v Országos Idegenrendesszeti Föigazgatóság Dél-alföldi Regionális Igazgatóság and Országos Idegenrendeszeti Föigazgatóság* ECLI:EU:C:2020:367.

[75] Case C-554/*13 Z. Zh. v Staatssecretaris van Veiligheid en Justitie and Staatssecretaris van Veiligheid en Justitie v I. O* ECLI:EU:C:2015:377.

[76] Case C-648/11 *The Queen, on the application of MA and Others v Secretary of State for the Home Department* ECLI:EU:C:2013:367.

[77] Joined cases C-411/10 *NS v Secretary of State for the Home Department and ME and Others v Refugee Applications Commissioner and Minister for Justice, Equality and Law Reform* ECLI:EU:C:2011:865.

[78] See A Küçüksu, 'Adjudicating Asylum as a Technical Matter at the European Court of Justice: Neglecting Human Rights When the CEAS Appears to be in Jeopardy?' in E Kassoti and N Idriz (eds), *The Informalisation of the EU's External Action in the Field of Migration and Asylum, Global Europe: Legal and Policy Issues of the EU's External Action* (Springer Publishing, 2022) 172.

[79] See A Desmond, 'The Return Directive: Clarifying the Scope and Substance of the Rights of Migrants facing Expulsion from the EU' in Russell King and Katie Kuschminder (eds), *Handbook of Return Migration* (Edward Elgar, 2022) 140.

[80] D Thym, 'A Bird's Eye View on ECJ Judgments on Immigration, Asylum and Border Control Cases,' (2019) 21 *European journal of migration and law* 167.

[81] See D Thym, 'Between "Administrative Mindset" and "Constitutional Imagination": The Role of the Court of Justice in Immigration, Asylum and Border Control Policy' (2019) 44 *European Law Review* 156.

broader teleological perspectives on rights and EU integration. In my view, the unwillingness of the Court to do so is explained by its limited view of its role relative to the political actors. The Court seems to be of the view that it is up to the political actors, and not the Court, to decide on sensitive policy issues. It is focusing on upholding existing rules rather than re-examining fundamental values, which could enable the Court to reign in the Member State governments.

This position of restraint is likely a result of the political sensitivity of migration law and the risk of non-compliance, which limits the possibility of judicial expansiveness. For instance, no EU actor was keen on taking authorship of the EU–Turkey Statement and in the case of *X & X* on humanitarian visas, 13 Member States and the EU Commission intervened, and all of them opposed the idea that there could be an obligation to grant humanitarian visas. Thomas Spijkerboer noted in his analysis of the cases that if the Court would apply its 'usual anti-formal, teleological methods of interpretation this could easily lead to a series of highly controversial judgments, resulting, for example, in the annulment of the EU–Turkey Statement or an obligation to issue humanitarian visas to Syrian refugees'.[82] The ECJ is likely aware of these political controversies, which contribute to its accommodating and formal style of argumentation. Attempts to develop constitutional values are, generally, only successful if they are embedded in the political processes.[83]

However, it cannot only be for the executive actors to decide on the road to be taken within the confines of migration law. The Court's task is to interpret the scope of permissible actions within the Treaties. If the Court merely defers to the executive's formulation of policy rather than determining itself what a rule means, the system of separation of powers and the realisation of control and democratic will-formation is threatened as not all three branches are involved in the legal development. As the Court often leaves it to the political actors to decide on the meaning and scope of EU law, we lack the legal counterbalance needed for political measures overreaching. When the Member States go to great lengths to control and limit migration through informality and externalisation, it is all the more important that the ECJ emphasises the constraints of law, including human rights and constitutional principles.

In essence, I argue that the case law demonstrates that the Court has a cautious understanding of its role within the separation of powers framework, which limits the scope of review. While human rights could empower the ECJ to conduct a more substantive review of legal acts and measures against the Treaties, the Court rejects this option. It becomes clear based on the case law that the Court often seeks to align its decisions with the position of the EU executive. This approach reflects the Court's commitment to preserving the delicate balance of power and upholding a formal rule of law in the EU legal system. The deferential nature of the ECJ's legal reasoning hides the conflicting nature of the cases and the different interests and values at stake. Rather than taking this as an opportunity for conceptualisation and scrutiny of human rights, the Court

[82] Spijkerboer (n 5) 16.

[83] G Rosenberg, *The Hollow Hope: Can Courts Bring about Social Change?*, 2nd edn (University of Chicago Press, 2008) 31.

shies away from broader constitutional perspectives. Ultimately, this here empowers the executive relative to the EU legislature and judiciary.

V. Conclusion

In this chapter, I aimed to show and explain how the ECJ responds to challenges to the separation of powers in the development of the external dimension of migration law. It is an area where executive actors, mostly Member State governments, seek to develop relationships with third countries to improve management and control of migration. In this process, legislative institutions such as the European Parliament and judicial actors like the ECJ are sidelined. These power shifts are all the more concerning as human rights are at stake. I, therefore, see it as important that the ECJ exercises substantive judicial review to reign in the executive by observing fundamental constitutional principles.

The overall perception is that potential mechanisms for conceptualisation, scrutiny and enforcement of migration law have been eschewed by an endeavour to remain close to the position of the Member States. The cases analysed suggest that human rights are not identified as a priority and are rarely brought in as a distinct perspective to constrain the executive. By its interpretation of the 'essential elements' doctrine in light of human rights protections, the Court empowered the European Parliament, representing the legislative branch, and restricted executive actors, which in this case was the Council.[84] Yet generally when it comes to interpreting substantive law, the Court is exercising self-restraint. This is demonstrated by the accommodating readings of development projects,[85] and readmission agreements,[86] and by the doctrinal reading of secondary law in the case of humanitarian visas that does not consider the Treaty's aims of protecting human rights.[87] This approach means that strong executive powers are not counter-balanced by the judiciary.

The ECJ's orientation at the executive branch means that constructive will formation and control are weakened, as not all three government branches are engaged. While the legal reasoning may be compelling, the ECJ is not using its full potential for structuring and constraining executive powers. By limiting its review to formal assessments of secondary law and by giving weight to the views of Member State governments, the Court does not give due consideration to competing interests that ought to be balanced and protected. As the Court seeks to avoid highly political issues by a formal and accommodating approach to solving legal issues, it supports a consensual model of decision-making that weakens judicial opposition and control. This chapter thus demonstrates how the Court's legal reasoning strengthens the executive branch relative to the legislative and judicial branches. Even prominent human rights are insufficient to guard against executive competence creeps, thus showing how the law is formed as the executive likes it.

[84] *European Parliament v Council* (n 30).
[85] *Commission v Council* (*PCA with the Philippines*) (n 31).
[86] *NF v European Council* (n 32); *NG v European Council* (n 32); and *NM v European Council* (n 32).
[87] *X and X v Belgium* (n 33).

9

Litigating Monetary Policy: 'The Limits are Ours'. A Study of the ECB's Institutional Transformation from the Euro Zone Sovereign Debt Crisis to the COVID-19 Pandemic

ANTTI RONKAINEN[1]

I. Introduction

In his famous speech that practically ended the Euro area sovereign debt crisis in 2012, European Central Bank (ECB) President Mario Draghi described the euro as a bumblebee. According to Draghi, the euro had to graduate as a real bee because of the financial and sovereign debt crises, and promised that 'within our mandate, the ECB is ready to do whatever it takes to preserve the euro'.[2]

As the ECB unleashed extraordinary crisis measures, it transformed institutionally. This process has led to wide-ranging debates over its graduation as a 'new central bank' and its influence over the broader integration of the Economic and Monetary Union (EMU).[3] Some have suggested that the ECB's preoccupation with stability culture pushed the Member States into structural reforms and fiscal austerity.[4] Others

[1] My thanks to Jens van 't Klooster, Tuomas Saarenheimo and Jan von Gerich for useful comments.

[2] European Central Bank, 'Verbatim of the remarks made by Mario Draghi. Speech by Mario Draghi, President of the European Central Bank at the Global Investment Conference in London 26 July 2012', at www.ecb.europa.eu/press/key/date/2012/html/sp120726.en.html.

[3] T Beukers, D Fromage and G Monti, *The New European Central Bank: Taking Stock and Looking Ahead* (Oxford University Press, 2022); M Brunnermeier, H James and J-P Landau, *The Euro and The Battle of Ideas* (Princeton University Press, 2016); D Ioannou, P Leblond and A Niemann, 'European Integration and the Crisis: Practice and Theory' (2015) 22 *Journal of European Public Policy* 155.

[4] P Hall, 'The Economics and Politics of the Euro Crisis' (2012) 21 *German Politics* 355; CR Henning, 'The ECB as a Strategic Actor: Central Banking in a Politically Fragmented Monetary Union' in J Caporaso and M Rhodes (eds), *The Political and Economic Dynamics of the Eurozone Crisis* (Oxford University Press, 2015); J Yiangou, M O'Keeffe and G Glöckler, '"Tough Love": How the ECB's Monetary Financing Prohibition Pushes Deeper Euro Area Integration' (2013) 35 *Journal of European Integration* 223.

have argued that the EMU's inadequate institutional architecture and non-action by the Member States forced the ECB to introduce unconventional measures and engage with looser monetary policy, suggesting both fiscal and financial dominances, but also the 'loneliness' of the ECB.[5]

The ECB's institutional transformation reflects the 'increased institutional variation' of the EMU legal order.[6] Regarding fiscal policies, the EMU's crisis governance has followed the German ordoliberal tradition, where bailout programmes and mechanisms have been created as path-dependent processes copying previous institutional structures that reflect German national interests.[7] In the area of monetary policies, the ECB has distanced itself from these ordoliberal and monetarist ideas that have been constitutionalised in its mandate.[8]

The ECB's transformation has been perceived mainly critically as reflecting covert economic integration, serious democratic authorisation gaps, greater reliance on technocracy and the emergence of central bankers and legal experts alongside EU judges as the main drivers of economic integration.[9] After the Euro crisis, the ECB has been understood to have taken advantage of its institutional transformation. While it stood alone during the crisis, it has been able to engage in inter-crisis and intra-crisis learning and expand its crisis measures to help Member States and EU institutions to respond to the COVID-19 pandemic.[10] ECB board member Benoît Cœuré described the ECB's broad discretion granted by the ECJ with the phrase: 'the limits are ours'.[11]

[5] S Diessner and G Lisi, 'Masters of the 'Masters of the Universe'? Monetary, Fiscal and Financial Dominance in the Eurozone' (2020) 18 *Socio-Economic Review* 315; A Niemann and D Ioannou, 'European Economic Integration in Times of Crisis: A Case of Neofunctionalism?' (2015) 22 *Journal of European Public Policy* 196; M Matthijs and M Blyth, 'When Is It Rational to Learn the Wrong Lessons? Technocratic Authority, Social Learning, and Euro Fragility' (2018) 16 *Perspectives on Politics* 110; D Mabbett and W Schelkle, 'Independent or Lonely? Central Banking in Crisis' (2019) 26 *Review of International Political Economy* 436.

[6] B de Witte, 'Euro Crisis Responses and the EU Legal Order: Increased Institutional Variation or Constitutional Mutation?' (2015) 11 *European Constitutional Law Review* 434.

[7] F Schimmelfennig, 'Liberal Intergovernmentalism and the Euro Area Crisis' (2015) 22 *Journal of European Public Policy* 177; A Verdun, 'A Historical Institutionalist Explanation of the EU's Responses to the Euro Area Financial Crisis' (2015) 22 *Journal of European Public Policy* 219; M Ryner, 'Europe's Ordoliberal Iron Cage: Critical Political Economy, the Euro Area Crisis and Its Management' (2015) 22 *Journal of European Public Policy* 275.

[8] K McNamara, *The Currency of Ideas: Monetary Politics in the European Union* (Cornell University Press, 1998); H James, *Making the European Monetary Union* (Harvard University Press, 2014); N Jabko, 'Contested Governance: The New Repertoire of the Eurozone Crisis' (2019) 32 *Governance* 493; J van 't Klooster, 'Technocratic Keynesianism: a paradigm shift without legislative change' (2022) 27 *New Political Economy* 771.

[9] A Héritier, 'Covert Integration in the European Union' in J Richardson and S Mazey (eds), *European Union. Power and policy-making*, 4th edn (Routledge, 2015); N de Boer and J van 't Klooster, 'The ECB, the Courts and the Issue of Democratic Legitimacy After Weiss' (2020) 57 *Common Market Law Review* 1689; N Scicluna and S Auer, 'From the Rule of Law to the Rule of Rules: Technocracy and the Crisis of EU Governance' (2019) 42 *West European Politics* 1420.

[10] L Quaglia and A Verdun, 'Explaining the Response of the ECB to the COVID-19 Related Economic Crisis: Inter-Crisis and Intra-Crisis Learning' (2023) 30 *Journal of European Public Policy* 635; W Bateman and J van 't Klooster, 'The Dysfunctional Taboo: Monetary Financing at the Bank of England, the Federal Reserve, and the European Central Bank' (2023) *Review of International Political Economy*; D Gabor, 'Revolution Without Revolutionaries: Interrogating the Return of Monetary Financing' (2021) SocArXiv, Transformative Responses to the crisis.

[11] C Jones 'Interview with Benoît Cœuré' *Financial Times* (12 June 2019), at www.bis.org/review/r190617g.htm.

The specific interest of Germany in these developments relates to its agreement to abandon the *Deutsche Mark* after German reunification on the condition that the ECB was to mirror the German Central Bank (the *Bundesbank*).[12] Under the leadership of the German chief economist Otmar Issing, the ECB adopted a stability-oriented monetary policy strategy heavily inspired by the *Bundesbank* and monetarist money aggregates.[13] It is no surprise that the ECB measures taken to combat the Euro crisis faced fierce resistance from German politicians, central bankers and politicians.[14] Most importantly, the German Federal Constitutional Court (*Bundesverfassungsgericht*, BVerfG) referred the ECB's government bond purchase programmes to the European Court of Justice (ECJ) for two preliminary rulings.[15] The BVerfG argued that without judicial review of the ECB's crisis measures, the ECB would autonomously determine the powers assigned to it and expand its mandate at its own discretion.[16] In the references, the German court suggested that exceeding the ECB's mandate would constitute an ultra vires act and an infringement of German voters' democratic rights. This would result in the *Bundesbank*'s *de facto* withdrawal from the ECB's crisis measures and Germany's partial exit from the eurozone.

The constitutional dispute between the German court and the ECB reflects Europe's 'independence wars' – a critical juncture in which Europe's constitutional settlement is redefined, broadened and deepened through questioning the distribution of competences.[17] The EMU has a specific rule-based economic constitution relying on social market economy, market discipline and price stability-oriented monetary policy.[18] The model is based on the separation of fiscal and monetary policies: Article 119 TFEU defines economic policies as the responsibility of Member States and the conduct of monetary policy in the Euro area as the responsibility of the ECB. The ECB's mandate is laid down in Article 127 TFEU, which defines its primary objective as maintaining price stability and, 'without prejudice' to this objective, supporting the EU's general economic policies. Article 130 TFEU guarantees the ECB's operational independence: the ECB can define both inflation target and monetary strategy for achieving it and its decisions cannot be vetoed.[19] Market discipline should guarantee the sustainability of public finances. The Stability and Growth Pact limits public deficits to three per cent

[12] K Dyson and K Featherstone, *The Road to Maastricht: Negotiating Economic and Monetary Union* (Oxford University Press, 1999); D Marsch, *The Euro. The Battle for the New Global Currency* (Yale University Press, 2011).

[13] O Issing, *The Birth of Euro* (Cambridge University Press, 2008).

[14] 'German central bank chief in resign threat' *Irish Examiner* (31 August 2012) at, www.irishexaminer.com/business/arid-30565143.html; S Wagstyl and C Jones 'German court refers ECB bond-buying programme to European justice' *Financial Times* (7 February 2014), at www.ft.com/content/3feab440-8fd5-11e3-aee9-00144feab7de; S Wagstyl and C Jones 'Germany blames Mario Draghi for rise of rightwing AfD party' *Financial Times* (10 April 2016), at www.ft.com/content/bc0175c4-ff2b-11e5-9cc4-27926f2b110c.

[15] BVerfG, *Order of the Second Senate of 14 January 2014 – 2 BvR 2728/13* [2014] (OMT reference); BVerfG, *Order of the Second Senate of 18 July 2017 – 2 BvR 859/15* [2017] (PSPP reference).

[16] OMT reference (n 15) para 60.

[17] A Vauchez, 'The Genie of Independence and the European Bottle: How Independence Became Europe's Most Contentious Legal and Political Category' (2022) 20 *International Journal of Constitutional Law* 2032.

[18] C Joerges, 'What Is Left of the European Economic Constitution?' (2004) EUI-LAW Working Papers 13, at papers.ssrn.com/sol3/papers.cfm?abstract_id=635402.

[19] J de Haan, 'The European Central Bank: Independence, Accountability and Strategy: A Review' (1997) 93 *Public Choice* 395.

and public debts to 60 per cent of GDP. Article 123 TFEU further prohibits the ECB from financing the Member States and Article 125 TFEU prohibits bailouts. The ECJ confirmed in 2005 that while the ECB is bound in general by secondary legislation, it is allowed broad independence to conduct monetary policy.[20] As the one of the most independent central banks in the world, the ECB has substantial leeway to interpret its own mandate.[21] It is also carefully shielded from public scrutiny through its highly confidential decision-making.[22]

Due to the EMU's institutional peculiarities, the independence wars turned the ECB, the Commission and the ECJ into close collaborators in broadening the ECB's mandate. As the ECB's Treaty based mandate is difficult to amend, the ECJ's preliminary rulings make the Court a powerful actor concerning the EMU's economic integration.[23] The Commission systematically intervenes in all preliminary rulings as it sees itself as representing the general European interest in the Court by defending the validity of EU law.[24] The Commission has the broadest resources in terms of access to *travaux préparatoires* and technical details. Under the Court's Rules of Procedure, the Commission is allowed to submit statements or written observations to all cases submitted to the ECJ,[25] and it leads the Court towards more legal integration as it has tendency to win its cases.[26]

This chapter further argues that the ECJ's landmark *Gauweiler* and *Weiss* rulings[27] not only authorised the ECB's government bond purchase programmes, but also modified the general concept of the EMU's economic constitution.[28] While Euro crisis management has been studied as a path-dependent process between the Member States and EU institutions, horizontal cooperation between EU institutions has received less scholarly attention. The ECB's transformation into a real bee 'within its mandate' poses interesting research dilemma: what has been the nature of the cooperation between the ECB, the Commission and the ECJ throughout the dispute over the ECB's mandate? To what extent has the ECJ followed the ECB's and the Commission's legal and economic reasoning in reviewing the legality of ECB's crisis measures? And how have the ideas of

[20] Case C-11/00 *Commission v ECB* ECLI:EU:C:2003:395.

[21] M van der Sluis, 'The Role of Constitutional Law for the ECB: Past, Present, and Future' in T Beukers, D Fromage and G Monti, *The New European Central Bank: Taking Stock and Looking Ahead* (Oxford University Press, 2022).

[22] P Leino-Sandberg, 'Public access to ECB documents: are accountability, independence and effectiveness an impossible trinity?' in *Building bridges: central bank law in an interconnected world: ECB Legal Conference 2019* (European Central Bank, 2019); D Curtin, '"Accountable independence' of the European Central Bank: seeing the logics of transparency' (2017) 23 *European Law Journal* 28.

[23] G Davies, 'The European Union Legislature as an Agent of the European Court of Justice' (2016) 54 *Journal of Common Market Studies* 846.

[24] P Leino-Sandberg, 'The Commission Legal Service' in P Leino-Sandberg (ed), *The Politics of Legal Expertise in EU Policy-Making* (Cambridge University Press, 2021).

[25] Rules of Procedure of the Court of Justice [2012] OJ L 265/1.

[26] E Stein, 'Lawyers, Judges, and the Making of a Transnational Constitution' (1981) 75 *American Journal of International Law* 1.

[27] Case C-62/14 *Peter Gauweiler and Others v Deutscher Bundestag* ECLI:EU:C:2015:400 (*Gauweiler*); Case C-493/17 *Henrich Weiss and Others* ECLI:EU:C:2018:1000 (*Weiss*).

[28] H Lokdam and MA Wilkinson, 'The European Economic Constitution in Crisis: A Conservative Transformation?' in G Grégoire and X Miny (eds), *The Idea of Economic Constitution in Europe* (Brill, 2022); K Tuori, 'The ECB's Quantitative Easing Programme as a Constitutional Game Changer' (2019) 26 *Maastricht Journal of European and Comparative Law* 94; V Borger, 'The Transformation of the ECB in Sovereign Bond Markets' in T Beukers, D Fromage and G Monti, *The New European Central Bank: Taking Stock and Looking Ahead* (Oxford University Press, 2022).

market discipline and monetary financing been interpreted and how do they affect the EMU's economic constitution more generally?

The chapter examines the strategic cooperation between the ECB, the Commission and the ECJ in the *Gauweiler* and *Weiss* preliminary rulings. The research data includes the ECB's written responses to both the BVerfG and the ECJ, the Commission's pleadings, and finally the ECJ's *Gauweiler* and *Weiss* judgments. The Commission's pleadings[29] have been gathered through an access to document request. The ECB's written responses to the BVerfG's questions in the *Gauweiler* and *Weiss* cases have been gathered through access to ECB documents requests. When responding to my initial request in 2020, the ECB provided the written responses regarding the OMT,[30] but refused to even partially disclose those related to the Public Sector Purchase Programme (PSPP). According to the Bank, disclosure would reveal the strategy, preparation and implementation of the PSPP, which could create misperceptions about the ECB's conduct of monetary policy.[31] However, based on a new confirmatory application, the ECB decided to disclose its PSPP responses in 2023,[32] albeit with significant portions redacted.[33] This demonstrates that the ECB is sensitive to a discussion about the legal arguments it uses and considers that these arguments are relevant also for its future operations.

The unique research data is analysed through the historical institutionalist approach.[34] Section II summarises the BVerfG's arguments against government bond purchase programmes. Section III studies the strategic cooperation between the Bank, the Commission and the Court by mapping out the similarities between these institutions' legal reasoning in *Gauweiler* and *Weiss*.[35] The study finds that the Commission has provided the legal arguments for finding government bond purchases to be compatible with the Treaties and the ECB's mandate. Relying on this argumentation, the ECJ allowed the ECB to provide the economic reasoning based on its monetary expertise. Section IV reviews more closely the economic reasoning used in *Gauweiler* and *Weiss*. The analysis suggests that the argumentation further increases the ECB's discretion over the market conditions and the financing conditions of the Member States. The final section provides a contribution to the literature on separation of powers by arguing that instead of operating as a 'classic' court on the basis of a legal standard independent from the executive, the ECJ has acted as a cooperative partner of the ECB and the Commission.[36] This dualistic cooperation between the executive and judicial branches concentrates public power in the hands of technocratic central bankers, Commission legal experts and judges with no direct democratic mandate.[37]

[29] Commission, 'Schriftsatz zu dem Vorabentscheidungsersuchen C-62/14' [2014] (OMT pleadings); Commission, 'Schriftsatz zu dem Vorabentscheidungsersuchen C-493/17' [2017] (PSPP pleadings).

[30] European Central Bank, 'Schriftliche Erklärung in der Rechtssache C-62/14' [2014] (OMT responses).

[31] European Central Bank, 'Reply to access to ECB documents request, 19.10.2020' LS/PS/2020/56.

[32] European Central Bank, 'Reply to confirmatory application for public access to ECB documents, 6.7.2023' LS/CL/2023/135.

[33] European Central Bank, 'Schriftliche Erklärung in der Rechtssache C-493/17' [2017] (PSPP responses).

[34] R Smith, 'Historical Institutionalism and the Study of Law' in GA Caldeira, RD Kelemen and KE Whittington (eds), *The Oxford Handbook of Law and Politics* (Oxford University Press, 2008).

[35] On the method, see also L Leppävirta, 'What is the purpose of Regulation 1049/2001? An empirical analysis of Member State positions' in M Hillebrandt, P Leino-Sandberg and I Koivisto (eds) *(In)visible European Government. Critical Approaches to Transparency as an Ideal and a Practice* (Routledge, 2023).

[36] C Möllers, *The Three Branches. A Comparative Model of Separation of Powers* (Oxford University Press, 2013).

[37] Leino-Sandberg and Minkkinen, ch 2 in this volume.

II. The German Defence of a Price Stability-oriented ECB

Since the Euro crisis the ECB has introduced five government bond purchase programmes, due to which its balance sheet has expanded by almost five trillion euros.[38] Securities Markets Programme (SMP), Outright Monetary Transactions (OMT) and Transmission Protection Instrument (TPI) are all intended to restore the appropriate functioning of the monetary policy transmission mechanism but with different policy settings: SMP purchases were limited in advance, the OMT includes unlimited purchases of crisis countries with fiscal adjustment programmes of either the European Financial Stability Facility (EFSF) or the European Stability Mechanism (ESM), and the TPI includes longer maturities and looser conditionality than the OMT.[39] In turn, the PSPP and the Pandemic Emergency Purchase Programme (PEPP) are quantitative easing (QE) programmes for countering deflationary threats and increase liquidity.[40] The PEPP combines both rationales of protecting monetary policy transmission and countering deflation and hence it diverts significantly from the technical features and self-imposed limits of the PSPP.

The debate on the ECB's role in the Euro crisis management has been manifold, but there is no doubt that it has become broader than leading policy-makers in Germany wished. The ECB's government bond purchase programmes have drawn strident criticism from German central bankers: *Bundesbank* president Axel Weber, ECB chief economist Jürgen Stark and ECB board member Sabine Lautenschläger all resigned as a protest against bond purchases.[41] More than 11 000 signatories brought constitutional actions against the OMT in Germany, and *Bundesbank* president Jens Weidmann testified against it in proceedings.[42] At the time of writing, the ECJ has ruled on the OMT

[38] D Lombardi and M Moschella, 'The Government Bond Buying Programmes of the European Central Bank: An Analysis of Their Policy Settings' (2016) 23 *Journal of European Public Policy* 851. European Central Bank, 'Annual consolidated balance sheet of the Eurosystem', at https://www.ecb.europa.eu/press/annual-reports-financial-statements/annual/balance/html/index.en.html.

[39] European Central Bank, 'ECB decides on measures to address severe tensions in financial markets' (Press Release, 10 May 2010), at www.ecb.europa.eu/press/pr/date/2010/html/pr100510.en.html; European Central Bank, 'Technical features of Outright Monetary Transactions' (Press Release, 6 September 2012), at www.ecb.europa.eu/press/pr/date/2012/html/pr120906_1.en.html; European Central Bank, 'The Transmission Protection Instrument' (Press Release, 21 July 2022), at www.ecb.europa.eu/press/pr/date/2022/html/ecb.pr220721~973e6e7273.en.html.

[40] European Central Bank, 'FAQ on the Public Sector Purchase Programme' (9 August 2023), at www.ecb.europa.eu/mopo/implement/app/html/ecb.faq_pspp.en.html; European Central Bank, 'ECB announces €750 billion Pandemic Emergency Purchase Programme (PEPP)' (Press Release, 18 March 2020), at www.ecb.europa.eu/press/pr/date/2020/html/ecb.pr200318_1~3949d6f266.en.html.

[41] Spiegel International, 'German Central Bank Head Axel Weber Resigns' (*Spiegel International*, 11 February 2011), at www.spiegel.de/international/germany/merkel-ecb-candidate-german-central-bank-head-axel-weber-resigns-a-745083.html; BBC 'Jürgen Stark in surprise resignation from ECB' (BBC, 11 September 2011), at www.bbc.com/news/business-14858155; T Escritt and F Canepa, 'ECB hawk Sabine Lautenschläger resigns amid policy backlash' (Reuters, 25 September 2019), at www.reuters.com/article/us-ecb-board-lautenschlaeger-idINKBN1WA2OH.

[42] 'ECB's Weidmann says bond buy conditions problematic' (Reuters, 21 January 2013), at www.reuters.com/article/uk-ecb-weidmann-idUKBRE90K00320130121; J Weidmann, 'Eingangserklärung anlässlich der mündlichen Verhandlung im Hauptsacheverfahren ESM/EZB' (Stellungnahme, Bundesbank, 11 June 2013), at www.bundesbank.de/de/presse/stellungnahmen/eingangserklaerung-anlaesslich-der-muendlichen-verhandlung-im-hauptsacheverfahren-esm-ezb-662878.

and the PSPP after references from the BVerfG. Complaints against the PEPP are pending in Germany.[43]

As government bond purchase programmes have significant economic consequences over the financing conditions of Member States, fiscal redistribution and overall financial stability, the BverfG questioned whether the OMT and the PSPP overstep the ECB's monetary mandate and infringe the monetary financing prohibition.[44] The following briefly summarises the BVerfG's legal argumentation expressed in the OMT and PSPP references.

First, the BVerfG argued that government bond purchases exceed the ECB's monetary mandate because both programmes constitute more economic than monetary policies.[45] As the ECJ had held in *Pringle* that the ESM cannot be treated as equivalent to a monetary measure merely because monetary policy might also have indirect economic effects,[46] the BVerfG stated that the OMT does not qualify as monetary policy because it pursues monetary objectives only indirectly.[47] The BVerfG suggested that the programme constitutes financial assistance, which, according to the *Pringle* judgment, falls within economic policy.[48] It argued that neutralising interest rate spreads and dividing them into rational and irrational parts was a political declaration to safeguard the current composition of the Euro area, which is the responsibility of politicians.[49] Furthermore, it argued that due to the selective nature of purchases, the conditionality to the fiscal adjustment programmes and the risk of undermining their objectives, the OMT oversteps the ECB's responsibilities to support the EU's economic objectives.[50]

Similarly, the BVerfG argued that the PSPP is an economic policy measure because it affects the balance sheets of commercial banks by transferring government bonds to the balance sheet of the ECB and improving the financing conditions of Euro Member States.[51] The BVerfG stated that these economic steering effects were intended as part of the programme's design and were at least comparable to the intended monetary policy objectives.[52] It also questioned the programme's proportionality by stating that the ECB had not balanced the intended monetary policy effects with the foreseeable economic policy effects.[53]

Second, the BVerfG argued that both programmes infringed the monetary financing prohibition as they significantly loosened the financing conditions of the Euro Member

[43] K Matussek, 'ECB's Covid Rescue Program Attacked in Suit at Top German Court' (Bloomberg, 11 March 2021), at www.bloomberg.com/news/articles/2021-03-11/ecb-s-covid-rescue-program-attacked-in-suit-at-top-german-court.

[44] A Thiele, 'The Independence of the ECB: Justification, Challenges, and Possible Threats' in T Beukers, D Fromage and G Monti (eds), *The New European Central Bank: Taking Stock and Looking Ahead* (Oxford University Press, 2022).

[45] OMT reference (n 15) para 69; PSPP reference (n 15) para 120.

[46] Case C-370/12 *Thomas Pringle v Government of Ireland and Others* ECLI:EU:C:2012:756 (*Pringle*) [56].

[47] OMT reference (n 15) para 64.

[48] *Pringle* (n 46) [65].

[49] OMT reference (n 15) paras 70–72.

[50] ibid paras 73–83.

[51] PSPP reference (n 15) paras 120–121.

[52] ibid paras 119.

[53] ibid paras 123.

States. In its OMT referral, it argued that the prohibition from purchasing government bonds directly on the primary markets cannot be circumvented by 'functionally equivalent measures', like risky government bond purchases on the secondary markets, holding them until maturity with possible debt cuts and encouraging private market operators to purchase government bonds.[54] Additionally, purchasing government bonds shortly after their emission or pre-announced purchases would interfere with free price formation on the government bond markets.[55]

Regarding the PSPP, the BVerfG argued that pre-announced information on the monthly purchases and duration of the programme provides sufficient certainty for market participants and the Member States, hence disrupting the functioning of both primary and secondary markets and infringing the monetary financing prohibition.[56] Additionally, the ECB's ability to purchase bonds with negative yields and hold them until maturity reduces Euro Member States' incentives to pursue sound fiscal policies.[57] Lastly, it claimed that in the event of default, the ECB would engage in full risk-sharing between central banks and thus create new risk-sharing regime that would infringe the monetary financing prohibition.[58]

III. EU Institutions' Strategic Cooperation During the Independence Wars

This section analyses the strategic cooperation between the ECB, the Commission and the ECJ during the *Gauweiler* and *Weiss* cases by mapping the similarities in their legal argumentation and economic reasoning. The analysis is structured into thematic entities according to the doubts raised by the BVerfG in its referrals for preliminary rulings, with the first section focusing on the ECB's monetary mandate and the second on the monetary financing prohibition. The final subsection concludes the still unresolved questions.

A. Compliance with the ECB's Monetary Mandate

In their written responses, both the ECB and the Commission disagreed with the BVerfG's interpretation of the scope of the ECB's monetary mandate. For the ECB, not only government bond purchases but all monetary policy measures pursue monetary policy objectives only indirectly through different monetary transmission mechanisms.[59] Every monetary measure influences the behaviour of economic agents, so the ECB would be practically disarmed if measures with economic steering effects were classified

[54] OMT reference (n 15) paras 86–91.
[55] ibid para 92.
[56] PSPP reference (n 15) paras 81–92.
[57] ibid paras 96–99.
[58] ibid paras 130–131.
[59] OMT responses (n 30) para 51.

as economic policy measures.[60] Both institutions referred to *Pringle* in arguing that the nature of the measure should be reviewed based on its objectives instead of its indirect steering effects or the fact that the ESM can also purchase government bonds on the secondary markets.[61]

Moreover, the ECB explained that the OMT's objective was to restore the monetary transmission mechanism, which was malfunctioning because of financial market distortions in 2011–12 and fears of the Euro area breaking up.[62] Hence, the OMT was not about 'eliminating' the convertibility premium completely, but instead bringing interest rates back to their 'normal' market conditions.[63] It also downplayed the BVerfG's accusations of economic steering effects by focussing on the technical features that limit the OMT's influence on the financing conditions of the Euro Member States, namely the eligibility criteria of one–three-year bonds of countries committed to the EFSF/ESM assistance programme.

Most importantly, both the Commission and the ECB suggested that the ECB's actions should be subject to limited judicial review in which the ECJ only assesses whether the ECB's measures are appropriate without going beyond what is necessary to achieve their objectives.[64] The ECB stated that the ECJ should not substitute the ECB's economic assessments with its own or any another institution's assessment, and that it should examine only 'the factual accuracy, completeness and coherence of available evidence and the plausibility of the conclusions drawn from it'.[65] The Commission stated that the ECJ can scrutinise whether the ECB's reasoning appears plausible, but it must accept the ECB's assessment in principle.[66]

The ECJ followed the ECB and the Commission in its *Gauweiler* judgment. It stated that the nature of a measure should be assessed based on its objectives and chosen instruments.[67] It agreed that government bond purchases could not be treated as an economic measure simply because of their indirect effects, and that the ESM can conduct government bond purchases in the area of economic policy.[68] The ECJ ruled that whether government bond purchases respect the principle of proportionality must be assessed in a three-step process: 1) they contribute to the ECB's monetary objectives;[69] 2) they go beyond what is necessary to achieve the programme's objectives;[70] and 3) the ECB has weighed the interests involved to avoid disadvantages manifestly disproportionate to its objectives.[71] By relying entirely on the ECB's reasoning, the ECJ found the OMT to fall within the area of monetary policy as it accepted that safeguarding appropriate policy transmission was a valid monetary policy

[60] ibid paras 52, 55.
[61] ibid para 53; OMT pleadings (n 29) para 47.
[62] OMT responses (n 30) para 62.
[63] ibid para 66.
[64] ibid paras 38–42; OMT pleadings (n 29) paras 62–66.
[65] OMT responses (n 30) para 61.
[66] OMT pleadings (n 29) para 65.
[67] *Gauweiler* (n 27) [46].
[68] ibid [61], [63].
[69] ibid [72]–[80].
[70] ibid [81]–[90].
[71] ibid [91]–[92].

objective[72] and that the ECB had ensured that the OMT did not infringe the principle of proportionality.[73]

The Court also followed the ECB and the Commission by accepting that it should not question the ECB's economic reasoning nor consider any other institutions' analyses more credible. As monetary policy requires decision-makers 'to make choices of a technical nature and undertake forecasts and complex assessments', the Court allowed the Bank broad discretion to provide economic reasoning for its government bond purchases.[74] It obliged the ECB to examine 'all the relevant elements of the situation in question and to give an adequate statement of the reasons for its decisions' but did not require the ECB 'to go into every relevant point of fact and law'.[75] Additionally, the Court required the ECB to 'use its economic expertise and the necessary technical means at its disposal to carry out that [reasoned] analysis',[76] and compliance with the obligation to state reasons should be assessed on the basis not only of the wording of the act, but also its context.[77] The ECJ replied to the BVerfG by repeating the Commission's argument that challenging the ECB's economic analysis does not call its reasoning into question, as questions of monetary policy are 'usually of a controversial nature'.[78]

Based on case law established in *Gauweiler*, the ECB and the Commission argued that the PSPP was also in compliance with the three-step proportionality assessment. Both institutions reasoned along similar lines:[79] the necessity of the programme, its extensions and adjustments,[80] and finally that the ECB had balanced the various interests to avoid undue disadvantages.[81] For the Commission, it remained unclear whether the PSPP had improved the economic situation of banks significantly when the ECB's other measures were taken into account, and that the programme's economic influence over the Member States' financing conditions should be related to its monetary policy objectives.[82] The ECB noted that it had set up safeguards to ensure market neutrality on the secondary markets and the Member States' incentives to uphold sound fiscal policies, as well as to limit potential losses for the ECB in several ways, including eligibility criteria, purchases limits, credit risk mitigation and other special guarantees.[83]

Following the Commission and the ECB, the ECJ disagreed with the BVerfG's argumentation that the PSPP should be deemed an economic measure based on its steering effects. In its *Weiss* judgment, it stated that the ECB's mandate is to support general economic policies in the EU 'without prejudice' to its primary objective of price stability.[84] As all monetary policy measures affect the real economy, precluding the measures with economic steering effects would prevent the ECB from using all the means provided by the Treaties for maintaining price stability.[85]

[72] ibid [48]–[49].
[73] ibid [92].
[74] ibid [68].
[75] ibid [69]–[70].
[76] ibid [75].
[77] ibid [70].
[78] ibid [75]; *Weiss* (n 27) [91].
[79] PSPP responses (n 33) paras 152–54; PSPP pleadings (n 29) paras 138–42.
[80] PSPP responses (n 33) paras 155–63; PSPP pleadings (n 29) paras 143–59.
[81] PSPP responses (n 33) paras 164–67; PSPP pleadings (n 29) paras 160–62.
[82] PSPP pleadings (n 29) paras 143–57.
[83] PSPP responses (n 33) paras 168–80.
[84] *Weiss* (n 27) [58]–[60].
[85] ibid [61]–[67].

Hence, the ECJ held that the PSPP was an appropriate and necessary measure to counter deflationary threats,[86] that the programme and its extensions and adjustments had not gone beyond what was necessary[87] and that the ECB had weighed up the interests involved appropriately.[88] Thus, providing monetary accommodation through a QE programme falls within the area of monetary policy and the PSPP does not infringe the principle of proportionality.[89]

The analysis suggests that the ECJ not only accepted the economic justification and rationale of OMT and PSPP, but also granted the ECB considerable discretion to introduce new purchase programmes. The ECJ established a new legal framework for assessing the proportionality of government bond purchases, subject to the ECB's own economic reasoning and a narrow proportionality analysis: although government bond purchases have broad economic implications, the ECJ required the ECB only to demonstrate the appropriateness and necessity of purchases and that it had considered all possible disadvantages. As the Court does not question the ECB's economic expertise, the technical features of programmes or the economic justification for purchases, it becomes highly unlikely that the ECJ would find new purchase programmes introduced after *Gauweiler* and *Weiss* to exceed the ECB's mandate.

However, in its national judgment after the ECJ's *Weiss* ruling, the BVerfG questioned both the ECB's and the ECJ's legal reasoning. According to the German court, as the ECJ did not require the ECB to examine the actual and expected economic consequences of PSPP, the ECB could engage directly in economic policy-making as long as it justified these actions with its price stability objective which would allow the ECB to determine its own competences.[90] The BVerfG judged that both the ECB and the ECJ had acted ultra vires and obliged the German *Bundestag* to assess the adequacy of the ECB's proportionality analysis. Although the *Bundestag* accepted the *Bundesbank*'s participation in the PSPP,[91] the BVerfG response underlines the possibility that it would again oblige the *Bundestag* to review the proportionality of new government bond purchase programmes.

B. Teleological Interpretation of the Monetary Financing Prohibition (Article 123 TFEU)

In response to the BverfG's interpretation of the monetary financing prohibition, the ECB argued that the monetary financing prohibition is crucial to the legal architecture of the EMU, as it maintains fiscal discipline and preserves the ECB's independence.[92]

[86] ibid [71]–[78].

[87] ibid [79]–[92].

[88] ibid [93]–[99].

[89] ibid [70], [100].

[90] BVerfG, *Judgment of the Second Senate of 5 May 2020 – 2 BvR 859/15* [2020]; MP Maduro, 'Some Preliminary Remarks on the PSPP Decision of the German Constitutional Court' (*Verfassungsblog*, 6 May 2020), at verfassungsblog.de/some-preliminary-remarks-on-the-pspp-decision-of-the-german-constitutional-court.

[91] B Jennen 'German Parliament Backs ECB Bond-Buying After Court Standoff' (Bloomberg, 2 July 2020), at www.bloomberg.com/news/articles/2020-07-02/german-parliament-backs-ecb-bond-buying-ending-court-standoff.

[92] OMT responses (n 30) para 115.

However, government bond purchases can be conducted on secondary markets if they serve the objective of price stability, the ECB decides independently on these purchases and they are not intended to finance Member States independently of the capital markets.[93]

However, it was the Commission that provided the legal argumentation for the ECJ to review the compliance of government bond purchases with the monetary financing prohibition. First, it interpreted Article 123 TFEU prohibiting only 'direct acquisition of debt instruments' to mean that the ECB cannot engage in purchases on secondary markets that would have the same economic effect as primary market purchases.[94] Second, *qua Pringle*, the objective of Article 123 TFEU was to ensure sound budgetary discipline by subjecting the financing of Euro Member States to the logic of the financial markets.[95] Hence, the Commission suggested that the ECJ should review whether the ECB has provided sufficient safeguards to ensure that: 1) purchases on secondary markets do not have equal effects as primary market purchases; and 2) the Member States remain subject to the logic of the financial markets and cannot rely on ECB financing.[96]

The ECJ accepted the Commission's teleological interpretation of Article 123 TFEU and specified two requirements to comply with the monetary financing prohibition. As proposed by the Commission, the Court stated that purchases on secondary markets cannot have an equivalent effect as purchases on primary markets.[97] This would arise if potential purchasers of government bonds were to know the timing and scope of the ECB's purchases of specific government bonds for certain, which would allow them to act as *de facto* intermediaries between the ECB and Member States, thus impeding free market price formation.[98] Second, the Treaties do not prohibit secondary market purchases of government bonds as long as they do not constitute financial assistance to Euro Member States.[99] Again, following the Commission's interpretation, the Court clarified that the aim of Article 123 TFEU was 'to encourage the Member States to follow a sound budgetary policy' and that the ECB is therefore required to set up safeguards to ensure that government bond purchases do not lessen the impetus to do so.[100]

Both the ECB and the Commission argued similarly that the OMT has sufficient safeguards to avoid the infringement of the monetary financing prohibition. First, quantitative *ex ante* limits would constrain the efficacy of the OMT, but eligible bonds have been limited to countries with the EFSF/ESM programmes with maturities of only one–three years.[101] Second, the OMT does not impair the market price formation of government bonds, as the ECB imposes a blackout period between the issuance of bonds on the primary markets and their purchase on the secondary markets.[102] Third,

[93] ibid para 120.
[94] OMT pleadings (n 29) paras 111–13.
[95] ibid para 114.
[96] ibid paras 115, 124.
[97] *Gauweiler* (n 27) [97].
[98] ibid [104].
[99] ibid [103].
[100] ibid [99]–[102].
[101] OMT responses (n 30) paras 122–24; OMT pleadings (n 29) paras 137–42.
[102] OMT responses (n 30) paras 125–33; OMT pleadings (n 29) paras 118 and 143.

holding purchased bonds until maturity does not interfere with market logic, as the ECB's mandate does not prohibit it from holding bonds until their maturity.[103] Fourth, a risk of default would not constitute indirect monetary financing, as the ECB has limited the risks of open market operations through the eligibility criteria and the conditionality requirement.[104] Fifth, concerns over possible haircuts constituting illegal monetary financing were unfounded as the ECB would not agree to them voluntarily.[105] Lastly, the OMT does not encourage private operators to purchase government bonds on the primary markets, as the ECB does not announce purchases in advance.[106]

The ECJ found that the OMT respects both limits. First, it established that OMT purchases do not have equivalent effects as purchases on primary markets. The blackout period, the ECB's independent decision-making on the scope, start, continuation and suspension of purchases, and the fact that the ECB refrains from making any prior announcements concerning purchases or their volume, ensure free market price formation.[107] Second, the OMT does not lessen the impetus to follow sound budgetary policies, as Member States cannot rely on the ECB's government bond purchases when determining their budget policies. The eligibility criteria of one–three-year bonds limits influence over financing conditions and the ECB has the option of selling purchased bonds. Additionally purchases are conditioned on the ESFS/ESM programme, which requires fiscal austerity and structural reforms.[108] Finally, the Court stated that purchases cannot be used for the harmonisation of interest rates.[109] The ECJ concluded that the other features of the OMT do not call these conclusions into question.[110]

Finally, the ECJ disagreed with the BVerfG that purchasing bonds with a risk of debt cut would automatically infringe the monetary financing prohibition. It noted that open market operations expose the ECB to the risk of losses and that Article 33 of the ECB's Protocol defines how the ECB's losses should be allocated, without delimiting possible risks.[111] It accepted that the ECB is exposed to the risk of debt cuts because it does not have privileged creditor status, but did not specify how the ECB should act in the event of debt restructuring.[112] However, the mention that debt cuts would be 'decided upon by other creditors of the Member State concerned' might indicate that a national central bank agreeing to debt restructuring would constitute a violation of the prohibition of monetary financing.[113]

[103] OMT responses (n 30) paras 134–39; OMT pleadings (n 29) paras 144–47.
[104] OMT responses (n 30) paras 140–44; OMT pleadings (n 29) paras 148–52.
[105] OMT responses (n 30) paras 145–48; OMT pleadings (n 29) paras 153–59.
[106] OMT responses (n 30) paras 149–50; OMT pleadings (n 29) paras 160–65.
[107] *Gauweiler* (n 27) [105]–[108].
[108] ibid [109]–[120].
[109] ibid [113].
[110] ibid [122].
[111] ibid [125].
[112] ibid [126].
[113] ibid [126]. Detailed legal discussion on the ECB and debt restructurings: S Grund and F Grle, 'The European Central Bank's Public Sector Purchase Programme (PSPP), the Prohibition of Monetary Financing and Sovereign Debt Restructuring Scenarios' (2016) *European Law Review*. The General Court had already indicated that the ECB's participation in the restructuring of Greek public debt as part of its second bailout package would have constituted a violation of the prohibition on monetary financing. Case T-79/13 *Accorinti and Others v ECB* ECLI:EU:T:2015:756 (*Accorinti*) [114].

The ECJ's guidelines on safeguards left many open questions. As already mentioned, the difference between the OMT and the PSPP is that while the OMT is intended to repair the monetary transmission mechanism, the PSPP is a QE programme intended to counter deflationary threats. As the PSPP aims to boost inflation, its policy-setting differs from the OMT by containing pre-announced information on the monthly purchase volumes and the duration of the programme, with much longer maturities than the OMT without the EFSF/ESM conditionality. Additionally, as purchases include all eligible countries instead of given crisis countries, purchases are conducted throughout the Euro area by national central banks based on the ECB's capital key.

Both the ECB and the Commission underlined these differences in their written submissions before the Court. The Commission argued that the BVerfG had misunderstood the legal requirements set out in *Gauweiler*.[114] According to the Commission, the ECB can purchase government bonds as long as private operators cannot be certain that the ECB will purchase a certain bond at a certain time (first requirement) and purchases do not lessen the Member States' impetus to follow sound budgetary policies (second requirement).[115] The Commission disagreed with the BVerfG that the absence of a single safeguard accepted in *Gauweiler* would lead to a breach of Article 123 TFEU.[116] According to the Commission, sufficient safeguards established in *Gauweiler* do not set minimum standards for all government bond purchase programmes. Instead, the required safeguards must be adapted to the respective programme and therefore they can vary depending on the programme's objectives.[117] The ECB shared the Commission's view and derived two additional conclusions from Advocate General Cruz Villalón's opinion in *Gauweiler*. First, safeguards should be assessed 'not in detail, but in their interaction' as to whether they prevent the circumvention of Article 123 TFEU.[118] Second, the ECB should be granted a margin of discretion to balance the objectives of Article 123 TFEU and the effectiveness of its government bond purchase programmes.[119]

In its *Weiss* judgment, the ECJ accepted the Commission's and the ECB's interpretation of *Gauweiler* that the ECB has discretion to design safeguards. It judged that adequate safeguards 'depend both on the particular features of the programme under consideration and on the economic context in which that programme is adopted and implemented'.[120] Hence, the ECB is required to prevent certainty of purchases among private operators and avoid reducing the impetus to follow sound budget policies, but meeting these requirements does not require exactly the same safeguards that have been deemed sufficient in *Gauweiler*.[121]

The ECB and the Commission proved the PSPP's compliance with the first requirement with very similar arguments, although the ECB demonstrated the sufficiency of chosen safeguards in more detail.[122] The ECB listed six safeguards that prevent

[114] PSPP pleadings (n 29) para 69.
[115] ibid.
[116] ibid para 68.
[117] ibid para 67.
[118] PSPP responses (n 33) para 56; Case C-62/14 *Peter Gauweiler and Others v Deutscher Bundestag* ECLI:EU:C:2015:7, Opinion of AG Cruz Villalón [231].
[119] PSPP responses (n 33) para 56; AG Opinion *Gauweiler* (n 118) [253].
[120] *Weiss* (n 27) [113].
[121] ibid [106]–[107].
[122] PSPP pleadings (n 29) paras 74–92.

certainty among private operators about exact bond purchases: the blackout period and the ability to purchase after it; issue and issuer limits, without a requirement to meet upper limits; the requirement to purchase at the most favourable market price; and limited published information on asset purchases.[123] It stated that pre-announced information on the monthly purchase volumes, expected programme duration, issue and issuer limits, and allocation of purchases according to the ECB's capital key do not undermine these safeguards. The announcement of these modalities should be understood as communication on the future monetary policy orientation (forward guidance), which reinforces the PSPP's efficiency without leading to microeconomic predictability.[124] These sections of the ECB's written responses were heavily redacted especially regarding the blackout period in the version that was publicly disclosed, making their assessment difficult.

The ECJ accepted the economic justification of the sufficiency of designed safeguards provided by the ECB and the Commission. Regarding the first requirement, the ECJ accepted that chosen safeguards ensure that private operators cannot act as intermediaries between the ECB and the Member States.[125] The Court admitted that pre-announced information could enable private operators to foresee 'significant aspects of purchases', but referred to the ECB and the Commission that this was an intended feature of the programme.[126] Hence, the ECB is not required to refrain from making prior announcements if purchases are conducted in the context of QE programme.

Regarding the second requirement, the ECB listed four safeguards to ensure Member States' incentives to follow sound budgetary policies: purchases being based on monetary policy objectives; the eligibility criteria excluding Member States with poor credit ratings (albeit only Greece was excluded); the issue and issuer limits restricting the amount of available assets; and the capital key allocation of purchases ensuring that they are made regardless of Member States' overall debt levels.[127] It also explained that the issuer limit ensures that the ECB will not become a dominant creditor of the Euro Member States and that it would not have a blocking minority in the case of debt restructuring.[128]

Additionally, the ECB replied to the BverfG's claims regarding the holding of bonds until maturity and purchasing them with negative yields. The Bank stated that holding bonds until maturity does not reduce incentives to follow sound fiscal policies, as such actions would be conducted only as long as necessary to achieve the programme's monetary targets, and the ECJ has already held in *Gauweiler* that such action is not prohibited by the Treaties.[129] The Bank also stated that the principle of market neutrality requires it to purchase bonds with both positive and negative yields. As purchasing of bonds with negative yields would result in losses for the ECB, potential losses associated with purchases should be reviewed based on the principle of proportionality instead of

[123] PSPP responses (n 33) paras 66–81.
[124] ibid paras 83–86.
[125] *Weiss* (n 27) [113]–[128].
[126] ibid [111]–[112].
[127] PSPP responses (n 33) paras 93–106.
[128] ibid para 103.
[129] PSPP responses (n 33) paras 107–13.

incentives to pursue sound fiscal policies.[130] Finally, the ECB stated that it had found no effect on the functioning of government bond markets or the formation of government bond market prices, nor detected any anomalies in bond issuance or the implementation of fiscal policies.[131]

The ECJ found the safeguards also to respect the second requirement. The Court noted that although the PSPP makes it foreseeable that the ECB will purchase member state bonds for years ahead, it may not necessarily reduce the impetus to follow sound budget policies.[132] Referring to *Gauweiler*, the Court stated that the impetus is not reduced as long as the Member States cannot rely on future purchases when determining their budget policies.[133] It accepted the ECB's argument that safeguards ensure that the Member States cannot abandon sound budgetary policy without risking their bonds being excluded from the PSPP or the ECB selling already purchased bonds.[134] As the ECJ had required in *Gauweiler* that OMT purchases cannot be used for the harmonisation of interest rates, in *Weiss* it waived this requirement for QE purchases.

The ECJ also replied to the BVerfG's question regarding holding bonds until maturity and purchasing bonds with negative yields based on the arguments of the Commission and the ECB. The ECJ stated that holding bonds until maturity does not lessen the impetus to follow sound budgetary policies, as the ECB is not obliged to purchase the bonds of a member state that has ceased to do so.[135] Regarding negative yields, it concluded that the Treaties do not forbid the ECB from purchasing them on secondary markets; purchasing them makes it harder to identify the bonds that the ECB is purchasing, and in any case negative yields reflect Member States' positive assessment in the sovereign debt markets.[136] Based on these considerations provided by the ECB and the Commission, the ECJ held that the PSPP does not either reduce the impetus to follow sound budgetary policies.

The ECJ dismissed the BverfG's question on losses, defaults and recapitalisation of central banks as inadmissible, because the question was 'at this stage' hypothetical.[137] Additionally the ECJ did not clarify the question of possible debt restructurings. It found that the maximum amount of national central banks' holdings of their governments' debt cannot be over 50 per cent by stating that 'in every case only a minority of the bonds issued by a Member State can be purchased under the PSPP'.[138] Hence, the ECJ accepted that the ECB could exceed its current 33 per cent issuer limit, but did not specify whether the ECB should refuse, abstain from or accept possible debt cuts. Hence, a more detailed judicial review of debt cuts will take place either in future preliminary rulings or if the ECB incurs losses as a result of the debt restructurings.

The acceptance of various safeguards regarding the monetary financing prohibition suggests that the ECB has significant discretion to 'balance' the objectives of

[130] ibid paras 115–20.
[131] ibid paras 124–31.
[132] *Weiss* (n 27) [131].
[133] ibid [132]; *Gauweiler* (n 27) [113].
[134] *Weiss* (n 27) [133]–[144].
[135] ibid [145]–[152].
[136] ibid [152]–[158].
[137] ibid [159]–[167].
[138] ibid [141].

Article 123 TFEU and the effectiveness of its government bond purchases, in line with the Bank's own submissions to the Court. The rulings in *Gauweiler* and *Weiss* practically diluted Article 123 TFEU, from a concrete monetary constraint within which the ECB's monetary policy objectives would be pursued to a more general objective to be considered when the ECB conducts its monetary policy.

C. Open Questions for Future Preliminary Rulings

As the ECJ accepted different safeguards based on the different policy objectives of purchase programmes, only possible future preliminary rulings will clarify how much deviation from the required safeguards the ECJ accepts between different programmes with the same policy objective.

Since the *Gauweiler* and *Weiss* judgments, the ECB has introduced two new government bond purchase programmes that diverge significantly from the elements discussed in these rulings. The TPI includes unlimited purchases of one-ten-year bonds without EFSF/ESM conditionality. The pandemic-related PEPP diverges even more from the PSPP: it contains the total amount of purchases, purchases can be conducted flexibly over time and across asset classes, the eligibility criteria have been loosened (for including Greek bonds in the programme) and national central banks can divert from the capital key allocation regarding purchases and reinvestments.[139] Most importantly, the PSPP's issue and issuer limits do not apply, which was confirmed by President Christine Lagarde that the PEPP holdings will not be consolidated with other purchase programmes.[140] No new preliminary rulings are currently pending, which has further broadened the Bank's leeway in choosing measures that it deems appropriate.

If the TPI is referred for a preliminary ruling, the ECJ needs to decide whether the loosened conditionality is still sufficient to ensure sound fiscal policies. The programme includes a significant degree of undefined and undisclosed conditionality to the EU's fiscal framework, but the ECB Governing Council judges independently whether countries comply with the fiscal rules and Next Generation EU recovery plans and whether they have excessive macro-economic imbalances or sustainable debt levels. It is unlikely that the ECJ would find the TPI to infringe the monetary financing prohibition, which in turn would increase the ECB's discretion over the Member States' fiscal policies even further and seriously threaten the separation of fiscal and monetary policies. As ING

[139] The announcement of PEPP states that although the capital key will be benchmark for purchases, 'purchases will be conducted in a flexible manner on the basis of market conditions and with a view to preventing a tightening of financing conditions that is inconsistent with countering the downward impact of the pandemic on the projected path of inflation.' European Central Bank, 'Pandemic Emergency Purchase Programme (PEPP)', at www.ecb.europa.eu/mopo/implement/pepp/html/index.en.html.

[140] Decision (EU) 2020/440 of the ECB of 24 March 2020 on a temporary pandemic emergency purchase programme (ECB/2020/17) [2020] OJ L91/1, 6: 'to the extent some self-imposed limits might hamper action that the Eurosystem is required to take in order to fulfil its mandate, the Governing Council will consider revising them to the extent necessary to make its action proportionate to the risks faced.'; C Lagarde, 'Letter from the ECB President to Ms Manon Aubry, MEP, on monetary policy' (European Central Bank, 22 December 2020) L/CL/20/315, at www.ecb.europa.eu/pub/pdf/other/ecb.mepletter201229_Aubry%7E82873a5b54.en.pdf.

Research macro analyst Carsten Brzeski concluded, while the OMT was a 'whatever-it-takes' tool, the TPI with the lighter conditions and increased discretion represents a 'whatever-we-want' instrument.[141]

As the PEPP deviates even more from the PSPP's safeguards, it is more challenging to argue that PEPP purchases do not lessen the Member States' impetus to maintain budgetary policies. First, as the Euro Member States' deficits fell after the introduction of the PSPP, the ECB was able to argue that the PSPP maintained the commitment to sound budgetary policies and structural reforms.[142] However, as the Euro area's public indebtedness increased heavily after the COVID-19 pandemic and the ECB purchased almost all pandemic-related government bonds, it is harder to argue that the PEPP did not lessen the Member States' incentives to maintain sound budgetary policies. Second, the capital key allocation ensured that purchases influence the overall financial conditions of the Euro area and are not selective. The ECB has conducted PEPP purchases mainly based on the capital key allocation, but since its interest rate hikes it has deviated somewhat from the benchmark in its reinvestment policies.[143] As higher spreads are a result of its normalisation policy and the deviation from the capital key is helping especially highly indebted countries, the ECB and (the ECJ) would need to argue that this flexibility does not meet the specific financing needs of certain Member States.

Third, the ECJ would need to clarify its stance on the question of maximum debt holdings. The limited publication of information on asset purchases makes it harder to assess the ECB's total debt holdings, but estimates suggest that national central banks have already become dominant creditors of their respective governments, as the combined PSPP and PEPP holdings exceed 40 per cent in the euro area.[144] Hence, national central banks own more than the ECB's self-imposed 33 per cent threshold and the German and Dutch central banks have even temporarily passed the 50 per cent upper limit set in *Weiss*.

If the Court were to accept that the ECB can purchase only a minority of issued government bonds under all purchase programmes, as indicated in *Weiss*, the combined PSPP and PEPP holdings restrict significantly the monetary accommodation provided by the OMT and the TPI.[145] Alternatively, the ECJ could guarantee the ECB more monetary leeway by accepting that the PEPP holdings will not be consolidated with the other purchase programmes. However, excluding one emergency measure from the legal framework of reviewing the compliance of government bond purchases with the monetary financing prohibition would seriously undermine the credibility of established case law set in *Gauweiler* and *Weiss*.

[141] C Brzeski, 'More News from the ECB Press Conference after First Rate Hike since 2011' (*ING Think*, 21 July 2022), at think.ing.com/articles/more-news-from-the-ecb-press-conference-after-first-rate-hike-since-2011.

[142] PSPP responses (n 33) paras 34, 129–31.

[143] 'The ECB used this flexibility between June and July 2022 by injecting €17 billion into Italian, Spanish, and Greek bonds while allowing its portfolio of German, French and Dutch debt to fall by €18 billion': N Asgari, 'ECB injects billions of euros into weaker eurozone debt markets' *Financial Times* (7 August 2022), at www.ft.com/content/b53f2254-9409-432a-9755-62c621e3f552.

[144] K-J Gern, N Sonnenberg and U Stolzenburg, '"whatever it takes": the ECB remains busy with crisis management' (In-Depth Analysis, Monetary Dialogue Papers, European Parliament, June 2022), at www.europarl.europa.eu/cmsdata/249535/Kiel_DEF.pdf; J von Gerich, 'Nordea's assessment of the ECB's holdings' (*X*, 8 December 2023), at twitter.com/JanVonGerich/status/1733160183071719645.

[145] K Whelan, 'The Past, Present and Future of Euro Area Monetary-Fiscal Interactions' (2022) 19 *International Economics and Economic Policy* 557.

Lastly, as the ECB has become dominant creditor of Member States, the ECJ also needs to clarify its position towards debt restructurings. The ECJ could rule in accordance with *Accorinti* and *Gauweiler* that debt restructurings infringe the monetary financing prohibition. The ECB would then be forced to block possible debt restructurings, which would seriously damage the resolution regime established after the Euro crisis. The rejection of debt restructuring could result in a chaotic default, which would also seriously harm financial stability.

IV. The Economic and Political Implications of the Interpretation of Monetary Financing

The previous section demonstrated that the ECJ relied entirely on the Commission's legal arguments and the ECB's monetary expertise in its judgments and rejected all the claims raised by the BVerfG on the monetary financing prohibition. Even though Article 67 of the ECJ's Rules of Procedure allows the Court to hear independent experts,[146] the ECJ heard only the appellants, the German authorities, the ECB, the Commission, the European Parliament and intervening governments of Member States (consisting of more southern than northern Member States) in *Gauweiler* and *Weiss*. As the Court clearly limited itself to the expertise supporting a specific institutional position towards the ECB, this section reviews the economic concepts of 'free market price formation' and 'impetus to sound budgetary policies' used in the ECJ's legal argumentation and the political implications of its reading.

First, the teleological interpretation of the monetary financing prohibition was based on the assumption that the ECB's government bond purchases must not infringe free market price formation of government bonds. However, the understanding of the free price formation used in the ECJ's preliminary rulings is very limited in an economic sense.

The ECJ clarified that purchases do not infringe the free price formation of government bonds either on the primary or secondary markets as long as market participants cannot know for certain when and what specific bonds the ECB will purchase. In *Weiss*, it established that the blackout period, the diversity of eligible bonds and limited information on purchases ensure this uncertainty among market participants. However, the primary dealer markets are highly concentrated and the operators that purchase bonds from the Member States on the primary markets are the very same actors that sell these same bonds to the ECB on the secondary markets. As the time of issuance is a crucial contractual provision, the primary dealers will know when specific bonds are issued. Additionally, they sell these same bonds to the ECB, so they will also know when the ECB makes purchases. Hence, based on their trading with the Member States on the primary markets and with the ECB on the secondary markets, primary dealers are the only market operators aside from the ECB who can really

[146] See also E Barbier de la Serre and A-L Sibony, 'Expert Evidence Before the EC Courts' (2008) 45 *Common Market Law Review* 941.

determine the blackout period under different bond purchase programmes. Hence, although the market operators cannot foresee 'for certain' which bonds the ECB will purchase, this 'designed uncertainty' does not guarantee that primary dealers could not deduce the ECB's purchasing behaviour and act as intermediaries between the ECB and Member States.

The legal argumentation falters in suggesting that the designed uncertainty based on the blackout period will guarantee free market price formation. The ECJ itself admitted that, regardless of various safeguards, the ECB's inventions may still have 'some influence on the functioning of the primary and secondary sovereign debt markets' but added, referring to Advocate General Cruz Villalón, that this influence is not decisive when reviewing the ECB's compliance with Article 123 TFEU as it reflects only the effective use of government bond purchases.[147] The ECJ's caselaw on the circumvention of Article 123 TFEU is indeed based on the very limited understanding on the functioning of government bond markets. Although the ECJ allowed national central banks to hold 50 per cent of their governments' debt in *Weiss*, the Court did not contemplate at all how the ECB becoming dominant creditor would influence the functioning of government bond markets. 'Certainty' among primary market dealers is in no way a necessary condition for the primary markets to be affected. Instead of knowing for certain which bonds the ECB will buy, the sole knowledge that the ECB will intervene provides near certainty that the bonds purchased can be sold at a reasonable price. Moreover, any perceived probability of ECB intervention on the secondary markets will influence the expectations and behaviour of market participants, and hence encourage primary market purchases – higher probability increasing purchases, and lower probability decreasing them. Although the ECB can always ensure that secondary market purchases do not have an 'equivalent' effect as primary market purchases, they will have a very similar effect that can be exploited to achieve the same goals as primary market purchases.

By focusing on the limited interpretation of the circumvention of Article 123 TFEU, the ECB has in practice the right to intervene in government debt markets based on its own judgment on what market behaviour is normal and which bond spreads fracture its monetary transmission mechanism. Hence, the continuation of free market price formation is increasingly influenced by the ECB's economic judgments about the functioning of the government bond markets and its interventions to 'protect' the functioning of the market mechanism. The ECB has still not specified a framework for differentiating 'normal' from 'abnormal' market behaviour. When ECB President Christine Lagarde was asked to specify the framework for assessing anomalies in the financial markets, she replied that the ECB reacts to the 'fragmentation' when the risk arises and that the chosen measures will be appropriate, effective, proportionate and within the ECB's mandate as requested by the ECJ, refusing to elaborate further.[148]

Second, the ECJ also stated that sufficient safeguards are needed to ensure that government bond purchases do not reduce the Member States' impetus to maintain sound fiscal policies. A closer look at the ECJ's review of safeguards reveals that the ECJ

[147] *Gauweiler* (n 27) [108]; *Weiss* (n 27) [152].

[148] M Arnold 'Christine Lagarde defends ECB plan to counter bond market panic' *Financial Times* (20 June 2022), at www.ft.com/content/fdbbc613-3ae9-4fd6-b3d7-cc68ee52ae16.

established a new reading of the assumptions of the relationship between market discipline and Member States' fiscal policies.

The Court considered the influence over the financing conditions only as a side-effect of unconventional monetary policy and ignored the fact that to the extent that purchase programmes succeed in calming the financial markets, they also ease budget constraints and hence weaken the impetus to maintain sound budgetary policies. Purchases have had significant influence over the Member States' financing conditions: the announcement of OMT alone decreased interest rates across the Euro area from 2012 onwards; PSPP purchases worth almost €3 trillion have loosened the budget constraints further; and the ECB purchased under the PEPP practically all the Euro Member States' pandemic-related government debt issuance during 2020–21. Additionally, the Member States do not pay interest on bonds that the ECB holds until their maturity, as national central banks remit their profits back to their finance ministries after covering their expenses. Although purchases benefit the Member States as long as the bonds stay on the ECB's balance sheet, the ECJ repeated the Commission's argument in *Weiss* that this influence is not decisive as the extensions of PSPP 'covered relatively short periods'.[149] Lastly, purchasing bonds with negative yields constitutes a fiscal transfer from the central bank to the Member States.

Instead of considering whether government bond purchases provide prohibited financial support for the Member States, the Court reviewed the impetus to maintain sound budgetary policies based on the predictability of the continuation of purchases. Based on *Gauweiler* and *Weiss*, the ECJ established that purchases do not reduce the impetus to maintain sound budgetary policies as long as Member States cannot rely on ECB financing. Under the new established caselaw, the ECB can easily ensure this uncertainty with the temporary nature of purchases, limiting the scope of purchases with the eligibility criteria, and underlining its ability to either halt purchases or sell already purchased bonds if it detects abuse.

However, it is unclear what 'temporary' means when the ECB has continued purchases for years and has managed to reduce only minimally the number of bonds held in its balance sheet. More importantly, as the decisive factor regarding compliance with the monetary financing prohibition was the ECB's independent decision-making on purchases, the *Gauweiler* and *Weiss* judgments significantly increased the Bank's discretion over Member States' fiscal policies. As the ECB not only judges whether government bond purchases are needed, but also whether the Member States fulfil the criteria of purchase programmes, it has considerable discretion to judge to what extent the market discipline applies to the Member States.

V. Conclusions

The independence wars over the ECB's mandate underline the political problems associated with the litigation of monetary policy. Both the BVerfG and the ECJ have faced

[149] *Weiss* (n 27) [86]–[89].

difficulties in defining the limits of monetary policy clearly, and their different interpretations have major political consequences for the EMU. If the BverfG had won the argument over government bond purchases, the ECB's unconventional measures would have been emasculated. In turn, this could have led to the break-up of the eurozone in its current form, either through crisis countries exiting the single currency or the *Bundesbank* withdrawing from the ECB's crisis measures. Justices Gertrude Lübbe-Wolf and Michael Gerhardt underlined this in their dissenting Opinions by stating that the legality of the OMT was more a political than a judicial question.[150]

The study demonstrates that when powerful EU institutions ally, the ECJ does not question them. Both the ECJ and the Commission helped the ECB to remain 'within its mandate' as the Commission provided the legal argumentation for reviewing the legality of government bond purchases and the ECJ adopted it in the case law. Instead of the classical understanding of the separation of powers, the strategic cooperation between the ECB, the Commission and the ECJ reflects a dualist model in which the Court acts as a cooperative partner with the EMU's executive branch.[151] This strategic cooperation made it possible for the ECB to transform institutionally into a 'real bee', which was necessary to save the single currency in its current form. The ECJ not only expanded the ECB's expert powers but also loosened the constraints of monetary policy. Like ECB Board member Benoît Cœuré concluded after *Weiss*:

> The limits are there to guard against monetary financing and to protect the price discovery process. On the other hand, the ECJ has also affirmed the principle that we should have broad discretion in designing our instruments. The limits are ours.[152]

To reconcile the ECB's government bond purchases with the prohibition on monetary financing, the ECJ needed to establish a framework for reviewing their legality that simply ignores the actual functioning of government bond markets, the indirect financing of Member States and broader economic steering effects. Although the Bank, the Court and the Commission all emphasised the continuity of the EMU's economic constitution, the teleological interpretation of Article 123 TFEU essentially changed the background assumptions of the EMU's economic constitution, most importantly the free market price formation and the market discipline. However, a closer analysis of the safeguards suggests that Court's understanding of sovereign debt markets is very limited at best. Additionally, established case law left many unresolved questions regarding the deviation of safeguards, the debt restructurings and the ECB's overall ability to conduct government bond purchases.

In addition to the credibility problems of the established case law in *Gauweiler* and *Weiss*, the analysis demonstrates the flexibility of the EMU's economic constitution. The Commission's and the Court's ability to transform the prohibition on monetary financing from a constraint into a more general policy objective suggests that Article 123 TFEU has not been as restrictive as it had previously been interpreted,

[150] OMT reference (n 15) Abweichende Meinung der Richterin Lübbe-Wolff und Abweichende Meinung des Richters Gerhardt.

[151] P Leino-Sandberg, *The Politics of Legal Expertise in EU Policy-Making* (Cambridge University Press, 2021).

[152] Jones (n 11).

especially in Germany. It only forbids the ECB from purchasing government bond purchases on the primary markets or offering overdraft and credit facilities to EU institutions or Member States, but does not include any precise definition of monetary financing. Although there have been attempts to prohibit the ECB from financing Euro Member States, it has not been possible to ban the open market operations that modern central banks have used throughout their existence and especially after the Global Financial Crisis and the COVID-19 pandemic. The fact that the ECB has been practically allowed to introduce crisis measures that indirectly finances the Member States seriously questions the meaning of Article 123 TFEU and the functioning of the EMU's economic constitutions.

The ECJ's difficulties in balancing the ECB's operational independence and respecting the principles of the EMU's economic constitution demonstrates more general problems of rule-based economic governance. The Court's ability to find government bond purchases to fall within the area of monetary policy regardless of their economic steering effects suggests that the strict separation of economic and monetary policy cannot be credibly maintained. Not only do government bond purchases have significant economic influence over financing conditions, redistribution and financial stability, but the legality of purchases was fundamentally based on the ECB's assessment of the normal functioning of government bond markets and the sustainability of Member States' fiscal policies. Hence, the ECJ significantly allowed the ECB to intervene in the sovereign debt markets as well as to decide how much market discipline affects the financing conditions of the Member States. Although this must have been necessary to 'preserve the euro', it is highly problematic from the viewpoint of the separation of powers, as no democratic or constitutional processes were involved in the legislative or executive branches to expand the ECB's independence or modify the EMU's economic constitution.

Considering the political integration of the EMU, it is questionable whether it is sufficient to leave the leading expert role to the ECB and the Commission, both of which pursue the same institutional agenda in favour of integration. As the ECB, the Commission and the ECJ share the same principles, there is a high risk that, without reviewing dissenting opinions, EMU integration is happening through the back door with the ECB's privileged understanding of monetary issues. Without political approval and commitment, such integration risks leading to a populist backlash.

When deciding on future actions, the Bank still needs to consider a possible German veto on its monetary decision-making as the BVerfG can again mandate that the *Bundestag* decide on the *Bundesbank*'s participation in the ECB's unconventional policies. Additionally, the BVerfG's extraordinary claims that not only the ECB but also the ECJ had acted ultra vires might also escalate independence wars on other fronts, for example by inspiring more open attacks against the EU's legal order in other EU countries. The ECJ's difficulties in balancing the efficiency of the ECB's actions and the principle of separation of powers suggest that the ECB's rules will need to be reviewed and reformed to allow the ECB to act like other modern central banks that do not need to rely on legal hocus pocus for their most significant actions.

10

Constitutional Courts as Part of the Separation of Powers' Arrangement in the Member States: From the Euro Crisis to the NGEU

CRISTINA FASONE

I. Introduction

Seventy years after the process of EU integration was set in motion, there is little doubt of the long-term effects it has produced on national constitutional bodies. The executive branch is 'structurally overreaching' and 'Parliaments are weakened'.[1] This exposes that the idea of separation of powers 'in a tripartite government is designed for domestic action' and that supranational policies foster 'the adaptation of domestic structures'.[2]

This conclusion is further strengthened when looking at the specific domain of European economic governance, a field where the EU is formally competent to coordinate national economic policies and that comprises measures related to taxation, government spending, income redistribution and the job market.[3] Yet, 'normalisation' of crisis management, technocratisation, informalisation, and various forms of 'fuzziness' in the creative use of legal tools[4] have significantly limited the margin of manoeuvre of domestic legislatures both in terms of timing and discretion of their fiscal choices – in spite of the traditional motto 'no taxation without representation!'.[5]

Since 2010, with the inception of the Euro crisis, the resort to legal solutions outside the EU Treaties and the bureaucratisation of domestic budgetary procedures under the European Semester, the parliamentary control of the economic governance has

[1] Eckes, Leino-Sandberg and Ghavanini, ch 1 in this volume.

[2] C Möllers, 'Separation of Powers' in R Masterman and R Schütze (eds), *The Cambridge Companion to Comparative Constitutional Law* (Cambridge University Press, 2019) 250.

[3] Monetary policy, instead, remains out of the scope of this chapter, but see Ronkainen, ch 9 in this volume.

[4] Eckes, Leino-Sandberg and Ghavanini (n 1).

[5] V Ruiz Almendral, 'The Spanish Legal Framework for Curbing the Public Debt and the Deficit' (2013) 9 *European Constitutional Law Review* 189.

faced unprecedented challenges.[6] In systems of government based on the confidence relationship – in place in all EU Member States but Cyprus – a 'close cooperation between government and parliamentary majority is indeed necessary to facilitate the realization of the democratic will'.[7] Particularly in the budgetary domain, the national legislative and the executive authorities appear as merged in several instances to the advantage of executive dominance and against the classical tripartite model of separation of power.[8] This leads me to the guiding question of this chapter: is adjudication in front of constitutional courts an effective tool to redress parliamentary marginalisation in the economic governance? What approach has been followed by these courts and with which consequences?

In the aftermath of the Euro crisis and in the following 10 years of enforcement of economic governance reforms, constitutional courts have been faced with a number of disputes on the use and misuse of budgetary powers by parliaments and governments.[9] Pragmatism seems to have informed the attitude of the courts on these cases[10] while the constitutional courts have given priority to the protection of parliamentary prerogatives (against the executive) on budgetary decisions only on very few occasions.[11]

Following a 'relational conception of separation of powers which emphasizes interaction, collaboration, and conflict between branches', where 'conflicts can have a distinct value in democratic will-formation',[12] the assessment of the relevant case law reveals a limited capacity of constitutional courts to cope with executive dominance in the design and implementation of the economic governance reforms. Overall, there has been little constitutional collaboration by courts with parliaments to safeguard their prerogatives.

The constitutional case law in the aftermath of the Euro crisis reforms will be compared to the situation following the COVID-19 pandemic. The NGEU and the implementation of the Recovery and Resilience Facility (RRF)[13] provide a new test bench to explore the triangular relationship between parliaments, governments and constitutional courts on budgetary decisions as legislatures have been further sidelined in the governance of these instruments.[14]

This chapter focuses on constitutional courts specifically, and it does so by looking at their case law in Southern EU Member States (France, Italy, Portugal and Spain), given the position of these countries during the Euro crisis and the decline they have

[6] See M Moschella, 'When Some Are More Equal than Others: National Parliaments and Intergovernmental Bailout Negotiations in the Eurozone' (2017) 52 *Government and Opposition* 239.

[7] C Möllers, *The Three Branches: A Comparative Model of Separation of Powers* (Oxford University Press, 2013) 113.

[8] Eckes, Leino-Sandberg and Ghavanini (n 1).

[9] M Markakis, *Accountability in the Economic and Monetary Union: Foundations, Policy, and Governance* (Oxford University Press, 2020) ch 6.

[10] K Kombos, 'Constitutional Review and the Economic Crisis: In the Courts We Trust? – Part Two' (2019) 25 *European Public Law* 229.

[11] C Fasone, 'Do Constitutional Courts care about Parliaments in the Euro-crisis? On the precedence of the "identity constitutional review"' (2018) 10 *Italian Journal of Public Law* 2, 352.

[12] Eckes, Leino-Sandberg and Ghavanini (n 1).

[13] Regulation (EU) 2021/241 of the European Parliament and of the Council of 12 February 2021 establishing the Recovery and Resilience Facility [2021] OJ L57/17.

[14] P Leino-Sandberg and T Raunio, 'From Bad to Worse: The Continuous Dilemma Facing Parliaments in European Economic and Fiscal Governance' (2023) *Government and Opposition*, first view, 1.

experienced in democratic governance.[15] This allows us to control for cross-country variation in the comparative analysis. The analysis covers countries under financial assistance (Portugal and Spain), financial support only by the European Central Bank (Italy), and (just) under excessive deficit procedure (France), and takes into account the differences between the respective constitutional courts. Moreover, the four countries are among the most advanced in the implementation of the national recovery and resilience plans (NRRPs). Some occasional references will be made to the German Federal Constitutional Court (GFCC)'s case law as it has become a traditional benchmark in this field.[16]

First, the chapter explains why constitutional courts are the object of comparison when assessing parliamentary powers in the economic governance and constitutional adjudication of eminently political-democratic procedures such as those on the budget (section II). Next, the chapter refers to 'collaborative constitutionalism'[17] as a useful benchmark against which separation of powers in economic governance matters can be assessed (section III). Then, the analysis of the most significant and representative judgments of the French, Italian, Portuguese and Spanish Constitutional Courts on Euro crisis measures points to similarities and differences (section IV). Following that, the chapter deals with the NGEU and the NRRPs' first implementation in the four countries, which has proved to be equally problematic from the perspective of parliamentary deliberation (section V). Finally, the chapter concludes on the questionable lack of effective remedy to parliamentary marginalisation offered by constitutional courts as a critical issue for today's constitutional democracy in the EU (section VI).

II. Constitutional Courts as the Guardians of Democratic Budgetary Procedures?

The process of European integration has been generally regarded as strengthening domestic (and European) courts, which have managed to empower themselves, notably due to the preliminary reference procedure.[18]

However, such a conclusion is less straightforward for the 'special courts' set up to perform constitutional adjudication as their main task, following the Kelsenian model of judicial review. When the process of integration started, the constitutional courts of the founding Member States, where established, were brand new institutions and needed to build an authoritative reputation as interpreters of their Constitutions. This has also been the case for the new countries joining the then European Community and equipped with a constitutional court after a democratic transition. Possibly, the last hurdle these courts were willing to overcome during their institutionalisation process

[15] M Matthijs, 'Integration at what price? The erosion of national democracy in the Euro Periphery' (2017) 52 *Government and Opposition* 266.

[16] N de Boer, *Judging European Democracy. The Role and Legitimacy of National Constitutional Courts in the EU* (Oxford University Press, 2023) and now ch 15 in this volume.

[17] A Kavanagh, *The Collaborative Constitution* (Cambridge University Press, 2023).

[18] JHH Weiler, 'The Transformation of Europe' (1991) 100 *The Yale Law Journal* 2403.

was to engage with another body of law, namely EU law, that could interfere with the alleged supremacy of the Constitution. In the meantime, the *Simmenthal* doctrine marginalised constitutional courts in supranational litigation.[19]

The 'specialty' of constitutional courts has been neglected in the European system, which serves to explain why at least some of them have been rather reticent in fulfilling their 'European mandate'.[20] As Jan Komarek puts it, 'The ECJ's doctrine, based on an orthodox understanding of the primacy of EU law, fails to acknowledge the difference between constitutional and ordinary national courts implementing the distinction between ordinary and constitutional legality'.[21] Unlike other tribunals, 'specialized constitutional courts maybe understood best as hybrid entities that are neither appropriately described as courts nor as purely political actors'.[22] In contrast with ordinary and supreme courts, constitutional courts entertain a special relationship with parliaments. First, the appointment procedure of constitutional courts' judges differs from that of the other courts. The Parliament is always involved either in the selection and election of a share of constitutional court's members (eg in France, Italy and Spain) or in the appointment of the whole Court (eg in Germany and in Portugal). Second, parliamentary minorities are usually entitled to bring challenges before constitutional courts. This is the case in France, Portugal and Spain, although not in Italy. Hence, a direct link is established between constitutional adjudication by these courts and parliaments, whenever a minority wants to overturn the legislative output endorsed by the majority. Third, the special relationship between constitutional courts and parliaments is also reflected in the fine-tuning of the effects of the declarations of unconstitutionality by constitutional courts.

Indeed, a declaration of unconstitutionality leads to the annulment of the unconstitutional norm with retroactive and *erga omnes* effects. Thus, a decision of a constitutional court sanctioning a violation of the Constitution is deemed to produce a sort of 'earthquake' in the legal and – depending on the financial implications of the decision – economic system, unless the court itself modulates the temporal effects of its judgments. The adjustment of the temporal effects of the unconstitutionality is provided for by the Portuguese Constitution[23] and was indeed used in some judgments during the Euro crisis to allow the Parliament to amend the relevant legislation and to confine the financial implications of the case law.

The Spanish Constitutional Court has since 1989 reinterpreted its powers so as to grant itself the opportunity to declare a norm unconstitutional *ex nunc*, in order to not affect pre-existing legal positions and, wherever possible, not to put the Parliament in the difficult position to regulate the fiscal consequences of the Court's intervention.[24]

[19] M Dani, 'National Constitutional Courts in supranational litigation: A contextual analysis' (2017) 23 *European Law Journal* 212.

[20] See M Claes, *The National Courts' Mandate in the European Constitution* (Hart, 2006).

[21] J Komárek, 'National constitutional courts in the European constitutional democracy' (2014) 12 *International Journal of Constitutional Law* 525. See also D Lustig and JHH Weiler, 'Judicial review in the contemporary world – Retrospective and prospective' (2018) 16 *International Journal of Constitutional Law* 319.

[22] Möllers (n 7) 141.

[23] Art 282 Portuguese Constitution.

[24] Spanish Constitutional Court, judgment 45/1989, 2 March 1989.

In France, with the introduction of the ex post constitutional review of legislation in 2008, the effects of a declaration of unconstitutionality are produced just for the future. In order to apply the effects of the relevant judgment at least to the parties in the main proceeding, the *Conseil constitutionnel* can exceptionally attach some limited retroactive effects to its decision.[25] Complaints relating to budgetary procedures, however, are filed almost exclusively under the *ex ante* review mechanism whereby the unconstitutional provision is prevented from entering into force.

Finally, in Italy, retroactivity of the declaration of unconstitutionality has always been the rule.[26] Since 2015 the Constitutional Court has admitted that the effects of its decisions of unconstitutionality can have only *pro futuro* effects.[27] However, this applies under specific conditions, notably the duty to limit the fiscal implication of the case law and the need to respect the proportionality principle.

As a matter of deference to the parliaments, constitutional courts often try to avoid issuing a declaration of unconstitutionality. To this end, they may interpret the admissibility requirements very strictly, adopt an interpretation in conformity with the Constitution, or include specific warnings directed at the parliament in their judgments, essentially requesting the parliament to amend what is considered, although not declared, unconstitutional.

When constitutional courts are asked to act as guardians of budgetary procedures, they typically find themselves in an uncomfortable position. On the one hand, they are called to engage with the procedural guarantees of democracy, which may be considered to lie at the core of separation of powers. On the other hand, due to their design and powers, constitutional courts are better at protecting individual rights than at improving the legislative process.[28] The latter fulfils a general interest for the political community so that representative democracy and the legislative–executive relationship work properly.

Typically, the justification for constitutional review of democratic procedures is very context-dependent and is affected by the status of minorities and opposition within and outside Parliament and on the degree of the majoritarian imprinting shaping the decision-making.[29] Yet, when entering fields with a high level of saliency and politicisation like that of budgetary politics, the risk for constitutional courts is either that of being accused of exceeding their competence if challenging the discretionary choice of budgetary authorities or, on the opposite end, doing too little to address problems of legislative–executive imbalance.

At the one end of the scale, representing courts keen to replace the vacuum left by political institutions, is the case of legislative omissions whereby the Constitution sets specific legal requirements to be fulfilled to protect civil or social rights, but the

[25] See the comparative analysis provided by P Popelier et al (eds), *The Effects of Judicial Decisions in Time* (Intersentia, 2013).

[26] Art 136 Italian Constitution.

[27] Italian Constitutional Court, judgment no 10/2015, 9 February 2015. See P Faraguna, 'The Economic Crisis as a Threat to the Stability of Law. Recent Developments in the Case Law of the Italian Constitutional Court' (2016) 8 *Hague Journal on the Rule of Law* 249.

[28] Möllers (n 7) 129.

[29] See, famously, JH Ely, *Democracy and Distrust* (Harvard University Press, 1980) on the theory of representation reinforcement for minorities in the US.

parliament does not act. If the parliament fails on this duty, constitutional courts are required to intervene. In these circumstances, it has been argued that when such an omission by the parliament is found unconstitutional, 'the constitutional court effectively assumes the right of legislative initiative',[30] thus going as far as taking up a role that is normally fulfilled by democratic representative actors.

At the other end of the scale, where constitutional courts side-step their role to correct the malfunctioning of budgetary procedures, especially when the parliament is sidelined, the difficulty for these courts in EU Member States also lies in making sure that EU law (and international law enforced by EU institutions) is complied with. This requires that the economic governance rules set, for example, in the rescue programmes, in the Stability and Growth Pact, and in the NRRPs in agreement with the Commission, are duly enforced. In this context, notwithstanding the limitations of parliamentary prerogatives ascertained, the deferential approach by a constitutional court may be triggered by the will not to incur in a violation of the supranational standards – be it the country-specific recommendations of the European Semester or the balanced budget clause or strict conditionality. Part of the problem also lies in the changing landscape of legal instruments produced by the EU, many of which are not formally binding. This creates uncertainty as to what the parliament is asked to do and on the treatment of these sources of law in the domestic judicial review.

All in all, the adjudication of Euro crisis measures by constitutional courts has been met with scepticism in the literature due to the nature of the law reviewed[31] and for the pragmatic[32] and erratic approach the courts have followed.[33] Daniel Kelemen has harshly criticised the judicialisation of EU austerity measures in the Member States. In his view, this has prompted more policy controversy and interinstitutional conflict,[34] and such review triggered a populist backlash against constitutional courts.[35]

However, the rise of tensions between constitutional courts and representative institutions is not necessarily bad per se. It may, for example, have merit when the parliamentary majority remains inactive following the governmental diktat and relinquishes its responsibility toward the people.

> When Constitutional Courts constrain the majoritarian political process by protecting the right of the political opposition inside or outside the formal political process, they may *even politicize the political process* meaning that they open up the space of political alternatives and political discourse.[36]

[30] Möllers (n 7) 138.

[31] See eg I Pernice, 'Domestic Courts, Constitutional Constraints and European Democracy: What Solution for the Crisis?' in M Adams, F Fabbrini and P Larouche (eds), *The Constitutionalization of European Budgetary Constraints* (Hart, 2014); S Bardutzky and E Fahey, 'Constitutional Courts, Preliminary Rulings and the "New Form of Law": The Adjudication of the European Stability Mechanism' (2015) 16 *German Law Journal* 1771.

[32] Kombos (n 10) 229.

[33] C Fasone, 'Constitutional Courts facing the Euro crisis: Italy, Portugal, and Spain in comparative perspective' (2014) 25 *EUI Working Paper MWP*.

[34] RD Kelemen, 'Commitment for Cowards. Why the Judicialization of Austerity is Bad Policy and Even Worse Politics' in T Ginsburg, MD Rosen and G Vanberg (eds), *Constitutions in Times of Financial Crisis* (Cambridge University Press, 2019) 146.

[35] ibid.

[36] Möllers (n 7) 141–42.

III. The Benchmark of 'Collaborative Constitutionalism'

Viewing separation of powers in a relational perspective (see section I) implies considering the interdependence between the branches of government when fulfilling their legislative and adjudicatory functions, for both parliaments and constitutional courts. It requires that constitutional adjudication of budgetary procedures remain respectful of representative democracy.[37]

This is also the underlying assumption of Aileen Kavanagh's notion of 'collaborative constitutionalism' as '"coordinated institutional effort between branches of government" in the service of good government'.[38] A well-functioning collaborative Constitution needs '"mutual self-restraint" and "mutual support"[39] as much as a "healthy opposition" and creative constitutional tensions between branches of government, precisely so that they can hold each other to account'.[40] If contestation, correction and competition are a central part of a collaborative constitution in the making,[41] the rise of fiercely antagonistic dynamics should remain exceptional, in order to avoid a democratic decay. And, in principle, constitutional courts have several tools at their disposal to build 'constructive criticism',[42] balancing self-restraint and mutual support to legislatures against their displacement from the new economic governance procedures.

Moving on from the normative ideal to the practice, however, reveals how complex it is to enforce the model of collaborative constitution when the rate of constitutional conflicts escalates. As clearly illustrated by Nik de Boer in chapter fifteen of this volume, the GFCC's case law on the new economic governance measures has been regarded as a benchmark, given the number of constitutional complaints received and the arguments built in relation to the budgetary authority of the *Bundestag*. The GFCC has stood as a protector of the budgetary powers of the *Bundestag* in a series of cases decided since 2010 where the democratic principle has been connected to the overall budgetary responsibility of Parliament in the face of the attempt of the Government to marginalise the legislative branch. The GFCC has followed an interpretation in conformity with the Basic Law on the EU and international Euro crisis measures. It has not hesitated to declare domestic acts of implementation unconstitutional, where information rights of the Parliament have been disregarded or the transparency regime of the parliamentary body involved has failed to meet certain standards.[43] At times a too-paternalistic stance towards the Parliament has been detected,[44] protecting the *Bundestag* against itself

[37] D Kyritsis, 'Constitutional Review in a Representative Democracy' (2012) 32 *Oxford Journal of Legal Studies* 297.

[38] A Kavanagh, 'The Constitutional Separation of Powers' in D Dyzenhaus and M Thorburn (eds), *Philosophical Foundations of Constitutional Law* (Oxford University Press, 2016) 234 ff.

[39] For these two concepts, Kavanagh (n 17) 98 ff.

[40] ibid 107. See also E Carolan, *The New Separation of Powers. A Theory for the Modern State* (Oxford University Press, 2009) 186–87, who speaks of 'sceptical cooperation' between branches.

[41] Kavanagh (n 17) 106. On the value of correction, in particular by constitutional courts vis-à-vis the domestic impact of supranational law, see Dani (n 19) 189.

[42] Kavanagh (n 17) 107.

[43] De Boer, ch 15 in this volume.

[44] Dissenting opinion Lübbe-Wolff, GFCC, Case 2 BvR 2728/13 et al OMT, order of 14 January 2014, para 12.

and its alleged passivity. This is the case when the GFCC contemplated the prospect of unconstitutionality by legislative omission.[45]

Even where the Court did not find evidence of unconstitutionality, in 2014 it did not forget to recall its warning against the self-marginalisation of the *Bundestag* in the budgetary process and the risk of imprecise budgetary authorisations to other entities:

> Art. 38 sec. 1 GG is violated in particular if the German *Bundestag* relinquishes its budgetary responsibility with the effect that it or a future *Bundestag* can no longer exercise the right to decide on the budget on its own (BVerfGE 129, 124 <177>; 132, 195 <239>, n. 106). Deciding on public revenue and public expenditure is a fundamental part of the ability of a constitutional state to democratically shape itself (cf. BVerfGE 123, 267 <359>; 132, 195 <239>, n. 106). The German *Bundestag* must therefore make decisions on revenue and expenditure with responsibility to the people (para 161).[46]

IV. The Place of Parliaments in the Constitutional Adjudication of the Economic Governance Measures Following the Euro Crisis

The dissensus against the reforms triggered by the EU's new economic governance have been channelled before constitutional courts in France, Italy, Portugal and Spain. The contention has been primarily directed at national austerity measures adopted to protect the principle of balanced budget, as required by the Fiscal Compact, and to implement country-specific recommendations (mostly in France and Italy) as well as the rescue packages according to Memoranda of Understanding negotiated by the Portuguese and the Spanish Governments in exchange for financial assistance.[47]

The cases have usually been solved by constitutional courts in line with their pre-crisis decisions. Concerns for the powers of national parliaments in the crisis have rarely surfaced in the judgments of these courts, even when a reference to them was made in the constitutional challenge or complaint. Is this a sign of a problem with separation of powers and a lack of commitment to a collaborative constitutional model by courts?

A. The Self-restraint of the French and Spanish Constitutional Courts

Both the French *Conseil Constitutionnel* and the Spanish Constitutional Tribunal have shown an evident strategy of self-restraint, directly or indirectly endorsing the political

[45] On this point, see in detail M Wendel, 'Exceeding Judicial Competence in the Name of Democracy: The German Federal Constitutional Court's OMT Reference' (2014) 10 *European Constitutional Law Review* 281.

[46] German Constitutional Tribunal, Second Senate, BVerfG, 2 BvR 1390/12, 18 March 2014, confirming the validity of the EU Council decision of 2011 to amend Art 136 TFEU, of the ESM Treaty, of the TSCG, and of their national acts of implementation.

[47] Memorandum of Understanding on specific economic policy conditionality for Portugal, 17 May 2011; Memorandum of Understanding on financial-sector policy conditionality for Spain, 20 July 2012.

directions set by the Government and regardless of the protection of the value of parliamentary deliberation.

During the Euro crisis, the *Conseil constitutionnel* did not intentionally concur to undermine the budgetary authority of the Parliament, but it certainly did not struggle to protect parliamentary powers either. Its decisions on the domestic measures implementing the reform of the economic governance appear much more oriented to preserve the autonomy and the political discretion of the government than to protect parliamentary budgetary powers.[48]

In continuity with the pre-crisis case law, the principle of budgetary sincerity has been constantly used by the *Conseil* as the standard of review when judging fiscal measures. The concept appeared for the first time in France in the constitutional case law in 2000. It was codified one year later in the *loi organique relative aux lois de finances* (LOLF)[49] and through the obligation to have a reliable budget.[50]

In its pre-crisis case law, the *Conseil* related the principle of sincerity to the quality of parliamentary scrutiny carried out on the law under review; for example, the sincerity of the budgetary measure at stake depends on whether the Parliament, also through its committees, is promptly informed by the Government about the budgetary measures to be adopted and is able to control them.[51] Yet, this condition has not been ascertained in the post-crisis scenario. Instead, in the 2012 judgment dealing with the *Loi organique relative à la programmation et à la gouvernance des finances publiques*, the *Conseil* connected the positive evaluation of the measures by the *Haut Conseil des finances publiques* with the proper enforcement of the principle of budgetary sincerity.[52]

However, although parliamentary minorities have repeatedly lamented the Government's lack of compliance with the assessment of the *Haut Conseil* before the *Conseil Constitutionnel*, according to Article 61 of the Constitution, these cases have never succeeded.[53]

On 13 July 2012, the new President of the French Republic, François Hollande, requested the *Conseil Constitutionnel* to decide on whether the authorisation to the ratification of the Fiscal Compact had to be preceded by a constitutional reform. The Court's reasoning regarding the consequences for parliamentary powers remained very superficial. The *Conseil* considered the constitutionalisation of the balanced budget clause unnecessary and consequently its inclusion in an organic law sufficient.[54]

[48] As Stone Sweet points out, only in a few – though significant occasions – the Constitutional Council ruled against legislation implementing governmental programmes. See A Stone Sweet, *The Birth of Judicial Politics in France. The Constitutional Council in Comparative Perspective* (Oxford University Press, 1992) 140–91.

[49] An organic law in France is a law whose adoption is prescribed by the Constitution to regulate the organisation and functioning of public powers, is passed by absolute majority in Parliament and is subject to the mandatory *ex ante* review of the *Conseil*.

[50] French *Conseil Constitutionnel*, Décision n° 2000-441 DC du 28 décembre 2000. As the *Conseil* affirmed, 'la sincérité se caractérise par l'absence d'intention de fausser les grandes lignes de cet équilibre [financier]; … la sincérité s'entend comme imposant l'exactitude des comptes'. See French *Conseil Constitutionnel*, Décision n° 2005-519 DC du 29 July 2005.

[51] French *Conseil Constitutionnel*, Décisions n° 2001-453 DC du 18 décembre 2001 and n° 2001-456 DC du 27 décembre 2001.

[52] French *Conseil Constitutionnel*, Décision n° 2012-658 DC du 13 décembre 2012.

[53] See French *Conseil Constitutionnel*, Décision n° 2013-682 DC du 19 décembre 2013; Décisions n° 2014-698 DC and 2014-699 DC du 6 août 2014; Décision n° 2014-707 DC du 29 décembre 2014.

[54] French *Conseil Constitutionnel*, Décision n° 2012-653 du 9 août 2012.

It briefly touched upon the protection of the budgetary autonomy of the Parliament affirming that the implementation of the Fiscal Compact could not be fulfilled in a way that encroached upon the prerogatives of this institution without further specifications. In support of the idea that the Fiscal Compact did not violate parliamentary powers, the Court cited Article 3.2 of this Treaty, which provides that the correction mechanism cannot breach the prerogatives of the national parliaments. However, this provision appears to be merely programmatic.[55] Furthermore, in the subsequent judgment on the organic law on the Programming and Governance of Public Finances,[56] for the implementation of the Fiscal Compact, the *Conseil Constitutionnel* clearly stated that the new law did not encroach upon parliamentary prerogatives in budgetary matters.[57]

In Spain, most constitutional challenges on budgetary and fiscal measures, brought by means of a preliminary reference of constitutionality or by the Autonomous Communities, were declared inadmissible by the Constitutional Court in the aftermath of the Euro crisis.[58] The Court is known to suffer from a backlog of cases despite the reform of the individual complaints in 2007. It is also very cautious in striking down parliamentary legislation. Between two and nine years usually elapsed from passing a piece of legislation to a judgment on its merits. So, judicial deference, rather than being pursued in an attempt to protect the legislative discretion of the Parliament, is often dictated by the need to protect legitimate expectations deriving from the legal status and positions consolidated years before, since the legislation entered into force.[59]

This very approach was confirmed when the Spanish Constitutional Court declared the Budget for 2009 partially unconstitutional. This was almost five years after a constitutional challenge by a parliamentary minority was filed. The Court clarified that the declaration of unconstitutionality did not entail retroactive effects upon already established legal situations, ie, those in which a final judgment had been delivered or those in which the administrative situation had been settled.[60]

Nevertheless, at least when dealing with decree-laws, ie, measures adopted by the executive to be converted into legislation by the Parliament, frequently used to implement austerity reforms prompted by the EU, the Constitutional Court did not defend the position of the Parliament and indirectly endorsed that of the Government.[61] According to Article 86 of the Spanish Constitution, a decree-law cannot 'affect the legal system of the basic State institutions, the rights, duties and freedoms of the

[55] ibid [25].

[56] *Loi organique n° 2012-1403 du 17 décembre 2012 relative à la programmation et à la gouvernance des finances publiques.*

[57] French *Conseil Constitutionnel*, Décision n° 2012-658 DC du 13 Décember 2012 [12].

[58] According to Art 37.1 of the Organic Law on the Constitutional Tribunal (LOTC), a reference is inadmissible when it does not meet the procedural requirements provided by law (eg the nature of the body that makes the reference, how the order of reference is drafted, etc) or when the challenged violation of the Constitution is patently non-grounded.

[59] LM Díez-Picazo, 'Introducción a la Mesa 2: Tribunal Constitucional y derechos fundamentales' in P Pérez Tremps (ed), *La reforma del Tribunal constitucional*. Actas del V congreso de la asociación de constitucionalistas de España (Tirant lo Blanch, 2007) 507.

[60] Spanish Constitutional Court, judgment 206/2013 [3](h) and (j).

[61] See L Díez Sanchez, 'Spain: Dealing with the Economic Emergency through Constitutional Reform and Limited Parliamentary Intervention' in T Beukers, B de Witte and C Kilpatrick (eds), *Constitutional Change Through Euro Crisis Law* (Cambridge University Press, 2017) 199.

citizens contained in Part 1, the system of Autonomous Communities, or the general electoral law.' A preliminary reference of constitutionality reached the Court on Decree-law no 8/2010, which reduced public salaries in violation of an existing collective agreement and of the right to collective bargaining in connection with the right to freely join a trade union (Article 8.1 Spanish Constitution).[62] The Court declared the preliminary reference inadmissible on procedural grounds and did not consider the question of the illegitimate use of decree-laws by the Government when implementing measures prompted by the reform of the EU economic governance in this or subsequent cases.[63]

By the same token, an order of inadmissibility was issued by the Court upon a referral by parliamentary minorities that contested the procedure chosen in 2011 to amend the Constitution, revising its Article 135, with a view to introduce the balanced budget clause. The negotiation of the Fiscal Compact was ongoing at the time, but the constitutionalisation of the clause was required in exchange for financial support by the ECB.[64]

The constitutional amendment procedure raised many concerns as for the respect of the constitutional prerogatives of the Parliament due to the shortened and urgency procedure followed and to the tight timeline.[65] The overall majority of the two Chambers agreed on the reform, with the support of the socialist government and the main opposition party, *Partido Popular*. Some MPs from the minority group of *Esquerra Republicana-Izquierda Unida-Iniciativa Per Catalunya Verds* were unable to reach the quorum of one-tenth of MPs to hold a constitutional referendum. They filed a complaint before the Spanish *Tribunal constitucional* on procedural grounds that was declared inadmissible.[66] The case is interesting because it illustrates a separation powers dynamic that is fairly frequent in Spain, as well as in France. In this dynamic, the parliamentary majority sides with the Government in supporting the reform under review, while minority groups in Parliament challenge the violation of parliamentary prerogatives.

Judgment n 119/2014 explicitly emphasised the discretion of the Parliament when upholding the validity of the labour reform contested, which was referred to both in the Memorandum of Understanding and in the EU country-specific recommendations. The Constitutional Court confirmed its previous case law and stated that the Spanish Constitution – Article 37 – does not foresee a specific model of collective bargaining and thus the Parliament enjoys a wide discretion on how to regulate it. The dismissal of the case confirms that the Court has not departed from its deferential approach to representative institutions, as the legislature here strictly followed the input of the Government in a collaborative effort. The Court justified its decision by interpretating the contested reform in conformity with the Constitution and referring to the significant powers of Parliament in this field.

Thus, the Spanish constitutional case law examined has not aimed to protect or strengthen parliamentary powers directly and specifically. Yet, it has had the effect

[62] See, respectively, Arts 37 and 28.1 of the Spanish Constitution.

[63] See Spanish Constitutional Court, order 85/2011.

[64] See the exchange of letters on 5–6 August 2011 between the then President of the ECB Trichet and the President of the Spanish Government Zapatero, at www.ecb.europa.eu/ecb/access_to_documents/document/correspondence/shared/data/ecb.dr.cor20110806Zapatero_reply.en.pdf.

[65] See F Balaguer Callejón, 'Presentación' (2011) 8 *Revista de derecho constitucional europeo* 16.

[66] See order 9/2012, para 152.

of preserving legislative discretion in general, in particular the choice made by the Government, with the endorsement of the parliamentary majority. To this end, the Court relied on declarations of inadmissibility and interpretations in conformity with the Constitution. The position of the Spanish Constitutional Court, therefore, stands somewhat halfway between self-restraint and mutual support for the legislature according to the scheme of the collaborative Constitution.

B. The Italian Constitutional Court's Relationship with the Parliament, between 'Constructive Criticism' and Correction

The Italian Constitutional Court's case law in the aftermath of the Euro crisis mainly dealt with measures implementing EU country-specific recommendations. Its relations with the legislature oscillated between 'constructive criticism' to correction of the legislature's position when legislation was declared unconstitutional.

At least since the 1990s, when the country went through a serious financial crisis, the Italian Court paid much attention to the financial sustainability of its decisions, adopting a high level of self-restraint.[67] Like in Spain, the balanced budget clause was constitutionalised in 2012, anticipating the requirements of the Fiscal Compact.[68] Its constitutionalisation also featured among the conditions posed for financial support by the ECB. Since the entry into force of the constitutional reform of 2012, and in spite of the fact that the balanced budget clause has only been in operation since January 2014, the Constitutional Court has started to refer more often to the compelling interest in having a balanced budget and sound public accounts. Occasionally, the Court annulled legislation on this ground.

The actual need for the Court to combine the application of the balanced budget clause, enshrined in new Article 81.1 of the Italian Constitution, with other constitutional principles, notably equality and the independence and autonomy of the judiciary,[69] has led the Court to decisions that have not always appeared very consistent with one another.[70] For instance, provisions of decree-laws adopted during the Euro crisis under Article 77 of the Italian Constitution with the aim of redistributing resources among workers and pensioners have been declared unconstitutional on some occasions and constitutional on others. The Court has been very strict on the reduction of the allowances for magistrates – on the freezing of their salary adjustment to the inflation rate – as a form of 'solidarity contribution'. It declared the relevant legislation

[67] V Onida, 'Giudizio di costituzionalità delle leggi e responsabilità finanziaria del parlamento' in AA VV, *Le sentenze della Corte Costituzionale e l'art. 81, u.c., della Costituzione* (Giuffrè, 1993) 19; D Tega, 'Welfare Rights and Economic Crisis before the Italian Constitutional Court' (2014) *European Journal of Social Law* 63. eg, see Italian Constitutional Court, decision no 455/1990.

[68] Italian Constitutional Law 1/2012.

[69] Arts 3 and Arts 100,101,104, and 108 of the Italian Constitution, respectively.

[70] In judgment no 457/1997, despite lacking a constitutional balanced budget clause, the Italian Constitutional Court had tried to develop a test aiming to combine these competing principles and values by stating that the limitation of welfare rights is consistent with Art 3 Italian Constitution provided that they were exceptional, transient, non-arbitrary and relevant to the purpose achieved.

unconstitutional insofar as it imposed a deterioration of their standard of living and considered that the independence and impartiality of the judges also derive from their income.[71] By contrast, it did not consider the freezing of the salary adjustment mechanism for non-contracted people working in the public sector as a form of taxation nor as an unreasonable sacrifice.[72]

The Court has affirmed that it is for the Parliament, in the exercise of its legislative discretion, to balance compliance with budgetary requirements and competing constitutional values.[73] Yet, in what can be seen as a collaborative effort vis-à-vis the Parliament, the Italian Constitutional Court tried to provide some guidance as to when the cut to social spending by the legislature could be upheld. This followed the criticism triggered by judgment no 223/2012. Thus, in order to respect the Constitution, the freezing of the salary and pension adjustment has to be reasonable, transient, and justified in the light of domestic and supranational mandatory requirements to contain public spending.[74]

Quite unexpectedly, the Court departed from this standard in judgment no 70/2015. It annulled – at the benefit of the greatest majority of pensioners – the blocking of the pension adjustment to the inflation rate in 2012 and 2013. The decision forced the political authorities to give billions of euros back to pensioners in an effort to redistribute resources. In such circumstances, it was the Parliament that was forced to 'correct' and address the effects of a declaration of unconstitutionality.

Surprisingly, in this case, the Court did not declare the effects of the decision as *pro futuro* as it did in judgment no 10/2015 – just a few weeks earlier (section II) and a couple of months later[75] – by way of derogation from the rule of retroactivity.

Thus, power and discretion of the legislature in fiscal decisions incidentally feature in the case law of the Italian Constitutional Court. The protection of the democratic principle through the Parliament has never been used as a standard of review. This has not changed since the avenues to access constitutional adjudication were broadened. In 2018, a group of senators challenged on procedural grounds the adoption of the budget act for 2019. They had been unable to scrutinise and amend the bill due to the intertwinement between late formation of the Government post-election and the timeframe of the European Semester. Despite considering the action inadmissible for the lack of *locus standi*, the Constitutional Court acknowledged for the first time ever the possibility for MPs individually as 'powers of the state' to challenge abusive legislative practices, which could be considered a patent and direct violation of their individual constitutional prerogatives.[76] However, to date, this precedent has never led to a decision on merit.

[71] See Italian Constitutional Court, judgment 223/2012.

[72] Italian Constitutional Court, judgment 310/2013.

[73] See Italian Constitutional Court, decisions no 304 and no 310/2013, and no 154/2014 [5.3], and no 10/2015.

[74] See Italian Constitutional Court, judgments no 7 and no 154/2014.

[75] Italian Constitutional Court, judgment 178/2015, dealing however with a case of supervening unconstitutionality. On these cases see C Bergonzini, 'The Italian Constitutional Court and Balancing the Budget' (2016) 12 *European Constitutional Law Review* 177.

[76] Italian Constitutional Court, order 17/2019 and, then, order 60/2020.

C. The Portuguese Constitutional Tribunal between Correction and Open Conflict with the Parliament

The judgments of the Portuguese Constitutional Court on economic governance measures linked to the Memorandum of Understanding show a clear lack of consideration of their effects on the authority of the Parliament. The Court engaged in an effort to correct the effects of the (unconstitutional) austerity measures adopted, which at times triggered an open conflict with the legislature (and the Government).[77]

Some justifications for the case law of the Portuguese Court can nonetheless be provided. Many institutional actors were equally concerned by the challenged measures, first of all parliamentary minorities, the Ombudsman and the President of the Republic, who repeatedly brought cases before the Constitutional Court. Also, before striking down sections of the Budget Acts, the Constitutional Court had warned the Parliament not to adopt budgetary provisions which introduced a non-reasonable discrimination against public workers and pensioners, annual permanent curtailments to public wages and pensions, or retroactive measures.[78] Those provisions were found unconstitutional and the Court, in the exercise of its powers,[79] decided to suspend the effects of the declaration of unconstitutionality so as not to affect the ongoing execution of the budget in the fiscal year.

The Portuguese Constitutional Court contended that the Parliament could have used less restrictive and more proportionate and equitable measures to reduce public spending in the light of the avenues provided by the Memorandum of Understanding.[80] However, the Court failed to take into account the context in which the Parliament was acting, first under the extraordinary situation of a bailout and then under the ex post surveillance programme, with the periodical review missions of the Troika representatives. It did not discuss the protection of parliamentary powers, which had to rubber-stamp the governmental decisions to ensure the commitment for financial assistance.

The Court has not shown a very cooperative approach towards the legislature either. In judgment no 413/2014 the Portuguese Constitutional Court held that a further reduction of public salaries, provided for by the Budget Act 2014, was in contrast with the principle of equality. Its judgment did not establish retroactive effects and the wage cuts were annulled *ex nunc* starting from the date of the ruling. Following this decision, the Portuguese Parliament, as the institution that had passed the contested Budget Act 2014, referred several questions to the Court seeking clarifications on the temporal

[77] Portuguese Constitutional Court, judgment n° 187/2013, which forced the Government to renegotiate internationally the terms of the Financial and Assistance Programme.

[78] See Portuguese Constitutional Tribunal, judgments n° 396/2011 and n° 353/2012, on which see M Nogueira De Brito, 'Comentário ao Acórdão nº 353/2012 do Tribunal Constitucional' (2012) *Direito & política* 108; A Dos Santos, C Celorico Palma, 'O Acordão do Tribunal Constitucional nº 353/2012 de 5 de julho: a prevalência da razão juridica sobre a razão económica' (2012) *Revista e finanças públicas e direito fiscal* 31.

[79] Art 278.4, Portuguese Constitution.

[80] F Pereira Coutinho, 'A natureza jurídica dos memorandos da "Troika"' (2013) *Themis Ano XIII* 147. While recognising the binding nature of the Memoranda un understanding (judgments no 187/2013, no 413/2014 and no 574 and 575/2014), the Court considered that there was a margin left for parliamentary discretion.

effects of this judgment.[81] Some practical aspects of the implementation of the Court's decision about the quantification of holiday allowance and the timing of its payments remained unclear according to the Parliament, which was in charge of the follow-up of the ruling. However, the Court stated that the judgment was unambiguous and that no further instructions could be offered. Interestingly, from a separation of powers perspective, the Constitutional Court claimed that was not a legislature and it was beyond its mandate to define the aspects requested, which concerned the administrative competence of the Government and the exercise of rule-making powers. Nor, according to the Court, could the principle of inter-institutional cooperation be invoked by the Parliament to this end. Thus, the doubts remained unaddressed. The judgment proved how tense the relationship between the Parliament and the Constitutional Court can be, moving away from the very idea of a collaborative Constitution.

V. The NGEU as a New Test Bench for the Constitutional Courts–Parliaments Relationship? The Case of the National Recovery and Resilience Plans

The Euro crisis has shown significant problems in the capacity of courts to act as 'guardians of democracy' and of the role of Parliaments as budgetary authorities, particularly in the countries where the economic measures implemented were stricter due to the financial situation. Has the first implementation of the NGEU (2021–23) led to a different conclusion?

By setting common EU priorities, through the NGEU and, in particular, the RRF, the EU institutions committed themselves to granting or to lending EU money across the Union. Within the broad framework of EU common targets and the country-specific recommendations, Member States have remained reasonably free to decide how to design their NRRPs in a constant negotiation with the Commission, up to the point that the NGEU has been criticised for 'nationalising' the determinations on how EU funds are spent.[82] EU money is thus financing national investments and reforms in a variety of different policy areas excluding only security and defence and financial markets' regulation.[83]

Therefore, one could expect an active participation of national parliaments in such strategic budgetary decisions. Some national parliaments have tried to adapt and to strengthen ex-post oversight on the implementation of the NRRPs,[84] but the governance of the RRF and the NRRPs is entirely executive-driven, between the national Governments and the Commission.[85] The result has been, in many cases, the worsening

[81] M Canotilho, T Violante and R Lanceiro, 'Austerity measures under judicial scrutiny: the Portuguese constitutional case-law' (2015) 11 *European Constitutional Law Review* 155.

[82] E Cannizzaro, 'Editorial: Neither Representation nor Taxation? Or, 'Europe's Moment'– Part I' (2020) 5 *European Papers* 704.

[83] Leino-Sandberg and Raunio (n 14) 9.

[84] E Griglio, 'National Parliaments' Resilience under the Euro-Zone and the Covid-19 Crises: Continuity and Discontinuity in the Euro-National Scrutiny' (2022) 28 *Journal of Legislative Studies* 313.

[85] Leino-Sandberg and Raunio (n 14) 9.

of the level of parliamentary involvement compared to the Euro crisis economic governance reform.[86]

The execution of the plans is still at an early stage in most Member States,[87] and for this reason there has been very little judicial scrutiny on the domestic acts requested for the NRRPs' implementation. Except for the cases that will be briefly recalled below, executives have remained basically unbound in their action.

Such status quo is of a concern, again, from a separation of powers perspective, especially for those countries that are already quite advanced in the implementation of the plans. At the time of writing, Italy and Portugal are the only two countries to have already received the payment of four instalments, Spain has received three instalments, while France two. It is possible that the lack of contestation of the NRRPs' measures in the courts also depends on the circumstance that Italy, France, Portugal and Spain are the countries that, in relation to their GDP, are going to benefit the most from the RRF. This is certainly an incentive that prompts the fast and smooth implementation of the plan against any delay dependent on judicial proceedings.

Time considerations may also explain why the EU legal instruments that underpinned the operation of the RRF, including the Own Resource Decision (ORD),[88] were not subject to constitutional challenges in these countries. The ORD entered into force in the record time of six months, compared to the usual timespan of two years that was needed for domestic parliaments to complete the national stage of the approval procedure under Article 311 TFEU for previous ORDs. Only in Germany was the ORD, through the national Act ratifying it, subject to the review of the GFCC, which eventually gave its green light subject to the necessarily temporary nature of NGEU and the RRF and constraining the possibility for the Parliament in the future to confer fiscal sovereignty to the Union.[89]

Another element to take into account when appreciating the (to date) low level of constitutional conflicts before courts surrounding the implementation of NRRPs in the four countries is the limitation relating to the reversal of measures foreseen in the RRF Regulation.[90] As also clarified by the Commission,[91] the domestic measures put in place to fulfil targets and milestones cannot be reversed by the Member States once they have been satisfactorily achieved. Such reversal could also involve a judgment annulling the

[86] COSAC, *35ème Rapport semestriel L'évolution des procédures et pratiques de l'Union européenne en matière de contrôle parlementaire* (Lisbon, 2021) 14–15; European Parliament, *Survey on the role of national parliaments in the implementation of the Recovery and Resilience Facility* (Economic Governance Support Unit (EGOV) PE 699.524, 7 April 2022) 5.

[87] Commission, 'Annual Report on the implementation of the Recovery and Resilience Facility: Moving forward' COM(2023) 545 final/2.

[88] Council Decision (EU, Euratom) 2020/2053 of 14 December 2020 on the system of own resources of the European Union and repealing Decision 2014/335/EU, Euratom [2020] OJ L424/1.

[89] BVerfG, Judgment of the Second Senate of 6 December 2022 – 2 BvR 547/21. The ruling was preceded by a decision of 26 March 2021, BVerfG, Beschluss des Zweiten Senats vom 26. März 2021 – 2 BvR 547/21, and by BVerfG, Order of the Second Senate of 15 April 2021 – 2 BvR 547/21, rejecting a request for temporary injunction against the Act. Eigenmittelbeschluss-Ratifizierungsgesetz, ERatG allowing the President of the Republic to sign the Act of ratification into law.

[90] Art 24(3).

[91] Commission (n 87) annex II.

effects of one of those measures.[92] In such circumstances, no further RRF payments could be granted, and the payments already made could be reduced proportionally according to the Commission's methodology.[93]

No judgment of the Spanish Constitutional Court has engaged with measures implementing the NRRP so far, whereas there is at least one relevant judgment to be mentioned for the other jurisdictions.

The Italian Constitutional Court was asked to review the constitutionality of a decree-law meant to revise, amongst other things, the strategic planning for the national port system in compliance with the NRRP. The measure was challenged in front of the Court also because, when converting the decree-law into a legislative act, the Parliament had included provisions inconsistent with the original text, thereby triggering the alleged violation of the constitutional limits for decree-laws and an abusive parliamentary procedure of conversion.[94] The Court dismissed both pleas, arguing, amongst other things, that the final content of the decree-law fulfilled the need to comply with one of the first milestones of the NRRP as soon as possible.[95]

Here the NRRP is used to justify the rationale of the measure under the review. However, the Court failed to engage with the nature of the plan and of the legal constraints under the operational arrangements and the discretion left to the Parliament and Government. The plan is considered a 'given' that trumps any further consideration on the legality of the measure adjudicated in a way that, in this particular case, left parliamentary procedures untouched.[96]

The Portuguese Constitutional Tribunal followed exactly the same approach as the Italian Constitutional Court, on the revision of the framework law on national associations. The President of the Republic filed an *ex ante* constitutional challenge before the Tribunal questioning the compatibility of some provisions of the new Act[97] with several constitutional principles and rights. The Court dismissed the action on every ground and argued that for years the European Commission had recommended to the Portuguese authorities to lower the legal restrictions on the regulated professional activities; a reform that is now enshrined into the NRRP as a milestone. The Constitutional Tribunal found the reform under review to be instrumental to fulfil it. No further details were provided on the nature of the obligations stemming from the NRRP or on the leeway left to the Parliament, which for the Court acted within the constitutional boundaries.

Thus, in the two judgments briefly analysed, the Italian and Portuguese Constitutional Courts, respectively, have shown a deferential approach vis-à-vis the

[92] ibid. Of course, not every judgment of unconstitutionality of measures implementing the NRRP entails a reversal as long as it does not impair the fulfilment of the relevant milestone or target: see, eg Italian Constitutional Court, judgment 223/2023.

[93] Commission, 'Recovery and Resilience Facility: Two years on. A unique instrument at the heart of the EU's green and digital transformation' COM(2023) 99 final, 10 ff and annex II.

[94] See, respectively, Arts 77 and 72 of the Italian Constitution as the standards of review.

[95] Italian Constitutional Court, judgment 6/2023, on decree-law 121/2021. In the end, the Court invalidated certain (marginal) provisions of the decree-law that encroached upon the competences of regions and municipalities.

[96] A Lauro, 'Quando le censure formali delle Regioni entrano in porto, ma non approdano (a causa del PNRR)' (2023) *Giurisprudenza costituzionale* 123.

[97] See *Decreto nº 30/XV da Assembleia da República.*

measures formally adopted by the Parliaments, but substantially predetermined by the Government (in cooperation with the Commission) in the NRRPs, with little or no parliamentary control, as anticipated.

A final example of case law to highlight in the post-NGEU governance refers to the 2023 *Conseil Constitutionnel*'s decision on the disputed French pension reform. The Commission had insisted on the need for a pension reform in France since the 2019 country-specific recommendations. The French Government has repeatedly tried, without success, to introduce such a reform resulting in the rise of the retirement age. As the reform is politically very controversial, the national executive did not list it in the NRRP, which the Commission criticised on this point.[98] After the required reform reappeared in the first country-specific recommendation of 2022, the long-awaited reform returned on the political agenda.[99]

It was harshly contested outside and within the Parliament, also inside the majority, and could only pass in the National Assembly based on a combination of controversial procedural and substantive choices. It was included in the bill rectifying the 2022 social security (annual) budget, despite having a financial impact on the coming decades, bypassing the ordinary legislative procedure and by using the accelerated legislative procedure.[100] Moreover, it combined the *vote bloqué* with the engagement of the confidence of the Government.[101] While each of these instruments (singular) had been used in the past, they had never been applied jointly, which triggered an obvious degradation of parliamentary deliberation.

The pension reform was immediately subject to multiple constitutional challenges, by minorities in both the Assembly and the Senate, and by the same Prime Minister. While in the end just a few provisions were struck down, all the claims targeting the undemocratic nature of the mixed procedure and the qualification and substance of the Act were dismissed. EU law and the country-specific recommendations were absent from the decision, but the Court confirmed its long-standing claim that it is not for the *Conseil Constitutionnel* to replace the legislature in the appreciation of political discretionary choices.[102]

While scholars had unanimously predicted the outcome of the decision, drawing on the *Conseil*' consolidated approach, positions diverge on how it should be assessed. Some have argued that the Court has just managed to keep the existing inter-institutional balance provided for by the Constitution in favour of the executive;[103] many have argued that this was a missed of opportunity to rebalance a too-asymmetric relationship between Parliament and Government;[104] finally, others have considered

[98] Commission, 'Staff working document, Analysis of the recovery and resilience plan of France accompanying the document Proposal for a Council implementing decision on the approval of the assessment of the recovery and resilience plan for France', SWD/2021/173 final, 40–41.

[99] K Chatzilaou, 'National Recovery and Resilience Plan: France' (2022) 15 *Italian Labour Law e-Journal* 8.

[100] Art 47-1 French Constitution.

[101] See, respectively, Arts 44-3 and 49-3 French Constitution.

[102] Décision n° 2023-849 DC du 14 avril 2023 [11].

[103] D Maus, 'La leçon de droit parlementaire appliqué du Conseil constitutionnel sur la réforme des retraites devrait servir de modèle' *Le Monde* (19 April 2023), at www.lemonde.fr/idees/article/2023/04/19/didier-maus-la-lecon-de-droit-parlementaire-applique-du-conseil-constitutionnel-sur-la-reforme-des-retraites-devrait-servir-de-modele_6170126_3232.html.

[104] D Baranger, 'Réforme des retraites: «Le Conseil constitutionnel a perdu une chance de rétablir un degré d'équilibre entre les pouvoirs»' *Le Monde* (16 April 2023), at www.lemonde.fr/idees/article/2023/04/16/

that the judgment has worsened the inter-institutional imbalance further jeopardising the Parliament.[105] As already highlighted when commenting other decisions in this chapter, the deferential approach of the Constitutional Court very often implies deference to the executive but more constraints on the legislature.

VI. Conclusion

This chapter reviewed the constitutional case law on thc Euro crisis reform of the economic governance and on the initial implementation of the NGEU in France, Italy, Portugal and Spain. It reveals that constitutional courts have not acted effectively as guardians of the democratic process nor of Parliaments as budgetary authorities. Problems of separation of powers between the legislative and the executive branch in the field of economic governance have not been addressed by these courts and the case law tends to develop in continuity with the past.

The idea of a 'collaborative Constitution'[106] combining deference and mutual support with constructive criticism, conflict and correction between constitutional courts and legislatures has not materialised. Judicial deference in most cases runs in favour of governments, thus strengthening the long-standing path to executive dominance. In the aftermath of the Euro crisis, political tensions and conflicts on principles and rights have been channelled through courts. Yet they have seldom been turned into opportunities to correct and revise the malfunctioning of separation of powers' relationships. The legal techniques used to fine-tune the implications of constitutional judgments and their effects over time have not been decisive.

The marginalisation of domestic parliaments has been perpetuated and even worsened in the implementation of the RRF, also due to the stabilisation of procedures and instruments of emergency politics in ordinary time.[107] The window of opportunity offered to the four countries by the financing of the NRRPs and their mode of governance disincentivise contestation before constitutional courts. In the few instances where they have been called to intervene, the approach followed by the courts has been very deferential vis-à-vis the Government. The quality of democratic procedures is not valued. constitutional courts lack critical reflection on the source – the nature and scope – of the legal constraints, emerging as a by-product of the negotiation between the EU and the national executives. Where cited, the contents of the NRRPs are taken as a *fait accompli*, not suitable for judicial review.

At least in the post-Euro crisis and post-NGEU economic governance, the consideration that 'European constitutional courts have in many respects been remarkably

reforme-des-retraites-le-conseil-constitutionnel-a-perdu-une-chance-de-retablir-un-degre-d-equilibre-entre-les-pouvoirs_6169737_3232.html.

[105] E Bottini, M Bouaziz and S Hennette-Vauchez, 'Un juge activiste ? Les choix du Conseil constitutionnel dans les décisions n° 2023-4 RIP et n° 2023-849 DC du 14 avril 2023' (2023) *La Revue des droits de l'homme* 2, who analyse this judgment together with French *Conseil Constitutionnel*, Décision n° 2023-4 RIP du 14 avril 2023, declaring unconstitutional the parliamentary initiative to lower the retirement age at 62 years via Referendum (RIP).

[106] Kavanagh (n 17).

[107] Leino-Sandberg and Raunio (n 14) 2.

successful in implanting constitutional restraints on governments in systems long inhospitable to such restraints'[108] no longer holds. As argued by Marco Dani just a few years ago 'constitutional courts contribute to the sustainability of a comprehensive institutional setting corroding the idea of constitutional democracy on which they are premised'.[109] With Parliaments unable to defend themselves and constitutional courts unwilling to step in to correct the executive imbalance, economic governance procedures have become a test bench for the entrenchment of democratic values and separation of powers' dynamics.

[108] J Ferejohn and P Pasquino, 'Constitutional Adjudication: Lessons from Europe' (2004) 82 *Texas Law Review* 1672 drawing on M Cappelletti, *The Judicial Process in Comparative Perspective*, in collaboration with P J Kollmer and JM Olson (Clarendon Press, 1989) 118–81.

[109] Dani (n 19) 189.

11

Bolstering the Executive Through Judicial Review: Diagonal Separation of Powers with Multilevel Effects in the Field of Migration

ANNA W GHAVANINI, ALLISON ÖSTLUND AND ANNA WALDENSTRÖM

I. Introduction

The policy field of migration possesses many of the traits that pose particular challenges for the separation of the powers between the legislature, the executive and the judiciary. Migration law and the debate surrounding it are still marked by what is sometimes referred to as the '2015 migration crisis' – an ongoing high-stakes development annually affecting countless individuals and triggering challenging political negotiations at all levels of government.[1] Rife with political controversy, the field is in acute need for the representative public decision-making that can be guaranteed only through parliament, whereas the continuous state of crisis necessitates the rapid and decisive response associated with the executive. Furthermore, migration policy and its national implementation activates fundamental rights considerations of uttermost pertinence given that the futures of populations of migrants are at stake throughout the whole process: from transport and reception to international protection, residence or return. These strong human rights implications create both an exigency and an impetus for judicial safeguards against abuse of political (including administrative) power. Against this background, the Pact on Migration and Asylum, consisting of legislative measures including a proposal for a new Regulation[2] on situations of crisis and *force majeure* as well as executive tools designed to consolidate migration procedures in

[1] On EU migration law 'politicization', its sensitivity and contradicting objectives and interests therewithin, see Westlund, ch 8 in this volume. On EU migration law 'crisisification, see Gnes and Sormunen, ch 4 of this volume.

[2] Commission, 'Proposal for a Regulation of the European Parliament and of the Council addressing situations of crisis and force majeure in the field of migration and asylum' COM(2020) 613 final.

the EU, is a welcome development that promises to replace ad hoc crisis action with comprehensive legislation. It remains to be seen, however, how these measures will play out in practice. The Pact is currently being negotiated, with the expectation of final adoption in early 2024.[3]

In this chapter, we examine the European Court of Justice's (ECJ, or 'the Court') exercise of control of legislative and executive action at Member State level in the field of migration law. We do so through a systematic study of 142 ECJ judgments rendered in the field between 1 January 2010 and 31 December 2020, using an empirical approach which allows us to examine how the Court proceeds not only in the politically charged cases that draw the most controversy, but also in the cases of everyday exercise of legislative and administrative powers shaping the policy field and thus directly affecting migrants. We aim to establish, first, how, and with what intensity, the Court exercises control of the Member State political branches and, second, whether it makes any distinction between the legislative and the executive branch in its exercise of that control function.

We find that the Court's judicial review is predominantly of a 'middle ground' standard, going beyond a mere competence check but stopping short of engaging thoroughly with substantive choices. We furthermore find that the judgments tend to use more direct language when reviewing legislative measures than when reviewing executive application. On this basis, we argue that EU judicial control of decentralised executive and legislative power is functional, hampered neither by judicial overreach nor by undue docility and at least to some extent resisting a trend of conflating the two political branches. However, placing the findings in the broader perspective offered by this volume, we question whether the Court's comparatively more active role vis-à-vis the national legislative and executive branches, when not coupled with the same level of scrutiny of the Union political branches, may not in fact amplify the position of the Union political powers, reinforcing the authoritative effects of EU law in the Member States.

The argument proceeds as follows. After this introduction, section II sets out the role of the judiciary in a separation of powers regime within EU migration law. Section III describes our dataset and analysis method (section III.A) before outlining the most significant findings of the empirical analysis: that the Court typically engages in a *limited substantive review* of national legal acts (section III.B); that it is more likely to engage in *direct review* of legislative than of executive acts (section III.C); and that it tends to defer final decision-making to the decentralised judiciaries in the Member States (section III.D). Section IV discusses the implications of these findings for the conception of separation of powers within EU migration law at large, arguing that a reasonably well-functioning judicial control of the Member State legislatures and executives does not make up for but may indeed, paradoxically, accentuate shortcomings in the separation of powers at the Union level.

[3] For an overview of the content of the Pact and legal developments, see home-affairs.ec.europa.eu/policies/migration-and-asylum/pact-migration-and-asylum_en.

II. Judicial Control in Diagonal Relationships

As pointed out by Möllers, the judiciary sits somewhat apart from the other branches insofar that it is not vested with its own political power and therefore serves not the interests of collective will-formation or democratic accountability, but rather the need to scrutinise the exercise of political power.[4] Thus, the main judicial function from a separation of powers perspective is one of *control*, contributing to democratic will-formation mainly by ensuring the two political branches' compliance with constitutional decision-making procedures and other constraints laid down in EU primary law.

As pointed out in the introduction to this volume, the Union's institutional structure is both multilevel and polycentric. Although the preliminary reference procedure does not formally allow the Court to engage in judicial review of national law, in practice the Court has often used this procedure to ascertain whether national policy or enforcement of law is in compliance with EU law. The preliminary reference procedure thus often functions as an avenue for centralised judicial review of decentralised political and administrative decision-making, with the national courts as intermediaries.

Conversely, national courts fulfil control functions vis-a-vis the political branches not only within their Member State but also in relation to the Union political branches, in particular through the obligation to hear actions against the validity of acts of secondary EU law brought by actors not able to take such complaints directly before the ECJ under Article 263(4) TFEU.[5] The Court of Justice also engages in direct review of national legislative and executive (or, exceptionally, judicial)[6] actions through the infringement procedure laid down in Articles 258 and 259 TFEU. We designate these interactions across both branches and levels of governance *diagonal* relationships.[7]

As has been demonstrated elsewhere in this volume, the EU legislative branch is traditionally weak, and risks being overpowered by a strong executive.[8] While similar trends, as observed by Minkkinen and Leino-Sandberg in chapter two, can be observed at least in some Member States, the legislative branch tends to be relatively stronger at national level. For this reason, the national legislatures appear to have important functions to fulfil as regards the process of democratically legitimate will-formation within an EU still plagued with accusations of a democratic deficit rendered more acute through a series of recent crises.[9] Migration has been and remains a highly controversial topic within the EU, with southern border States experiencing different problems than the northern 'final destinations', challenging the Member States' unity and commitment

[4] C Möllers, *The Three Branches: A Comparative Model of Separation of Powers* (Oxford University Press, 2013) 18.

[5] Case C-50/00 P *UPA* ECLI:EU:C:2002:462 [44].

[6] Case C-416/17 *Commission v France* ECLI:EU:C:2018:81.

[7] C Joerges, 'The Impact of European Integration on Private Law: Reductionist Perceptions, True Conflicts and a New Constitutional Perspective' (1997) 3 *European Law Journal* 378.

[8] See in the migration context Gnes and Sormunen, ch 4 of this volume, finding in respect to readmission agreements that legislative oversight is diminished with Parliament being kept in the dark; and more generally, Minkkinen and Leino-Sandberg, ch 2 of this volume.

[9] AE Stie, 'Crises and the EU's Response: Increasing the Democratic Deficit?' in M Riddervold, J Trondal and A Newsome (eds), *The Palgrave Handbook of EU Crises* (Palgrave Macmillan, 2021).

to a common policy.[10] Tensions have also risen within Member States (as well as within the European Parliament), where the surge of right-wing populism has expanded the political spectrum, presenting particular challenges for collective will-formation in which this wide variety of political positions need to be heard.[11] The legislative decision-making process providing for open debate in a representative organ is inherently better equipped to meet this requirement.[12] Yet, the very fact of European harmonisation risks shifting the centre of gravity to the executive arena.[13] In a field increasingly governed by EU law, the national legislature is reduced to merely implementing supranational regulation – at best filling a few lacunae. The effect is that the practical difference between the national legislature and the executive is lessened; even if the decision is formally a legislative one, its function is mainly one of execution.

All this entails that EU judicial control mechanisms must cover not only Union but also, importantly, Member State actors. Judicial control exercised by the Court of Justice is crucial towards ensuring that the balance of powers within the EU is maintained insofar that the political branches stay within their powers as constitutionally conferred. Such judicial scrutiny can take various shapes, as illustrated in other contributions to this volume. While national judiciaries – as a part of the EU judiciary – have a central role to play in this regard, the Court of Justice retains its function as the key judicial player in the field.

III. Exploring Diagonal Judicial Control in Migration Law

A. Methodological Remarks

This chapter presents the results of a systematic analysis of judgments in migration law cases rendered by the Court of Justice in the post-Lisbon era. In order to examine the Court's review of legislative and executive action on migration, we relied on the SepaRope Judiciary Dataset, an original dataset encompassing Court of Justice judgments in migration cases decided between 1 January 2010 and 31 December 2020. In all, the data comprised 142 rulings constituting a total selection of judgments categorised in the Court of Justice's Curia database as belonging to the 'Area of Freedom, Security and Justice' and one of the subcategories 'Immigration Policy', 'Border Checks', and 'Asylum Policy'.[14] For the purposes of conducting the analysis, each judgment in the dataset was

[10] P Slominski and F Trauner, 'How Do Member States Return Unwanted Migrants: The Strategic (non-) use of Europe during the Migration Crisis' (2018) 56 *Journal of Common Market Studies* 101; F Infantino, 'Practices of External Control: Is There a North-South Divide?' in C Finotelli and I Ponzo (eds), *Migration Control Logics and Strategies in Europe* (IMISCOE Research Series, Springer, 2023).

[11] G Falkner and G Plattner, 'EU Policies in Times of Populist Radical Right Euroscepticism: Which Future?' in C Rauchegger and A Wallerman (eds), *The Eurosceptic Challenge* (Bloomsbury, 2021).

[12] See, however, S Novak, 'The surprising effects of transparency on the EU legislative process' (2014) 51 *Cuadernos Europeos de Deusto* 63.

[13] See further, Gnes and Sormunen, ch 4 in this volume.

[14] For a detailed description of research methods for compiling the SepaRope judiciary dataset for the analysis, see A Wallerman Ghavanini et al, 'An Empirical Approach to Separation of Powers in the EU' (2022) 1 *CERGU Working Paper Series*.

subdivided into smaller units that we call *legal issues*, each reflecting a distinguishable legal problem decided by the Court.[15] In all, the 142 judgments were found to contain 283 such legal issues, roughly corresponding to the bullet points in the operative parts of the judgment and the reasoning pertaining to each.

Of these cases, the vast majority of judgments emanated from the preliminary reference procedure, with only four having been brought before the Court in other types of proceedings.[16] As is natural in the preliminary reference procedure, the majority of the issues (252 issues) concerned the interpretation of EU law. This interpretation is however necessarily situated mainly in a national context.[17] Specifically, the purpose of the requests is often to establish whether national legislation is compatible with Union law.[18] This purpose was made explicit in 100 of the legal issues in the dataset, most often in relation to regulations or directives in the field, but sometimes also relative to primary law articles, including in the Charter of Fundamental Rights. All in all, this renders the data ideal for the analysis of the diagonal relationship outlined above between the EU judiciary and the national executives and legislatures.

The legal issues were systematically analysed (hand-coded) by a team of research assistants with the aid of a system of set questions (variables) with pre-defined answer alternatives (values). The variables included inter alia whether the judgment implied that an executive or legislative actor had failed to adhere to their EU law obligations, whether the Court engaged in judicial review of a legislative or an executive measure, and whether or not that review resulted in the measure being upheld. For instances in which the Court engaged in judicial review of legal measures, we coded this review as either explicit or implicit and graded the standard of review applied on a three-grade scale of intensity. We furthermore coded whether the Court's ruling displayed deference towards another actor – ie, whether it left part of the decision-making to be determined by another body – and if so, whether it deferred within the judicial branch to a national court or to actors belonging to another branch of government as well as whether deference was minimal, partial, or full. These variables will be explained in more detail as we describe the findings in the following subsections.

The analysis of the coded dataset was exploratory and data-driven. We did not formulate preconceived hypotheses to test using the data. Instead, we relied on the data to tell us how the Court typically acts on the matters covered by our variables. In addition to calculating the average approach or the commonality of various approaches, we also divided the dataset into two subsets depending on whether the actor under scrutiny belonged to the legislative or the executive branch. This allowed us to compare the Court's exercise of control of each branch – both with that of the other branch and with its approach in the field as a whole, thus helping to bring out patterns of atypical or otherwise remarkable behaviour.

[15] For a more thorough discussion of legal issues as units of analysis for ECJ judgments, see eg P Schroeder and J Lindholm, 'From One to Many: Identifying Issues in CJEU Jurisprudence' (2023) 11 *Journal of Law and Courts* 163.

[16] Two in the infringement procedure under Art 258 TFEU and two as validity challenges under Art 263 TFEU.

[17] Requests for purely abstract interpretations would be declared inadmissible; see M Broberg and N Fenger, *Preliminary References to the European Court of Justice*, 3rd edn (Oxford University Press, 2021) 122.

[18] A Wallerman Ghavanini, 'Mostly harmless: the referring court in the preliminary reference procedure' (2022) *European Law Review* 310.

B. Neither Activism nor Passivism

Exploring the intensity of scrutiny to which the ECJ subjects national acts, we found indications neither of an activist court leaning towards furthering Union law implementation at the expense of national legislative or executive autonomy, nor of a passivist judiciary allowing the political powers to exercise their discretion freely. Two observations support this inference.

First, the analysis shows that, out of the 283 legal issues in the dataset, 212 legal issues involved judicial review of a legal act taken by a legislative or executive actor. In 92 of these legal issues (43 per cent), the act was ultimately struck down as contrary to EU law, and in another nine (four per cent) the act was partially struck down. Only in a minority of the cases did the Court hence find the reviewed national acts to be contrary to EU law. Since there is no independent control group to indicate how large a proportion of incompatibility rulings would be 'normal', it is of course difficult to make an assessment as to what these figures tell us. Considering, however, that the cases that reach the Court are those where the question of incompatibility has been raised by either the parties or the referring court, it would be reasonable to expect these legal acts to be in violation of EU law more often than acts not subject to litigation before the ECJ. In this light, it can perhaps be considered redeeming that even in these cases, compliance findings were more often made than not. Whether this reflects a reticence on the part of the Court or that legal actors generally do act in accordance with the law, remains open to discussion.

Whereas the Court found that the legislative acts scrutinised were incompatible with Union law in 42 per cent of the legal issues examined, the corresponding figure for actors representing the executive power was 45 per cent. This appears to indicate that the Court does not take a *dramatically* different approach vis-a-vis the respective branches. If that is the case, it may however be taken to reveal something about the patterns of will-formation on the side of the respective political branches. In the highly contentious field of migration law, one might expect that the strong national interest and pressure from national public opinion would influence national decision-making. Such influence should then, in theory, be most visible in the legislature, whose mission it is to push forward political will at the impetus of their constituencies and who is directly accountable to them through regular elections. The executive, on the other hand, whose main task is to implement and enforce the legislature's political will, should in general be relatively more insulated from public opinion and thus more likely to keep a high level of compliance even in fields of controversy. The fact that legislative acts were yet observed to be incompatible with Union law marginally less often than executive ones might suggest that the national legislatures manage to remain loyal to their EU law obligations at a level that is more or less on par with the national executive–even in the face of domestic pushback.

Second, the standard of review most often adhered to by the Court in its review of legislative and executive acts was mostly found to conform to what we call *limited substantive review*, which is the middle option on the three-grade scale we used for coding the standard of review – the other two being *procedural review only* at the lower end of the scale and *strict substantive review* at the higher.[19] Limited substantive review was used by the Court in 69 per cent of all legal issues examined, and slightly more commonly used vis-à-vis the legislature than the executive (72 per cent and 62 per cent, respectively).

The limited substantive review standard is characterised by going further than merely ensuring that the disputed measure has been adopted in accordance with formal rules of procedure, so as to also examine whether the measure in substance conforms to higher-ranking norms (ie, for the purposes of this chapter, any rule of EU law that enjoys primacy over national law). It stops short, however, of a full examination of that conformity, satisfying only that there are no *clear* infringements of substantive obligations imposed on the legislature. Typically, the substantive examination takes as its point of departure the reasons provided in support of the challenged act in order to establish whether they fulfil basic requirements of adequacy in the sense that they are intelligible and relevant to the decision to be taken.

The Court itself gives an example of this standard of review in case C-69/10, *Samba Diouf*. The case concerned minimum standards for granting or withdrawing refugee status under Directive 2005/85/EC. The national executive authority had rejected an individual's application for international protection under an accelerated procedure that did not allow for appeal, and it fell to the ECJ to consider whether this was justified due to the interest in expediency in decision-making. The Court spelled out what the right to an effective judicial remedy required in terms of standards of judicial review:

> *It is, however, for the national court to determine* … whether that element is such as to justify, on its own, upholding the action brought indirectly against the decision to examine the application for asylum under an accelerated procedure … The [Directive] and the principle of effective judicial protection do not preclude national rules such as those at issue in the main proceedings, under which no separate action may be brought against the decision of the competent national authority to deal with an application for asylum under an accelerated procedure, *provided that the reasons which led that authority to examine the merits of the application under such a procedure can in fact be subject to judicial review in the action which may be brought against the final decision rejecting the application – a matter which falls to be determined by the referring court.*[20]

In other words, the Court of Justice examined whether the expedited procedure fulfils what we here refer to as 'basic requirements of adequacy' – stopping short, though, of making a proportionality assessment, rejecting the national decision-making authority's conclusions on fact or as a matter of national law, or substituting the national body's assessment for its own.[21]

The Court's preference for the limited substantive review standard may be partially explained by the preliminary reference procedure. In the review of national legal acts,

[19] This classification is lightly based on R Widdershoven, 'The European Court of Justice and the Standard of Judicial Review' in J de Poorter et al (eds), *Judicial Review of Administrative Discretion in the Administrative State* (TMC Asser Press, 2019) 57.

[20] Case C-69/10 *Samba Diouf v Ministre du Travail* ECLI:EU:C:2011:524 [68]–[70] (emphasis added).

[21] As per our codebook; Wallerman Ghavanini et al (n 18) 12–13.

a purely procedural review would have to involve examining Member State constitutional arrangements as well as the legislative history of the challenged act, both of which patently fall outside the competence of the Court of Justice. Such considerations will also rarely be the reason that the referring court raises doubt of the measure's compatibility with Union law. Thus, it is hardly surprising that procedural review only was relatively uncommon among the cases we analysed.[22]

Similarly, we found only a few judgments to classify as entailing full substantive review (7.5 per cent of all legal issues where a review was conducted). Two factors may explain the Court's reticence in this regard. First, the competence limitations inherent in the preliminary reference procedure, specifically the fact that the Court is not permitted to interpret national law in preliminary rulings, may make the Court less inclined to apply a more intrusive standard of review, which would necessitate a more intimate understanding of the national measure at hand. This, however, would of course not exclude that the Court might have prescribed this standard and left it to the national court to carry the review out. Secondly, since the basis for the review was often a directive coupled with provisions of primary law or general principles (as for example in *Samba Diouf*, discussed above), it is also possible that the Court prefers, in these cases, to provide legislatures with some margin of appreciation.[23] However, as neither of these explanations entail that the Court would be prevented from conducting or requiring full substantive review, they still imply that the lower standard of review is a choice made by the Court, reflecting the level of control it sees fit to exercise in relation to the Member State executives and legislatures.

C. More Explicit Review of the Legislature

Although the results of our analysis on the whole demonstrated only little difference between the treatment of the two political branches at the hands of the Court, a more detailed study into the mode of judicial control revealed that the Court tended to review legislative acts in a more direct or explicit language, than it did acts of the executive. As the judicial review of national acts typically occurs through preliminary rulings, direct disapplication, or invalidation of an executive or legislative provision is not possible as a matter of law. It is therefore not surprising that review in the preliminary reference context was found overall to be primarily implicit. Still, even within the preliminary reference procedure, the Court does have the option of engaging directly with the character of a national legal act, thus making the ruling explicitly about that act's compatibility with EU law, rather than providing only broad and generic guidance for the national court to apply. We considered review to be explicit where the ECJ's ruling directly engaged with the character of a national legal measure, even where this did not formally lead to a direct requirement to disapply that measure.

[22] That procedural review showed itself to be uncommon is also explained by the fact that our coding scheme allowed only one standard of review to be selected (the least intrusive one), meaning that review combining limited substantive review with procedural review would have to be coded as limited substantive review.

[23] See also Westlund, ch 8 in this volume.

Only 36 per cent of the reviews conducted in our dataset were coded as explicit. As noted above, this is mainly explained by the nature of the preliminary ruling procedure. However, explicit review was found to be markedly more common in relation to national legislative acts. For the legal issues on which review of a legislative act was conducted, that review was coded as explicit judicial review in 45 per cent of the cases, compared to only 25 per cent for executive acts.

One example of explicit review of legislative measures is presented by case C-651/19, *JP v Commissaire général aux réfugiés et aux apatrides*, where an application for international protection had been dismissed due to its tardiness. The key issue for the preliminary ruling was whether the time-limit was compatible with the right to an effective remedy and secondary legal provisions to that effect. In reference to the length of the contestation period that national law prescribed for challenging a refusal to grant international protection, the Court held that

> the drafting of such an initiating application is not, a priori, of such particular complexity as to require a period greater than 10 days[.] … [S]ubject to what that court may determine, a period of 10 days, including public holidays, does not appear to be insufficient in practical terms to enable an effective remedy to be prepared and submitted challenging a decision declaring a subsequent application for international protection to be inadmissible.[24]

The ruling continued by outlining that an additional *pro forma* extension allowing margin for postal delays and public holidays rendered the prima facie strict time limit more favourable and therefore compliant with the right to an effective remedy.[25] The examination of national administrative law, including casuistic features of application by national authorities, corresponded to what we term explicit review, ie, the type of direct engagement with technical aspects thereof in terms of its compliance with EU rules and principles.

In this case the Court of Justice engaged in detail with the modalities of the national administrative rules on which the applicable time-limit hinged.[26] The Court set out specific and concrete requirements primarily relating to the relevant domestic context even where no such specific requirements existed in (codified) EU law, for instance in reference to formal receipt of a decision:

> [S]uch legislation makes it easier for those applicants to exercise their right to an effective remedy and helps to ensure respect for their rights of defence. That legislation may, however, have such an effect only if each of two conditions are met, namely, first, that the applicant is properly informed that, where he or she has not provided an address in the Member State concerned, the letters which the responsible authorities in connection with the examination of his or her application for international protection may send will be addressed to him or her at the head office of the CGRS and, second, the conditions for access to that head office are not such that the receipt of those letters is excessively difficult.[27]

By contrast, when the Court provides only broad guidance for the national court's legality review but refrains from engaging with the specifics of the act in question, the review

[24] Case C-651/19 *JP v Commissaire général aux réfugiés et aux apatrides* ECLI:EU:C:2020:681 [61], [64].
[25] ibid [65].
[26] ibid [36]–[47].
[27] ibid [45]–[46].

was in our analysis considered *implicit*. The case C-233/18, *Zubair Haqbin*, concerning Belgian reception of applicants for international protection, provides an example of this. The referring court had essentially asked whether and under what conditions EU secondary law permitted Member States to withdraw or reduce substantive conditions for reception as a punitive sanction on asylum-seekers – in particular minors – behaving violently and in serious breach of the rules of the accommodation centres. Although the Court of Justice was ultimately firm in its findings that such material sanctions were not permitted to entail withholding most basic human needs,[28] in order to reach this conclusion, the Court mainly referred to provisions of EU secondary law and its own jurisprudence, declining to closely and concretely scrutinise the contested national rules and their application.[29]

The two considered examples illustrate on the one hand explicit review of a legislative act and on the other implicit review of an executive one. To be sure, implicit review remained more common than explicit review across both branches in the dataset. As has already been pointed out, this is not surprising considering that the cases examined were almost exclusively brought under the preliminary reference procedure, in which the Court is not allowed to engage in the interpretation of national legal measures and is therefore – at least in theory – prevented from exercising direct judicial review of such measures.[30] Against this background, it may instead be considered remarkable that as often as once in three legal issues the Court still does engage in such explicit review. It is, however, already known that the Court takes some liberties with these limitations and examples of this behaviour have been registered, albeit sometimes critically, in previous literature.[31]

The difference in attitude displayed towards the executive and the legislative branches is noteworthy. On the one hand, this can be easily understood in relation to the Court's assignment in the preliminary reference procedure: to *interpret*, but not to apply. If scrupulously followed, it should lead the Court to take a greater interest in the more abstract legislative level and be more cautious of extending its review into the territory of application – ie, execution – of rules. On the other hand, however, the Court's competence is also limited to the interpretation of *EU law*. In the cases where the Court engages in explicit review of national legal measures, it has already exceeded this mandate. The Court has justified this apparent overstep by stating that it engages in explicit review only where the referring court has provided information about the national provisions in question and the relevant facts in such detail that the outcome of the review follows immediately from the interpretation of EU law.[32] One might expect these conditions to be fulfilled more often in situations handled by the executive, whose actions and following implications are easier to overlook, than in situations involving legislative provisions that typically have a broader scope and with regards to which it

[28] Case C-233/18 *Zubair Haqbin* ECLI:EU:C:2019:956 [56].
[29] ibid [32]–[55].
[30] *cf* Art 267 TFEU.
[31] Broberg and Fenger (n 17).
[32] H Rasmussen, 'Remedying the crumbling EC judicial system' (2000) 37 *Common Market Law Review* 1071, 1102; GT Davies, '*The Division of Powers Between the European Court of Justice and National Courts: A Critical Look at Interpretation and Application in the Preliminary Reference Procedure*' (University of Groningen, 2006).

is therefore more difficult for the Court to foresee the consequences of its judgments. From this perspective, the Court's greater propensity to engage in explicit review of legislative, compared to executive, acts cannot so easily be explained by the procedural context. It might instead be understood as indicative of a stricter scrutiny of the national legislature, compared to the executive.

D. The Court's Deference of Final Decision-Making

A difference in the Court's attitude towards executive and legislative actors was also visible as regards the extent to which it deferred final decision-making to others. As explained above, we understand deference as meaning that the Court does not conclusively deal with the legal issue but leaves some aspects of it to be determined by another actor.[33] When the Court reviewed the legality of a legislative act, it deferred final judgment to another actor in about a third of the issues (35 per cent), compared to approximately a quarter of executive actions (26 per cent) and across all issues (24 per cent). The actor to whom final decisions were deferred was overwhelmingly one belonging to the national judiciary. This is an expected consequence of the division of competences between the Court of Justice and the national court in the preliminary reference procedure, where it falls to the national court to ultimately determine the outcome of the case including any possible setting aside of national provisions found incompatible with Union law by the ECJ.[34]

An example of this behaviour can be found in case C-517/17, *Milkiyas Addis v Bundesrepublik Deutschland*. In that case, an application for asylum had been rejected by German authorities without the applicant having been granted, as prescribed in the Procedures Directive,[35] a personal interview. The Court found that while the absence of an interview could be compensated for with a hearing at the appeals stage, the applicable national rules failed to guarantee that such a hearing would be held or, even if it were, that the hearing would comply with the conditions for personal interviews laid down in the Directive.[36] The effect of this ruling was, at any reasonable interpretation, that the national legislation failed to live up to the requirements of Union law. Instead of spelling this out, however, the Court deferred final judgment in the case to the referring court:

> Ultimately, it is for the referring court to determine whether, in the procedure at issue in the main proceedings, the opportunity was, or could still be, given to [the applicant] to be heard in full compliance with the conditions and fundamental guarantees applicable to the case in the main proceedings, in order to allow him to present, in person and in a language with which he is familiar, his view.[37]

In the operative part of the judgment, the Court then held that the Directive precluded the application of the national legislation in question, *unless* the legislation allowed for

[33] See Wallerman Ghavanini et al (n 18) 14–15.

[34] 72% of the issues where deference was detected concerned deference to the judiciary.

[35] Directive 2013/32/EU of the European Parliament and of the Council on common procedures for granting and withdrawing international protection [2013] OJ L180.

[36] Case C-517/17 *Milkiyas Addis v Bundesrepublik Deutschland* ECLI:EU:C:2020:579 [71]–[72].

[37] ibid [73].

a personal interview at a later stage. Thus, in this case, deference allowed the Court to refrain from outright requiring the setting aside of national legislation, leaving it to the national court to deliver the final blow.

Interestingly, however, the greater propensity on the part of the Court to defer to other actors when reviewing legislative measures, appears to be driven almost entirely by cases in which the Court's review resulted in the reviewed measure being upheld. In those cases, the Court deferred to other actors in 46 per cent of instances of upholding legislative measures and in 27 per cent of the issues where it upheld executive acts. Where it instead *struck down* the legislative measures reviewed, the frequency of deference was significantly lower (20 per cent), and indeed quite comparable to the corresponding figure for executive measures (17 per cent). Interestingly, this seems to indicate that the Court does not resort to deference as a means of conflict avoidance, as it has been found to do in other contexts.[38] If anything, the results of our analysis appear to indicate the opposite: what we are observing is not conflict avoidance on the part of the ECJ, but rather conflict support insofar that national courts might find themselves more inclined to take the politically controversial stance of ruling against their own political branches after having received a preliminary ruling where the ECJ's non-deferential judgment – by leaving little margin of discretion – effectively leaves the national judiciary no choice. Where there is conflict with the legislature (or with the executive, although the difference in this regard is less dramatic), the Court is more likely to give a firm ruling spelling out for national courts what to do to promote compliance with Union law.

IV. Conclusions

This chapter set out to explore how the Court acts when exercising its control functions in the field of migration and in particular vis-a-vis the political branches operating at the national level. It did so on the basis of a systematic, empirical analysis of the ECJ's case law during the 11 years following the entry into force of the Lisbon Treaty.

The analysis revealed three tendencies on the part of the Court. First, we found that the Court takes a rather tepid approach to the exercise of executive and legislative power in these politically fervent issues. On the one hand, it avoids a full substantive review of acts of the legislature and executive by which it could keep the political actors closely within the limits of their powers, while on the other hand, it similarly avoids a formal procedural review that would allow it to escape entering politically controversial issues. Instead, it carries out a middle-way *limited substantive review* where it checks that the act under review does not manifestly conflict with substantive EU law. As the Treaties fail to prescribe a standard for the review of illegality, there is no legal ground for criticism against this practice. Nevertheless, as has been demonstrated elsewhere, the constitutional protection of fundamental rights in the field does provide support for

[38] U Šadl and A Wallerman, '"The referring court asks, in essence": Is reformulation of preliminary questions by the Court of Justice a decision writing fixture or a decision-making approach?' (2019) 25 *European Law Journal* 416.

a more active approach.[39] The Court's own case law in some aspects of migration law, such as asylum-seekers' right to be heard, demonstrates its capacity for bolder stances.[40] The resort to limited substantive review as the default mode in these cases must, therefore, be understood as just that: a choice on the part of the Court.

Secondly, at a closer look at the wording of the judgments, we found that the Court is more explicit in its review of national legal acts when it examines acts of the legislature than when it examines acts of the executive. As the cases are mostly brought before the Court under the preliminary reference procedure, which strictly speaking does not provide for judicial review of national law, the Court's engagement in explicit judicial review must be seen as deliberate.

Third, the Court clearly prefers to leave the final decision to the national court. It is more careful to do so when reviewing an act by the legislature than one by the executive, but in particular when it does not find an incompatibility with EU law. The latter two observations, we argue, can be understood as a way for the Court to bolster judicial power at the national level in the confrontations with the political branch enjoying the strongest democratic legitimacy and where the unelected judicial branch's need for legitimacy is highest.[41] At the same time, they demonstrate that the Court does not shy away from conflict with the national legislatures.

The findings support two conclusions. First, the analysis revealed no evidence for the activism encroaching on national competences that the Court has sometimes been accused of,[42] nor for the passivist stance that other contributions to this book have demonstrated in relation to the Union political institutions. The Court's attitude, as revealed in this chapter, appears to strengthen the judicial branch nationally while predominantly exercising a medium level of judicial review against the national political branches. Diagonal judicial control in the migration field can in this sense be said to be functional and designated to ensure the enforcement of EU law in the Member States. Second, our analysis shows that in diagonal relationships, the Court does appear to uphold a distinction between the legislative and the executive powers at the national level by approaching these two branches differently. While such differentiation is justifiable and indeed satisfactory from a separation of powers perspective, a more comprehensive analysis is needed in order to fully understand the reasons and effects of the Court's strategy in this regard.

Overall, our contribution paints the picture of a Union Court that will safeguard EU law. In this sense, the Court could be said to be true to its mandate as laid down in the Treaties, fulfilling the role of a constitutional court expressing itself only on the matter of law (as opposed to the matter of fact). From a formal point of view, the Court of Justice

[39] See Westlund, ch 8 in this volume; as well as M Westlund, 'The Road Less Travelled in EU Asylum Law: The CJEU's Restrictive Way of Reasoning and How a Different Approach Could Strengthen Human Rights' (2023) 6 *Nordic Journal of European Law* 3 (forthcoming).

[40] See M Moraru, 'The European Court of Justice Shaping the Right to Be Heard for Asylum Seekers, Returnees, and Visa Applicants: An Exercise in Judicial Diplomacy' (2022) 13 *European Journal of Legal Studies* 21.

[41] *cf* A-M Burley and W Mattli, 'Europe Before the Court: A Political Theory of Legal Integration' (1993) 47 *International Organization* 41.

[42] M Dawson et al (eds), *Judicial Activism at the European Court of Justice* (Edward Elgar, 2013); M Adams et al (eds), *Judging Europe's Judges* (Hart, 2013).

is of course precluded from interpreting, and by extension also from reviewing, national law in this procedure; Article 267 TFEU confers upon it only the competence to rule on the interpretation and validity of Union legal acts. As a matter of positive law, this approach of the Court's is therefore difficult to criticise. On the other hand, as review of national executive and legislative acts have come to constitute a main function of the preliminary reference procedure,[43] entirely refusing to meaningfully engage with these issues would be unhelpful in instances where that question is at the heart of the referring court's query, and would risk alienating national courts.[44] Previous research has demonstrated that lack of clarity is what national judges find most problematic in ECJ judgments, and migration law has been identified as one of the areas where the Court is particularly prone to ambiguity.[45] Increased clarity, inter alia of the kind observed in the Court's review of legislative acts in this study, will most likely improve receiving national courts' capacity and thus proclivity to correctly translate ECJ jurisprudence into national judicial outcomes. Indeed, explicit language is not only necessary in terms of efficient communication, but also in order to lend normative support and, so to speak, embolden the referring court in its move to set aside national legislation.[46]

If the Court's actions are in line with Treaty objectives, there is, however, one remaining problem from the perspective of separation of powers: the Treaties do not provide for it. This relatively well-functioning, albeit decidedly less than rigorous, review of Member States' implementation of EU law, when coupled with the lack of effective control vis-à-vis the Union lawmaker that has been demonstrated elsewhere in this volume,[47] rather reinforces the problem. The Court's particular diligence when scrutinising the legislature at the national level, while not reacting to examples of sidelining the Union legislature,[48] appears to amplify an executive overload in the Union as a whole. As will-formation at the national level is more often set aside in favour of decisions made at Union level, where controversial policy issues will be settled through decision-making procedures crippled by lesser democratic legitimacy, the Court's approach results in rendering the effect of EU law in the Member States more authoritative. Scrutinising the political branches at national level while refusing to engage in similar scrutiny of the power exercised by the corresponding branches at Union level effectively entails that the Court sides with the Union institutions against the Member States.

[43] B de Witte, 'The preliminary ruling dialogue: three types of questions posed by national courts' in B de Witte et al (eds), *National courts and EU law: new issues, theories and methods* (Edward Elgar, 2016).

[44] *cf* S Lefèvre, 'Réponse utile dans le contentieux des aides d'État' in E Neframi (ed), *Renvoi préjudiciel et marge d'appréciation du juge national* (Larcier, 2015) 261, 275–76.

[45] J Krommendijk, 'The preliminary reference dance between the CJEU and Dutch courts in the field of migration' (2017) 10 *European Journal of Legal Studies* 144.

[46] *cf* Burley and Mattli (n 41).

[47] See Gnes and Sormunen, ch 4 in this volume.

[48] See eg A Wallerman Ghavanini, 'The CJEU's give-and-give relationship with executive actors in times of crisis' (2023) 2 *European Law Open* 284.

12

Judicial Control of the European Union and the Member States' Trade and Investment Relations

CHRISTINA ECKES

I. Introduction

Trade and investment have become increasingly subject to controversy within public debate. Sustainability and economic growth are understood to stand in an intrinsic tension.[1] Trade agreements are intended to increase the production and transport of goods, which inevitably produces emissions, and, at least potentially, has other unsustainable consequences, such as intensifying deforestation and lowering animal welfare and labour standards. These are fundamental tensions which go deeper than the past tensions caused by sectorial interests and national prioritisation of certain industries. The mantra of ever freer trade and economic growth as a value per se has found its limits. Critics see the crossing of international boundaries and growing inequalities *also* as a result of globalised trade relations.[2]

[1] L Ankersmit, 'The EU's strategy for more "rules-based" trade and the EU's withdrawal from the Energy Charter Treaty' (2023) 50 *Legal Issues of Economic Integration* 117; M Ossewaarde and R Ossewaarde-Lowtoo, 'The EU's Green Deal: A Third Alternative to Green Growth and Degrowth?' (2020) 12 *Sustainability* 9825; Fundamentally: D Rodrik, 'Has Globalization Gone Too Far?' (1998) 41 *Challenge* 81; On the sustainability of EU trade agreements: D van 't Wout, 'The enforceability of the trade and sustainable development chapters of the European Union's free trade agreements' (2022) 20 *Asia Europe Journal* 81; J Orbie et al, 'Promoting sustainable development or legitimizing free trade? Civil society mechanisms in EU trade agreements' (2016) 1 *Third World Thematics* 526; Specifically on the UK–Australia FTA: MA Young and G Clough, 'Net Zero Emissions and Free Trade Agreements: Efforts at Integrating Climate Goals by the United Kingdom and Australia' (2023) 72 *International and Comparative Law Quarterly* 393; A Marhold, 'Externalising Europe's energy policy in EU Free Trade Agreements: A cognitive dissonance between promoting sustainable development and ensuring security of supply?' (2019) *Europe and the World: A Law Review*; C Eckes, R Verheyen and P Krajewski, 'Treaty-Making by Afterthought: Can the EU-Mercosur Association Agreement Be Saved by the Joint Instrument?' (2024) *Archiv des Völkerrechts*.

[2] J Hickel, *Less is More – How Degrowth Will Save the World* (Penguin, 2021). See on the planetary boundaries: J Rockström, J Gupta and D Qin, 'Safe and just Earth system boundaries' (2023) 619 *Nature* 102.

Trade and investment play an important role in the EU's relations with the rest of the world. The EU's main tool in organising its trade and investment relations is the conclusion of international agreements. However, the negotiation and conclusion of trade agreements has become more difficult.[3] Also, with an eye to the international paralysis in the World Trade Organization (WTO), one can safely conclude that international trade is in crisis.

Positions both in favour and against free trade and investment protection can often be traced to the different EU institutions, with the Parliament generally more willing to push for the inclusion of other (non-trade) values and the Commission, above all Directorate-General (DG) Trade, committed to the logic that economic exchange is a value as such.[4] The Council, as the institution representing the Member States, is often politically split on issues of trade and investment. This level of controversy requires democratic decision-making procedures that, on the one hand, allow will-formation that is free of domination by one actor and, on the other, ensure that the different views are not sidelined.

In the context of EU treaty-making, the European Court of Justice (ECJ) is vested with exceptional judicial powers that allow it to review prospectively the compatibility of envisaged international agreements with the EU Treaties. The opinion procedure pursuant to Article 218(11) TFEU differs from other mechanisms of judicial review in that it invites the court to offer a general and abstract *ex ante* assessment rather than deciding ex post an individual case. The opinion procedure can only be triggered by privileged applicants, ie, the EU institutions and the Member States. Hence, the ECJ – as any court – cannot exercise its exceptional review powers out of its own volition. In other words, the ECJ depends in the opinion procedure on the other branches to request an opinion, including in trade and investment.[5] The assessment of the Court comprises both procedural and substantive compliance with EU law.

Historically, the Court of Justice has played an important role in establishing the legal framework for the EU and its Member States' international treaty-making.[6] The relevance of judicial interpretation for EU treaty-making has not been diminished after the entry into force of the Lisbon Treaty. On the contrary, changed provisions required judicial interpretation and the Member States have brought many legal challenges to the Court, aiming to protect their role as international actors. In response, the Court has interpreted and further developed the post-Lisbon arrangements in Articles 207 and 218 TFEU. It has protected the prerogatives of the different EU institutions, from each other, from the Member States, and from international law.[7] Judicial challenges by privileged applicants demonstrate a move from the political to the judicial, ie, 'politics

[3] See eg CETA and EU–Mercosur. See also C Eckes, 'The Autonomy of the EU Legal Order: The Case of the Energy Charter Treaty' (2023) *European Papers*, pp 1465–1494.

[4] See eg Eckes (ibid); Ankersmit, ch 5 in this volume.

[5] Opinions 1/13 ECLI:EU:C:2014:2303; 2/15 ECLI:EU:C:2017:376; 2/13 ECLI:EU:C:2019:341; 1/17 ECLI:EU:C:2019:72; and 1/20 ECLI:EU:C:2022:485.

[6] J Wouters, F Hoffmeister, G De Baere and T Ramopoulos, *Law of EU External Relations: Cases, Materials, and Commentary on the Eu as an International Legal Actor* (Oxford University Press, 2021).

[7] C-399/12, *Germany v Council*, ECLI:EU:C:2014:2258; Opinion 2/15 (n 5); Case 284/16 *Slowakische Republik v Achmea BV* ECLI:EU:C:2018:158; Case 626/15 *Commission v Council* ECLI:EU:C:2018:925; Opinion 1/17 (n 5); Case 741/19 *Republique de Moldovie v Komstroy LLC* ECLI:EU:C:2021:655; Opinion 1/19 ECLI:EU:C:2021:198; Opinion 1/20 (n 5).

with legal means' conducted by those that did not achieve their political objectives in the political decision-making process.[8] This illustrates the agonistic dimension of separation of powers. When accepting the justiciability of these inter-institutional disputes the Court paves the way to an even greater recourse to legal means.

This chapter examines the Court's role against a relational understanding of separation of powers, pursuant to which the three branches of government interact in mutual control and collaboration to facilitate will-formation.[9] The independence of the judiciary forms part and parcel of any concept of separation of powers. The judiciary generally rests its claims to legitimacy on consistency of its decisions with standards of law that have been adopted and developed in a democratic (inclusive?) fashion. Its powers are also legitimised by multiple constraints, eg, by the fact that it can only act if prompted to do so by other actors and the ex post perspective (that stands in the way of prospective law-making). Separation of powers is here understood as a procedural principle that does not impose any substantive limitations on what courts can or cannot rule.[10] It does not offer or demand a clean division between law (application) and politics, but aims at perpetuating and containing law and politics' continuous attempts to dominate each other.[11] To achieve its purpose, separation of powers requires that powers and responsibilities are reasonably clearly allocated.[12] This allows cooperation as well as conflict. Importantly, it also allows the tracing of positions to national and European actors, who find their legitimacy claims endorsed by citizens as national or European citizens (two-pronged structure of legitimation).[13]

When the other branches turn to the Court they invite it to impose legal constraints on each other's powers. Under the rule of law, when a court in last instance declares a certain action to be legally required or prohibited in an individual case, this should end the political debate for that case. This is required by legal certainty. Political institutions are expected to comply. Judicial decisions can limit the space for politics in this way. However, the courts can also widen the wiggle room for democratic decision-making within the framework of the law. They may reopen the debate on the limits to political discretion – ie, by establishing distinguishing factors or a context in which an earlier ruling is not applicable. They may decide that an action is neither prohibited nor required by law. They may explicitly carve out prerogatives of the legislature or discretion of the executive. All this is an expression of judicial self-restraint and contributes to limiting the Court's role for the future because parties will refrain from bringing these questions to court. In this way, the Court protects the political autonomy of the institutions or the Member States.

[8] For an inspiring account, see Joanna Kusiak, *Radically legal politics*; see summary at: ninedotsprize.org/extracts-from-joanna-kusiaks-winning-entry.

[9] C Eckes, P Leino-Sandberg and A Wallerman Ghavanini, 'Conceptual Framework for the Project Separation of Powers for 21st Century Europe' (SepaRope, 2021) No 2021-06, Amsterdam Centre for European law and Governance Research Paper, 1–2.

[10] C Möllers, *The Three Branches: A Comparative Model of Separation of Powers* (Oxford University Press, 2013) 95.

[11] Eckes, Leino-Sandberg and Wallerman Ghavanini (n 9).

[12] See also Chamon, ch 7 in this volume.

[13] C Eckes, 'The Paradox of EU External Relations: Taking Back Control', inaugural lecture 601 of 9 November 2018, at dare.uva.nl/search?identifier=583073d2-e0a1-42ba-b10e-4ae112ad6394.

Separation of powers is important in a controversial and contested context. At least potentially, separation of powers with an independent judiciary can contribute to making dissensus productive, allowing for justification, and achieving reasonable outcomes. At a time in which the EU commits to deep socio-economic changes in the Green Deal, the controversies surrounding the EU trade and investment deals are unlikely to calm down. On the contrary, it may be expected that the Court will find itself ever more often in the position that actors request it to oppose the conclusion of trade and investment agreements.

The chapter briefly considers all opinions of the Court and then focuses on those post-Lisbon opinions that have the potential to shape the institutional interaction in EU treaty-making in trade for the future. These are Opinions 1/13, 2/15, 1/17, 1/19 and 1/20. In addition, the chapter considers several post-Lisbon inter-institutional challenges (actions for annulment) where they are relevant to understand the powers of the institutions in the negotiation and conclusion of trade agreements.

This chapter argues that the Court, while acting as the guardian of the internal power relations, demonstrated judicial restraint to protect the autonomy of the EU institutions. It carved out *political* space that is not subject to legal assessment. At the same time, the Court allowed Member States to continue to remain at the table, for example when agreements include highly controversial Investor–State Dispute Settlement (ISDS) mechanisms. In light of the growing controversy about the desirability of (certain contents of) trade agreements and investment protection, the Court is walking a tightrope of ringfencing the EU's autonomous decision-making capacities while protecting the Member States' visibility and influence. Separation of powers requires allocating reasonably concretely responsibilities between the different actors, while at the same time avoiding political *paralysis* and complete judicialisation. In principle, this allocation should be established in law, ie in the European Treaties, but often the Treaty provisions require further judicial interpretation, and that interpretation should also keep the requirement of concretely identified responsibilities in mind. Where the multi-layered polycentric EU acts under the state-centric rules of international law, this is an increasingly tall order for the Court.

Section II outlines the role of the Court in determining the power relations in EU treaty-making. It examines the boundaries of the opinion procedure and sketches the particularities of EU treaty-making. Section III examines the case law of the Court with particular attention to the powers of the different branches. It identifies the Court's commitment to carve out greater political autonomy for the Council while protecting Member States' involvement. Section IV reflects on the implications of the Court's case law for the separation of powers within the EU. Section V concludes.

II. Creating a Legal Framework for International Treaty-Making

With every amendment of the EU's founding treaties the EU has obtained greater external competences and extended its ability to conclude international agreements. Article 218 TFEU is a general procedure for the negotiation and conclusion of international agreements by the EU.[14] For trade agreements in particular, Article 207 TFEU on the Common Commercial Policy (CCP) is *lex specialis*. The internal rules have significantly changed under the Lisbon Treaty. The exclusive competence of the EU for CCP has been extended to cover all trade aspects (beyond trade in goods)[15] and more trade-related issues, including foreign direct investment (FDI). This directly affects the power relations between the EU and the Member States. In addition, every amendment of the EU's founding treaties, including the Lisbon Treaty, has strengthened the role of the European Parliament (EP).[16] The EP now holds veto powers for the conclusion of trade and investment agreements, as well as a more powerful position in their negotiation and ratification. The Court's exceptional review powers over envisaged agreements under Article 218(11) TFEU form part and parcel of the conception of separation of powers that the EU adheres to in trade relations.

The following subsections explain relevant particularities of EU treaty-making that flow from its peculiar multilayered and polycentric nature (section A) and the law and practice of the Court's exceptional powers under the Article 218(11) TFEU procedure (section B).

A. Constitutional Particularities of EU Treaty-making Practices

The EU legal framework for international treaty-making is complex and dynamic. The Commission, the Council and, regularly, the Member States represent the top-level split executive that concludes international treaties for the territory of the Member States, in the name of the EU and, regularly, the Member States. Together, the Commission and the Member States individually and jointly as Council share, in trade and investment, the task to negotiate and enter into international obligations, as well as to implement them.

Tension arises from the fact that the Member States remain under international law the only primary and sovereign actor while the EU, with its exclusive CCP competence, is the recognised international trading partner. Formally, the EU institutions are autonomous in their ability to pursue trade policy. In practice, the Commission, as the Council's top-level executive counterpart, is *exceptionally* autonomous when negotiating trade agreements.[17] At the same time, the EU depends on the Member States, certainly for implementation of agreements, but also often for the conclusion of the agreements when these agreements are mixed.

These autonomous actors, from an international law perspective, represent one territory and therefore need to act as one party to international treaties, while they participate individually and in their own right. To do so, they are necessarily intricately interconnected. This explains why the EU's treaty-making practices are characterised

[14] See Krajewski, ch 6 in this volume.

[15] As confirmed by the Court in Case 414/11, *Daiichi Sankyo Co. Ltd and Sanofi-Aventis Deutschland GmbH v DEMO Anonimos Viomikhaniki kai Emporiki Etairia Farmakon* ECLI:EU:C:2013:520 and Case 137/12, *European Commission v Council of the European Union* ECLI:EU:C:2013:675.

[16] See for more details on the expanded powers of the European Parliament: Chamon, ch 7 in this volume, III.B.

[17] Krajewski, ch 6 in this volume.

by several particularities that do not find their counterparts in state practices. These particularities are procedural attempts to accommodate the complex power divisions within the EU. Mixed agreements are the most prominent and still not fully explored example.

Mixity is seen as 'a creature of pragmatic forces – a means of resolving the problems posed by the need for international agreements in a multilayered system'.[18] Mixity offers a political and legal construction that allows the Union and the Member States to act jointly as one party when they conclude international agreements. This results under international and EU law in a – seemingly permanent – suspension of the question of who is competent. It obscures who is in charge and responsible for which part of the agreement, ie, the EU or the Member States. By extension, it also obscures whether the European Parliament or national parliaments are responsible for any particular part.[19] Seemingly, this permanent suspension can only be brought to an end when one of the involved parties seeks a judicial decision on the competence division in a specific case.

To what extent does mixity retain its relevance for trade and investment agreements in light of the extended EU competences under CCP and after Opinion 2/15? Article 207 TFEU establishes encompassing exclusive competences of the EU for CCP. This provision has further been interpreted very widely by the Court, holding that 'an EU act falls within [CCP] if it relates specifically to such trade in that it is essentially intended to promote, facilitate or govern such trade and has direct and immediate effects on it'.[20] The debate is ongoing about what this encompassing EU competence for CCP means for whether EU trade agreements should be 'EU-only' or 'mixed'.[21] Mixity used to be the default for deep and comprehensive trade agreements. Examples are Comprehensive Economic and Trade Agreement (CETA) and the EU–Mercosur Agreement. However, a new trend of EU-only agreements appears to be emerging: Singapore, Japan, Vietnam, and the UK TCA. The Commission, with a tacit acceptance of the Council, appears to pursue a strategy whereby investment protection is excluded from negotiation directives and the rest can be concluded as an EU-only agreement.[22] In other words, the future of mandatory (ie, legally required) mixity has come under pressure by the Court's wide interpretation of CCP. Yet, the increasing controversy surrounding trade and investment has also triggered a trend of including more and more norms relating to non-trade value into these agreements, which in turn justify involvement of the Member States.[23]

[18] Case 243/15 *Lesoochranárske zoskupenie VLK v Obvodný úrad Trenčín* ECLI: EU:C:2016:491 Opinion AG Kokott [56].

[19] C Eckes, *EU Powers Under External Pressure: How the EU's External Actions Alter its Internal Structures* (Oxford University Press, 2019) ch 5. Because of the dynamic development of EU powers, this is the case even if at the moment of conclusion for example the Finnish Parliament insists on a list of issues of national competence.

[20] Opinion 2/15 (n 5) [36] ff, referring inter alia to C 414/11 *Daiichi Sankyo and Sanofi-Aventis Deutschland* ECLI: EU:C:2013:520 [51].

[21] P Conconi, C Herghelegiu and L Puccio, 'EU Trade Agreements: To Mix or Not to Mix, That Is the Question', (2021) 55 *Journal of World Trade* 231.

[22] eg agreements with New Zealand, Chile an Australia; see data.consilium.europa.eu/doc/document/ST-8622-2018-INIT/en/pdf.

[23] Eckes, Verheyen, and Krajewski (n 1).

Few aspects of the EU's trade and investment relations are as controversial as ISDS mechanisms – both in terms of substance and competence. They have also been the focus of a growing body of case law.[24] This case law is not necessarily focussed on substance, but often challenges institutional or procedural aspects. Yet, it is motivated by a widening conviction that ISDS protects unsustainable extractive business interests.[25] In terms of competence division, Opinion 2/15 on the competence division in the EU–Singapore agreement demonstrates that the ECJ draws some lines around the EU's exclusive competence for CCP. It establishes that ISDS provisions are a 'shared competence'.[26] The EU cannot simply occupy the field by regulating ISDS, as would be the case under Article 2 TFEU. Opinion 2/15 explicates that Member States must *consent* to ISDS because it removes disputes from national judiciaries and, by extension, from the preliminary ruling procedure under Article 267 TFEU, which has been called the 'keystone' of European integration.[27] Opinion 2/15 hence requires involvement and consent of the Member States for each and every international agreement that sets up an ISDS mechanism. In other words, trade agreements that contain ISDS mechanisms cannot be concluded by the EU alone, as ISDS requires the Member States' consent via mixity.

Another example of an EU particularity that recently became subject of a judicial dispute is hybrid acts. Hybrid acts are the result of bringing 'together in a single decision' or adopting 'under a single procedure two different acts, one of which entails a consensus of the representatives of the Member States, and therefore their unanimous agreement, whereas the other must be adopted' by a qualified majority in the Council.[28] The Member States act alongside the Council in their capacity as sovereign actors under international law, not as part of the Council. The Court prohibited hybrid acts in one of the post-Lisbon interinstitutional disputes concerning external relations, because it undermines the decision-making procedures under the EU Treaties and interferes with the institutional autonomy of the EU institutions.[29]

The third example of an EU particularity in treaty-making is the 'common accord'. Concluding an agreement only with 'common accord' refers to the situation that the Council does not take a decision that it is formally able to take until and unless all Member States have indicated that they agree. This is a practice followed in areas of shared competence, which is not reflected in Articles 207 and 218 TFEU. In Opinion 1/19, the CJEU clarified that Article 218(2) (6) TFEU, on the role of the Council in authorising the opening of the negotiations, adopting the negotiating directive, authorising the signing of

[24] Opinion 2/15 (n 5); Case 284/16 *Slowakische Republik v Achmea BV* ECLI:EU:C:2018:158; Opinion 1/17 (n 5); Case 741/19 *Republique de Moldovie v Komstroy LLC* ECLI:EU:C:2021:655; Opinion 1/19 (n 7); Opinion 1/20 (n 5).

[25] DR Boyd, Report of the Special Rapporteur on the issue of human rights obligations relating to the enjoyment of a safe, clean, healthy and sustainable environment: 'Paying polluters: the catastrophic consequences of investor-State dispute settlement for climate and environment action and human rights'(A/78/168), at www.ohchr.org/en/documents/thematic-reports/a78168-paying-polluters-catastrophic-consequences-investor-state-dispute.

[26] Opinion 2/15 (n 5), [36].

[27] Opinion 2/15 (n 5); L Ankersmit, 'Regulatory autonomy and regulatory chill in Opinion 1/17' (2020) 4 *Europe and the World: A Law Review* 1; Eckes (n 3).

[28] Opinion 1/19 (n 7) [243]. See: Case 28/12 *European Commission v Council of the European Union* ECLI:EU:C:2015:282.

[29] Case 28/12 *European Commission v Council of the European Union* ECLI:EU:C:2015:282.

agreements, and adopting the decision concluding the agreement, *do not accord any role to the Member States*.[30] Hence, common accord cannot be a legal requirement (but only a political option).

Article 218 TFEU sketches the conclusion of an international agreement by the Union as 'an autonomous act'.[31] This is also the case for mixed agreements for the part that falls within EU competences and for which the Council, rather than the Member States, must agree. Prohibiting hybrid acts and declaring that 'common accord' is not a legal requirement ensures the autonomous capacity of the Union to act externally without allowing a minority of (or even individual) Member States to hinder its actions. The limits of the EU's autonomous capacity to conclude trade and investment agreements lie in the division of competences as established by the EU Treaties, procedurally and substantively by Articles 207 and 218 TFEU.

The ideal of separation of powers requires that powers are *reasonably concretely allocated*, ie, that it is possible to identify who exercises which powers.[32] While all constitutional frameworks aim to lay down rules on the exercise of public powers, they can only give limited guidance that requires filling in and enacting through institutional practices. A certain level of ambiguity is not only unavoidable to ensure the needed flexibility of the institutional actors; it also arises from the healthy relational and collaborative practices of mutually reinforcing, challenging and demanding further justification for each other's acts. However, the three examples of particular procedural practices that arose in the EU's external relations go beyond the usual level of ambiguity. These particularities allow the EU to act internationally without being debilitated by its own complex constitutional set-up as a non-state actor with state-like external powers. They are hence an intrinsic feature of the EU as an international legal actor. However, they are *designed to intertwine powers* in a way that does not permit tracing them to the individual entity or actor. An illustrative example is mixity and pre-emption. Merijn Chamon argued that when the EU and MS conclude a mixed international agreement covering matters of shared competence, mixity allows them to 'suspend' the field pre-emption that would otherwise kick in if the agreement was concluded as EU-only.[33] This is problematic in terms of separation of powers, and the Court holds the constitutional mandate to develop and apply the legal standards in the Treaties in order to ensure reasonably clearly allocated responsibilities.

B. Opinion Procedure under Article 218(11) TFEU

The first decade after the entry into force of the Lisbon Treaty has been characterised by an increasing number of judicial disputes about the Union's exercise of external powers.[34] The tone and intensity of these legal battles was pointedly criticised by AG

[30] Opinion 1/19 (n 7) [237], emphasis added.
[31] Opinion 1/19 (n 7) [246].
[32] See ch 1 of this volume.
[33] M Chamon, 'Provisional Application's Novel Rationale: Facilitating Mixity in the EU's Treaty Practice' in W Douma, C Eckes, P Elsuwege, E Kassoti, A Ott and RA Wessels (eds), *The Evolving Nature of EU External Relations Law* (Springer, 2021).
[34] eg Eckes (n 19), Intro.

Kokott, stating that legal actions are fought with 'astonishing passion' and 'allegation [s are made] that the Commission wished to do everything possible to prevent international action by the Member States', as well as that 'the Council [was] compulsively looking for legal bases that always permit participation by the Member States'.[35] In many of these cases, large numbers of Member States intervened.[36] The increased number of legal challenges is also the result of leaving choices open in the negotiation of the Lisbon Treaty. Textual ambiguities necessarily vest the judiciary with the powers to clarify, detail and interpret.[37] At the same time, when the Court develops more detailed rules from the Treaties' text, it reduces the scope for political manoeuvre of the EU institutions. Notably, relevant for the context of trade, the Court widened the substantive (CCP) and procedural (treaty-making in general) autonomy of the EU on several occasions, arguably in the most far-reaching manner under the opinion procedure.[38]

The EU Treaties give the Court the exceptional power to review envisaged international agreements (Article 218(11) TFEU) to avoid external (entrenched) commitments that run counter to EU law. This 'removes the pressure of subsequent costs from courts, which the *ex post* review of international commitments otherwise entails. It represents a workable mechanism for channelling foreign commitments back into a system of separated powers.'[39] The timing of *ex ante* opinions on the compatibility of the envisaged legal commitments should allow the institutions to negotiate substantive amendments or procedurally comply with internal rules *before* making legally binding commitments. Incompatibility with EU law often also affects the division of powers, eg, because the EU commits to something that goes beyond its substantive competence or one EU institution infringes the prerogatives of another institution. The timing of the Court's involvement *during* the decision-making also requires thinking about who wins and who loses powers and influence when the opinion procedure is triggered. To do this, we should first reflect on *who* uses this procedure and *why* through a lens of separation of powers.

Marise Cremona sketched in 2020 the development of the opinion procedure over time.[40] Building on Cremona's analysis and updating it to December 2023, we count 23 opinions in total,[41] including Opinion 1/20, in which the Court rejected the request to examine the compatibility of the EU text proposal for the Energy Charter Treaty (ECT) reform for its compatibility with EU law. Nine of these opinions were given post-Lisbon. Seven of the opinions directly concern trade or investment agreements.[42] The general trend is that the Court's opinions become longer and longer.[43] In addition, the Court

[35] Opinion of AG Kokott, Joined Cases C-626/15 and C-659/16 *Commission v Council* ECLI:EU:C:2018:362 [75].

[36] Opinions 1/19 (n 7), 1/17 (n 5), 2/15 (n 5) but also references from Eckes (n 19).

[37] Arnull et al, *The European Union and its Court of Justice* (Oxford University Press, 2006) 89.

[38] Opinions 2/15 (n 5) and 1/19 (n 7).

[39] Möllers (n 10) 164.

[40] M Cremona, 'The Opinion procedure under Article 218 (11) TFEU: Reflections in the light of Opinion 1/17.' (2020) 4 *Europe and the World – A Law Review* 1.

[41] Excluding proceedings under the Treaty establishing the European Coal and Steel Community.

[42] EU–Singapore FTA Opinion 2/15 (n 5); CETA Opinion 1/17 (n 5); ECT Opinion 1/20 (n 5); Opinion 1/94 ECLI:EU:C:1994:384; Opinions 2/91 ECLI:EU:C:1991:490 and 1/92 ECLI:EU:C:1992:189; Opinion 3/94 ECLI:EU:C:1995:436.

[43] Opinion 1/19 (n 7) is 338 paragraphs; Opinion 1/17 (n 5) is 245 paragraphs; Opinion 2/13 (n 5) was 258 paragraphs; Opinion 2/15 (n 5) was 305 paragraphs. This is not counting the rejection of the request in Opinion 1/20 (n 5).

has moved from considering matters of competence to also engaging with substantive issues.[44] In other words, the role of the Court under the opinion procedure has quantitatively and qualitatively increased over time.

Another still nascent development appears to be requests by the European Parliament. While it does not have the same influence in treaty-making as the Commission and the Council,[45] in the opinion procedure it is a privileged applicant on a par with the other institutions and the Member States. One could hence argue that a move from the political to the judicial realm comparatively empowers the EP. So far, the EP has (only) twice triggered the Opinion procedure: once in 2015 (Opinion 1/15), which was the first substantive engagement; and once in 2019 (Opinion 1/19), which had great implications for the role of the Court, the Council and the Member States in international treaty-making.

In other words, it is mainly the Commission that involves the Court via the opinion procedure. The opinion procedure appears to be a tool used by the Commission to prevent the Council from taking decisions on division of powers that are not in line with its own interpretation of that division – for example, when the Council claims political autonomy to decide that an agreement requires mixity. It appears that the existence and practice of this powerful review procedure during decision-making empowers the Commission (as the EU part of the split-level top executive) vis-à-vis the Council and the Member States' Governments, when it protects the autonomy of the Union.

The two most recent opinions concern highly politicised international agreements: the Istanbul Convention (Opinion 1/19) and the ECT (Opinion 1/20). In both cases, the Court took a stand that may contribute to reducing the judicializsation of political power struggles. The Court paraphrased the preventive purpose of the Article 218(11) TFEU procedure as 'forestalling complications which would result from legal disputes concerning the compatibility with the Treaties of international agreements that are binding on the European Union'.[46] 'Complications' refers specifically both to the 'internal EU context' and 'international relations'.[47] The potential seriousness of such 'complications' justifies that 'the *mere risk* of an invalidation [of the envisaged agreement] suffices'.[48] At the same time, the Court does not assess the *compatibility* of the decision on conclusion *with international law*.[49] The scope of the opinion procedure is compatibility with EU law only.

The Court can only find incompatibility with the Treaties *before* an international agreement becomes legally binding on the EU. In the most recent Opinion 1/20 on what is probably the most controversial (mixed) investment agreement, ECT, the Court offered a restrictive interpretation of 'envisaged agreement', which excludes the judicial involvement of the ECJ in the early stage of negotiations. The Court's interpretation protects the political space of the negotiating parties by excluding judicial engagement before an actional text is politically agreed. The 'preventive intent' of the opinion

[44] In Opinion 1/15 ECLI:EU:C:2017:592, the Court examined the substantive compatibility of envisaged agreements with amongst other things fundamental rights.

[45] C Eckes, 'How the European Parliament's Participation in International Relations Affects the Deep Tissue of the EU's Power Structures' (2004) 12 *International Journal of Constitutional Law (ICON)* 904.

[46] Opinion 1/19 (n 7) [193].

[47] ibid.

[48] ibid [194], emphasis added.

[49] ibid [272].

procedure can also 'no longer be achieved' with regard to a signature decision that has already entered into force.[50] This temporal limitation stands in open contrast with the Court's willingness three decades ago to examine 'the system of judicial supervision which it is proposed to set up under the [European Economic Area] agreement'.[51]

The Court's recent position highlights the strict boundaries of Article 218(11) TFEU: the Court's extensive general and prospective powers are strictly confined to the short timeframe between the moment where there is sufficiently clear and explicit political agreement between the parties on the 'envisaged agreement' and the moment that the agreement is concluded. In the past, the Court has once rejected an opinion request as inadmissible, ie 'devoid of purpose', after conclusion, and once a request has been withdrawn after conclusion.[52] Furthermore, the opinion procedure is *not* intended to avoid difficulties associated with implementation.[53] The latter point is a considerable limitation of the reach of the opinion procedure as many *internal* difficulties may directly relate to implementation.[54]

The opinion procedure, different from the other judicial routes, is aimed to protect the *interest of the EU* rather than the particular party requesting the procedure.[55] The requesting party is not required to identify a 'harmful conduct' by the other actors.[56] At the same time, the Court of Justice always accepted and confirmed the potential agonistic nature of the procedure by emphasising that the power to involve the Court 'can be exercised individually' and does not require 'any coordinated action', nor does it require the requesting party to wait 'for the final outcome of any related legislative procedure'.[57] In other words, the opinion procedure offers the different branches and layers a channel to translate their disagreement between the negotiation and the conclusion of international agreements into the language of law and try to convince the Court that their concern is a legal concern.

Because of the rigid and cumbersome context of bilateral and even more so multilateral treaty-making, the EU cannot easily renegotiate core aspects of international agreements. In other words, the Court is de facto in the position to determine whether the EU can become a party to a treaty in an often semi-permanent way.[58] As such, the opinion procedure is exceptional in light of the most common task of Courts to rule on individual cases from an ex post perspective, ie, 'adjudicat[ing] individualized cases on external initiative, retrospectively'.[59] This exceptional nature of the opinion procedure explains the strict procedural limits to the window of opportunity during which parties can bring requests, to the nature of the analysis, and to the potential group of applicants, which is confined to privileged applicants.

[50] ibid [218].
[51] Opinion 1/91 (n 42).
[52] Opinion 3/94 (n 42) [22] and Opinion 1/04 (withdrawn), respectively. In both cases, follow-up procedures were brought to challenge the *legality* of the agreement: Case 122/95 *Germany v Council* ECLI:EU:C:1998:94 and Joined Cases C-317/04 and C-318/04 *European Parliament v Council* ECLI:EU:C:2006:346.
[53] Opinion 1/19 (n 7) [196].
[54] See for examples: Eckes, Leino-Sandberg and Wallerman Ghavanini (n 9).
[55] Opinion 1/19 (n 7) [195].
[56] ibid [221].
[57] ibid [204].
[58] See Opinion 2/14 ECLI:EU:C:2014:2454 on the accession of the EU to the ECHR.
[59] Möllers (n 10) 89.

As in all courts, the ECJ draws its 'legitimacy' from its 'commitment to legal standards'[60] and exercises its powers highly formally proceduralised. The reasoning in the language of law and the formality of its procedure are what distinguishes the judiciary from the other branches. In that sense, the opinion procedure is no exception. It presupposes that reasoning founded in legal standards can generate a distinct logic beyond the political process before this process has led to a legally binding decision. It also confirms the EU's sincere commitment to abide by international law, ie by avoiding entering into international legal obligations with which it cannot comply, unless it accepts a breach of its own law. The strict limits outlined above ensure that from a procedural understanding of separation of powers the Court acts in line with the 'desideratum of distinctiveness'[61] and within the boundaries of its mandate.

III. Vesting the Council with Greater Political Autonomy

When deciding disputes on boundaries of public powers, courts must decide what is and what is not a legal issue. In the EU, the issue of which authority, ie, which EU institution or the Member States, may exercise political discretion, is legally circumscribed. Opinions 2/15 offers a broad interpretation of the boundaries of the EU's exclusive competence for matters of trade but ringfences Member States' responsibility for ISDS. Opinion 1/19 protects the EU's political autonomy in the conclusion of mixed agreements. Together, they establish the complex legal framework that governs how the different branches and layers collaborate and control each other in trade and investment policy.

Section A below demonstrates how the Court has empowered the Council with autonomous decision-making capacity, and section B considers the potential international law consequences of ringfencing the powers of the different actors of the top-level split executive.

A. Political Discretion and its Procedural Limits

The ECJ bolstered the Council's capacity to act autonomously on the international plane and protected its internal decision-making procedures from external influences.[62] This is in line with and reflects the EU's ambition to shape the world in its image.[63] The Commission is a powerful autonomous actor in the negotiation and conclusion of EU trade and investment agreements.[64] However, the Council's autonomy as an institution from its national parts is central to the EU's particularity of having – different

[60] Möllers (n 10) 90.
[61] A Kavanagh, *The Collaborative Constitution Cambridge* (Cambridge University Press, 2023) ch 3.
[62] eg Opinions 1/17 (n 5) and 1/19 (n 7); see on the former Eckes (n 3). See also Case 280/93 *Germany v Council* ECLI:EU:C:1994:367.
[63] Art 3(5) TFEU; see also J Borrell, 'Why European Strategic Autonomy Matters' (2020) *HR/VP Blog*, at www.eeas.europa.eu/eeas/why-european-strategic-autonomy-matters_en.
[64] See Krajewski, ch 6 in this volume.

from the usual arrangements in federations – a top-level split executive, where the Commission, the Council and the Member States are charged to collaborate with and control each other.

On the boundaries between the Commission and the Council's executive powers, the Court held that 'both the decision [of] whether or not to act on the proposal to conclude an international agreement, and, if so, to what extent, and the choice of the appropriate time to adopt such a decision fall within the Council's political discretion'.[65] In other words, the law does not require the Council to act upon the Commission proposal to conclude an international agreement.

Further bolstering the Council's political discretion, the ECJ showed judicial self-restraint by delegalising certain issues and excluding certain grounds for the future.[66] Opinion 1/19 is illustrative in this respect. It concerned the conclusion of the Council of Europe Convention on preventing and combating violence against women and domestic violence ('the Istanbul Convention'). One question raised was whether the Council must wait for the Member States' common accord, ie, agreement of all Member States that the Convention should be concluded, before taking that step. The Court held that the issue of whether the Council waits for the common accord of all the Member States is *not prescribed by law*. Such practice is neither prohibited nor required by Article 218 TFEU. Consequently, the Council is allowed but not required to either wait or go ahead, irrespective of the intentional difficulties that may potentially emerge from the decision to go ahead. However, this distinction between 'allow' and 'require' common accord is less clear than it may appear at first glance. The Council has the discretion to wait and build a bigger majority in a continuous scale to consensus (common accord) – in principle, indefinitely. Waiting also serves a justified objective and is not just a strategy for delay. Securing Member States' commitments to as many ratifications as possible of an international agreement strengthens the international position of the EU, its credibility, and its political weight as composite actor, speaking with one voice.

However, a vote can be forced under its own rules of procedure.[67] In matters subject to qualified majority vote, qualified majority is sufficient for the formal decision in favour of moving forward. In other words, the possibility (rather than requirement) of waiting for a common accord does not affect the voting requirements in the Council and does not make the Council hostage to each and every dissenting state. Opinion 1/19 firmly links political discretion to *qualified majority in the Council*. This addresses the European Parliament's concern that requiring common accord would 'amount … to applying, in practice, an unanimity rule within the Council despite the fact … only qualified majority rule applies'.[68] Ultimately, it ensures that the qualified majority of the Council can act on eye-level with the other parts of the EU's split top-level executive, ie the Commission and national governments.

By way of conclusion, the Council may autonomously exercise its prerogatives under Article 218 TFEU, irrespective of the fact that the Member States are the primary actors under international law and the EU may have to rely on them for the implementation

[65] Opinion 1/19 (n 5) [252].
[66] ibid.
[67] ibid [253]–[255].
[68] ibid [60].

of the agreement. The Court was willing to protect that autonomous space of decision-making of the Council, emphasising that the procedural rules of will-formation require qualified majority. It also limited the relevance of the law and its own influence by firmly placing the decision within the discretion of the qualified majority of the Council. In other words, it protects the autonomy of the EU institutions vis-à-vis the Member States and, by doing so, it ensures the continuous need for political collaboration between the different parts of the top-level split executive in order to work towards a mutually acceptable and viable position.

B. International Law Consequences of Vesting the Split Executive with Autonomous Powers

The Court assesses the legality of EU international agreements exclusively in light of EU law, both procedurally and substantively. International law and the potential consequences from a breach of international law *are not the yardstick* of its assessment. This position is in line with the ECJ's understanding of the (jurisdictional) autonomy of EU law.[69] It protects and promotes, not only the autonomy of the EU legal order from international law but also the ECJ's room for manoeuvre to prioritise the political autonomy of the EU institutions. If the Court were also willing to review compliance of envisaged agreements with international law, this would – at least potentially – create a conflict by allowing the EU and its institutions to act independently from the Member States.

Excluding international law as a yardstick allows for the end result of 'incomplete mixity'. Incomplete mixity refers to the rare case when an international agreement is concluded by one or more but not all of the Member States alongside the Union.[70] It raises complex legal questions concerning for example the application of the international agreement by virtue of EU law within those Member States that are not party to the agreement or international responsibility of the Union for non-compliance.[71] In absence of a detailed declaration of competences explaining which parts fall within the powers of the Union and the Member States, respectively, incomplete mixity creates legal uncertainty.

The practical consequences of impending incomplete mixity in the context of trade and investment relations can currently be witnessed in the context of the withdrawal from the ECT.[72] After a long period of deliberation, in July 2023, the Commission tabled a proposal for coordinated withdrawal.[73] 'Coordinated withdrawal' refers to the legally clearest situation that the EU and all 27 Member States withdraw together from the

[69] C Eckes, 'The autonomy of the EU legal order' (2020) 4 *Europe and the World: A law review*; C Eckes, 'EU Autonomy: Jurisdictional Sovereignty by a Different Name?' (2020) 5 *European Papers* 319.

[70] J Heliskoski, and G Kübek, 'A Typology of EU Mixed Agreements Revisited' in N Levrat, Y Kaspiarovich, C Kaddous and RA Wessel (eds), *The EU and its Member States' Joint Participation in International Agreements* (Hart Publishing, 2022) 23–42, 34.

[71] ibid.

[72] See also on the Energy Charter Treaty, including the difficulties of withdrawal: Eckes and Ankersmit, report Client Earth; Eckes (n 3); and Ankersmit, ch 5 in this volume.

[73] Commission proposal for a Council decision on the withdrawal of the Union from the Energy Charter Treaty of 7 July 2023, available at eur-lex.europa.eu/legal-content/EN/TXT/PDF/?uri=CELEX:52023PC0447.

ECT, to which they have been (with the exception of Italy) a party since the 1990s.[74] However, at the time of writing, Member States have widely signalled that they want to leave the decision to withdraw to the individual Member State. This is likely to result in a situation that the EU and a large number of Member States, certainly representing the majority of the EU population(s) and territory/ies, will withdraw, while some Member States remain party to the ECT. While arguably possible under EU law, the uncoordinated withdrawal has highly undesirable consequences for all involved parties under international law.[75] What is more, the lack of clarity about responsibilities and powers to take autonomous decisions is further obscured by the unwillingness of the EU institutions to share with the public their understanding of the *legal* allocation and boundaries of responsibilities and powers between the EU and the Member States.[76]

In Opinion 1/19, the Court gave the Council the political discretion to opt for incomplete mixity and accept at the time of signature and conclusion by the Union that one or more Member States have no intention to ratify the Istanbul Convention.[77] The political possibility of partial rather than coordinated withdrawal appears to be the flipside of this coin. While this approach offers political space and autonomy to all parties, ie, the EU and the Member States, it places the burden of understanding the boundaries between the Union and the Member States of the application of and responsibility for the international agreement on the other (non-EU) contracting parties to the agreement. The ECJ's position arguably prioritises the political autonomy of the Council, as well as the sovereignty of those Member States that do not wish to ratify the Istanbul Convention or withdraw from the ECT, above the interests of the other (non-EU) contracting parties and legal certainty.

The Council and – by analogy – the Member States remain free to knowingly accept that their own autonomous choice breaks up the collective of the EU and its Member States as one party to international agreements, creating legal uncertainty about who is in charge of and, more importantly, whether anyone is responsible for, compliance and implementation. Irrespective of the occurrence or a breach of international law, the externalisation of the internal competence complexities weakens the rule of law and democratic legitimacy, simply by creating grey zones of uncertainty on the fundamental issue of who does what and in whose name. Such lack of reasonably clear allocation of responsibilities undermines the two-pronged democratic legitimation of the EU. It blurs responsibility between and shifts the burden of mutual control to the partially competing actors of the top-level split executive. At least potentially, this comes at the expense of non-EU parties for whom the division of responsibility remains obscure or at the expense of the credibility of the EU as a unitary actor.

[74] At the time of writing (November 2023), Poland, Germany and Luxembourg have unilaterally notified their withdrawal to the Secretariat of the Energy Charter Treaty.

[75] L Ankersmit, 'Withdrawal from mixed agreements under EU law: the case of the Energy Charter Treaty' (2023) 7 *Europe and the World: A Law Review* 1.

[76] P Leino-Sandberg and C Eckes, 'The European Commission's Assessment of EU Withdrawal from the Energy Charter Treaty: Legal analysis or confidential strategy?', Blogpost 41/2022, 28 SEPTEMBER 2022, at europeanlawblog.eu/2022/09/28/the-european-commissions-assessment-of-eu-withdrawal-from-the-energy-charter-treaty-legal-analysis-or-confidential-strategy.

[77] See more broadly: P Koutrakos and V Soneca, 'The Future of the Istanbul Convention before the CJEU' in N Levrat, Y Kaspiarovich, C Kaddous and RA Wessel (eds) *The EU and its Member States' Joint Participation in International Agreements* (Hart Publishing, 2022).

In trade, the power division is reasonably clear: the EU holds exclusive competence. Yet, concluding and ending participation in ISDS mechanisms requires consent by the Member States. Similarly, the powers to agree on non-trade issues are usually shared and dynamic. In light of the fact that international agreements are negotiated and concluded as one whole, third parties and citizens are left guessing who is responsible for which substantive part of the agreement. An illustrative example of this is the scope of provisional application of comprehensive trade agreements. In principle, provisional application should be limited to matters covered by the CCP, but the institutional practice has been more confusing and inconsistent.[78]

IV. Political Autonomy Amongst Separated Powers

Article 218(11) TFEU empowers the Court to review and, if need be, delimitate the EU's ability to commit to international obligations, based on general, prospective and sometimes even hypothetical considerations of where conflicts with EU law could arise.[79] Exercising this power, the ECJ has assumed a central and powerful role in shaping the EU legal order and in protecting the legal and political autonomy of that order and its actors.

The following sections examine the role of the Court and the political institutions in facilitating constructive will-formation (section A), as well as the case law's capacity to channel disagreement and dissent into the decision-making (section B).

A. Counter-balancing Political Autonomy

With the increased powers of the EU, the widening and deepening of trade agreements, and the strengthening of the European Parliament, the constitutional and institutional conditions have never been more conducive for a greater claim to political autonomy of the EU and its institutions. At the same time, the EU is constructed as a multilayered, polycentric legal order and the issue of trade has become fundamentally contested. This entails that the three branches are present not only within the 'EU layer' but also within the national layer. Particularly, in international treaty-making this brings multiple, partially overlapping executive actors to the table that do not stand in a hierarchical relationship. This lack of hierarchy raises on the one hand the demand for judicial solutions, while on the other it makes the solution of conflict by the judiciary more difficult. The decentralised enforcement of the preliminary ruling procedure is not available. Opinions and rulings given by the Court on the power division between the EU and the Member States depend on the compliance of the national and European political actors.

[78] P Krajewski, *Separation of Powers and the EU Treaty-Making: The Case of Trade Agreements*, ch 3 (unpublished thesis, to be defended in 2024); J Heliskoski, 'Provisional Application of EU Free Trade Agreements' in M Hahn and G Van der Loo (eds), *Law and Practice of the Common Commercial Policy* (Brill, 2020) ch 25.

[79] Opinion 2/13 (n 5), see also C Eckes, 'EU Accession to the ECHR: Between Autonomy and Adaptation' (2013) 76 *Modern Law Review* 254.

Opponents of the EU's trade and investment policy challenge the EU's exercise of powers in Court to stop the adoption of international agreements that they consider substantively harmful, eg, for non-trade values.[80] This empowers the Court but can the Court offer a counterbalance to the powerful multi-actor executive in international treaty-making?

While the Court has demonstrated its willingness to substantively review politically salient agreements, e. in the area of data protection, it has also throughout emphasised the political autonomy of the EU institutions. The permission to wait for common accord, the obligatory consent of the Member States' in the conclusion of ISDS mechanisms, and the Court's restraint in refusing to rule on a treaty-text before it is 'envisaged' require the different actors to work together towards political solutions. At the same time, the prohibition of hybrid acts and the rejection of a legal requirement to wait for common accord aim to ensure that responsibilities can be traced back to individual actors. From a separation of powers perspective, the Court is in a difficult position to strike the balance between concretising the legal standards to ensure reasonable clarity of responsibility and protecting a political space in which all actors can participate in their role of will-formation in the EU. Arguably, the Court seems to leave the counter-balancing executive power to the other executive actors, ie, it seems to rely on the multilayered system, assuming that national executive powers counterbalance EU executive powers and vice versa. While this raises questions from a separation of powers perspective, the Court can also only step in if it can rely on sufficient support and legitimation by the other actors, including not only the judicial but also the executive branches of the Member States. The Court can only resolve political conflicts between the different layers and autonomous executive actors if it can rally up support that the conflict concerns a legally resolvable matter.[81]

Externally, only the Member States are primary actors under international law. In recognition of the Member States' position as primary actors and in order to ensure their full commitment and support, the EU had developed the general practice of common accord for mixed agreements. However, this practice renders the requirement and hence possibility of taking a Council decision by qualified majority de facto void. Member States obtain additional powers to postpone, veto, and – as a result also – to exercise pressure on the content of the whole agreement, ie beyond the areas of national competence.[82] The political autonomy of the Council is internationally compromised.

Moreover, it is questionable what legal consequences may flow from the formless expression of agreement, ie common accord, by the government of a Member State. From the perspective of separation of powers, it appears difficult to argue that a formless statement of government can bind parliament to adopt a formal decision pursuant to a

[80] See eg the lobby activities leading to the submission of the request in Opinion 1/17 (n 5). See also Opinion 1/20 (n 5).

[81] See similarly on the rule of law: Möllers, ch 3 in this volume.

[82] Internally, a parallel could be drawn to the same situation when legal bases with different decision-making procedures are combined and as a result the roles of institutions are strengthened. However, internally both the EU institutions and the Member States are bound by the decisions of the Court and the primacy of EU law. Externally, international commitments with third parties that are not bound by EU law create a different dynamic.

procedure that is specifically intended to give parliament a veto power. National parliaments, whose positive vote is required in the national ratification of a mixed agreement, do still have the power to vote no.

In principle, protecting Council's political autonomy affirms its role as the EU institution representing the Member States. The Council, different from the Commission and the Parliament, is the EU institution in which the national interests are directly represented. However, the focus of the Council as the politically autonomous actor, representing the voices of the Member States, potentially sidelines national parliaments. This is 'potentially' the case because the influence of national parliaments then fully depends on their ability to give their national representative in the Council a mandate and control its execution. It is far from obvious that the different executive layers constrain each other. Quite to the contrary, when taking concerted action they may be even more overpowering for the legislature. Amongst many reasons, this may be why the European Parliament has started turning to the Court under the opinion procedure.

B. Capturing Dissenting Voices

Legally required mixity and common accord rely on the ability to achieve political consensus. These constructions have therefore the potential to paralyse EU treaty-making. Post-Lisbon, the Court has confirmed that for shared competences, whether previously exercised or not, the choice for facultative mixity or EU-only conclusion of an agreement is a *political* choice, and neither of the two is legally required.[83] The legal constraints on the political decision on mixity or EU-only conclusion have been discussed both in general and with regard to individual agreements.[84] Opting for mixity has far-reaching practical consequences that illustrate the risk of political paralysis: large numbers of Commission proposals to conclude mixed agreements are blocked in the Council.[85] In other words, in a climate of controversy, the legal requirement of consensus in decision-making may practically paralyse EU action. When the different top executive actors are in a stalemate the EU and its Member States are paralysed. We can witness this in the great difficulties of the EU and its Member States in dealing with the ECT, which has been found (partially) incompatible with EU law, but coordinated withdrawal remains complicated and uncoordinated withdrawal triggers many undesirable consequences, such as legal uncertainty and potentially international liability. The EU simply lacks a unified executive actor that can decide – limited by procedures and separation of powers – for the EU and its Member States as one party.

Reasonable disagreement about what is a 'good life' and hence the impossibility of identifying an uncontroversial public good lie at the core of why we need separation of

[83] Opinion 2/15 (n 5).

[84] M Chamon, 'Constitutional limits to the political choice for mixity' in E Neframi and M Gatti (eds), *Constitutional issues of EU external relations law* (Nomos, 2018); L Prete, 'The constitutional limits to the choice of mixity after EUSFTA, COTIF I, MPA Antarctic and COTIF II: towards a more constructive discourse?' (2020) 1 *European Law Review* 113; C Eckes and P Leino-Sandberg 'The EU-UK Trade and Cooperation Agreement – Exceptional Circumstances or a new Paradigm for EU External Relations?' (2022) *Modern Law Review*.

[85] Opinion 1/19 (n 7) [152].

powers to ensure procedures of will-formation that take into account differing views.[86] These procedures also ensure the continuity of democracies. Perpetual consensus would render democracies ultimately futile.[87] Creating scope for political discretion gives room for confrontation and captures dissenting voices within the decision-making process. Both in the current political climate in the Council and because of the increased controversy surrounding trade and investment policies, conflictual exchanges are likely to stay. At the same time, we need some level of consensus between the top level-split executive in order to avoid paralysis or breaking that paralysis at the cost of international liability.

Externally, the Council may, when exercising its political discretion, decide to hazard the consequences of incomplete mixity and potential international liability for being unable to implement part of the agreement, as explained above. Besides international liability, this burden-shifting has the potential to trigger political backlash by non-EU states and controversy about the Union's 'exceptionalism'. The Court's argument in Opinion 1/19 that the Council of Europe 'is aware' of the competence division between the Union and the Member States[88] remains a vague attempt to justify this burden, which is unlikely to legally convince beyond the EU legal order.[89] This creates the possibility of conflicts both of a legal and political nature that reach beyond the EU legal order and that the opinion procedure is intended to avoid.

In the case of the ECT, legal uncertainties of who can stay and who can go, and who must stay and who must go, depending on what the other chooses, have overshadowed the political discussion of whether or not the EU and its Member States should want to be parties to the ECT in the first place.[90] This case, more than anything, demonstrates how uncertainties over who holds power to do what can also be politically held responsible for what stands in the way of open debate and will-formation on substance. While democratic decision-making procedures must allow for reasonable disagreement on substance, they also need a reasonable level of agreement on procedure, including the allocation of responsibilities.[91] Disagreement must have its place in institutional decision-making, but only reasonably concretely allocated powers and responsibilities allow engaging with disagreement or even dissensus without paralysis and confusion. The particular construction of the EU, in which not only the Commission and the Council but also the Member States have (part of the) ultimate executive say under international relations, are more prone to stalemates than the traditional separated powers between the different branches.

The Court has erred rather on the side of creating the legal framework conditions for *collaboration* than in stepping in with strict procedural legal standards. This may allow for more disagreement and dissensus in the political arena, ie, amongst executive actors and potentially at least with the input of the legislature. It does not strengthen the judicial channel for challenging consensus and controlling the collaborating actors. Nor does it empower the European or national parliaments.

[86] E Carolan, *The New Separation of Powers* (Oxford University Press, 2009).
[87] Möllers (n 10) 76.
[88] Opinion 1/19 (n 7) [261].
[89] See also G Kubek, 'Facing and embracing the consequences of mixity: Opinion 1/19 Istanbul Convention' (2022) 59 *Common Market Law Review* 1465, 1482.
[90] Eckes (n 3); Ankersmit (n 75).
[91] Möllers (n 10) 76.

V. Conclusions

Examining the Court's case law, this chapter demonstrates first that the Court relies on the various executive actors to balance themselves. Yet, instead of controlling each other, they could also jointly overpower the legislature. Second, the Court's confirmation of autonomy of the involved actors necessarily opens up new space for political controversy in an already politicised area. This comes with the danger of overcoming paralysis at the cost of international liability.

External actions put the EU's internal power structures under pressure.[92] The joined international commitments of the Union and the Member States are inseparably intertwined as they relate to the same territories and peoples. Within the EU governance structures, the top-level split executive that consists of the Commission, the Council and the Governments of the Member States aims to coordinate the different positions into one. Yet, EU treaty-making regularly requires complicated legal arrangements to allow for joined representation. Complicated and fragile constructions are required to ensure that, on the one hand, the practice complies with the Treaty rules and, on the other, the EU can act autonomously as a unified actor and is not taken hostage by the potentially paralysing positions of individual Member States.

In international treaty-making this becomes particularly apparent because of the EU's weak position under international law as a derivative actor and the complexity of the power division between the EU and its Member States. In trade and investment, the EU enjoys an exceptional level of autonomy, which further complicates the picture. The growing controversies with regard to the desirability of (certain parts of) trade agreements and investment protection add to the complexity. Political struggles surround the negotiation and conclusion of trade and investment agreements. In this context, it is difficult to overestimate the relevance of the Court's powers to frame the EU's treaty-making procedure, and the need for involvement of both the Member States and the different EU institutions in that procedure.

In this complex landscape of institutional collaboration and political controversy, separation of powers is an *ideal* may help the EU and its Member States, on the one hand, to channel disagreement or even dissent into the process of will-formation and, on the other, to balance the political autonomy of EU institutions and the Member States with judicial control of its constitutional principles. The ECJ is a central actor in the legal landscape shared between the EU and the Member States. In the context of international treaty-making, the opinion procedure under Article 218(11) TFEU gives the Court even greater powers and hence responsibility to control the externally empowered executive actors.

The Court has used that power to protect the autonomy of EU will-formation. By exercising judicial restraint and opening up political autonomy of the EU institutions (and the Member States), the Court does not take up the invitation to become the final arbiter of political controversy. It created a situation where the Treaty procedures in Article 218 TFEU establish the legal procedural boundaries of what is possible while protecting the institutional actors within that framework. This also protects the

[92] Eckes (n 19).

positions of the other institutions, ie the European Parliament and the Commission. From a separation of powers perspective, this strengthens the European layer (above all the Council, but also the European Parliament and the Commission) vis-à-vis the national one (both governments and parliaments). However, in the context of mixed agreements, national parliaments continue to hold their direct (national ratification) and indirect (mandate for and control over national representatives in Council) powers of influence and control. Opinion 1/19 leaves the EU institutions and the Member States, both as part of the Council and independently, free to decide politically how to position themselves in the network of partially conflicting powers and obligations under national, EU and international law.

In trade and investment, Opinion 2/15 precisely excludes that the EU can conclude a treaty with an ISDS mechanism on its own. This must logically also exclude partial conclusion by the EU and some Member States. In other words, when international agreements with ISDS clauses are concluded, the Council does not possess the powers to conclude the agreement without the 'consent' of all Member States. At the same time, as has convincingly argued, this cannot prohibit individual Member States from withdrawing from an existing treaty containing an ISDS mechanism.[93] Greater scope for the autonomy of European actors (and the Member States) is likely to create tensions with international law, which treats territories as governed by one uniform sovereign actor.

However, whether the Court can and does offer a counterbalance to the dominance of externalised multi-actor and top-level split-executive powers in EU treaty-making is another question. In the multilayered nature of the EU, the Court rather emphasises that the Council as the European representation of the national executives needs to collaborate not only with the Commission and the European Parliament but also with the Member States. Taking the position that the multilayered nature of the EU offers sufficient constraints amongst executive actors, however, seems problematic from a separation of powers perspective, which emphasises the distinctness of the different branches and insists that not all power can be concentrated in one of them – even if this branch consists of different autonomous actors.

[93] Ankersmit (n 75).

PART IV

Cross-cutting Considerations

13

Separation of Powers Failures: The EU Expert–Executive Nexus

MARTA MORVILLO

I. Introduction

Expertise and separation of powers are topics that seldom intersect in constitutional law debates in the European Union (EU) and beyond. While perhaps surprising, this is telling: surprising, considering that both expertise and separation of powers are centre stage in contemporary liberal democracies: the former as a 'fact' deriving from both technical progress and increased technical and societal complexity,[1] the latter as a key organising principle for the exercise of public authority;[2] telling, as it signals a difficulty with both integrating expertise within the three branches and analysing them in light of the current expert dependency.

The relatively rare literature engaging with expertise from a separation of powers perspective conceptualises expertise as a self-standing branch, relegated outside the classical tripartition.[3] Regardless of the perspective from which expertise is approached,[4] authors tend to acknowledge the extensive power it exerts: comparable, at least on the rhetoric level, to legislative, executive and judiciary, and portrayed as autonomous from them. Conceptualising expertise as a form of power that does not fit within the triad and the ensuing legitimising and control mechanisms justifies a focus on how to otherwise

[1] C Holst and A Molander, 'Epistemic democracy and the accountability of experts' in C Holst (ed), *ARENA Report No 1/14*, 13, 16; C Holst, 'What is Epistocracy?', in S Andersen Øyen, T Lund-Olsen and N Sørensen Vaage (eds), *Sacred Science? On Science and Its Interrelations with Religious Worldviews* (Wageningen Academic Publishers, 2012) 41–54, 51.

[2] C Möllers, *The Three Branches. A Comparative Model of Separation of Powers* (Oxford University Press, 2013). Eckes, Leino-Sandberg and A Wallerman-Ghavanini, ch 1 in this volume.

[3] S Jasanoff, *The Fifth Branch. Science Advisers as Policymakers* (Harvard University Press, 1998); F Vibert, *The Rise of the Unelected. Democracy and the New Separation of Powers* (Cambridge University Press, 2009).

[4] eg Vibert (n 3) from a positivist, ontological perspective, according to which expertise and politics can and should be separated; Jasanoff (n 3) from a post-positivist, constructivist perspective, whereby the two are intimately intertwined. See section II in this chapter.

legitimise and control experts in democracies.[5] EU expert governance literature, on the other hand, emphasises expertise's institutional embedding. While refraining from an explicit engagement with the separation of powers framework, here expertise is approached 'from within' the branches, the expert–executive nexus being by far the most researched juncture.[6] Studies on expertise in the European Courts and within the European Parliament have also flourished, confirming that experts' involvement in legislative and judicial decision-making is no longer a matter of *if* but rather of *how*.[7] EU separation of powers literature has also touched upon expertise, yet only tangentially. Here, expertise is treated as one of the features of a branch (most commonly the executive),[8] operating as a justification for conferring powers upon it and giving rise to specific inter-branch relationships.[9]

This chapter integrates these approaches and considers expertise as *one of the ways* in which the three branches exercise their powers and control each other. Steps in this direction have been taken in the context of EU constitutional and administrative law scholarship, focusing on how the availability and deployment of expertise affect inter-institutional dynamics of power and accountability.[10] Building on this literature, the chapter makes the separation of power focus explicit, along the relational understanding articulated in this volume,[11] and fully incorporates 'the fact of expertise' into a

[5] A Arcuri and F Coman-Kund (eds), *Technocracy and the Law. Accountability, Governance and Expertise* (Routledge, 2021); S Maasen and P Weingart, *Democratization of Expertise? Exploring Novel Forms of Scientific Advice in Political Decision-Making* (Springer, 2005); SA Langvatn and C Holst, 'Expert accountability: What does it mean, why is it challenging – and is it what we need?' (2022) *Constellations* 1; M Heazle and J Kane (eds), *Policy Legitimacy, Science and Political Authority Knowledge and action in liberal democracies* (Routledge, 2016); T Christiano, 'Rational deliberation among experts and citizens' in J Parkinson and J Mansbridge (eds), *Deliberative Systems: Deliberative Democracy at the Large Scale. Theories of Institutional Design* (Cambridge University Press, 2012) 27–51; A Moore, *Critical Elitism, Deliberation, Democracy, and the Problem of Expertise* (Cambridge University Press, 2017); J Christensen, C Holst and A Molander, *Expertise, policy-making and democracy* (Routledge, 2022).

[6] A Gornitzka and C Holst, 'The Expert–Executive Nexus in the EU: An Introduction' (2015) 3 *Politics and Governance* 1 and the literature cited therein; M Weimer and A De Ruijter (eds), *Regulating Risks in the European Union: The Co-production of Expert and Executive Power* (Hart Publishing, 2017). See more in detail section III.

[7] See eg E Barbier de la Serre and AL Sibony, 'Expert evidence before the EC Courts' (2008) 45 *Common Market Law Review* 941; T Christiansen, E Griglio and N Lupo, 'Making representative democracy work: the role of parliamentary administrations in the European Union' (2021) 27 *The Journal of Legislative Studies* 4.

[8] D Curtin, *Executive power in the European Union* (Oxford University Press, 2009) esp chs 5 and 6.

[9] eg the doctrine of technical discretion in the context of executive–judiciary relations. See further section III.

[10] Judicial review and parliamentary accountability of expert-based executive measures appear as the main focusses of this scholarship. On the former see eg C Anderson, 'Contrasting Models of EU Administration in Judicial Review of Risk Regulation' (2014) 51 *Common Market Law Review* 2, 425; M Morvillo and M Weimer, 'Who shapes the ECJ regulatory jurisprudence? On the epistemic power of economic actors and ways to counter it' (2022) 1 *European Law Open* 510; A Kalintiri, 'What's in a name? The marginal standard of review of 'complex economic assessments' in EU competition enforcement' (2016) 53 *Common Market Law Review* 1283. On the latter see D Fromage, 'The Parliamentary Accountability of EMU Decisions: Between Informality and Fragmentation' (2021) 6 *European Papers* 1415; B Crum, 'Parliamentary Accountability in Multilevel Governance: what Role for Parliaments in Post-crisis EU Economic Governance?' (2017) 25 *Journal of European Public Policy* 268; M Morvillo, 'From contestation to accountability in EU pesticides regulation? The case of glyphosate' in Arcuri and Coman-Kund (n 5) 197–222; LC Blichner, 'Epistemic Dependence and the EU Seal Ban Debate' (2015) 3 *Politics and Governance* 49.

[11] Eckes, Leino-Sandberg, and Wallerman-Ghavanini, ch 1 in this volume; see also J Mendes and I Venzke, 'Introducing the Idea of Relative Authority' in J Mendes and I Venzke (eds), *Allocating Authority. Who Should Do What in European and International Law?* (Bloomsbury, 2018) 13.

dynamic analysis of the relations between the branches in terms of both will-formation and control.[12] In terms of will-formation, expertise is essential to ensuring the 'truth-sensitivity' and epistemic quality of decision-making.[13] In terms of control, expertise plays a crucial role in guarding against arbitrary decisions.[14] Against this background, the overarching question is therefore: in what way(s) is each of the three branches empowered and/or disempowered by 'the fact of expertise'? In other words, in what way(s) does the availability and deployment of expertise affect the relations, and in particular the power balance, between the three branches in terms of both will-formation and control?

Answering this question presupposes addressing two preliminary issues: the concept of expert and expertise; and the type of power experts exert over decision-making processes (section II). Section III outlines the *static* institutional background of the inquiry. It identifies the executive as the 'place of expertise' in EU governance and considers how the other two branches have responded to the consolidation of the expert–executive nexus.[15] Section IV focusses on the *dynamics* of expertise and separation of powers in the three areas considered in the SepaRope project: Economic and Monetary Union (EMU), trade and migration. Starting from each of the three areas' most emblematic configuration of the expert–executive nexus, it considers the different modes and degrees to which the legislative and the judiciary engage with it. Since each of the three areas presents a different institutional and legal build-up,[16] the analysis is illustrative rather than fully comparative. It does however yield a concerning picture, whereby the executive tends to monopolise expertise, encountering a very limited and erratic counterbalance from the other two branches. When it comes to expertise, the EU is an example of separation of powers failure. This has broader implications in so far as it undermines expertise's capacity to effectively deploy its role in terms of both will-formation and control (section V). Section VI concludes and outlines further lines of inquiry into expertise and separation of powers in the EU.

II. Regulatory Experts at the Juncture of Epistemic and Political Power

Who are the experts that citizens and institutions depend so much on? What type of power do they exert? The world of experts and expertise is extremely diverse, ranging from laboratory scientists to commissions for constitutional reform.[17] When

[12] Möllers (n 2).

[13] Christiano (n 5) 31.

[14] J Corkin, 'Science, Legitimacy and the Law: Regulating Risk Regulation Judiciously in the European Community' (2008) 33 *European Law Review* 359.

[15] This chapter focusses on the horizontal dimension of separation of powers in the EU and on the European Parliament as expression of the legislative branch, the Commission of the executive, and the ECJ of the judiciary.

[16] In terms of both type of competences and of epistemic actors involved. See further section IV.

[17] In general terms, an expert is an entity (individual or organisation) endowed with specialised knowledge on a subject or field; see AI Goldman, 'Experts: which ones should you trust?' (2001) 1 *Philosophy and Phenomenological Research* 85, 92; M Morvillo, 'Why Should Citizens Trust EU Regulatory Expertise? Legal Warrants, Science and Politics in EU Food Governance' in R Barradas de Freitas and S Lo Iacono (eds), *Trust matters. Cross-disciplinary essays* (Hart Publishing, 2023) 229–50.

embarking on an inquiry into expertise and separation of powers, the focus is however on a peculiar type of experts: regulatory experts.[18] This category emerged in the context of Science and Technology Studies (STS) with regard to scientific expertise, and refers to the expertise 'produced with the explicit aim of having a political impact'.[19] More specifically, regulatory expertise is practice-oriented, aiming at the development of 'techniques, processes and artifacts that further the task of policy development'.[20] Due to its close links to policy, regulatory expertise is essentially intertwined with government, society and the economy.[21]

Regulatory expertise is far from unitary. First, there is a broad array of expert institutions: not only do they differ in terms of composition, but also of powers and mandates. Limiting the scope of inquiry to the EU, think of the difference between the Commission expert groups and the European Central Bank (ECB). The former are composed of external experts, exercise non-binding advisory powers, and serve the goal of collecting technical information within an inclusive governance framework. The latter is composed of central bankers and EU officials, it has legally binding powers (including the adoption of legal acts) enshrined in the Treaties and pursues the primary aim of independently running the EU's monetary policy. In other words, both are independent expert bodies, yet this is arguably the only trait they share.[22]

Second, experts working *within* the institutions are only part of the world of regulatory experts. We can therefore speak of a strict and a broad understanding of regulatory expertise.[23] In the strict sense, regulatory expertise refers to experts working within institutions and expert institutions themselves (eg the economists working at the ECB and the ECB itself as an expert body).[24] In its broad sense, regulatory expertise entails a more pluralistic approach, including also private actors (economic actors, think tanks, consulting firms) and civil society (NGOs, activists, affected communities). What they have in common is the possession of specialised, yet not always independent, knowledge over an issue, which is relevant for decision-makers and makes them actual or potential contributors to decision-making processes.[25] When adopting a separation of

[18] Regulatory expertise is defined in opposition to research expertise by Jasanoff (n 3) 76.

[19] A Jung, RL Korinek and H Straßheim, 'Embedded expertise: a conceptual framework for reconstructing knowledge orders, their transformation and local specificities' (2014) 27 *Innovation: The European Journal of Social Science Research* 398, 403–04.

[20] Jasanoff, (n 3) 76. In terms of content, regulatory science is the outcome of three different types of scientific activity: knowledge production, synthesis and prediction (ibid 77).

[21] ibid 78.

[22] This chapter focusses on non-legal expertise, but the diversity increases further when broadening the analysis to legal expertise. See P Leino-Sandberg, *The Politics of Legal Expertise in EU Policy*-Making (Cambridge University Press, 2021); E Korkea-Aho and P Leino-Sandberg (eds), *Law, Legal Expertise and EU Policy-Making* (Cambridge University Press, 2022).

[23] This distinction has been made also in terms of 'location' of expertise, namely inside or outside government: J Halligan, 'Policy Advice and the Public Sector' in B Guy Peters and DT Savoie (eds), *Governance in a Changing Environment* (McGill-Queen's University Press, 1995) 138–72; J Craft and M Howlett, 'Policy formulation, governance shifts and policy influence: location and content in policy advisory systems' (2012) 32 *Journal of Public Policy* 79, 81.

[24] In its narrow sense, regulatory expertise largely overlaps with the Weberian expert-bureaucrat (or technocrat): Curtin (n 8) 105; F Fischer, *Technocracy and the Politics of Expertise* (Sage, 1990) 17.

[25] On knowledge as an asset to gain access to decision-making: P Bouwen, 'Corporate Lobbying in the European Union: The Logic of Access' (2002) 9 *Journal of European Public Policy* 365.

powers perspective on expertise, the focus is on expertise in the strict sense. I will argue, however, that the line between expertise in the strict and in the broad sense is often porous.

Regulatory experts exert what Archer et al label as epistemic power, meaning 'the ability to influence what others believe, think, or know' and 'to enable and disable others from exerting epistemic influence'.[26] Epistemic power operates through the provision of data that inform decision-making, and, more subtly, through framing. It is conferred on experts by the legal frameworks under which they operate, eg Article 29 of Regulation 1896/2019 establishing that Frontex, the European Border and Coast Guard Agency, carries out risk analyses, which form the basis of the agencies' activities.[27]

What is often neglected is that, because of its specific collocation, regulatory expertise in the strict sense does not operate solely within the epistemic realm but rather at the juncture of political and epistemic authority. It has 'the competence to validate and justify knowledge claims ("epistemic authority") and the capability to make these knowledge claims relevant for collectively ordering and evaluating society ("political authority")'.[28] Understanding regulatory experts' authority in these terms challenges the positivistic assumption of the epistemic and the political as neatly separate realms.[29] In this view, issues which are 'merely technical' can be separated from political issues and entrusted to expert judgment alone. Cases of politicisation of expertise or expertisation of politics expose the limits of this approach. The former occurs when technically complex issues, eg sanitary standards in the technical annexes of trade agreements, become the target of public contestation, bringing expertise into the political arena; the latter occurs where politically divisive issues, eg who should bear the costs of a sovereign debt crisis, are removed from the political realm and entrusted to experts. These episodes, which positivist approaches fail to capture or at best consider as aberrations, reveal the complex and often unnoticed intertwinement of facts and values that characterises the workings of regulatory expertise. Most importantly, they rule out the possibility of understanding regulatory expertise as a politically neutral feature of decision-making, but rather as a form of power operating at the juncture of politics and knowledge, where the two are often impossible to disentangle.

The EU is a fertile ground for inquiries into expert governance. Reliance on expertise has historically been a 'constitutional' feature of the EU, expertise being considered one of the key legitimising factors for a polity relying, at least in its early days, primarily on output legitimacy.[30] A technocratic bias was seen as a consequence of both the EU's very institutional design (namely the unelected Commission's central role and the absence of

[26] A Archer, A Cawston, B Matheson and M Geuskens, 'Celebrity, Democracy, and Epistemic Power' (2020) 18 *Perspectives on Politics* 27, 28. See also Morvillo and Weimer (n 10).

[27] See section IV.C.

[28] H Strassheim 'Behavioural Expertise and Regulatory Power in Europe' in Weimer and De Ruijter (n 6) 157; this approach is rooted in the concept of co-production: S Jasanoff, 'The idiom of co-production' in S Jasanoff (ed), *States of Knowledge: The Co-Production of Science and Social Order* (Routledge, 2004) 2–3.

[29] See above all RK Merton, 'Science and the Social Order' (1938) in RK Merton, *The Sociology of Science. Theoretical and Empirical Investigations* (The University of Chicago Press, 1973) 254.

[30] V Abazi, J Adriaensen and T Christiansen, 'The Role of Scientific Expertise in EU Policy-Making: Ever Greater Contestation?' in V Abazi, J Adriaensen and T Christiansen (eds), *The Contestation of Expertise in the European Union* (Routledge, 2020) 2; FW Scharpf, *Governing in Europe: effective and democratic* (Oxford University Press, 1999).

a directly elected government, the proliferation of non-majoritarian institutions, from agencies to the ECB) and of the substance of its policies, often highly technical.[31] The 'technocracy in the EU' debate has been flourishing.[32]

Different political and constitutional developments (from the Lisbon treaty to the Euro-crisis) have gradually increased the politicisation of EU policy-making.[33] Yet, the initial technocratic bias remains, and the role of expertise in decision-making has generally increased,[34] from the proliferation of agencies to the turn to evidence-based decision-making and the institutionalisation of impact assessments.[35] As Jasanoff argues, the EU is structurally characterised by a reverse legitimation mechanism.[36] Episodes of 'expertise as justification',[37] whereby epistemic arguments are used as surrogates for weak democratic credentials in politically contentious yet technical fields, abound in the EU's recent history: from the establishment of the European Food Safety Authority (EFSA) as a response to the BSE crisis,[38] to the enlargement of the European Medicines Agency (EMA)'s remit in the aftermath of the COVID-19 pandemic,[39] to the very management of the Euro-crisis.[40] Expertise therefore remains a characterising feature of EU integration.

Against this background, and keeping this situated understanding of expertise in mind, the following sections investigate how expertise's epistemic power intersects the power exercised by each of the three branches and how it affects the relations between them.

III. Expertise and Separation of Powers in the EU

Whereas an exhaustive mapping of the expert bodies operating within and alongside EU law and policy-making is yet to be accomplished, the expression 'expert ecosystem'[41]

[31] C Radaelli, *Technocracy in the European Union* (Routledge, 2013) 7. One of the most influential accounts in these regards remains that by G Majone, *Regulating Europe* (Routledge, 1996).

[32] Radaelli (n 31), in particular the literature cited at 30 ff.

[33] P De Wilde, 'No Polity for Old Politics? A Framework for Analyzing the Politicization of European Integration' (2011) 33 *Journal of European Integration* 555; P Leino and T Saarenheimo, 'Discretion, Economic Governance, and the (New) Political Commission' in J Mendes (ed), *EU Executive Discretion and the Limits of Law* (Oxford University Press, 2019) 132–54.

[34] Gornitzka and Holst (n 6) 7; Vibert (n 3) 5; J Metz, 'Expert groups in the European Union: A sui generis phenomenon?' (2013) 32 *Policy and Society* 267, 268.

[35] Commission of the European Communities, 'European Governance – A White Paper' COM(2001) 428, 19; 'Better regulation: Joining forces to make better laws' COM(2021) 219 final, 12; M Busuioc, *European Agencies Law and Practices of Accountability* (Oxford University Press, 2013); A Renda, *Impact Assessments the EU: The State of the Art and the Art of the State* (CEPS, 2006).

[36] S Jasanoff, 'Constitutions of Modernity: Science, Risk and Governable Subjects' in Weimer and De Ruijter (n 6) 19–36, 33.

[37] M Weimer and G Pisani, 'Expertise as Justification: The Contested Legitimation of the EU 'Risk Administration' in Weimer and De Ruijter (n 6) 167–92.

[38] D Chalmers '"Food for Thought": Reconciling European Risks and Traditional Ways of Life' (2003) 66 *Modern Law Review* 532, 544, esp fn 72; EIL Vos and FA Wendler, 'Food Safety Regulation at the EU Level' in EIL Vos and FA Wendler (eds), *Food Safety Regulation In Europe. A Comparative Institutional Analysis* (Intersentia, 2006) 122.

[39] E Brooks, A de Ruijter, SL Greer and S Rozenblum, 'EU health policy in the aftermath of COVID-19: neofunctionalism and crisis-driven integration' (2023) 30 *Journal of European Public Policy* 721, 730.

[40] M Everson, 'Politicising Europe: liberating the technocratic?' in PJ Cardwell and MP Granger (eds), *Research Handbook on the Politics of EU Law* (Edward Elgar Publishing, 2020) 144–61.

[41] Strassheim (n 28) 400.

conveys the intricate and not always visible network of experts and expert bodies. They cut across different decision-making stages, institutional settings, private and public sources of information, legal frameworks, and often even hard and soft law.[42] This ecosystem spans across the three branches but, similarly to nation-states, it has deep historical roots in the executive. In national contexts, the first stable involvement of expertise in decision-making has taken place through the development of specialised bureaucracies, reflecting the qualitative and quantitative expansion of the public administration's tasks.[43] The executive branch's dominance within the EU's institutional system[44] can be seen as going hand-in-hand with the latter being expert-intensive.

The manifestations of the expert–executive nexus in the EU are multifarious, ranging from the Commission itself, and its various internal articulations, including expert groups[45] and comitology committees,[46] to 'detached' independent bodies such as decentralised agencies[47] and the ECB, acting with varying degrees of executive autonomy.

How does the EU executive's coessential reliance on such an extensive network of expert bodies affect the exercise of its powers? There is growing evidence that the different configurations of the expert–executive nexus result in an expert-powered expansion of the executive's remit, whereby the executive's availability of the epistemic power granted by expertise translates into an expanded political power. With regard to the Commission, this occurs not only in relation to fields in which its role is well established,[48] but also in areas where the Commission would formally have only a limited role. In foreign policy, for example, the Commission has been found to strategically steer the discussions towards areas where it enjoys expert authority. This allows it to expand its influence over decision-making processes that would in principle be intergovernmental.[49] European agencies have been recently found to adopt a similar 'expert-based' strategy.[50] These findings suggest that the availability and deployment of expertise by the EU executive has an empowering effect (formally, by expanding mandates, or informally, by increasing influence over a policy area or decision-making process). How do the other two branches react to this expert-based executive empowerment?

[42] D Curtin and M Egeberg, 'Tradition and innovation: Europe's accumulated executive order' (2008) 31 *West European Politics* 639.

[43] M Weber, *The theory of social and economic organization* (Oxford University Press, 1947). See also Möllers (n 2) 98.

[44] Curtin (n 8); Gornitzka and Holst (n 6) 2.

[45] The Commission uses expert groups in at least one-third of its policy initiatives, see B Van Ballaert, 'The Politics behind the Consultation of Expert Groups: An Instrument to Reduce Uncertainty or to Offset Salience?' (2015) 3 *Politics and Governance* 139, 144; J Metz, *The European Commission, Expert Groups, and the Policy Process* (Palgrave, 2015); R Jennings, 'The Use of Scientific Evidence in Precautionary Decision-Making in EU Environmental Law' (2022) 24 *European Journal of Law Reform* 24, fn 123.

[46] T van Den Brink, 'Danger! Glyphosate may Expose Weaknesses in Institutional Systems: EU Legislation and Comitology in the Face of a Controversial Reauthorisation' (2020) 11 *European Journal of Risk Regulation* 436; A Greppi, 'Practical authority and epistemic authority: comity, expertise and public understanding' (2020) 11 *Jurisprudence* 437.

[47] There are currently 39 agencies, presenting a wide variety of mandates and powers, but sharing independence and specialised nature. See Busuioc (n 35); C Ossege, *European Regulatory Agencies in EU Decision-Making. Between Expertise and Influence* (Palgrave Macmillan, 2016).

[48] eg trade; see further section IV.B.

[49] MH Chou and M Riddervold, 'The Unexpected Negotiator at the Table: How the European Commission's Expertise Informs Intergovernmental EU Policies' (2015) 3 *Politics and Governance* 61.

[50] eg Frontex; see section IV.C and TN Fjørtoft, 'More power, more control: The legitimizing role of expertise in Frontex after the refugee crisis' (2022) 16 *Regulation & Governance* 557.

If the executive has historically been the 'place of expertise', legislatures are often latecomers in the expertise game. Parliaments originated as generalist institutions, concerned with representation and political and budgetary accountability rather than with the technicalities of implementation. However, they are not immune from 'the fact of expertise' and the increased complexity of legislation has meant that a properly functioning parliament needs to have access to good expertise. Parliamentary chambers across the board have therefore gradually strengthened their internal bureaucracies.[51] The features of EU law-making exacerbate these considerations: first, the technical content of EU legislation, which can be traced back both to the nature of the conferred competences and to the Commission's monopoly over legislative initiative, meaning that all legislative proposals originate from an expert-powerhouse;[52] second, the progressive expansion of the European Parliament's role, which required it to develop its own expert infrastructure in order to fully exercise its newly acquired powers, both in terms of law-making and ex post oversight.[53] Compared to the executive, in the case of the European Parliament the relationship between expertise and power seems to be reversed: while the executive has expertise, hence power, the Parliament has power, hence needs expertise.[54]

The European Parliament's expert infrastructure, while less articulated than the executive's and in particular the Commission's, revolves around the European Parliament secretariat and comprises both generalist (eg the European Parliament Research Service – EPRS, active since 2013) and specialised sites of knowledge production (eg the Economic Governance Support Unit, since 2012, or the Scientific and Technology Options Assessment).[55] Parliamentary committees also represent an important site for the collection and processing of policy-relevant knowledge within the European Parliament.[56] In recent years, committee secretariats have been registering a steady increase in size.[57] Committees gather information mainly through hearings, inviting representatives from civil society, economic interests and scientific experts.[58]

[51] Christiansen, Griglio and Lupo (n 7) 477–93, 480–81.

[52] In this sense, see also ibid 483.

[53] J Greenwood and C Roederer-Rynning, 'Power at the expense of diffuse interests? The European Parliament as a legitimacy-seeking institution' (2020) 21 *European Politics and Society* 118, 120–22; M Dobbels and C Neuhold, 'Who Selects What and How? How the European Parliament Obtains and Processes Information for Policy-Making' in T Blom and S Vanhoonacker (eds), *The Politics of Information. The case of the European Union* (Palgrave, 2014) 78; I Anglmayer and A Scherrer, 'Ex-post evaluation in the European Parliament: an increasing influence on the policy cycle' (2020) 26 *The Journal of Legislative Studies* 405–26, 422.

[54] More specifically, the strengthening of the European Parliament in-house expertise has been linked to the Parliament embracing comitology (C Roederer-Rynning and J Greenwood, 'The European Parliament as a developing legislature: coming of age in trilogues?' (2017) 24 *Journal of European Public Policy* 735, 744) and to a broader process of institution- and authority-building (Greenwood and Roederer (n 53) 122).

[55] On the European Parliament Secretariat, see Christiansen, Griglio and Lupo (n 7) 484–85; on the EPRS and the Impact assessment directorate, see Roederer and Greenwood (n 54) 744; Dobbels and Neuhold (n 53) 83.

[56] DA Alexander, 'Expertise, turnover and refreshment within the committees of the European Parliament: as much like Sisyphus pushing the boulder up the mountain as we may think?' (2022) 44 *Journal of European Integration* 899–917, 900.

[57] Greenwood and Roeder (n 53) 123. More critically on the quality of their work see, however, D Marshall, 'Do rapporteurs receive independent expert policy advice? Indirect lobbying via the European Parliament's committee secretariat' (2012) 19 *Journal of European Public Policy* 1377, 1385.

[58] Christiansen, Griglio and Lupo (n 7) 484.

Their selection is a highly political exercise, which serves both coordination and epistemic goals.[59] Besides the work carried out in-house, both committees and parliamentary DGs often outsource epistemic activity by commissioning studies to academics and practitioners. This is particularly relevant for information of a technical nature,[60] which the European Parliament struggles to autonomously produce, due to both time and resources constraints.[61]

The results of this process of expertise- and authority-building by the Parliament are mixed. While the Parliament has been on occasion able to exert influence on highly technical issues, namely in the environmental field,[62] significant asymmetries with the executive's knowledge base persist. The Commission, in particular, remains the Parliament's main source of expertise and information.[63] European Parliament empowerment through expertise is thus the exception rather than the rule.

If parliaments are latecomers to the expertise game, courts are its 'victims'. The increasing complexity of legal acts has inevitable repercussions on the judicial branch. The European Court of Justice (ECJ) is confronted increasingly regularly with legal disputes hinging on technically complex legislative contents and challenging the very expertise underpinning the contested measure. While this trend is particularly clear in areas such as risk regulation, it has also been documented in the context of environmental law, competition law and the EMU.[64] The Court has also acknowledged the importance of science for decision-making and its own role in reviewing its excellence, independence and transparency.[65] Yet, while the Court is a legal expert, it is not endowed with the non-legal expertise required to engage with the technical assessments it needs to decide such cases.

While this tension has become more acute in recent years, it is far from novel and has affected domestic courts and the ECJ alike. In the ECJ's case, ways to mitigate it exist in the books, but have in practice been left largely unexplored.[66] There are in fact several channels through which the Court could strengthen its access to in-house or external non-legal expertise. As to the former, the brief experience of the in-house economist

[59] D Coen and A Katsaidis, 'Between cheap talk and epistocracy: The logic of interest group access in the European Parliament's committee hearings' (2019) 97 *Public administration* 754, 755–756; P Leino-Sandberg, 'Transparency and Trilogues: Real Legislative Work for Grown-Ups?' (2023) 14 *European Journal of Risk Regulation* 271, 281; P Leino-Sandberg, 'Enchantment and critical distance in EU legal scholarship: what role for institutional lawyers?' (2022) 1 *European Law Open* 231, 237.

[60] C Burns, 'The European Parliament' in A Jordan and C Adelle (eds), *Environmental Policy in the EU* (Routledge, 2013).

[61] Dobbels and Neuhold (n 53) 80–83; See also European Parliament, DG IPOL, *Annual Activity Report 2019*, 4.

[62] See eg Alexander (n 56) 904; Greenwood and Roederer (n 53) 123; Morvillo (n 10); Anglmayer and Scherrer (n 53).

[63] Dobbels and Neuhold (53) 82; P Leino-Sandberg, 'Transparency and Trilogues' (n 59) 280–81 and 285.

[64] Jennings (n 45) 10–27; Kalintiri (n 10); Ronkainen ch 7 in this volume.

[65] Case T-13/99 *Pfizer Animal Health SA v Council of the European Union* ECLI:EU:T:2002:209 [159].

[66] The most exhaustive analysis remains Barbier de la Serre and Sibony (n 7). More recently see also S Baroncelli and A Mooij, 'What kind of judicial review for the European Central Bank? All institutions are equal but some are more technical than others' (2022) 29 *Maastricht Journal of European and Comparative Law* 413, 430; on *ex ante* impact assessments: E Alblas and JL Castro-Montero, 'Competence versus competency: Judicial review of impact assessments by the court of justice of the European union' (2018) 6 *The Theory and Practice of Legislation* 25, 51; A Alemanno, 'The Better Regulation Initiative at the Judicial Gate: A Trojan Horse within the Commission's Walls or the Way Forward?' (2009) 15 *European Law Journal* 382. See also Ronkainen (n 64) 13.

operating at the ECJ to assist the justices in competition cases has proved inconclusive.[67] As to the latter, the appointment of court-appointed experts is explicitly provided for in Article 25 of the Statute of the ECJ. The provision, while being somewhat frequently invoked by the parties, is rarely enacted by the Court: before 2008 external experts were appointed 25 times;[68] but just once from 2008 to 20 December 2023.[69] The Court's reluctance to share its authority with non-legal experts ultimately results in the ECJ relying either on its own experience, or on that of the parties.

These 'material' limitations to the acquisition of technical information are met by the Court's doctrinal approach to the review of technically complex assessments. The ECJ has extensively relied on what is perhaps the most sophisticated 'coping mechanism' that courts have deployed vis-à-vis technical complexity: the doctrine of technical discretion. At its core, the doctrine is premised on the separation of technical and policy choices. Where the former are at stake, for example in the form of complex technical – scientific or economic – assessments, the decision-maker is granted broad discretion, which the court respects by engaging in a limited, light-touch review of the measure based on such assessments, usually carried out by expert bodies such as EU agencies or the ECB.[70] This judicial doctrine has its roots in the emergence of the administrative state at domestic level, and is extremely well established in the European judicial culture.[71] It is however not immune from criticism, on both epistemic and normative grounds. On epistemic grounds, it suffers from the same difficulty of all positivist approaches to expertise, namely the difficulty of drawing the line between facts and values, on which the separation between technical and policy choices rests.[72] On normative grounds, it has been criticised for its effects, as it risks leaving important exercises of power unchecked, by labelling them as technical and '*as such* – not entailing policy choices'.[73] This is problematic in light of the trend discussed above, whereby expertise tends to result in a silent empowerment of the executive branch.

Both criticisms have been voiced with regard to the ECJ, in particular in the context of the Euro crisis,[74] and several alternatives have been put forward to ensure a meaningful review of expert–executive measures. Among them, procedural review has been seen as holding the promise of reconciling expert–executive accountability with institutional balance concerns, with courts engaging with technical complexity as 'information catalysts'.[75] The overcoming of the very distinction between technical discretion and discretion proper has also been advocated, in favour of a unitary, and public interest oriented approach to judicial review of discretion.[76] Yet, the ECJ's case

[67] Barbier de la Serre and Sibony (n 7) 954, see also fn 91.

[68] ibid 949.

[69] See case Case T-31/18 DEP *Izuzquiza and Semsrott v Frontex* ECLI:EU:T:2021:173.

[70] eg Case T-134/13 *Polynt et al v ECHA* ECLI:EU:T:2015:254 [52].

[71] For an analysis of the doctrine's roots in domestic legal systems, see J Mendes, 'Bounded Discretion in EU Law: A Limited Judicial Paradigm in a Changing EU (2017) 80 *Modern Law Review* 443.

[72] See Case 9/56 *Meroni v High Authority* ECLI:EU:C:1958:7; more recently C-270/12, *United Kingdom v Parliament and Council* ECLI:EU:C:2014:18; P Schammo, 'The European Securities and Markets Authority: Lifting the veil on the allocation of powers' (2011) 48 *Common Market Law Review* 1879.

[73] Mendes (n 71) 448.

[74] See further section IV.A.

[75] J Scott and S Sturm, 'Courts as Catalysts. Re-Thinking the Judicial Role in New Governance' (2006) 13 *Columbia Journal of European Law* 565, 583; Corkin (n 14).

[76] Mendes (n 71) 469.

law seems to be firmly anchored on a traditional understanding of technical discretion, and its engagement with procedural review, while well established, has proven to be firmly rights-based rather than public interest-oriented.[77] In light of this, the ECJ could be seen as part victim of, part complicit to the empowerment of the expert–executive nexus: neither willing to change its deferential approach rooted in the doctrine of technical discretion, nor to compensate its structural epistemic weaknesses.

In addition, many manifestations of the expert–executive nexus escape the ECJ's jurisdiction, due to their 'soft' or informal nature. Impact assessments, for example, have been recognised by the Court as having the potential to *inform* its review,[78] but cases of direct engagement with their content remain exceptional and direct challenges are hard to envision due to their preparatory nature.[79] The same issues are exacerbated with regard to expert groups: even if formally established, their recommendations, opinions or reports have, at least legally, purely consultive nature.[80]

This 'static' picture suggests that the executive is still firmly the place of expertise. It also begs more nuance as to how the other two branches engage with the expert–executive nexus. Do they acritically accept the executive's expertise? Do they meaningfully scrutinise it? Do they even engage in autonomous (and competing) knowledge-production? I will seek to provide such nuance starting from the different configurations of the expert–executive nexus operating in the areas addressed by the Separope project: the ECB in the EMU, the Commission and its expert groups in the area of trade, and Frontex in relation to migration.

IV. Expertise and EU Separation of Powers in the EMU, Trade, and Migration Policy

A. The ECB's Expert–Executive Power between Emerging Parliamentary Oversight and Judicial Deference

The ECB's expert nature is reflected both in the composition of its governing bodies and of its staff. As to the former, its executive board is composed of persons 'of recognised standing and professional experience in monetary or banking matters'.[81] As to the latter, the ECB's decision-making is supported by an extensive cohort of in-house experts. Contrary to other expert–executive bodies, the ECB adopts an autarchic approach to the collection and processing of expertise, relying almost exclusively on its own research

[77] Morvillo and Weimer (n 10).

[78] eg Case C-58/08 *Vodafone v Secretary of State for Business, Enterprise and Regulatory Reform* ECLI:EU:C:2010:321 [55] ff; Joined cases T-424/14 and T-425/15 *ClientEarth v European Commission* ECLI:EU: T:2015:848 [87]–[89].

[79] Case C-310/04 *Spain v Council*, ECLI:EU:C:2006:521 [126]. On the various ways in which the ECJ could engage with impact assessments, see Alemanno (n 66). More recently, Alblas and Castro-Montero (n 66).

[80] Art 13(4) Commission Decision of 30.5.2016 establishing horizontal rules on the creation and operation of Commission expert groups C(2016) 3301 final. See also ibid, Framework for Commission expert groups: horizontal rules and public register, C(2016) 3300 final.

[81] Art 283(2) TFEU.

teams,[82] with the exception of occasional public and stakeholders consultations the ECB holds on its draft regulations.[83] The ECB has also developed a capillary outreach strategy towards academia: its researchers conduct research aimed at the academic audience[84] and its Legal Research Programme invites scholars to work on pre-selected topics, signalling a rather instrumental approach to academic research.[85] In a context of overall executive empowerment,[86] the Euro-crisis has resulted in a significant widening and deepening[87] of the ECB's portfolio in a formally unchanged Treaty framework. This expansion called into question the technical nature of the ECB: the potentially unlimited purchase of bonds on the secondary markets, the negotiation and monitoring of Memoranda of Understanding in the context of the ESM, and the measures adopted in the context of banking supervision and resolution all entail a balancing of competing interests. In other words, the post-crisis ECB has acquired an increasingly political role.[88] This sits uncomfortably with the very idea of a narrow mandate entailing limited discretion (ie, one goal (price stability) to be pursued through one tool (interest rate setting)).[89] The fact that the ECB's expanded and more political role emerged in the absence of any adjustment to its institutional make-up has triggered a lively and ongoing debate. In particular, scholars highlighted that the increased ECB powers have not been met with heightened accountability and called for more robust parliamentary and judicial oversight,[90] enhanced transparency[91] and even for a reconsideration of the ECB's independence.[92]

When considering the European Parliament's relationship with the ECB from a separation of powers perspective, the focus is necessarily on the control element rather

[82] See eg the economic, macroprudential and research bulletins prepared by ECB economists. Economic bulletins 'provide the foundations for the ECB's decisions in all policy areas': www.ecb.europa.eu/pub/html/index.en.html.

[83] Public consultations are framed both in terms of public trust and of acquisition of expertise: see www.ecb.europa.eu/stats/ecb_statistics/governance_and_quality_framework/consultations/html/index.en.html.

[84] eg the ECB's research papers, which 'create links to the academic community, sparking discussion and debate on topics of relevance to the ECB': www.ecb.europa.eu/pub/research/html/index.en.html.

[85] P Leino-Sandberg, 'Enchantment and critical distance' (n 59) 237–38.

[86] M Bauer and S Becker, 'The Unexpected Winner of the Crisis: The European Commission's Strengthened Role in Economic Governance' (2014) 36 *Journal of European Integration* 213; Leino and Saarenheimo (n 33); N Moloney, 'The European Securities and Markets Authority and Institutional Design for the EU Financial Market: A Tale of Two Competences: Part (1), Rule-making' (2011) 12 *European Business Organisation Law Review* 41–86; T Beukers, D Fromage and G Monti (eds), *The New European Central Bank* (Oxford University Press, 2022).

[87] S Diessner, 'The promises and pitfalls of the ECB's "legitimacy-as-accountability" towards the European parliament post-crisis' (2022) 28 *The Journal of Legislative Studies* 402, 404 identifies five areas of ECB mandate expansion; see also Ronkainen (n 64).

[88] F Amtenbrink, 'The European Central Bank's Intricate Independence versus Accountability Conundrum in the Post-Crisis Governance Framework' (2019) 26 *Maastricht Journal of European and Comparative Law* 165, 167.

[89] N de Boer and J van 't Klooster, 'The ECB, the Courts and the Issue of Democratic Legitimacy After Weiss' (2020) 57 *Common Market Law Review* 1689, 1695.

[90] F Amtenbrink and M Markakis, 'The Legitimacy and Accountability of the ECB at the Age of Twenty' in Beukers, Fromage and Monti (n 86) 265–91; D Fromage, P Dermine, P Nicolaides and K Tuori, 'ECB independence and accountability today: Towards a (necessary) redefinition?' (2019) 26 *Maastricht Journal of European and Comparative Law* 3.

[91] D Curtin, '"Accountable Independence" of the European Central Bank: Seeing the Logics of Transparency' (2017) 23 *European Law Journal* 28.

[92] De Boer and van 't Klooster (n 89) 1721.

than on will-formation, due to the independence enjoyed by the ECB, which should not 'seek or take instructions'.[93] While the Treaties provide limited avenues for the ECB's parliamentary accountability,[94] institutional practices have developed into a more articulated framework, consisting of the approval of the annual report, the possibility for the European Parliament to pose questions for written answer, and the monetary dialogue.[95] The quarterly monetary dialogues held at the ECON Committee, in particular, have consolidated as the primary avenue for parliamentary control of the ECB.[96] Here, the ECB President appears in front of the ECON and answers the questions posed by the MEPs on two preselected topics. The ECON has been striving to ensure a substantive exchange, eg by establishing a monetary expert panel composed of external experts (mostly from academia and think tanks) producing papers on the selected topics, which are then discussed with the authors in a preparatory meeting ahead of each monetary dialogue.

The picture is less clear-cut in terms of results. Before the Euro-crisis, there was widespread scepticism as to European Parliament's ability to engage in meaningful ECB oversight: the ECON's questions remained general[97] and triggered standard answers from the ECB, allowing it to retain a 'discursive monopoly' over most issues.[98] The Euro crisis led to a quantitative increase in the ECON's activity.[99] Some accounts suggest the emergence of a more emancipated, technical dialogue between the European Parliament and the ECB;[100] others, including MEPs themselves, confirm an insufficient European Parliament specialisation, leading to redundant, excessively open and ultimately ineffective questions.[101] The ECON monetary dialogues show that Parliamentary committees have the potential to engage in autonomous knowledge production, in particular when dealing with politically salient developments, such as the Euro-crisis. Yet, its translation

[93] Art 130 TFEU.

[94] See in particular Art 284(3) TFEU.

[95] For an overview of the European Parliament's oversight activities, see: European Parliament, Briefing Monetary Dialogue – November 2022. Summary of parliamentary scrutiny activities, PE 733.753 – December 2022.

[96] Art 284(3) TFEU; Art 15(3) ESCB statute; Art 135(3) and (5) Rules of Procedure, 9th parliamentary term, July 2019 OJ L 302, 22.11.2019, p 1. On the gradual development of monetary dialogue, see Diessner (n 87) 405.

[97] F Amtenbrink and K van Duin, 'The European Central Bank before the European Parliament: theory and practice after 10 years of monetary dialogue' (2009) 34 *European Law Review* 561, 580, 582. On a more positive note see S Eijffinger and E Mujagic, 'An Assessment of the Effectiveness of the Monetary Dialogue on the ECB's Accountability and Transparency: A Qualitative Approach' (2004) 39 *Intereconomics* 190.

[98] Amtenbrink and van Duin (n 97) 580–82; P De Grauwe and D Gros, 'Accountability and Transparency in Central Banking', European Parliament, IP/A/ECON/ST/2008-17, PE 416.220, 2009.

[99] D Coen and A Katsaitis, 'Governance, accountability, and political legitimacy: who participates in the European parliament's committee hearings (ECON 2004–2014)' (2022) 44 *Journal of European Integration* 475, 476; C Fasone, 'European Economic Governance and Parliamentary Representation. What Place for the European Parliament?' (2014) 20 *European Law Journal* 164.

[100] F Torres, 'The EMU's Legitimacy and the ECB as a Strategic Political Player in the Crisis Context' (2013) 35 *Journal of European Integration* 287, 295; S Collignon and S Diessner, 'The ECB's Monetary Dialogue with the European Parliament: Efficiency and Accountability during the Euro Crisis?' (2016) 54 *Journal of Common Market Studies* 1296.

[101] G Claeys, M Hallerberg, and O Tschekassin, 'Options for the Monetary Dialogue under an evolving monetary policy' European Parliament, IP/A/ECON/NT/2014-01, PE 518.753, 2014, 9–24; C Wyplosz, 'The Monetary Dialogue', European Parliament, IP/A/ECON/NT/2014-01, PE 518.753, 2014, 25–40; S Collignon, 'Central bank accountability in times of crisis. The Monetary Dialogue: 2009–2014', European Parliament, IP/A/ECON/NT/2014-01, PE 518.753, 2014, 65–84.

into an empowerment of the legislative branch, signalled by the capacity to sustain a technical conversation with the executive, is at best achieved only to a limited extent.[102]

The picture is grimmer when turning to the ECJ. In the first place, the occasions in which the Court has been asked to review measures pertaining to the ECB's monetary policy have been limited,[103] and many of them decided in the sense of inadmissibility.[104] When the Court decided on the merits, however, its decisions have been highly consequential in both legal and political terms, as discussed by Ronkainen in chapter nine.[105] From the perspective of expert–executive accountability, the ECJ's approach has been one of close adherence to the doctrine of technical discretion.

Gauweiler offers a textbook example of this approach.[106] When assessing the OMT's proportionality, the Court granted the ECB broad discretion, grounded on the need for the ECB to undertake complex assessments.[107] In line with its approach to technical discretion, it then considered that, in such cases, procedural review based on the duty of care and the duty to state reasons is of the essence.[108] Yet, when carrying out its review, the Court relied exclusively on the information and arguments provided by the ECB itself.[109] In a rather circular fashion, the ECB's assessment of the economic situation was considered sufficient to justify its own programme.[110] The Court acknowledged that the measure had been controversial, but considered the ECB's own expertise as a sufficient guarantee for its legal soundness, not deeming it necessary to inquire further.[111]

From an expert–executive accountability perspective, the Court's approach is unsatisfactory: first, the Court did not probe the ECB's expertise against a broader set of economic views. While unsurprising, in light of the Court's reluctance to engage with expertise beyond that submitted by the parties, it remains questionable how the Court could actually consider whether *all the relevant elements* had been taken into account, as required by the duty of care. Second, and perhaps more problematically, the Court acritically accepted the ECB's expertise, refraining from interrogating its justifications in any apparent way. In *Gauweiler*, judicial restraint met epistemic deference.

[102] Several proposals have been put forward to enhance the ECON's technical capacity: see S Jourdan and S Diessner, 'Positive Money Europe. From Dialogue to Scrutiny: Strengthening the Parliamentary Oversight of the ECB' (Positive Money Europe, 2019); R Lastra, 'Accountability Mechanisms of the Bank of England and of the European Central Bank. Study for the Committee on Economic and Monetary affairs' (European Parliament, 2020); M Chang and D Hodson, 'Reforming the European Parliament's Monetary and Economic dialogues: Creating accountability through a Euro area oversight subcommittee' in O Costa (ed), *The European Parliament in times of EU crisis: Dynamics and transformations* (Palgrave Macmillan, 2019) 343–64; S Grünewald and J van 't Klooster, 'New strategy, new accountability: The European Central Bank and the European Parliament after the strategy review', *EBI Working Paper Series 2023 – no 139*, 24. While the volume of the ECON's epistemic activity does not seem to have decreased in the 8th legislature, no adjustments to its knowledge-production processes have been implemented.

[103] See A Ronkainen and P Leino-Sandberg, 'The House Always Wins – an empirical analysis of ECJ case law relating to the Economic and Monetary Union (2010–2020)' (on file with the author) 5–6.

[104] ibid 9.

[105] See in particular Case C-62/14 *Gauweiler and Others* ECLI:EU:C:2015:400; Case C-493/17 *Weiss and Others* ECLI:EU:C:2018:1000.

[106] For a more detailed discussion of the case see Ronkainen (n 64).

[107] *Gauweiler* [68].

[108] ibid [69].

[109] ibid [72].

[110] ibid [72]–[77].

[111] ibid [75].

Weiss confirmed this approach.[112] From a separation of powers perspective, this suggests a disempowerment of the judiciary when confronted with technical monetary issues. While other areas of the EMU (eg, the Banking Union) present a partially different picture, *Gauweiler* and *Weiss* hint to separation of powers failure when it comes to the expert–executive nexus represented by the ECB. While this could be partly justified in light of the ECB's broad independence,[113] the fact remains that the picture discussed above is one of significant expansion of executive power which has not been met by effective judicial oversight, largely, if not exclusively, due to its expert nature.

B. Trade Agreements: Selective Visibility of the Expert–Executive Nexus

When it comes to international trade, the type of expertise involved is rather diverse. New generation trade agreements have a far-reaching nature, touching upon areas as diverse as social and environmental sustainability and fundamental rights.[114] In addition, their content has a highly technical nature, largely hinging on technical specifications of products and services.[115] Decision-makers' epistemic demand in this area therefore ranges beyond economic and legal expertise, including environmental, labour market, fundamental rights and intellectual property experts.[116]

In institutional terms, the most relevant configuration of the expert–executive nexus in the area is the Commission.[117] Expertise has been one of the enablers of the Commission's empowerment. Sustainability impact assessments, for example, are one of the ways in which the Commission has strengthened its political leadership through expertise, as discussed by Krajewski in chapter six. This largely occurs though framing: as a form of epistemic power, it allows the Commission to set the boundaries of the discussion and to filter what is relevant information and what is not.

The network of experts supporting the EU's trade policy in general, and the Commission as its protagonist, is extensive and consists of different in-house and external entities. At the core of the Commission's expert network lies DG Trade. One of the most powerful DGs,[118] it also hosts the Chief Economist team, the European Trade Economist Network (TEN), and various expert groups. The Chief Economist

[112] M Dawson and A Bobic, 'Quantitative Easing at the Court of Justice – Doing Whatever it Takes to Save the Euro: *Weiss and Others*' (2019) 56 *Common Market Law Review* 1005; F Amtenbrink and R Repasi, 'The German Federal Constitutional Court's Decision in Weiss: A Contextual Analysis' (2020) 45 *European Law Review* 757, 759 ff. See also Ronkainen (n 64).

[113] A Thiele, 'The Independence of the ECB. Justification, Challenges, and Possible Threats' in Beukers, Fromage and Monti (n 86) 237–64.

[114] B Rigod, '"Global Europe": The EU's New Trade Policy in Its Legal Context' (2012) 18 *Colum Journal of European Law* 277.

[115] See eg Comprehensive Economic and Trade Agreement (CETA) between Canada, of the one part, and the European Union and its Member States, of the other part [2017], OJ L 11, 23–1079.

[116] C Kimura and FG Nicola, 'The Negotiating Capital of Trade Experts: Transparency in EU-Asian Free Trade Agreements' in Leino-Sandberg and Korkea-aho (n 22) 173–95.

[117] Krajewski, ch 6 in this volume.

[118] D De Bièvre, 'Directorate-General for Trade of the European Commission' in KE Jørgensen et al (eds), *The SAGE handbook of European foreign policy* (SAGE Publications, 2015) 277–90, 281.

team carries out the economic analysis underpinning the EU's trade policy, if needed together with Commission-funded independent consultants. The TEN is an informal network of EU and national trade economists which 'discuss the economic impact of current trade policy issues, present their own analyses and papers, and share knowledge' in biannual meetings.[119] Finally, expert groups consist of business, labour and civil society organisations and operate both formally and informally.[120] A formally constituted expert group focusing on trade agreements operated between 2017 and 2019, providing advice during trade agreements negotiation and implementation.[121] Expert groups are entrusted with both the provision of technical expertise and interest representation,[122] combining the epistemic and the participatory dimension. The most tangible expression of the Commission's expert network are its impact assessments. Impact assessments bring together a variety of sources of information, including the Commission's own analysis, studies commissioned to external consultancies (eg LSE enterprise), and public consultations.[123]

Through this epistemic activity, the Commission is able to effectively set the tone of the discussion over trade agreements, which other institutional actors struggle to renegotiate. The European Parliament, in particular, suffers from a double dependency (institutional and epistemic) from the Commission.[124] Institutionally, it is dependent on the Commission for access to information on ongoing trade negotiations; epistemically, for the technical expertise needed to understand the content of the negotiations. The Commission has a duty to keep the European Parliament informed and the Parliament has relied on Article 218(10) TFEU and Article 25 of the Framework Agreement[125] to successfully obtain wide(r) access to information.[126] This however does not necessarily translate into a challenge to the Commission's epistemic monopoly, since the European Parliament remains a 'passive receiver' of expertise.[127]

Significant developments took place with regard to both the European Parliament's institutional and epistemic dependency over the 7th legislature. During this period, the parliamentary committee on international trade (INTA) has 'seen an impressive

[119] European Commission, policy.trade.ec.europa.eu/analysis-and-assessment/expert-groups_en.

[120] See section 3, fn 103.

[121] Commission decision of 13.9.2017 setting up the Group of Experts on EU Trade Agreements, C(2017)6113 Final.

[122] Expert groups are explicitly linked to the Commission's commitment to transparent and inclusive trade policy-making: policy.trade.ec.europa.eu/analysis-and-assessment/expert-groups_en.

[123] See eg European Commission, Commission staff working document – Impact assessment. Accompanying the document Recommendation for a Council Decision authorising the opening of negotiations for a Free Trade Agreement with New Zealand, SWD(2017) 289 final, 52ff. On sustainability impact assessments see Krajewski (n 117).

[124] In similar terms see also G Rosén and SH Tørnblad, 'How does expert knowledge travel between EU institutions? The case of the Transatlantic Trade and Investment Partnership' (2019) 20 *European Politics and Society* 32, 35; see also Krajewski (n 117) 2.

[125] Framework Agreement on Relations Between the European Parliament and the European Commission [2010], OJ L 304, provisions 23–29 and Annex III.

[126] K Meissner, 'Democratizing EU External Relations: The European Parliament's Informal Role in SWIFT, ACTA, and TTIP' (2016) 21 *European Foreign Affairs Review* 269–88; A Marx and G Van del Loo, 'Transparency in EU Trade Policy: A Comprehensive Assessment of Current Achievements' (2021) 9 *Politics and Governance* 261–71. See also Eckes, ch 12 in this volume, and Krajewski (n 117).

[127] Rosén and Tørnblad (n 124) 44.

evolution in the degree and quality of technical expertise and knowledge'.[128] Its administrative capacity has significantly increased, developing new modes of operation and strengthening its cooperation with the other in-house parliamentary expertise.[129] These developments did not happen in a vacuum, but rather in the very specific context of the Transatlantic Trade and Investment Partnership (TTIP) negotiations. These negotiations, although unsuccessful, triggered significant public attention and contestation, from both Member States and civil society.[130] The European Parliament, aware of the opportunity to consolidate its post-Lisbon position, responded to these calls and engaged, on the one hand, on a broad access to information campaign and, on the other, on significant epistemic activity, as shown by the INTA's expansion. It also set up specific monitoring groups to be briefed by the negotiators before and after the meetings, in order to follow the negotiations effectively.[131] The European Parliament's epistemic efforts resulted in 35 studies, mostly drawn up by the Directorate General (DG) external policies and by external experts (mostly academics and think tanks). INTA's epistemic activity in the context of the TTIP negotiations impacted the quality of the European Parliament's engagement with the Commission's expertise. Based on the two European Parliament resolutions on TTIP (2013 and 2015), Rosén and Tørnblad found the European Parliament to be gradually 'more skeptical towards the commission, including its expertise', relying on a more diversified knowledge base.[132]

TTIP was an exceptionally controversial case, especially for a policy area, such as trade, which had until then been removed from the limelight. Has the TTIP experience set the tone for future trade negotiations in terms of European Parliament engagement with the expert–executive nexus? While the institutional capacity developed by the European Parliament is now acquired, the level of epistemic activity deployed during the TTIP negotiations has remained unparalleled. When looking at subsequent and less politicised trade agreements, such as that between the EU and New Zealand, the difference is striking: against the 35 studies produced in the context of TTIP, the deal with New Zealand resulted in mere two studies. More generally, INTA's knowledge-production activity has now a more general character (eg issue specific and not trade agreement-specific).

Based on the TTIP experience and its aftermath, the European Parliament's epistemic engagement with the expert–executive nexus seems to be rather erratic and ultimately dependent on the political salience of the issue at stake.[133] TTIP was therefore rather the exception than the rule, the latter being the European Parliament rubber-stamping the Commission's position and the information it is based upon.[134]

[128] E Coremans and KL Meissner, 'Putting power into practice: Administrative and political capacity building in the European Parliament's Committee for International Trade' (2018) 96 *Public Administration* 561, 567.

[129] ibid 567.

[130] LJ Eliasson and P Garcia-Duran Huet, 'TTIP negotiations: interest groups, anti-TTIP civil society campaigns and public opinion' (2018) 16 *Journal of Transatlantic Studies* 101; I Mancini, 'The European Parliament and Civil Society in EU Trade Negotiations: The Untold Story of an Erratic Engagement' (2022) 27 *European Foreign Affairs Review* 241–62.

[131] Rosén and Tørnblad (n 124) 36; Coremans and Meissner (n 128) 567.

[132] Rosén and Tørnblad (n 124) 44.

[133] See also Mancini (n 130).

[134] Rosén and Tørnblad (n 124) 44–45.

To the contrary, the judiciary's engagement with the expert–executive nexus on trade-related matters is not affected by fluctuations, remaining constantly scarce. The epistemic activity carried out by the Commission's expert network falls largely beyond the reach of judicial review. In terms of direct review, expert groups' purely consultative nature firmly anchors their reports, opinions or recommendations in the policy or preparatory stage and excludes them from judicial scrutiny. The same consideration applies to the Chief Economist's and, even more, due to its informal nature, to the TEN's activities. The (unlikely) reviewability of impact assessments has already been discussed above. In terms of indirect review, however, it cannot be excluded that impact assessments, expert groups reports and the Chief Economist's studies could inform judicial review, when they constitute the evidentiary basis for the adoption of a measure in a proposed trade agreement. However, this has not been the case so far. Even though the Court has been deepening its review of trade agreements, as highlighted by Eckes in chapter twelve, it has not yet touched upon their epistemic underpinnings. In this case, the Court's failure to hold the expert–executive nexus accountable is at least in part rooted in formal and procedural reasons.

C. Migration: The Expert–Executive Nexus under the Radar

Migration is a field one would rather associate with political contestation than with technocratic decision-making, especially in the EU. Yet, Frontex plays an important epistemic role and represents an emblematic expression of the expert–executive nexus. Rijpma characterised Frontex as 'an agency with a dual nature':[135] the provision of technical and informational support to the Commission and Member States for the implementation of EU migration policy and more operative tasks, including the coordination of national border guards' activities but also migrants' identification and registration.[136] Under the former, Frontex operates as an epistemic actor. Namely, it collects, from both Member States and third countries,[137] and processes data concerning the situation at the EU external and internal borders in order to 'identify … key factors driving the situation at the external borders'.[138]

Risk analysis is 'the starting point for all Frontex activities'.[139] It is carried out by the Agency's Risk Analysis Unit and based on the Common Integrated Risk Analysis

[135] J Rijpma, 'Hybrid agencification in the Area of Freedom, Security and Justice and its inherent tensions: The case of Frontex' in M Busuioc, M Groenleer and J Trondal (eds), *The Agency Phenomenon in the European Union: Emergence, Institutionalisation and Everyday Decision-Making* (Manchester University Press, 2012) 84–99, 90.

[136] On Frontex, see also Coman-Kund, ch 14 in this volume.

[137] JP Kalkman, 'Frontex: a Literature Review' (2021) 59 *International Migration* 165, 169; M Takle, 'Migration and asylum statistics as a basis for European border control' (2017) 5 *Migration Studies* 267. F Coman-Kund, 'The international dimension of the EU agencies: Framing a growing legal-institutional phenomenon' (2018) 23 *European Foreign Affairs Review* 97.

[138] Frontex: www.frontex.europa.eu/what-we-do/monitoring-and-risk-analysis/risk-analysis/risk-analysis.

[139] Fjørtoft (n 50) 563; R Paul, 'Risk Analysis as a Governance Tool in European Border Control' in A Weinar, S Bonjour and L Zhyznomirska (eds), *The Routledge Handbook of the Politics of Migration in Europe* (Routledge, 2018) 227–38, 227–28. In addition, there are quarterly reports by the Frontex risk analysis network (FRAN) as well as special risk analyses on the Western Balkans and the EU's Eastern Border.

Model (CIRAM).[140] Similarly to other areas, such as risk regulation,[141] the risk-based approach has been seen as a 'move away from the political spectacle of the security emergency in favour of a quieter and more technocratic approach'.[142] This managerial turn is well reflected in Frontex's own definition of CIRAM's objectives, ie ensuring 'the optimal allocation of resources within constraints of budget, staff and efficiency of equipment'.[143] Frontex's risk analyses do not have binding effects: Member States should take them into account 'when planning their operations and activities at the external borders and their activities with regard to return'.[144] Yet, they underpin all Frontex's activities, including joint operations at the external borders. Besides risk analysis, Frontex's epistemic activity is also geared at producing vulnerability assessments and at managing the Eurosur platform.[145] The former are essentially supervisory tools, aimed at monitoring individual Member States;[146] the latter is a platform for real-life surveillance of the external borders. Vulnerability assessments, in particular, assess Member States' readiness to respond to challenges at the external borders and can lead to recommendations, including a deadline for their implementation. Non-compliance can lead to a binding decision of the Agency's executive board.[147] Further non-compliance can lead, upon Commission proposal, to a Council implementing act identifying the measures to be implemented by the Agency and requiring the Member State concerned to cooperate.[148]

Migration is a contested policy area and one characterised by a high epistemic complexity, offering a favourable environment for the strategic deployment of knowledge to substantiate policy preferences.[149] In this context, Frontex has successfully presented itself as a technical actor, not least through its managerial approach to risk analysis. In the context of the 2016 reform of the Frontex Regulation,[150] Fjørtoft has shown how 'appeals to neutral technical expertise [were] used to legitimise more supervisory and executive powers' to the Agency, relying in particular on quantification and objective indicators.[151] The Agency's legal framework was reformed again in 2019,

[140] Art 29(1) Regulation (EU) 2019/1896 of the European Parliament and of the Council, of 13 November 2019 on the European Border and Coast Guard and repealing Regulations (EU) No 1052/2013 and (EU) 2016/1624 [2016], OJ L 295/1 (Frontex Regulation); see also Frontex: www.frontex.europa.eu/what-we-do/monitoring-and-risk-analysis/ciram.

[141] See B Delogu, *Risk analysis and governance in EU policy making and regulation* (Springer International, 2016); for a comparison of risk analysis in Frontex and in the other risk regulation agencies, see Paul (n 139) 230.

[142] AW Neal, 'Securitization and Risk at the EU Border: The Origins of FRONTEX' (2009) 47 *Journal of Common Market Studies* 333, 348. For risk regulation see eg Chalmers (n 38); Vos and Wendler (n 38).

[143] Frontex: www.frontex.europa.eu/what-we-do/monitoring-and-risk-analysis/ciram. See also Frontex, 'Common Integrated Risk Analysis Model Summary booklet', Version 2.0, Reference number: 17600/2013 en.

[144] Art 29(7) Frontex Regulation. Strategic risk analysis informs Frontex' multiannual strategic policy: Arts 8(4) and 29(2) Frontex Regulation.

[145] ibid Arts 10(1)(f) and 18.

[146] ibid Art 32. Fjørtoft (n 50) 557.

[147] Art 32(10) Frontex Regulation.

[148] ibid Art 42(1).

[149] C Boswell, 'The political functions of expert knowledge: knowledge and legitimation in European Union immigration policy' (2008) 15 *Journal of European Public Policy* 471, 472.

[150] Regulation (EU) 2016/1624 of the European Parliament and of the Council of 14 September 2016 on the European Border and Coast Guard and amending Regulation (EU) 2016/399 of the European Parliament and of the Council and repealing Regulation (EC) No 863/2007 of the European Parliament and of the Council, Council Regulation (EC) No 2007/2004 and Council Decision 2005/267/EC [2016], OJ L 251, p 1.

[151] Fjørtoft (n 50) 568.

continuing the gradual expansion of the Agency's mandate and in particular of its executive powers.[152] Similarly to the examples considered in relation to EMU and trade, also in the case of Frontex, expertise has been a vehicle of executive empowerment (in this case in particular vis-à-vis Member States). Let us now turn to consider how the legislative and the judicial branch have reacted to it.

Whereas most commentators deem Frontex's accountability regime unsatisfactory,[153] also due to the Agency's rather poor track record in terms of both proactive and reactive transparency,[154] the Frontex Regulation envisages avenues for parliamentary accountability.[155] This takes place primarily in the context of the Committee on Civil Liberties, Justice and Home Affairs (LIBE).[156] In 2021, LIBE established a Frontex Scrutiny Working Group (FSWG), whose mandate is to 'permanently monitor all aspects of the functioning of Frontex',[157] including the evaluation of the Agency's compliance with fundamental rights and the promotion of its transparency and accountability towards the European Parliament.[158] From the outset, the FSWG focused on the operative side of Frontex's mandate, and one of its first initiatives was a fact-finding investigation over the allegations of fundamental rights violations and push-backs at EU external borders.

To what extent – if at all – does the FSWG address the epistemic facet of the agencies' activities? The European Parliament receives annually Frontex's annual risk analysis and vulnerability assessments.[159] Since its inception, the FSWG holds a hearing with the Agency's executive director to discuss the annual risk analysis. On these occasions, the questions asked by the MEP remain quite general, shying away from more technical aspects such as the CIRAM or the quality of the data collected.[160] This approach emerges also from the European Parliament's fact-finding investigation report: here, the FSWG noted that the risk analysis, which constitutes the main basis for the adoption of

[152] See Art 10 Frontex Regulation; M Fink and J Rijpma, 'The management of the European Union's external borders' in E Tsourdi and P De Bruycker (eds), *Research handbook on EU migration and asylum law* (Edward Elgar Publishing, 2022) 407–34, 418.

[153] See eg M Fink, *Frontex and Human Rights* (Oxford University Press, 2018); J Pollak and P Slominski, 'Experimentalist but not Accountable Governance? The Role of Frontex in Managing the EU's External Borders' (2009) 32 *West European Politics* 904–24.

[154] M Fink and M Hillebrandt, 'Access to documents and the EU agency Frontex: growing pains or outright obstruction?' in M Hillebrandt, P Leino-Sandberg and I Koivisto (eds), *(In)visible European Government: Critical Approaches to Transparency as an Ideal and a Practice* (Routledge, 2024); LJ Ruiz Diaz, 'The European Parliament's Oversight of the Agencies of the Area of Freedom, Security and Justice. Where are we Now and Where are we Heading' (2022) 6 *Cuadernos Europeos de Deusto* 29, 51. See also European Ombudsman, Case OI/4/2021/MHZ.

[155] Art 6 Frontex Regulation; see EPRS Briefing, European Parliament scrutiny of Frontex, PE 698.816 – September 2022; F Trauner, 'The European Parliament and Agency Control in the Area of Freedom, Security and Justice' (2012) 35 *West European Politics* 784, 793–94.

[156] Other Committees can also be involved in Frontex scrutiny, eg Budgetary Control Committee, Constitutional and Legal Affairs and foreign affairs, see Ruiz Diaz (n 154) 37.

[157] LIBE Committee, Report on the fact-finding investigation on Frontex concerning alleged fundamental rights violations, 2, at www.europarl.europa.eu/cmsdata/238156/14072021%20Final%20Report%20FSWG_en.pdf.

[158] LIBE Committee, Frontex Scrutiny Working Group (FSWG) Draft mandate, at www.europarl.europa.eu/meetdocs/2014_2019/plmrep/COMMITTEES/LIBE/DV/2021/02-04/Outcomeofwrittenprocedureof29January_EN.pdf.

[159] Arts 29(2) and 32(11) Frontex Regulation. See also Art 66(1) therein.

[160] eg 'Is Frontex taking into account reports from external groups while doing this risk analysis?'. The question was asked in the context of the Frontex scrutiny group, meeting 22/11/2022, at 10:04:35, available at multimedia.europarl.europa.eu/en/webstreaming/libe-committee-meeting_20221122-0930-COMMITTEE-LIBE.

joint operations, does not involve a fundamental rights analysis. Instead of, for example, recommending the mainstreaming of a fundamental rights assessment within the CIRAM,[161] it only recommended that the fundamental rights officer (FRO) is consulted prior to the decision to launch a joint operation and more generally advised strengthening the fundamental rights capacity of the agency, also in terms of in-house expertise.[162] While these are not negative developments per se, they signal a missed opportunity to critically engage with the technical underpinnings of Frontex's activities, and in particular with the managerial framing of risk analysis adopted by the agency, focusing instead directly on its operative dimension.

While the European Parliament seems to fall short in terms of autonomous knowledge-production (ie acquiring its own sources of expertise), it benefits from a broader institutional network. Both the European Data Protection Supervisor (EDPS) and the Court of Auditors questioned Frontex's epistemic practices and the European Parliament validated their concerns on multiple occasions, including by refusing to discharge the Agency's budget.[163] The EDPS criticised Frontex for undue personal data collection;[164] the Court of Auditors focused precisely on the quality of vulnerability assessments and questioned the completeness and quality of the data collected by the Agency, which affects its ability to follow the CIRAM in the elaboration of its vulnerability assessment.[165] The Court of Auditors' reports have fed into the European Parliament's assessment of Frontex's activities, allowing it to also address, at least to a limited extent, its epistemic dimension.

Frontex's legal accountability is even more problematic than its parliamentary counterpart. The structural limits of the system of remedies offered by the EU integrated border management regime have been widely exposed[166] and also emerged more recently in the ECJ's decision in *WS and others v Frontex*.[167] One of the main issues encountered by applicants in actions for damages, for example, is the very attribution of potentially illegal acts to the agency, due to the cooperative nature of its operations.[168] Considering these obstacles, the likelihood of the Court directly or indirectly reviewing the risk analysis underpinning Frontex's operations is at present remote.[169] However, it

[161] LIBE Committee Report (n 157) 7; Draft motion for a resolution on Frontex building on the fact-finding investigation of the LIBE Working Group for Frontex Scrutiny (2023/2729(RSP)) 5. See also L Karamanidou and B Kasparek, 'Fundamental Rights, Accountability and Transparency in European Governance of Migration: The Case of the European Border and Coast Guard Agency Frontex' *Global Migration: Consequences and Responses – RESPOND Working Paper Series, Paper 2020/59* [2020] 36.

[162] LIBE Committee Report (n 157) 7.

[163] LIBE Committee, Opinion on discharge in respect of the implementation of the budget of the European Border and Coast Guard Agency for the financial year 2019 (2020/2167(DEC)) 3; see www.europarl.europa.eu/news/en/press-room/20220429IPR28235/discharge-meps-delay-signing-off-on-accounts-of-frontex.

[164] EDPS, Supervisory opinion on the rules on processing of operational personal data by the European Border and Coast Guard Agency (Frontex), Case 2022-0147.

[165] Court of Auditors, Frontex's support to external border management: not sufficiently effective to date, report 8/2021, [2021] 24. The EP recommended the CoA to include fundamental rights in its analysis: LIBE Committee, Opinion on discharge (n 163) para 2.

[166] Fink (n 153).

[167] Case T-600/21 *WS and Others v Frontex* ECLI:EU:T:2023:492.

[168] J De Coninck, 'Relational Human Rights Responsibility' (2023) 45 *University of Pennsylvania Journal of International Law* 109.

[169] The only (cursory) references to risk analysis can be found in AG opinions and attributed to the parties: Joined cases Case C-715/17 *Commission v Poland*, Case C-718/17 *Commission v Hungary*, Case C-719/17 *Commission v Czech Republic*, Opinion of AG Sharpston ECLI:EU:C:2019:917.

is not to be excluded in principle. With regard to risk analysis, a helpful comparison can be drawn with other agencies, such as EFSA, EMA and ECHA. Here, risk assessments are routinely reviewed by the Court, since they form the basis for Commission's determinations.[170] Considering that Frontex's risk analysis, although non-binding, should be taken into account by both the agency and Member States when deciding not only their policies but also their concrete operations at the borders, the same line of reasoning could apply. This could lead to the possibility for the Court to examine, in a procedural fashion, whether the agency has taken into account all the relevant aspects of the situation (ie data quality and completeness).[171] The case is even stronger for vulnerability assessments, since they can form the basis for binding decisions.[172]

When it comes to migration, Frontex, as a manifestation of the expert–executive nexus, performs a key epistemic role which has been seen as shaping the whole policy area.[173] Yet, this remains largely under the radar of both European Parliament and ECJ. Frontex's legal accountability is facing serious obstacles, making the focus on its epistemic activity a second-order issue. The European Parliament, on the other hand, has been seeking to hold the Agency to account, most effectively by refusing to discharge its budget. However, in so doing, it has largely focussed on the operative aspect of the agency's activities, neglecting the epistemic background-work that underpins it. This could be due partly to its complexity or, perhaps more likely, to the higher political rewards attached to focussing on the more politically salient aspects of Frontex's activities.

V. The Expert–Executive Nexus: A Separation of Powers Failure

Regulatory expertise, operating at the juncture of epistemic and political authority,[174] can be an empowering or a disempowering factor: empowering for those who have access to it; disempowering for those who do not. If expertise is a key element for decision-making, thus affecting the way in which power is exercised, it should be distributed among the branches. Even if not in equal shares, its distribution is essential to allow for inter-branch will-formation and control. The areas considered above confirm that the executive remains the place of expertise and show that expertise empowers the executive, by allowing it to expand either its formal tasks (Frontex) or its de facto mandate (Commission and ECB). All three configurations of the expert–executive nexus have benefitted from presenting themselves as experts and technocratic arguments have been used to justify the expansion of their powers.

[170] eg Joined cases T-74/00, T-76/00, T-83/00 to T-85/00, T-132/00, T-137/00, T-141/00, *Artegodan GmbH et al v Commission of the European Communities* ECLI:EU:T:2002:283 [220] ff; Case T-539/10 *Acino v Commission* ECLI:EU:T:2013:110 [93] ff.

[171] M Gkliati, 'Frontex before the Judge: The Road to the Judicial Accountability before the ECJ, the ECtHR and National Courts' 2 EU *Responsibility in the International Legal Order* (Sakkoulas Publishers, 2023).

[172] See above fn 147–148.

[173] Paul (n 139); Neal (n 142); S Horii, 'The effect of Frontex's risk analysis on the European border controls' (2016) 17 *European Politics and Society* 242.

[174] Strassheim (n 28).

The legislative branch has not been a passive witness to this process, yet its engagement with the expert–executive nexus, in particular through parliamentary committees, has been at times discontinuous and often superficial. In some cases (EMU and trade), the European Parliament has engaged in autonomous knowledge production, seeking to step up its own expertise rather than simply relying on the executive's. The ECON has shown a constant and structured activity in the context of the monetary dialogues, which has led to mixed findings about its effectiveness. The INTA, on the other hand, has shown a successful yet discontinuous engagement, dictated by exceptional politicisation and salience in the context of the TTIP negotiations. Its 'ordinary' approach is rather one of near acritical acceptance of the Commission's expertise. The LIBE is active with regard to Frontex, but focusses on it as an executive, rather than expert–executive body. Its activities target the agency's epistemic dimension to only a limited extent. Resources and political salience seem to play an important role, suggesting that the European Parliament only invests in serious epistemic activity when the salience of the issue justifies it and concerns also technical aspects. In the case of TTIP, contestation hinged also on technical aspects of the proposed agreement; in the case of Frontex, public contestation is not directly targeted at the agency's risk assessments, but rather at its operations at the external borders. In the EMU, the European Parliament invests in its own expertise, but in a way that is not sufficiently focused to allow it to counterbalance the ECB's epistemic weight.

If one sees the glass half full, this means that in principle the European Parliament can be empowered by expertise vis-a-vis the executive, but this only happens under exceptional circumstances. If one sees the glass half empty, the European Parliament's empowerment is erratic and likely to remain such, against a background of epistemic subordination to the executive.

A pessimistic approach seems to be the only one available when turning to the judiciary. Here, a mix of structural and doctrinal features result in a disempowerment of the Court, which essentially does *not* engage with the expert–executive nexus (trade and migration). When it does (EMU), it acritically accepts the executive's epistemic monopoly. Among the structural obstacles that keep the expert–executive nexus at a distance from judicial review is the fact that its formal expressions (impact assessments, risk analyses, expert groups reports) are often informal and never legal acts, thus not subject to judicial review.[175] In principle, similarly to risk assessments in risk regulation, they could be indirectly reached by the Court, since their substance flows into the act subject to review. This has however not yet been the case, due to either a more general difficulty of ensuring legal accountability (Frontex) or to the fact that epistemic questions have not yet reached the Court (trade). In the EMU, the Court's reluctance to engage with the ECB's economic assessments has doctrinal roots, namely in the doctrine of technical discretion, to which the Court strictly adheres.

While it is legitimate to ask how far the Court should go into the review of technical assessments, the fact remains that those considered above are exercises of expert-based executive power which for a variety of reasons escape any meaningful judicial review.

This picture shows that 'the fact of expertise' is not constitutionally neutral, but rather results in a separation of powers failure, whereby the executive enjoys an almost

[175] Arcuri and Coman-Kund (n 5) 11 frame this issue as the 'nobody problem'.

unchallenged monopoly over expertise. Expert-based shifts of powers to the benefit of the executive branch in its various configurations occur, which are not counterbalanced by the other branches. From a separation of powers perspective, this is problematic both with regard to will-formation and to control. As to will formation, expertise plays an important role in ensuring the epistemic quality of decisions. If the other two branches, and in particular the legislative branch, do not meaningfully engage with the executive's expertise, it is likely that instrumental uses of expertise will neither be challenged nor complemented by other views. In terms of control, expertise can contribute to the detection of arbitrary decisions. Yet, if courts refrain from any meaningful engagement with expertise, these are going to remain unquestioned.

What is problematic is also that this monopolistic dynamic characterises all three areas considered: cases of autonomous knowledge production or even critical engagement with the executive's expertise remain rare if not exceptional. This state of things is not inevitable. The European Parliament is in principle capable of engaging meaningfully with the expert–executive nexus both in terms of will-formation and control, as the case of TTIP shows. This engagement however seems to be conditional on the availability of resources to support the development of autonomous expertise and on sufficient salience to politically justify their investment. The ECJ's position is more complex, being affected by both formal and doctrinal considerations, neither of which is however constitutionally insurmountable.

VI. Conclusion

This chapter examined whether the availability and deployment of expertise affects relations between the three branches. Its findings yield a concerning picture whereby the executive tends to monopolise expertise, encountering a very limited and erratic counterbalance from the other two branches. The European Parliament is only selectively empowered by the fact of expertise, relevant factors being the political salience of the issue at stake and the availability of resources. Courts, on the other hand, are generally disempowered by the fact of expertise. This can be due to how applicants and referring courts formulate their claims, or to how the Court itself meets the expert–executive nexus: either with judicial restraint based on the doctrine of technical discretion, or with inadmissibility based on lack of jurisdiction on the manifestation of the expert–executive nexus at stake.

While the three areas examined present significant variations, both in terms of legal and institutional make-up and of configurations of the expert–executive nexus, findings suggest a separation of powers failure when it comes to the expert–executive nexus. This has broader implications in so far as it undermines expertise's potential to effectively deploy its role in terms of both will-formation and control.

The analysis also revealed the relevance of broader institutional networks, which might help the European Parliament and the ECJ counterbalance the executive's monopoly over expertise. In migration, in particular, the Court of Auditors and the EDPS play an important role in supporting the European Parliament's oversight of Frontex: while the latter has been focussing mostly on the operative aspects of the Agency's activities, it relied on the finding of the CoA and the EDPS with regard to the agency's epistemic practices. In other contexts, it has been suggested that the European Ombudsman might be more suited than the ECJ in contexts of high technical complexity, also due to its looser procedural constraints.[176]

Lastly, the analysis shows that the label of 'expert' is not limited to institutions' in-house experts. External experts, involved through expert groups, hearings and commissioned studies are coessential both to the executive's and to the legislative's epistemic practices. Acting as experts grants consultancies, scholars, civil society and economic interests access to decision-making processes.[177] Yet, there is evidence that access to EU institutions is all but even,[178] raising questions as to whose voice counts as an expert voice.

To conclude, the largely dismal picture emerging from the analysis suggests that there is much to be gained from furthering a separation of powers lens to expertise – not only to address what looks like a concerning separation of powers failure, but also because an account of separation of powers that does not consider 'the fact of expertise' risks neglecting a crucial aspect of the reality of EU governance.

[176] J Mendes, 'Discretion, Care and Public Interests in the EU Administration: Probing the Limits of Law' (2016) 53 *Common Market Law Review* 419.

[177] Bouwen (n 25) 369.

[178] A Gornitzka and U Sverdrup, 'Societal Inclusion in Expert Venues: Participation of Interest Groups and Business in the European Commission Expert Groups' (2015) 3 *Politics and Governance* 151, 161; J Beyers and S Arras, 'Who Feeds Information to Regulators? Stakeholder Diversity in European Union Regulatory Agency Consultations' (2019) 21 *Journal of Public Policy* 1, 22; A Dür, 'Interest Groups in the European Union: How Powerful Are They?' (2008) 31 *West European Politics* 1212, 1215.

14

Separation of Powers within the EU Multilayered System and the Challenges of Hybrid Executive Governance

FLORIN COMAN-KUND

I. Introduction

Hybrid or composite procedures are characterised by complex decision-making and implementation processes that involve in increasingly intricate ways both Union and national actors.[1] The final decision taken in such procedures requires the active participation of both. Hybridity is most visible in the sphere of the executive. This is illustrated in various shapes and forms by the latest developments in the three EU policy fields examined in this book: Economic and Monetary Union (EMU), migration and trade.

This chapter examines how the hybridity of the EU multilayered framework, reflected particularly in the degree of the current advanced stage of EU executive/administrative integration, affects separation of powers. The chapter highlights the complex relationship and tensions between hybridity of executive powers and a relational conception of separation of powers.[2] It examines and compares manifestations of hybridity in the EMU, migration, and trade. It makes the case that the exercise of hybrid executive powers leaves gaps in terms of control of powers. As to the way forward in addressing this conundrum, the chapter puts forward two suggestions: (1) enhancing proper information and transparency regarding the ways in which such powers are exercised in

[1] See among others, European Central Bank, C Eckes and R D'Ambrosio, 'Composite administrative procedures in the European Union' (2020) ECB Legal Working Paper Series No 20 / November 2020, at data.europa.eu/doi/10.2866/08772; M Fink, 'EU Liability for Contributions to Member States' Breaches of EU Law' (2019) 56 *Common Market Law Review* 1227; F Brito Bastos 'Derivative illegality in European composite administrative procedures' (2018) 55 *Common Market Law Review* 101; M Scholten and M Luchtman (eds), *Law Enforcement by EU Authorities. Implications for Political and Judicial Accountability* (Edward Elgar, 2017); C Eckes and J Mendes, 'The right to be heard in composite administrative procedures: Lost in between protection?' (2011) 36 *European Law Review* 651; HCH Hofmann, GC Rowe and AH Türk, *Administrative Law and Policy of the European Union* (Oxford University Press, 2011) chs 11 and 26; D Curtin, *Executive Power of the European Union. Law, Practices and the Living Constitution* (Oxford University Press, 2009).

[2] See Eckes, Leino-Sandberg and Wallerman Ghavanini, ch 1 in this volume.

order to facilitate better public understanding of hybrid decision-making and accountability of executive actors; and (2) developing multilevel control mechanisms bringing together EU and national actors to cope with the (democratic) legitimacy and rule of law concerns raised by the hybrid executive governance phenomenon.

The chapter starts by introducing the (problematic) 'hybridisation' phenomenon that is increasingly visible in current EU governance, primarily in the field of the executive 'branch' (section II). It then illustrates (without normative claims to generalisation) various manifestations of this phenomenon, which is characterised by the complexity and plurality of actors involved across the layers of the EU legal system. For this purpose, the chapter relies on specific examples in the field of EMU (the operation of the Single Supervisory Mechanism (SSM)), migration (EU external border management)[3] and trade (the committee system implementing EU free trade and investment agreements (EUFTIAs), with a focus on the EU–Canada Comprehensive Economic and Trade Agreement (CETA)) (section III). Next, hybridisation of EU executive governance, viewed as symptomatic of an unprecedented degree of EU executive/administrative integration, is assessed against the (multidimensional) concept of separation of powers used in this volume. On the one hand, hybridity of executive powers within the multilayered EU legal system seems to fit with the collaborative dimension of separation of powers. On the other hand, the analysis reveals challenges and shortcomings regarding parliamentary and judicial controls, raising concerns for democracy and the rule of law. A reflection follows on different options to address the conundrum of insufficiently controlled hybrid executive power within the EU (section IV). Section V concludes.

II. (Problematic) EU Hybrid Executive Governance

In the EU, as in the Member States, one can identify legislative, executive and judicial functions.[4] Yet, the special features of the EU, as a regional international integration organisation with a pronounced supranational character, are reflected in EU governance. The underlying principle is arguably that of representation of different interests,[5] legally secured by the principle of institutional balance.[6] The multilayered nature of the

[3] The analysis of this example is partly based on F Coman-Kund, 'Hybrid EU External Border Management: Frontex, the Rule of Law and the Quest for Accountability', (2022) VerfBlog, 6 September 2022, at verfassungsblog.de/hybrid-eu-external-border-management.

[4] See ch 1 in this volume; K Lenaerts, 'Some Reflections on the Separation of Powers in the European Community' (1991) 28 *Common Market Law Review* 14 and F Coman-Kund, *European Union Agencies as Global Actors. A Legal Study of the European Aviation Safety Agency, Frontex and Europol* (Routledge, 2018) 14. The Lisbon Treaty further enhanced the identification of the three state-like functions at EU level, inter alia by labelling the former 'Community method' of decision-making as 'legislative procedure' and by marking a formal delineation between the legislative and non-legislative (delegated and implementing) acts adopted at EU level (see Arts 289–291 TFEU).

[5] The interests of the EU (Commission), the interests of the Member State (Council, European Council) and the interests of EU citizens (European Parliament (EP)); see G Majone, *Dilemmas of European Integration. The Ambiguities and Pitfalls of Integration by Stealth* (Oxford University Press, 2005) 46–48.

[6] See Coman-Kund (n 4) 14. One may thus argue that 'institutional balance' does not fulfil the same function as the principle of separation of powers within the Member States; for views maintaining that the principle of institutional balance accomplishes at EU level a similar function to the principle of separation of powers at state level, see S Prechal, 'Institutional Balance: A Fragile Principle with Uncertain Contents'

EU makes things even more complicated. In this respect, the full realisation of the EU level legislative,[7] executive and judicial functions[8] entails complex interactions with the relevant national actors in the Member States. This is mostly visible in the field of the executive.[9]

Within the EU executive branch, implementation of EU law has traditionally been carried out by the Member States.[10] This is known as 'indirect administration' as opposed to 'direct administration' (carried out by the EU institutions and bodies directly).[11] Being conceived essentially as a 'non-executive administration'[12] the EU level has focussed on coordinating, supporting and monitoring the implementation of EU law by national competent authorities, rather than on exercising executive powers directly. The EU has exercised, usually through the Commission, direct executive powers in a limited number of cases, for instance, in areas of EU exclusive competence, such as competition. The picture seems to have remained largely unchanged after Lisbon, at least if one looks at the level of EU primary law.[13] Article 291(1) TFEU seems to reconfirm the 'indirect administration' model by default through reflecting the primary role of the Member States to implement EU law. Direct implementing powers are to be exercised by the Commission as a rule, and more rarely by the Council, only when 'uniform conditions for implementing legally binding Union acts are needed'.[14] Such direct implementing powers, when exercised by the Commission, are subject to Member States' control, which is currently shaped in the form of the so-called 'comitology'.[15]

However, if we look at EU secondary legislation, the European Court of Justice (ECJ)'s relevant jurisprudence,[16] and EU institutional practice, a much more complex picture emerges. Intense interactions between EU institutions and bodies, and national actors[17] reflect an unprecedented degree of EU executive integration. One important feature of

in T Heukel, N Blokker and M Brus (eds), *The European Union after Amsterdam. A Legal Analysis* (Kluwer Law International, 1998) 280; J-P Jacqué, 'The Principle of Institutional Balance' (2004) 41 *Common Market Law Review* 384.

[7] See for instance the involvement of national parliaments in the EU legislative process according to Art 12 TEU.

[8] eg the cooperation/relationship between the ECJ and national courts within the preliminary ruling procedure under Art 267 TFEU.

[9] This holds even in the field of EU exclusive competences, such as competition, where the Commission works closely with the national authorities of the Member States and relies on their support in the exercise of its tasks and powers, see Council Regulation (EC) No 1/2003 of 16 December 2002 on the implementation of the rules on competition laid down in Articles 81 and 82 of the Treaty [2003] OJ L1/1.

[10] See currently Art 291(1) TFEU.

[11] See J Schwarze, *European Administrative Law*, revd 1st edn (Sweet & Maxwell, 2006) 25–37.

[12] AJG Ibáñez, *The Administrative Supervision and Enforcement of EC Law: Powers, Procedures and Limits* (Hart Publishing, 1999) 18.

[13] Coman-Kund (n 4) 15.

[14] Art 291(2) TFEU.

[15] Regulation (EU) No 182/2011 of the European Parliament and of the Council of 16 February 2011 laying down the rules and general principles concerning mechanisms for control by Member States of the Commission's exercise of implementing powers [2011] OJ L55/13; see also Coman-Kund (n 4) 15. See for a recent monographic study on 'comitology', Z Xhaferri, *Law and Practices of Delegated Rulemaking by the European Commission* (Brill Nijhoff, 2022).

[16] In particular, ECJ's judgment in ESMA, in which it affirms quite remarkably the possibility of the EU legislator to entrust powers on EU bodies (ie agencies) outside the 'delegation of powers' enshrined in Arts 290–291 TFEU, Case C-270/2012 *United Kingdom v Parliament and Council* ECLI:EU:C:2014:18 [78]–[86].

[17] Coman-Kund (n 4) 15.

this phenomenon entails increased involvement of EU institutions and bodies, alongside the Member States, in the exercise of direct administration tasks. This often leads to intricate relationships between the EU and national actors jointly involved in the decision-making process.[18] Such relationships are governed by an increasingly compound legal framework featuring a mix of EU law and national law. Different labels have been used to coin this phenomenon (or different aspects thereof), such as 'composite EU executive powers',[19] 'far-reaching mixed administration'[20] 'composite administrative procedures'[21] and 'sharedness' of EU law enforcement.[22]

For the purpose of this chapter, I will describe this phenomenon as 'hybridisation'. 'Hybrid' EU governance, and, more specifically, 'hybrid' executive power or administration, highlights in particular situations in which the tasks and powers of EU and national actors are increasingly entangled, often in obscure ways and under complex and hard-to-decipher legal frameworks. Hence, the decision-making process and final outcome can be seen as a 'joint product' of the various actors involved, making it increasingly difficult to distinguish the contribution of each actor to the decision-making process and the implementation of the resulting decisions. The term 'hybrid' in this context also begs a more normative follow-up inquiry: has the current degree of executive and administrative integration led to the creation of new and unprecedented merged multilayered decision-making procedures and cooperation frameworks? This, in turn, raises questions as to the full consistency of such developments with EU primary law: are these developments fully in line with the delineation of competences between the EU and the Member States enshrined in the Founding Treaties? Do they infringe fundamental values, principles and legal safeguards in EU primary law, such as rule of law, the principles of conferral, subsidiarity and proportionality, or fundamental rights? To what extent can executive hybridisation be effectively controlled from a separation of powers perspective? More specifically, are current control mechanisms adequate and sufficient, or do we need to design new controls for hybrid executive power?

III. Manifestations of EU Hybrid Executive Governance

Focussing on the policy areas examined in this volume, the chapter briefly examines three diverse examples of hybrid executive power. The first is the SSM. In this case, an EU actor – the European Central Bank (ECB) – instructs national actors with a view to support them in the exercise of their tasks. At the same time, the ECB heavily relies on the input of national actors and directly applies national law in order to fulfil its own tasks under EU law.

[18] See Eckes and Mendes (n 1).

[19] Curtin (n 1) 65–66.

[20] L Wissink, 'Challenges to an efficient European centralised banking supervision (SSM): Single Rulebook, joint supervisory teams and split supervisory tasks' (2017) 18 *European Business Organization Law Review* 434.

[21] See Brito Bastos (n 1).

[22] M Scholten, M Luchtman and E Schmidt, 'The proliferation of EU enforcement authorities: a new development in law enforcement in the EU' in Scholten and Luchtman (n 1) 19.

The second concerns EU external border management operations. In this case, an EU actor (the European Border and Coast Guard Agency, also referred to as 'Frontex') exercises its tasks and powers under EU law in close cooperation with competent national actors, including by acting under the instructions of Member States' actors. The legal framework governing this exchange displays a mix of EU and national legislation.

The third pertains to the 'joint committee' model implementing EUFTIAs. Here, the emphasis lies on the EU–Canada Comprehensive Economic and Trade Agreement (CETA), featuring a rather opaque executive hybridity in the field of EU external relations within the framework of a distinctive mixed agreement. A peculiar feature of the CETA Joint Committee, as compared to the previous two examples of 'internal' hybridity discussed in this chapter, is the participation of third country actors of the contracting party in this body.[23]

A. The Single Supervisory Mechanism (SSM)

Heralded as an instance of 'unprecedented transfer of supervisory powers from the national to the supranational level',[24] the SSM[25] features a complex sharing of tasks and intense interactions between the ECB and National Competent Authorities (NCAs) in the field of prudential supervision of credit institutions.[26]

On the one hand, the SSM Regulation entrusts the ECB with far-reaching and not entirely clearly delineated[27] supervisory tasks and powers, previously exercised by NCAs. Such tasks and powers are directly exercised in relation to significant credit institutions (SIs). As concerns all other (less significant) credit institutions, they are exercised indirectly, through the ECB's powers to issue general instructions to and take over supervisory tasks from the NCAs that are in charge of direct supervision.[28] This suggests a rather ECB-centred and hierarchical SSM model, raising questions as to the full compliance of this model with the principles of conferral,[29] subsidiarity and proportionality.[30]

[23] This holds for any other joint committee or body under a similar international agreement concluded by the EU alone or together with its Member States, see W Weiß, 'Delegation to treaty bodies in EU agreements: constitutional constraints and proposals for strengthening the European Parliament' (2018) 14 *European Constitutional Law Review* 532, 532–33.

[24] F Coman-Kund and F Amtenbrink, 'On the scope and limits of the application of national law by the European Central Bank within the Single Supervisory Mechanism' (2018) 33 *Banking & Finance Law Review* 139.

[25] Council Regulation (EU) 1024/2013 of 15 October 2013 conferring specific tasks on the European Central Bank concerning policies relating to the prudential supervision of credit institutions [2013] OJ L287/63 ('SSM Regulation' or SSMR).

[26] Coman-Kund and Amtenbrink (n 24), and Art 6 SSMR.

[27] Coman-Kund and Amtenbrink (n 24) 142. Regarding the 'blurring' of ECB's powers in monetary policy, with ECJ's endorsement, in particular through using unconventional monetary instruments, and giving rise to ultra vires accusations by the German Federal Constitutional Court, see Ronkainen, ch 9 in this volume.

[28] See Arts 4–6 and 9 SSMR, and Coman-Kund and Amtenbrink (n 24) 140–42.

[29] Especially if one compares ECB's tasks and powers in the SSM Regulation with the 'specific tasks' to be conferred upon ECB according to Art 127(6) TFEU.

[30] See in this vein also Case T-122/15 *Landeskreditbank Baden-Württemberg– Förderbank v European Central Bank* ECLI:EU:T:2017:337 [59]–[61].

On the other hand, the NCAs retain an important role in the decision-making procedures under the SSM.[31] The NCAs are closely involved in the supervisory process leading to a final decision by ECB.[32] For instance, the ECB's Supervisory Board, which is dominated by NCAs,[33] often prepares its (draft) decisions closely following the advice of the mixed Joint Supervisory Teams (JSTs), comprising ECB staff and staff from NCAs.[34] The JSTs, though headed by an ECB coordinator, are composed mostly of NCA staff who remain subject to national hierarchies.[35] More broadly, 'a dense web of expert networks, working groups, and drafting teams bringing together ECB staff and national supervisors'[36] has been established within the SSM. Some are led by NCA staff. These networks seem to be involved in all major SSM initiatives.[37] What is more, NCAs are directly involved in SSM decision-making procedures, as they adopt important preparatory acts, in particular draft decisions on the basis of which the ECB takes a final decision.[38] In this respect, the ECB's powers are actually shared (though not equally) with the NCAs, as the former cannot adopt a final decision without the preparatory input of the latter.[39] The exercise of the ECB's powers under SSM 'is embedded in a system of close cooperation and interaction with the NCAs'.[40] Jonathan Zeitlin's more empirical investigation into the actual functioning of the model characterises the SSM as a rather 'polyarchic governance structure'.[41] This entails that 'the ECB and the NCAs [are] ineluctably "condemned to cooperate" with one another'.[42]

The SSM is thus a highly complex hybrid model entailing the exercise of prudential supervisory and investigatory powers by the ECB and NCAs in an intricate interwoven fashion.[43] An additional complicating factor is the hybrid (EU and national) legal framework that characterises the SSM, enabling, most remarkably, the ECB to apply

[31] See TH Tröger, 'The Single Supervisory Mechanism-Panacea or Quack Banking Regulation? Preliminary Assessment of the New Regime for the Prudential Supervision of Banks with ECB Involvement' (2014) 15 *European Business Organization Law Review* 461.

[32] See C Eckes, 'Procedural rights in composite administrative procedures' in European Central Bank, C Eckes and R D'Ambrosio (n 1) 5.

[33] See J Zeitlin, 'Uniformity, Differentiation, and Experimentalism in EU Financial Regulation: The Single Supervisory Mechanism in Action', (2021) *RSC Working Paper 2021/74*, European University Institute, 10, at hdl.handle.net/1814/72859.

[34] Coman-Kund and Amtenbrink (n 24) 143–44.

[35] J Zeitlin (n 33) 12.

[36] ibid 11.

[37] ibid; see also J Gren, *The capacity for compliance within EU multilevel administration: the case of the Banking Union's Single Supervisory Mechanism (SSM)* (Doctoral dissertation, University of Luxembourg, 2018) 298–99.

[38] See Arts 6(3) and (7)(b) SSMR and Arts 90–91 Regulation 468/2014 of the European Central Bank of 16 April 2014 establishing the framework for cooperation within the Single Supervisory Mechanism between the European Central Bank and national competent authorities and with national designated authorities ('SSM Framework Regulation') (ECB/2014/17) [2013] OJ L141/1; see also Coman-Kund and Amtenbrink (n 24) 144 and F Brito Bastos, 'Judicial review of composite administrative procedures in the Single Supervisory Mechanism: Berlusconi' (2019) 56 *Common Market Law Review* 1355, 1368. Empirical work into the functioning of the SSM in practice suggests that (draft) decisions adopted by the ECB's Supervisory Board largely follow preparatory work undertaken by NCAs; see Zeitlin (n 33) 11.

[39] Brito Bastos (ibid) 1367. The importance of such preparatory work should not be underestimated, as it allows the NCAs framing and predetermining to some extent the ECB's final decision.

[40] Coman-Kund and Amtenbrink (n 24) 143–44.

[41] Zeitlin (n 33) 23.

[42] ibid.

[43] See Art 6 SSMR.

relevant national legislation in exercising its tasks and powers.[44] This makes it increasingly difficult to delineate precisely the actions and consequences attributable to each actor and holding them accordingly accountable for them. One may thus wonder to what degree the ECB and NCAs should be held accountable for final ECB decisions closely following the input of JSTs or the preparatory acts by NCAs, or for decisions adopted by NCAs upon ECB's instructions. While such composite or mixed administrative procedures are not new in EU law,[45] the highly hybrid SSM model makes it even more difficult to address the 'who for what?' accountability question and offers large leeway for 'blame-shifting' strategies.

The rather light accountability system under the SSM,[46] premised mainly on the idea of control by the EP and the Council over the ECB,[47] seems insufficient to address the complex intermingling between the ECB's and NCAs powers.[48] While some sort of communication channel between the ECB and national parliaments is enshrined in the SSM Regulation (SSMR), this does not seem to entail more than the possibility of a dialogue shaped to a large extent by the ECB's willingness to engage.[49]

Furthermore, legal review of acts adopted by the ECB and NCAs within the SSM framework and legal protection against such acts becomes increasingly difficult. Judicial review based on the traditional delineation between the jurisdiction of EU courts (exclusively competent to review acts of EU institutions and bodies) and national courts (primary fora for the review of acts of national authorities) does not seem well-suited for hybrid models like the SSM. Decision-making procedures, in which the ECB takes final decisions based on preparatory acts adopted by NCAs under national law or the controversial application of national law by the ECB under Article 4(3) SSMR, illustrate well the limits and problems of the current EU system of judicial review.[50] Recent attempts of the EU courts to bridge the judicial control gap by claiming jurisdiction over national preparatory acts supporting final ECB decisions under the SSM,[51] and by interpreting

[44] Art 4(3) SSMR. See in detail on the application of national by the ECB under SSM, Coman-Kund and Amtenbrink (n 24).

[45] See generally Brito Bastos (n 1).

[46] See for an extensive study on this, J Zeitlin and F Brito Bastos, 'SSM and the SRB accountability at European level: room for improvements? Banking Union Scrutiny' (2020) ECON PE 645.747 – May 2020, at www.europarl.europa.eu/RegData/etudes/IDAN/2020/645747/IPOL_IDA(2020)645747_EN.pdf.

[47] See Art 20 SSMR.

[48] For a similar observation, in the context of a thorough analysis of accountability in EU financial regulation and supervision, focussing on the European Supervisory Authorities (ESAs), see P Leino, 'Accountability dilemmas of regulating financial markets through the European Supervisory Agencies' in C Harlow, P Leino and G della Cananea (eds), *Research handbook on EU administrative law* (Edward Elgar, 2017) 209–37.

[49] See Art 21 SSMR. Whereas this loose accountability relationship could be said to reflect the strong independence of the ECB enshrined in Art 19 SSMR, one may argue that the specific mandate of the ECB within an area of shared competence and entailing far-reaching powers to interpret and apply national legislation could justify more extensive obligations on ECB to engage with national parliaments and address their questions and concerns.

[50] See for extensive analyses regarding Art 4(3) SSMR, Coman-Kund and Amtenbrink (n 24), and A Witte, 'The Application of National Banking Supervision Law by the ECB: Three Parallel Modes of Executing EU Law' (2014) 21 *Maastricht Journal of European and Comparative Law* 89.

[51] See Case C-219/17, *Silvio Berlusconi and Finanziaria d'investimento Fininvest SpA (Fininvest) v Banca d'Italia and Istituto per la Vigilanza Sulle Assicurazioni (IVASS)* ECLI:EU:C:2018:1023; see also Brito Bastos (n 38).

and applying national law with regard to the ECB's actions under national legislation,[52] not only fail to completely solve the issue, but also create considerable tensions concerning the delineation of adjudication powers between EU and national courts.

B. EU External Border Management Operations

EU external border management offers another example of 'hybrid' EU executive governance.[53] It is governed by an all-encompassing albeit fairly vague European Integrated Border Management concept.[54] Similar to the SSM, it exhibits a 'multi-actor' European Border and Coast Guard (EBCG)[55] bringing together national competent authorities on border management and return with the European Border and Coast Guard Agency (Frontex).[56] This conglomerate of EU-level and national actors interacts 'in convoluted and obscure ways, subject to heterogenous legal frameworks combining EU and national law'.[57] What is more, under the current EBCG Regulation,[58] Frontex and its staff may, along Member States' border guards, exercise executive powers during operations at the Union's external borders.

Against this background, EU external border management displays hybridity in three different ways.

First, the EBCG standing corps, in charge of operational activities at Union's external borders, consist of a mix of Frontex staff and – predominantly – Member State staff.[59]

Second, the exercise of operational and enforcement powers is shared between Frontex and the national competent authorities for EU external border management. Slightly different from the SSM, the EBCG model is formally premised on the principle that Member States retain ultimate control over their external borders.[60] Against this background, Frontex is playing a mainly supportive role, in the form of operational and technical assistance as well as coordination of Member States' external border management and return operations.[61] Hence, the EBCG seems to be less centralised and hierarchical than the SSM, with national actors in the lead and Frontex fulfilling

[52] See Case T-52/16 *Crédit mutuel Arkéa v European Central Bank* ECLI:EU:T:2017:902; Case T-712/15 *Crédit mutuel Arkéa v European Central Bank* ECLI:EU:T:2017:900; *Caisse régionale de crédit agricole mutuel Alpes Provence and Others v ECB*, T-133/16 to T-136/16, ECLI:EU:T:2018:219; Case T-502/19 *Francesca Corneli v European Central Bank* ECLI:EU:T:2022:627; see also Coman-Kund and Amtenbrink (n 24), and M Markakis, 'The General Court annuls an ECB decision for misapplying national law: Case T-502/19 Francesca Corneli v ECB', (2022) REALaw.blog, 8 November 2022, at realaw.blog/?p=1947.

[53] Coman-Kund (n 3).

[54] See Art 3 Regulation (EU) 2019/1896 of the European Parliament and of the Council of 13 November 2019 on the European Border and Coast Guard and repealing Regulations (EU) No 1052/2013 and (EU) 2016/1624 [2019] OJ L295/1 (EBCG Regulation).

[55] See M Fink, *Frontex and Human Rights. Responsibility in 'Multi-Actor Situations' under the ECHR and EU Public Liability Law* (Oxford University Press, 2018), esp 1–5.

[56] See Art 4 EBCG Regulation.

[57] Coman-Kund (n 3).

[58] See Art 82 EBCG Regulation.

[59] See Arts 5(2) and 54–61 EBCG Regulation.

[60] Art 7(1) EBCG Regulation.

[61] See Art 7(2)–(4) EBCG Regulation. Yet this delineation is not so clear-cut in practice, especially when Frontex and its staff become directly involved in the organisation, coordination and implementation of joint operations at Union's external borders.

a more complementary function. However, things become increasingly blurred when Frontex contributes more substantively, including through the exercise of direct executive powers, to operational activities.

Third, the legal framework governing external border management operations consists of 'a mix of EU law and national law, usually of the host Member State, whereby Frontex and its staff not only apply EU law but also relevant national legislation'.[62] Frontex does so when it coordinates return operations following individual return decisions by national competent authorities.[63] It also organises joint operations at the external borders based on an operational plan agreed with the relevant Member States.[64] Finally, it participates in such operations through its staff who exercise executive powers subject mainly to the national legislation of the Member State hosting the operation.[65]

These manifestations of hybridity raise serious questions. First, the intricate blending of Frontex and Member States' staff and powers makes it difficult to delineate the contribution of the various actors involved. This is combined with a general lack of transparency regarding Frontex's activities.[66] The 'fogginess' of this picture makes it rather difficult to exercise control over the EU and national actors involved and to hold them accountable. As such, it leaves room for blame-shifting.[67] Second, the mix of EU and national law that governs operational activities at the EU external borders makes judicial review a daunting task. One may wonder which EU or national court could exercise judicial review over the operational plan on joint operations agreed between Frontex and the host Member State, as well as other participating Member States. The same applies to operative measures such as rapid border interventions, return operations, or return interventions. This question can be extrapolated to all instances in which Frontex and its staff exercise powers that entail compliance with both EU and national law. The orthodoxy regarding the jurisdictional interplay between EU and national courts requires that EU courts exercise judicial review over acts of an EU agency like Frontex.[68] Yet the very same orthodoxy seems to curtail the competence of EU courts to interpret and apply national law upon which Frontex's actions are based.[69] Hence, the combination between a rather obscure and entangled operational environment and a hybrid legal framework results in arguably 'insufficiently checked discretionary

[62] Coman-Kund (n 3); this is well illustrated by the operational plan concluded between Frontex, the host Member State, and other participating Member States for each joint and return operation; see Fink (n 55) 59–61.

[63] See Arts 48, 50 and 52–53 EBCG Regulation.

[64] See Art 38 EBCG Regulation.

[65] See Art 82 EBCG Regulation.

[66] M Fink, 'Frontex: Human Rights Responsibility and Access to Justice, EU Immigration and Asylum Law and Policy', (2020) *EU Immigration and Asylum Law and Policy*, 30 April 2020, at eumigrationlawblog.eu/frontex-human-rights-responsibility-and-access-to-justice.

[67] M Fink, 'Why it is so Hard to Hold Frontex Accountable: On Blame-Shifting and an Outdated Remedies System?', (2020) *EJIL: Talk! Blog of the European Journal of International Law*, 26 November 2020, at www.ejiltalk.org/why-it-is-so-hard-to-hold-frontex-accountable-on-blame-shifting-and-an-outdated-remedies-system.

[68] See inter alia Case 314/85, *Foto-Frost, Ammersbek and Hauptzollamt Lübeck-Ost* ECLI:EU:C:1987:452 [20].

[69] See *inter alia* Case C-177/10, *Francisco Javier Rosado Santana v Consejería de Justicia y Administración Pública de la Junta de Andalucía* ECLI:EU:C:2011:557 [60] and Case C-433/13 *Commission v Slovakia* ECLI:EU:C:2015:602 [81].

executive power, with repercussions on the respect for the rule of law as well as for the fundamental rights emphatically stated in the Frontex Regulation'.[70]

C. The 'Joint Committee' Model Implementing EU Free Trade and Investment Agreements: The Case of CETA

Yet another quite peculiar form of hybridity is present in the Union's trade policy. It concerns the 'committee' governance framework designed for the implementation of EU free trade and investment agreements. The focus here is on the operation of the Joint Committee under the CETA as an example of overarching joint committees at the apex of the framework set up for the implementation of EUFTIAs. The Joint Committee under CETA is the oldest such structure in operation among the post-Lisbon EUFTIAs. It is seen by some as 'an embryo of how a well-functioning governance structure of mega-regionals could look like'.[71] Unlike other recent EU free trade agreements, CETA is a mixed agreement. This renders it more open to hybridisation processes, as reflected by the composition and operation of the CETA Joint Committee.

The CETA Joint Committee has been set up as a transnational executive–technocratic framework for the purpose of ensuring the centralised and consistent implementation of an overarching and complex mixed agreement. The CETA Joint Committee is competent to deal with all aspects pertaining to the implementation and application of CETA.[72] In fulfilling this role, it has significant powers to adopt decisions, including on the amendment of CETA, which are binding on the contracting parties.[73] The decisions of the CETA Joint Committee that entail legal effects are however subject to the procedure enshrined in Article 218(9) TFEU on establishing an EU position within a body established by an international agreement.[74] The power to amend the CETA is subject to the simplified amendment procedure in Article 218(7) TFEU.[75] In both cases, this entails an important role for the Council and the Commission. The Council adopts the decision establishing the Union's common position under Article 218(9) TFEU or authorising the Commission to approve simplified amendments to CETA under Article 218(7) TFEU. The Commission proposes the adoption of such decision by the Council under Article 218(9) TFEU, or approves the amendments under Article 218(7) TFEU) as regards the decisions ultimately adopted by the CETA Joint Committee.[76] In light of this, it can be argued that the CETA Joint Committee does not have genuinely autonomous powers, as its decisions are largely predetermined by

[70] Coman-Kund (n 3).

[71] R Repasi, 'Dynamisation of international trade cooperation. Powers and limits of Joint Committees in CETA' (2017) 41 *Questions of International Law* 95.

[72] See Art 26.1(3)–(5) CETA.

[73] See Art 26.3(1)–(2) CETA.

[74] Decisions supplementing or amending the institutional framework of an international agreements (eg extending or restricting the tasks and powers of a committee, creating new implementing committees) are, however, excluded from the scope of Art 218(9) TFEU.

[75] Council Decision (EU) 2017/38 of 28 October 2016 on the provisional application of the Comprehensive Economic and Trade Agreement (CETA) between Canada, of the one part, and the European Union and its Member States, of the other part (2017) OJ L11/1080; see also Weiß (n 23) 537–38.

[76] See Opinion 1/17 *Accord ECG UE-Canada* ECLI:EU:C:2019:341 [97] and [235].

the Council decisions under Article 218(9)[77] and (7) TFEU, and by the Commission's approval under Article 218(7) TFEU. It would hence appear that decisions are not adopted by the CETA Joint Committee as such, but by the CETA parties within the committee.[78] Yet, several arguments have been put forward in favour of the CETA Joint Committee's legally distinct decision-making powers: (1) the Council's decision on the EU position in the CETA Joint Committee is a preparatory act addressed to EU representatives, which does not produce independent legal effects in the absence of a formal committee decision; (2) formal committee decisions have the capacity to influence EU, as well as Member States' legislation; (3) the Council may grant some degree of discretion to the EU representatives in shaping decisions within the committee.[79]

Qua composition, the CETA Joint Committee is made up of representatives of the executive power of the contracting parties (Canada, on the one hand, and the EU together with the Member States, on the other hand).[80] From this perspective the CETA Joint Committee could be characterised as a hybrid structure with an extrinsic element (ie the involvement of the representatives of the third country with which the agreement was concluded).[81] This peculiarity adds another layer of complexity to the decision-making process; it arguably further complicates the delineation of the contribution of the actors involved, rendering control over the EU and Member States' representatives more difficult.

Article 26.1 (1) CETA clarifies that the Joint Committee is co-chaired by the Minister for International Trade of Canada and the EU Commissioner responsible for Trade. Yet the composition of the Joint Committee remains untransparent.[82] Though the CETA Joint Committee rules of procedure provide that each party to the CETA agreement must notify the list of its Joint Committee members to the other party,[83] a full list of

[77] eg Council Decision (EU) 2020/678 of 18 May 2020 on the position to be taken on behalf of the European Union in the CETA Joint Committee established under the Comprehensive Economic and Trade Agreement (CETA) between Canada, of the one part, and the European Union and its Member States, of the other part, as regards the adoption of a decision setting out the administrative and organizational matters regarding the functioning of the Appellate Tribunal (2020) OJ L161/1, based on which CETA Joint Committee adopted Decision 1/2021 of 29 January 2021 setting out the administrative and organizational matters regarding the functioning of the Appellate Tribunal; or Council Decision (EU) 2018/1062 of 16 July 2018 on the position to be adopted on behalf of the European Union within the CETA Joint Committee established by the Comprehensive Economic and Trade Agreement between Canada, of the one part, and the European Union and its Member States, of the other part as regards the adoption of the Rules of Procedure of the CETA Joint Committee and specialized committees (2018) OJ L 190/13, based on which CETA Joint Committee adopted Decision 1/2018 of 26 September 2018 adopting its Rules of Procedure and of the Specialised Committees.

[78] E Castellarin, 'The joint committees established by free trade agreements and their impact on EU law' in I Bosse-Platière and C Rapaport (eds), *The conclusion and implementation of EU free trade agreements. Constitutional challenges* (Edward Elgar, 2019) 205.

[79] See W Weiß, 'Joint organs in EU free trade agreements as a threat to democracy' in Bosse-Platière and Rapaport (ibid) 225–26.

[80] See Art 26.1 (1) CETA and Rule 1 of Decision 001/2018 of the CETA Joint Committee of 26 September 2018, adopting its Rules of Procedure and of the Specialized Committees ('CETA Committees RoP').

[81] Joint committees under EU free trade agreements, including the CETA Joint Committee have been characterised as 'bilateral executive bodies' without legal personality; see Castellarin (n 78) 203 and 205.

[82] Even for MEPs who addressed questions to the Commission on this matter, and received rather vague and general answers from the latter, see P-009059/2016 Answer given by Ms. Malmström on behalf of the Commission (23 February 2017).

[83] Rule 2 of the CETA Committees RoP.

the members is not readily available.[84] A reply from the Commission's DG Trade to this author's question on the composition of the CETA Joint Committee, laconically clarified that representatives of the EU Member States and of the Canadian provinces attend committee meetings.[85] Still, reports of the CETA Joint Committee meetings reveal that not all the Member States regularly participate at these meetings,[86] possibly because of the specific topics on the agenda of the meeting or the different importance attached by Member States to the trade relations with Canada.

Moreover, there is some ambiguity as to how tasks within the Joint Committee are discharged between the Commission and the Member States. What transpires from the little information provided by the Commission is that the composition of the CETA committees is established in accordance with the internal rules of each contracting party. As far as the EU and its Member States are concerned, the representation in the Joint Committee is determined by the delineation of competences between the EU and its Member States.[87] Thus, the Commission will represent the EU in the Joint Committee in matters within EU competence, while Member State representatives will participate in the adoption of decisions pertaining to national competence.[88] Yet things are not so clear-cut in practice. First, in view of the comprehensive scope of CETA, Member States are likely to be involved more extensively in Joint Committee decision-making. This involvement may cover, beyond non-direct investment and investor–state dispute settlement (ISDS),[89] issues pertaining to cooperation on sustainable development, labour, environment, science and research, and forestry, all of which remain largely within the realm of Member States' competences.[90] Second, even when the Joint Committee discusses issues within the EU's exclusive competences, it appears that the Member States are closely involved in the shaping of the decision within the Joint Committee.[91] And, while the decisions of the Joint Committee are made by mutual consent,[92] relatively little is known about the way in which consent is formed and expressed on behalf of the EU and its Member States.[93] It appears that more often than not ad hoc solutions, dictated by political and practical choices rather than legal concerns, apply as regards the internal coordination of the EU and its Member States

[84] According to Rule 2 of the CETA Committees RoP, the list of CETA Joint Committee is administered by the Secretariat of the CETA Joint Committee.

[85] Europe Direct Contact Centre, Your Europe Direct reply no #3150406 (7 December 2023).

[86] For instance, the CETA Joint Committee meeting on 26 September 2018 was attended by representatives of only 15 EU Member States, Summary Report of the Meeting of the CETA Joint Committee, 26 September 2018, Montreal (Canada), at www.international.gc.ca/trade-commerce/trade-agreements-accords-commerciaux/agr-acc/ceta-aecg/2018-09-26-summary_report-rapport_sommaire.aspx?lang=eng.

[87] See P-009059/2016 (n 82).

[88] ibid.

[89] See Opinion 2/15 *Free Trade Agreement between the European Union and the Republic of Singapore* ECLI:EU:C:2016:992.

[90] eg CETA ch 22 'Trade and sustainable development', ch 23 'Trade and labour', ch 24 'Trade and environment', ch 25 'Bilateral dialogues and cooperation'; see also M Chamon, 'Mixity in the EU's post-Lisbon free trade agreements' in Bosse-Platière and Rapaport (n 78) 42.

[91] See for an example pertaining to the amendment of the list of geographical indications (Annex 20-A CETA), Castellarin (n 78) 214.

[92] See Art 26.3(3) CETA and Rule 10 of the CETA Committees RoP.

[93] In this respect one may assume that decision-making within the CETA Joint Committee follows more or less the pattern for establishing common positions between the EU and its Member States participating in bodies set up under bilateral and or multilateral international agreements; see also Castellarin (n 78) 213–15.

within the Joint Committee. From the legal side, calls have been made, inter alia by the German Federal Constitutional Court, for an extended application of the unanimity requirement regarding the adoption of Joint Committee decisions, in view of the mixed nature of CETA and its provisional application.[94]

In view of the procedures in Article 218(9) and (7) TFEU, the Council and the Commission exercise important *ex ante* controls over the CETA Joint Committee as far as the adoption of binding decisions is concerned. Such controls are expected to ensure that Joint Committee decisions comply with EU primary law.[95] Member States' governments are also expected to monitor and control the matters within their own competences. While this provides for control mechanisms by both EU and Member State executive actors, things are different concerning judicial review[96] and parliamentary oversight. First, CETA Joint Committee decisions are not per se subject to judicial review by the ECJ.[97] That is because CETA itself is not directly applicable. As a result, the decisions of the Joint Committee established under this agreement, even if binding on the CETA contracting parties, do not have direct effect[98] and need to be implemented in order to become effective within the EU and domestic legal orders.[99] Second, CETA does not establish any role for parliaments with regard to the activity of its Joint Committee and specialised committees.[100] Hence, there is very little room for parliamentary scrutiny over the Joint Committee, with the European Parliament being at most informed about CETA Joint Committee work and decisions.[101] Additionally, the fact that the CETA Joint Committee remains quite an obscure hybrid decision-making body makes it difficult for the EP and Member States' parliaments to monitor its actions.

It thus appears that the Joint Committee works as a 'black box' subject almost exclusively to executive control. This may not be particularly problematic, as the management of external relations traditionally remains within the realm of the executive. In the case of the EU, this is reflected in the institutional balance in external relations enshrining the Council and the Commission as the main actors in this area.[102] From this perspective, the procedures in Article 218(9) and (7) TFEU may appear sufficient to ensure effective control over the Joint Committee's decision-making process. Yet, the lack of external control over the exercise of such hybrid untransparent executive power is worrisome,[103] not least because of the extensive and insufficiently defined formal powers granted to the CETA Joint Committee. According to Wolfgang Weiß, these powers go well beyond mere implementation, as they entail a large degree of discretion, and their execution

[94] See Castellarin (n 78) 214.

[95] Opinion 1/17 (n 76) [235].

[96] See extensively on the role and extent of judicial review in EU trade and investment relations, Eckes, ch 12 in this volume.

[97] See Castellarin (n 78) 220.

[98] According to Art 26.3(2) CETA, Joint Committee decisions are 'subject to the completion of any necessary internal requirements and procedures'.

[99] ibid; see also Weiß (n 79) 226.

[100] Weiß (n 23) 549.

[101] ibid 548–49.

[102] See for instance, Art 21(3) TEU and Art 207(3) TFEU.

[103] For similar concerns on unrestrained executive power in the field of voluntary regulatory cooperation under CETA, see Chamon, ch 7 in this volume.

may affect both legislative and regulatory functions.[104] This reveals yet another problematic dimension of executive hybridity: the Council, the Commission and Member States' executives, acting within a transnational body like the CETA Joint Committee, circumvent democratic control and unduly restrict the role of the European Parliament and national parliaments, through allegedly 'technocratic' decisions imposed from above. As a result, the current lack of parliamentary control over the operation of the CETA Joint Committee does not seem to meet the 'sufficient democratic legitimacy' threshold laid down by the German Federal Constitutional Court.[105] Hence, establishing fine-tuned (EU and/or national) parliamentary control over the operation of the CETA Joint Committee seems necessary in view of the significant powers entrusted to it, entailing decisions with far-reaching implications for the Union's and Member States' legal orders, as well as for EU citizens.[106]

IV. Hybrid EU Executive Governance and Separation of Powers: A Tense Relationship?

A. Framing Hybrid EU Executive Governance Through the Lenses of Separation of Powers

The relational conception of separation of powers is particularly relevant for assessing hybrid EU executive governance. It captures not only the relationships and mismatches between the legislative, judicial and executive functions seen *horizontally* at the level of the EU and Members States, but also the *vertical* interactions and interlinkages between the EU and Member State actors exercising these functions. In this respect, one may identify for analytical purposes a *tri-dimensional separation of powers* within the multi-layered EU legal order: (1) a horizontal EU level separation of powers, concerned with the exercise of the executive, legislative, and judicial functions by the EU institutions in line with the powers conferred on them by the Founding Treaties; (2) a horizontal Member State level separation of powers, concerned with the exercise of the executive, legislative and judicial functions by national authorities within the constitutional legal orders of the Member States; (3) a more atypical vertical EU–Member States separation of powers, shaped by the catalogue of EU competences in the Founding Treaties and the principles governing the exercise of EU competences, as well as by the delineation and relationship between EU and Member State actors entrusted with legislative, executive and judicial powers acting within the EU framework.

The EU level reflects quite a specific separation of powers entailing actors with a dual executive and legislative role (Commission and Council), as well as a complex geography of actors within the executive (European Council, Council, Commission, ECB, various EU agencies and bodies) and legislative functions (Commission, Council, European

[104] For an elaboration on this point and for some examples, see Weiß (n 23) 550 and 561–62.

[105] See on this Castellarin (n 78) 203 and 219, as well as BVerfG, Order of the Second Senate of 9 February 2022 – 2 BvR 1368/16, ECLI:DE:BVerfG:2022:rs20220209.2bvr136816, paras. 189–190.

[106] Repasi (n 71); Weiß (n 23) 561.

Parliament); only the judiciary, embodied by the ECJ is relatively well-delineated at EU level.[107] A look at the national level reveals a relatively different conception of separation of powers at least as far as the legislative and executive functions are concerned: national parliaments are as a rule the main depository of sovereignty and source of legitimacy, and *ergo*, also the quasi-exclusive authority in charge of the legislative function. Though interacting in complex ways with the legislature, national governments and public administration exercise the executive function under the control of the legislature and of the judiciary.

These different power distribution arrangements within the EU level and the Member States' level also entail differences as regards the design and exercise of control functions. The EU level separation of powers is functional rather than organic, whereas the Member States' separation of powers is more intelligibly both functional and organic. This mismatch is not per se problematic as long as the EU and Member States' levels remain relatively well delineated. But in case of increased executive integration through hybrid models for the implementation and enforcement of EU law, the control dimension of the separation of powers comes under threat, as it risks becoming diluted and lacunar.

An additional element that enriches the picture is the *multilayered nature of the EU* entailing complex interactions between the different conceptions of separation of powers at EU and Member State levels. This vertical dimension is mainly underpinned by the delineation and distribution of competences between the EU and its Member States, and the principles underlying this. The principles at stake are conferral, subsidiarity, proportionality, the principle of sincere cooperation enshrined in Article 4(3) TEU, as well as the so-called principle of national constitutional identity laid down in Article 4(2) TEU and envisaging the duty of the Union to respect the political and constitutional systems of the Member States.[108]

Two essential features can be observed in the vertical relationship between the EU and Member State levels.

First, the idea of delineation of powers between the two levels aims at ensuring the integrity of the EU level and Member States' legal orders.[109] This entails that, within the boundaries of the principle of conferral, EU competences are discharged by actors within the EU institutional framework. The acts so adopted by the EU institutions, and in line with the balance of powers in the Founding Treaties, are then given full effect in the legal order of the Member States by the national authorities exercising the legislative, executive and judicial functions according to their own constitutional systems. Additionally, separation of powers in this context includes intrafunctional delineations between EU level and Member State actors involved in the exercise of the same function. This jurisdictional delineation logic is quite well illustrated by the standard multilayered EU judicial control system, entailing that EU courts can only review EU acts and

[107] See Eckes, Leino-Sandberg and Wallerman Ghavanini, ch 1 in this volume.

[108] See for an analysis of the content and application of these principles, including the so-called principle of national constitutional identity, K Lenaerts and JA Gutiérrez-Fons, 'A Constitutional Perspective' in R Schütze and T Tridimas (eds), *Oxford Principles of European Union Law. Volume I* (Oxford University Press, 2018) 103–41.

[109] See Art 4(1)–(2) TEU.

measures, while Member State measures are reviewed by national courts.[110] The same holds for the distribution system of implementing powers between the Commission and the Member States in Article 291 TFEU.

Second, there is the idea of cooperation and gradual integration between and within the EU and Member States' layers. The principle of sincere cooperation encapsulates the need and duty of EU and Member States authorities to cooperate in order to ensure the full attainment of the objectives in the Founding Treaties and the effectiveness of the EU legal order. This has over time resulted in more or less structured forms of cooperation between EU level and national authorities belonging to the three branches.[111] Such structures of cooperation are likely to become enhanced and formalised – and thus more entangled – as the process of European integration evolves. The intensification of this cooperative feature in particular has led to unprecedented integration in the form of hybridity, irrespective of EU formal primary rules and the conception of separation of powers reflected therein.

As shown earlier,[112] arguably the most prominent manifestation of hybrid governance consists of the unprecedented concentration of executive power at EU level, which has taken place without Treaty reform. As illustrated in the examples discussed earlier,[113] EU institutions and bodies have been entrusted via infra-Treaty instruments with significant operational powers that they exercise in increasingly intermingled ways with the Member States. This marks a change of paradigm regarding the way in which executive power within the multilayered EU system is understood. It seems that, in dissonance with the Treaties,[114] the focus is no longer on delineation between EU level and Member State level executive action embodied in the interplay between the direct (exception) and indirect (by default) administration model. Instead, the emphasis lies on the increased integration and collusion between the EU and Member State actors involved in the implementation of EU law.

On the one hand, this phenomenon seems to fit well with the collaboration dimension of separation of powers. Yet, on the other hand, in addition to further blurring the lines between EU and Member States' competences, this executive/administrative hybridisation creates challenges from the perspective of the 'control' dimension of separation of powers. Control becomes increasingly difficult when the EU and Member States' executive actors are integrated and contribute in intricate ways to the decision-making-process, to the point that it is very hard to understand who does what and who is responsible for what in the implementation and enforcement of EU law and policies.

[110] As mentioned previously, the traditional orthodoxy regarding the jurisdictional delineation between the EU and Member States' judicatures is gradually eroded in response to the challenges raised by the ever-increasing executive/administrative hybridity characterising current EU governance.

[111] eg cooperation and dialogue between the ECJ and national courts within the framework of Art 267 TFEU; inter-parliamentary cooperation fora involving the EP and national parliaments, such as the mixed Joint Parliamentary Scrutiny Group established for monitoring Europol's activities; networks of EU level and national competent authorities involved in the implementation and enforcement of EU law (eg the network comprising the Commission and the national competition authorities, the SSM network comprising the ECB and national supervisory authorities, networks consisting of various EU agencies or bodies and their national counterparts).

[112] See section II of this chapter.

[113] See section III of this chapter.

[114] See Art 291(1)–(2) TFEU, and, more generally, Arts 4(1) and 5 TEU.

Under these conditions, ensuring effective control of the overall process and outcome of decision-making becomes virtually unattainable. Indeed, the ongoing executive hybridity phenomenon does not appear to be sufficiently matched by the development of corresponding fine-tuned controls on the legislative and judicial sides. The latter are still very much premised on the idea of a clear delineation between the powers of the EU and Member State actors.[115] An additional factor contributing to this is the lack of transparency obligations concerning EU hybrid administration. Such obligations, supported by effective enforcement mechanisms, could increase limpidity into the operation of hybrid executive governance, thereby enabling more effective accountability and control.

There is thus a tense relationship between current forms of hybrid EU (executive) governance and the control dimension of separation of powers. More specifically, the way in which EU hybrid executive governance is currently designed and operates largely undermines the possibilities to control executive power.[116] EU executive power is in any case difficult to control because of its technocratic character, especially in the form of expertisation leading to the so-called 'information asymmetry', where the legislature and judiciary become unable or unwilling to genuinely scrutinise the executive.[117] What adds to the problem is the marked composite, integrated and hybrid nature of EU executive governance, which makes it challenging to control via existing legislative and judicial control mechanisms largely operating within distinct EU level and national jurisdictions.

B. Controlling Hybrid EU Executive Power

The main message from the previous analysis is that hybrid EU executive governance (power), as it is shaped through infra-Treaties developments, seems de jure and de facto insufficiently controlled. The legal frameworks bringing about these developments only marginally, if at all, provide for effective control of such new configurations of executive power. It might well be that such arrangements reflect advanced forms of cooperation between executive actors across EU and Member States' layers pursuing more effective implementation of EU law and policies. However, from a separation of powers perspective, this should not come at the expense of effective control of executive power. If the latter aspect is not sufficiently considered, there is a great danger that ever-expanding but unrestrained executive power could significantly alter all three dimensions of separation of powers put forward in this chapter. This would have obvious detrimental

[115] There are punctual attempts to address this executive hybridisation phenomenon: ie the establishment of the mixed Joint Parliamentary Supervisory Group (JPSG) intended to enhance accountability in law enforcement cooperation between Europol and national competent authorities; the possibility to establish interparliamentary cooperation involving the EP and national parliaments ensuring scrutiny over the European Border and Coast Guard (see Art 112 EBCG Regulation); the self-extended ECJ jurisdiction over the interpretation and application of national law and measures within the SSM system; or the complementary system (involving the ECJ and national courts) of judicial review over the acts of the European Public Prosecutor's Office. Yet they are lagging behind the pace and degree of executive integration.

[116] This is particularly problematic when the exercise of executive powers within transnational bodies, such as the CETA Joint Committee and specialised committees, may significantly affect the exercise of the legislative function within the EU and its Member States' legal orders.

[117] See Morvillo, ch 13 in this volume.

consequences for democracy, the rule of law and fundamental rights. One may think of instances when far-reaching executive powers are exercised opaquely, without genuine public debate and contestation possibilities. Or when hybrid constellations of executive actors act ultra vires and it is impossible to put an end to the infringement and attribute responsibility to a certain actor. Or further when hybrid law enforcement results in breaches of fundamental rights but the victim is left with insufficient legal protection and remedies against such executive action.

This calls for urgent measures in order to prevent abuses of unchecked executive power and ensure democratic control, respect for the rule of law, and the legal protection of the individual. Two main scenarios could be envisaged in this respect.

A first possible scenario entails reversing the hybridity phenomenon, by going back towards ensuring a clearer separation of executive tasks and powers between EU and Member State actors. This would increase the effectiveness of legislative and judicial controls still largely delineated across EU and Member State levels. It would mean basically reverting to the indirect administration model by default, premised on the primary role of the Member States and a complementary role for the EU as far as implementation and enforcement of EU law and policies are concerned. After all, this scenario finds support in Article 291 TFEU and would also alleviate concerns regarding full compliance of current forms of hybrid executive governance with the principles of conferral, subsidiarity and proportionality. It would require disentangling EU hybrid executive powers configurations by undoing or adjusting the legal frameworks enshrining them. Since highly advanced hybrid executive powers are not enshrined in the Treaties, this could be done via EU secondary law instruments. By drawing more clearly the lines between the powers of EU and national executive actors, they could arguably be more effectively controlled politically and legally at EU level and within the Member States.

A second, perhaps more sensible, scenario consists of designing control mechanisms (parliamentary and judicial) that are capable of effectively controlling EU hybrid executive power. Such mechanisms could entail increased cooperation mechanisms between EU and Member States' courts and parliaments. The current EU legal framework features some meaningful attempts in this direction. One such attempt is the Europol model of parliamentary control through the Joint Parliamentary Supervisory Group (JPSG) composed of MEPs and members of national parliaments, and equipped, unlike previous EU joint parliamentary bodies, with a specific mandate and significant scrutiny powers.[118] In the same vein, the novel judicial review model (entailing judicial review by both EU and national courts) regarding the legal acts of the European Public Prosecutor's Office (EPPO)[119] marks a departure from the traditional judicial review archetype.[120] In other words, hybrid executive power should be contained by parallel

[118] See for an analysis of the JPSG set up to improve Europol's democratic accountability, F Coman-Kund, 'Holding Europol Accountable: The Promise and Limits of (Hybrid) Multilevel Accountability' in A Arcuri and F Coman-Kund (eds) *Technocracy and the Law: Accountability, Governance and Expertise* (Routledge, 2021) 285–314.

[119] Council Regulation (EU) 2017/1939 of 12 October 2017, implementing enhanced cooperation on the establishment of the European Public Prosecutor's Office [2017] OJ L 283/1, esp Art 42.

[120] The longstanding EU judicial control orthodoxy has also been called the principle of 'double-exclusivity'; see F Brito Bastos, 'An Administrative Crack in the EU's Rule of Law: Composite Decision-making and Nonjusticiable National Law' (2020) 16 *European Constitutional Law Review* 68.

effective (potentially hybrid) political and judicial control mechanisms. This would require devising closer forms of coordination between the European Parliament and national parliaments equipped with effective means to control the executive. It would also require increasingly shared judicial control models entailing, for instance, reliance of EU courts on determinations made by national courts[121] or national courts reviewing acts of EU institutions and bodies, when such acts are based on national law. One side-effect, in the longer term, is that this could lead to increased integration between the EU and Member States' levels across all three branches. This in turn prompts more existential questions: how far would such developments result in a substantive transformation of the EU in the future? How should this be reflected in the Treaties?

Additionally, hybridity could be tackled within the executive branch itself, through legislative design of administrative supervisory mechanisms specifically tailored for hybrid administrative procedures. An example of that effect is the supervisory model established in the field of personal data protection, featuring a European Data Protection Supervisor (EDPS) and a European Data Protection Board (EDPB) involved in the exercise of control functions over public authorities at both EU and Member State levels.[122] In order to be effective, such administrative review mechanisms should in principle display a sufficient degree of independence in carrying out their control functions, be equipped with appropriate resources, and themselves be subjected to effective political scrutiny and judicial review.[123]

Moreover, safeguards should be designed overall for hybrid executive power, such as increased and effective transparency, reporting and information obligations. This could enhance scrutiny by the legislative and judicial powers, and, in this way, prevent abuse of executive power in a hybrid setting.

V. Conclusion

This chapter draws attention to an ongoing phenomenon of integration within the EU: unprecedented forms of hybrid governance that increasingly feature complex decision-making processes whereby EU and national authorities act in a closely intertwined fashion. This phenomenon is most developed within the executive function of the EU

[121] This would entail some sort of a 'reversed preliminary ruling system' whereby ECJ reviewing the legal act of an EU-level actor would ask the competent national court questions pertaining to the interpretation and validity of the national law based on which the act of the EU level actor was adopted; see in this direction M Eliantonio, 'Judicial Review in an Integrated Administration: the Case of Composite Procedures' (2014) 7 *Review of European Administrative Law* 98.

[122] See Regulation (EU) 2016/679 of the European Parliament and of the Council of 27 April 2016 on the protection of natural persons with regard to the processing of personal data and on the free movement of such data, and repealing Directive 95/46/EC [2016] OJ L 119/1, esp Arts 68–70; and Regulation (EU) 2018/1725 of the European Parliament and of the Council of 23 Oct. 2018 on the protection of natural persons with regard to the processing of personal data by the Union institutions, bodies, offices and agencies and on the free movement of such data, and repealing Regulation (EC) No 45/2001 and Decision No 1247/2002/EC [2018] OJ L 295/39, esp Arts 52–62.

[123] See for a suggestion for judicial control by default of final determinations made by administrative review bodies at EU level, F Coman-Kund, 'Legal protection against fundamental rights breaches through factual conduct by the EU' in M Fink (ed), *Mechanisms to Redress Human Rights Violations by the EU* (Cambridge University Press, 2024), forthcoming.

multilayered system. The three examples discussed in this chapter illustrate various configurations of hybrid EU executive governance in three specific policy areas and expose some of the challenges and problems raised by hybridity.

The chapter argues that hybrid EU executive governance has far-reaching effects on the relational conception of separation of powers, analytically examined across three dimensions (two horizonal and one vertical) in view of the peculiarities of the EU multilayered system. On the one hand, increasingly hybrid executive governance can be seen as a form of cooperation within the executive functions across EU and Member States' legal orders, often serving pragmatically the effectiveness of EU law and policies. On the other hand, the bestowal of executive powers on EU level actors and the exercise of these powers in entangled and untransparent relationships with Member State executive actors poses great challenges for the control dimension of separation of powers. First, convoluted multi-actor executive networks acting in a cloudy operational environment make it difficult to understand from the outside who does what for the purpose of control and accountability. Second, the entangled hybrid web of EU and national executive actors can hardly be effectively controlled by parliamentary and judicial mechanisms largely delineated across EU and national lines.

Hence there is the danger that ever-expanding but unrestrained hybrid executive powers could significantly alter separation of powers within the EU, with detrimental consequences for democracy, the rule of law and fundamental rights. Two alternative solutions are suggested to address this conundrum. One entails reversing the hybridity phenomenon, by going back to the indirect administration as the default model as far as implementation and enforcement of EU law and policies are concerned. The other engenders tailored parliamentary, judicial and executive control mechanisms that are capable of effectively controlling EU hybrid executive power, in combination with commensurate legal safeguards, in particular as regards transparency, reporting and information obligations.

Looking forward, as a matter of principle, hybrid executive governance models should be established only together with adequate parliamentary, judicial and executive control mechanisms. From a separation of powers perspective, this is likely to improve control over the exercise of executive powers within a hybrid setting. However, if controlling hybrid executive power will entail replicating hybridity across the legislative and judicial functions, this would likely result in a more fundamental transformation of the Union that should be reflected accordingly in the EU Treaties.

15

Separation of Powers and the Role of National Constitutional Courts in the EU: German Lessons for Europe?

NIK DE BOER[1]

I. Introduction

The role of constitutional courts in the European Union (EU) is one of the most highly debated issues in EU legal scholarship. Constitutional courts from several Member States have articulated constitutional limits to the primacy of EU law and to further European integration through Treaty change. Critics argue that such review presents a problematic risk to the primacy of EU law and the stability of the EU legal order.[2] More recently, a number of authors have additionally stressed the dangers of abuse.[3] Nonetheless, a significant number of scholars have historically seen merit in the national constitutional courts' conditioning of primacy and of further European integration, although the debate knows many nuances.[4]

[1] This chapter builds on the author's recently published monograph, N de Boer, *Judging European Democracy: The Role and Legitimacy of National Constitutional Courts in the EU* (Oxford University Press, 2023). Efforts have been made not to use the same wording as in that book, but parts of the text may nonetheless bear a strong resemblance. I am very grateful for the insightful comments I received from Christina Eckes, Anna Wallerman Ghavanini and Päivi Leino-Sandberg on earlier drafts of this chapter. The usual disclaimer applies.

[2] eg D Kelemen, 'On the Unsustainability of Constitutional Pluralism' (2016) 23 *Maastricht Journal of European and Comparative Law* 136; D Kelemen et al, 'National Courts Cannot Override ECJ Judgments: A Joint Statement in Defense of the EU Legal Order' (*Verfassungsblog*, 26 May 2020), at verfassungsblog.de/national-courts-cannot-override-ECJ-judgments; JHH Weiler, *The Constitution of Europe: 'Do the New Clothes Have an Emperor?' And Other Essays on European Integration* (Cambridge University Press, 1999) ch 9.

[3] eg D Kelemen and L Pech, 'The Uses and Abuses of Constitutional Pluralism: Undermining the Rule of Law in the Name of Constitutional Identity in Hungary and Poland' (2019) 21 *Cambridge Yearbook of European Legal Studies* 59; F Fabbrini and A Sajó, 'The Dangers of Constitutional Identity' (2019) 25 *European Law Journal* 457.

[4] The idea of constitutional pluralism is often used as an umbrella term for such views although there are many different views and the debate is nuanced. For a number of influential views see N Walker, 'The Idea of Constitutional Pluralism' (2002) 65 *The Modern Law Review* 317; M Maduro, 'Contrapunctual Law: Europe's

Against the background of the ongoing debate on the role of constitutional courts in the EU, this chapter aims to critically assess whether and in what ways the review of European law by national constitutional courts can provide an appropriate answer to the EU's separation of powers problems.[5] The chapter studies the case of the German Federal Constitutional Court (GFCC), which is a national constitutional court that has engaged with EU law issues on several occasions and at important junctures of EU integration.[6] The GFCC's elaborate and sophisticated case law on the EU has put this court at the centre of debates on the role of national constitutional courts in the EU. While some have argued that the GFCC's review provides an answer to some of the EU's separation of powers problems, I argue that the GFCC's case law rather presents a problem in terms of separation of powers.[7] On the basis of the German case, I suggest that a more limited role, as adopted by some other national constitutional courts, is more appropriate. In this respect, I understand the notion of constitutional courts broadly, namely as all Member State courts with the power to engage in judicial review of legislation on constitutional grounds.[8] By these courts' review of European law I mean not just the review of EU law proper, but also that of EU Treaties before their entry into force, as well as instruments adopted under international law that strictly fall outside the scope of EU law, but are closely related to EU law. Examples of the latter are the Treaty on the European Stability Mechanism (ESM) and the Fiscal Compact. Some of the EU's separation of powers problems are associated precisely with the adoption of legal instruments outside the framework of EU law.[9] Using this broader notion of European law thus allows for a more balanced evaluation of the constitutional courts' role in relation to the EU.

The chapter builds on the contributions to this book that identify executive dominance and highly consensual policy making as key problems in the EU from a separation

Constitutional Pluralism in Action' in N Walker (ed), *European Constitutionalism* (Hart Publishing, 2003); M Kumm, 'The Jurisprudence of Constitutional Conflict: Constitutional Supremacy in Europe before and after the Constitutional Treaty' (2005) 11 *European Law Journal* 262; M Avbelj and J Komárek (eds), *Constitutional Pluralism in the European Union and Beyond* (Hart, 2012).

[5] The language of separation of powers or similar notions have been invoked in various influential publications on the role of constitutional courts in the EU. See eg A Von Bogdandy and S Schill, 'Overcoming Absolute Primacy: Respect for National Identity under the Lisbon Treaty' (2011) 48 *Common Market Law Review* 1417, 1453; Maduro (n 5) 523; H Schermers, 'The Scales in Balance: National Constitutional Court v. Court of Justice' (1990) 27 *Common Market Law Review* 97; D Grimm, 'The Role of National Constitutional Courts in European Democracy' in D Grimm (ed), *The Constitution of European Democracy* (Oxford University Press, 2017).

[6] More comprehensive overviews of the EU-related role of constitutional courts have been provided elsewhere, eg A Bobić, *The Jurisprudence of Constitutional Conflict in the European Union* (Oxford University Press, 2022); LFM Besselink et al, 'National Constitutional Avenues for Further EU Integration' (Study requested by the European Parliament's Committee on Legal Affairs and Constitutional Affairs Committee of the European Parliament, DG for Internal Policies Study, 2014), at www.europarl.europa.eu/RegData/etudes/etudes/join/2014/493046/IPOL-JURI_ET(2014)493046_EN.pdf.

[7] I discuss some of these positive evaluations of the GFCC's case law in sections II and III.

[8] The notion of constitutional courts adopted in this chapter thus encompasses both specialised constitutional courts, such as the German Federal Constitutional Court (GFCC) as well as ordinary courts with the power of constitutional review, such as the Danish Supreme Court.

[9] J Habermas, *The Crisis of the European Union: A Response* (Polity, 2012); B Crum, 'Saving the Euro at the Cost of Democracy?' (2013) 51 *Journal of Common Market Studies* 614. See also on informalisation, Gnes and Sormunen, ch 4 in this volume.

of powers perspective.[10] Such assessments echo familiar criticisms of the EU's decision-making procedures.[11] 'Executive dominance' refers to the problem that the key political actors on the European plane are institutions that would qualify as executive in a nation-state context, namely the European Council, the Council and the Commission, while the position of the directly elected European Parliament is relatively weak. The model of highly consensual policy making in the EU is a problem because it prevents political conflicts to be debated openly.[12]

Expanding on these evaluations, over-constitutionalisation and judicialisation have been regarded as important reasons why the EU lacks sufficient political conflict over different policy agendas.[13] Over-constitutionalisation concerns the problem that many policy decisions are laid down in the EU Treaties, while they would be ordinary law in the Member States. Such over-constitutionalisation removes these policy decisions from the ordinary political process. Over-constitutionalisation and the high-consensus requirements for adopting EU secondary law more generally, also empower the ECJ.[14] Authors such as Fritz Scharpf and Dieter Grimm argue that the ECJ's case law on the internal market has had a liberalising and deregulatory effect on the Member States. High consensus requirements for the adoption of EU secondary law, let alone the significant hurdles for amending the EU Treaties, make it difficult, however, to correct the ECJ's interpretations of EU law through decisions by the EU's political branches.[15] The result is that decisions of considerable political importance are made by the European court, instead of political institutions. In this sense the ECJ is often considered a motor of European integration. Leino-Sandberg and Minkkinen argue, moreover, that the ECJ has largely failed to take seriously its role of checking the EU's political branches, instead showing excessive deference.[16]

To fill the void left by the ECJ, one could argue that critical scrutiny of European law by national constitutional courts is warranted, including against the expansive case law of the European court itself. A challenge to this perspective, however, comes from the contested role of constitutional courts in a separation of powers perspective.[17] Constitutional courts are those courts equipped with the power to check the constitutionality of legislation. Yet whether courts should have that power is a matter of ongoing debate, because it allows independent judges to override the decisions of democratically

[10] On executive dominance, see Ankersmit, ch 5 in this volume, Eckes, ch 12 in this volume and Krajweski, ch 6 in this volume. On both issues, see Leino-Sandberg and Minkkinen, ch 2 in this volume.

[11] See eg: A Føllesdal and S Hix, 'Why There Is a Democratic Deficit in the EU: A Response to Majone and Moravscik' (2006) 44 *Journal of Common Market Studies* 533; similarly C Möllers, *The Three Branches: A Comparative Model of Separation of Powers* (Oxford University Press, 2013) 181–85; D Curtin, 'Challenging Executive Dominance in European Democracy' (2014) 77 *Modern Law Review* 1; Habermas (n 6) 6.

[12] Leino-Sandberg and Minkkinen, ch 2 in this volume.

[13] See also L van Middelaar, *Alarums & Excursions: Improvising Politics on the European Stage* (Agenda Publishing, 2019) ch 7; Möllers (n 11) 171–74.

[14] This can also be said about the ECB, which I leave out of the discussion here. See further: N de Boer and J van 't Klooster, 'The ECB, the Courts and the Issue of Democratic Legitimacy after Weiss' (2020) 57 *Common Market Law Review* 1689. On the ECB, see also Ronkainen, ch 9 in this volume.

[15] F Scharpf, 'Legitimacy in the Multi-Level European Polity' in P Dobner and M Loghlin (eds), The Twilight of Constitutionalism? (Oxford University Press, 2010); F Scharpf, 'The Asymmetry of European Integration, or Why the EU Cannot Be a "Social Market Economy"' (2010) 8 *Socio-Economic Review* 211; Grimm (n 5).

[16] Leino-Sandberg and Minkkinen, ch 2 in this volume, 11.

[17] Möllers (n 11) 128.

elected legislatures.[18] This democratic concern also applies to the role of constitutional courts in relation to the EU. Where a national court imposes constitutional limits on possible Treaty change, such limits constrain the leeway of its national legislature in deciding on further integration through Treaty change. Where a national court imposes constitutional limits on EU law, this can restrict the ability of the Member State's government to agree to secondary EU law or mean that certain provisions of EU law will be inapplicable within the national legal order.

In this chapter, I argue that the example of the GFCC does indeed affirm the risk that the national constitutional courts' review of European law can turn these courts into arbiters over contested political issues on the EU better decided by legislative institutions.[19] Rather than providing an adequate answer to the EU's separation of powers problems, the GFCC oversteps the bounds of its appropriate role. To avoid this dilemma, I suggest that the role of constitutional courts in relation to the EU should be limited and focus on safeguarding the space for legislatures to decide on fundamental constitutional questions regarding the EU. The GFCC has done so in some cases by countering executive dominance through demands of parliamentary participation and rights to adequate information at the national level. Possibly this is a role that constitutional courts could fulfil as well in other Member States.

My argument is structured as follows. Section II discusses the view that national constitutional courts introduce welcome opposition as a counterweight to the lack of political conflict over EU-related decisions. I argue that the judicial route is not the appropriate one for such opposition. Using the example of the German Constitutional Court (GFCC), I show that constitutional courts risk elevating a particular contested political viewpoint to the level of constitutional law, ultimately limiting rather than facilitating political contestation. Section III assesses whether constitutional courts should nonetheless act as a counterweight to the power of the ECJ, given the EU's over-constitutionalisation. I argue, however, that review by constitutional courts does not provide an obvious solution and can even exacerbate over-constitutionalisation. On a more positive note, section IV argues that constitutional courts can play a legitimate role in countering executive dominance. In this respect, I offer a number of positive examples from the GFCC's case law. The conclusion sums up the overall argument, discusses limitations that stem from this chapter's focus on the GFCC, and offers further reflections on how courts could possibly promote contestation and deliberation, while not limiting legitimate political choices.

[18] See for different views: J Rawls, *Political Liberalism* (Columbia University Press, 2005); R Dworkin, *Freedom's Law: The Moral Reading of the American Constitution* (Oxford University Press, 1996); R Bellamy, *Political Constitutionalism: A Republican Defence of the Constitutionality of Democracy* (Cambridge University Press, 2007); J Waldron, 'The Core of the Case Against Judicial Review' (2006) 115 *The Yale Law Journal* 1346; J Waldron, *Law and Disagreement* (Oxford University Press, 1999); M Tushnet, *Taking the Constitution Away from the Courts* (Princeton University Press, 2000).

[19] The German Federal Constitutional Court is more often accused of showing insufficient restraint towards the political branches in its EU-related rulings: F Mayer, 'Rebel Without a Cause? A Critical Analysis of the German Constitutional Court's OMT Reference' (2014) 15 *German Law Journal* 111; C Schönberger, 'Lisbon in Karlsruhe: Maastricht's Epigonies At Sea' (2009) 10 *German Law Journal* 1201; C Tomuschat, 'The Ruling of the German Constitutional Court on the Treaty of Lisbon' (2009) 10 *German Law Journal* 1259; C Möllers, 'Legalität, Legitimität Und Legitimation Des Bundesverfassungsgerichts' in M Jestaedt et al (eds), *Das entgrenzte Gericht. Eine kritische Bilanz nach sechzig Jahren Bundesverfassungsgericht* (Suhrkamp, 2011).

II. Constitutional Courts as Fora for Opposition?

One possible way to justify the national constitutional courts' review of European law is to argue that the proceedings before constitutional courts are a way to reintroduce the political conflict missing in the European political process. Such arguments have been voiced especially for the role of the GFCC in relation to the EU. Peter Huber, former Justice of the GFCC and rapporteur in several of the major cases on the EU, has contended that the Court functions as an 'opposition to the mainstream'.[20] This idea has been echoed in the context of the GFCC's *Maastricht-Urteil*. Reflecting on that judgment, Mattias Herdegen argued for example that the proceedings in Karlsruhe had been 'been widely conceived as a kind of substitute for a public debate on the monetary union before parliamentary approval', while the 'large consensus within Parliament did not allow for a profound discussion of Maastricht's implications, of the quality the political class of France and of other Member States has offered to its citizens.'[21] Similarly, Juliane Kokott evaluated the judgment as 'partly a compensation for the lack of a proper political debate on the implications of the Maastricht Treaty and the monetary union.'[22] In her view, such a debate 'took place too late and too superficially in Germany' furthering 'ambiguous feelings in the population' that the *Maastricht-Urteil* partly addressed, leading to better acceptance of European integration in Germany.[23]

These views, reflected in the arguments of other commentators, in fact appear to contain two justifications for a constitutional court's review of European law.[24] One is that the courts compensate for an apparent deficient *quality* of the political debate on European integration. The other is that the courts compensate for *a lack of opposition and political conflict* over European integration in the political process. Although these concerns about deficient quality and lack of opposition can be connected, they are conceptually distinct and stand in some tension. The idea that constitutional courts compensate for the deficient quality of political deliberations is familiar from legal constitutionalists' thought. Here the idea is that constitutional courts provide a better forum for deliberation on constitutional matters than the ordinary political process. Judicial review of legislation on this understanding is a way to ensure that issues of constitutional principle are duly considered. This feature justifies that constitutional matters are

[20] F Mayer, 'Rebel Without a Cause? A Critical Analysis of the German Constitutional Court's OMT Reference' (2014) 15 *German Law Journal* 142; see also M Wendel, 'Exceeding Judicial Competence in the Name of Democracy: The German Federal Constitutional Court's OMT Reference' (2014) 10 *European Constitutional Law Review* 263, 283.

[21] M Herdegen, 'Maastricht and the German Constitutional Court – Constitutional Restraints for an Ever Closer Union' (1994) 31 *Common Market Law Review* 235, 249.

[22] J Kokott, 'Report on Germany' in JHH Weiler, A Slaughter and A Stone Sweet (eds), *The European Court and national courts – doctrine and jurisprudence: legal change in its social context* (Hart, 1998) 131.

[23] ibid.

[24] For similar views see J Collings, *Democracy's Guardians: A History of the German Federal Constitutional Court, 1951–2001* (Oxford University Press, 2015) 280; M Claes, 'The National Courts' Mandate in the European Constitution' (PhD Thesis, Maastricht University, 2004) 10–11; Kumm (n 4) 282 fn 54. Perhaps such views are also echoed in J Reestman, 'Legitimacy through Adjudication: The ESM Treaty and the Fiscal Compact before the National Courts' in T Beukers, B De Witte and C Kilpatrick (eds), *Constitutional Change through Euro-Crisis Law* (Cambridge University Press, 2017). Reestman argues that the constitutional court judgments on the Euro crisis 'provided a legitimacy that the political process was unable to provide on its own' (267).

decided ultimately by constitutional courts instead of legislatures. Constitutional court judgments, in turn, are thought to have a subsequent salutary effect on the quality of public and political debate. So precisely because the political branches cannot be trusted to adequately address constitutional issues by themselves, it is justified to 'depoliticise' these matters by removing them from ordinary political contestation and leaving the 'final' say to constitutional courts.

This justification for the intervention of constitutional courts stands in tension, however, with the idea that a constitutional court can provide a forum for opposition. Here the argument appears to be that the political process is in fact not political enough and that the court intervention brings in political viewpoints not sufficiently considered in that political process. Yet, where a constitutional court starts acting as a forum for opposition, it risks elevating a particular and contested political viewpoint to the level of constitutional law in a way that will ultimately constrain the room for political contestation in the ordinary political process. The proceedings before a court may be seen as offering citizens an additional route of political participation. Yet, parties to a court case are not necessarily representative of all the societal interests affected, while the parties are not the decision-makers in any case: the judges decide. In this sense, representative political institutions have a better comparative democratic legitimacy.[25] That is the case even for the democratically deficient EU legislature. European citizens directly elect the European Parliament, while Member State representatives in the Council are democratically accountable to their national parliaments. However deficient in practice these mechanisms are for the EU institutions, no similar mechanisms of democratic accountability exist for constitutional court judges. The comparative legitimacy of courts and legislative institutions is the crucial issue here, as constitutional courts can override the assessments of legislatures based on a constitutional framework that binds ordinary politics. Constitutional courts police the limits of legitimate political action and this is a role that sits uneasily with facilitating opposition.

The GFCC's case law on the EU provides a practical example of this problem. The German experience highlights how the German court has acted as a forum for opposition. Yet it is much less clear that this Court has compensated for deficiencies in the quality of political debates, or that it improved the quality of subsequent political debates. In terms of the *quality* of the political debate, it is key to compare the constitutional issues raised by the GFCC with the prior deliberations of the relevant political branches and consider whether the GFCC's deliberations on these matters were of a better quality. Taking the *Maastricht-Urteil* as an example, the key question then becomes whether the Court compensated for lack of attention in the political process to the constitutional issue of democracy. The compatibility of the Maastricht Treaty with the constitutional principle of democracy was after all the key issue in the *Maastricht-Urteil*.[26] However, if one looks at the ratification debates in the *Bundestag* it becomes clear quite quickly that the issue of democracy was also a major topic of discussion in those political debates. There was widespread disappointment among the *Bundestag* members about

[25] On these arguments, see R Bellamy, 'The Democratic Qualities of Courts: A Critical Analysis of Three Arguments' (2013) 49 *Representation* 333.

[26] BVerfg, Judgment of 12 October 1993, 2 BvR 2134/ 92 (*Maastricht*) (translation in [1994] 1 CMLR 57).

the Treaty's democratic shortcomings. Some parties even called for quick revisions to the Treaty in order to strengthen the Union's democratic credentials.[27] Moreover, the aspiration to democratise the EU was laid down in the Constitution: a new Article 23 was introduced in the Basic Law which demanded that the EU would have to respect 'democratic, social and federal principles' in addition to the rule of law, the principle of subsidiarity and fundamental rights. The issue of democracy thus played an important role in the German ratification debates on the Maastricht Treaty. Yet, the Treaty was accepted by the *Bundestag* as a compromise, while its democratic shortcomings would have to be remedied in the future.[28]

Hence, the GFCC was not the first institution to raise the principled question of how the new EU Treaty had to be assessed in democratic terms. The key difference between the Court and the *Bundestag* was ultimately that the Karlsruhe judges relied on a more national understanding of democracy. The German Court voiced doubts about the idea that the EU could ever become fully democratic. It considered that the sociological preconditions for democracy – a sufficiently shared European collective identity and shared European public sphere – were missing at the European level. What shines through in the *Maastricht-Urteil* especially is that the powers of the EU would have to be limited in order to maintain a viable democracy in the Member States. Germany's politicians by contrast predominantly sought the answer for the EU's democratic problems in a strengthening of the European Parliament. Moreover, the link between democracy, people and statehood as drawn by the German Court was, and remains, contested.[29]

If one accepts that both the *Bundestag*'s more pro-European view of democracy and the German Court's more national reading are both legitimate interpretations of the constitutional principle of democracy, then it is difficult to argue that the GFCC compensated for a lack of attention to this principled issue in the political process. In that case, and as I have argued elsewhere, the German Court's *Maastricht-Urteil* is better understood as having provided an outlet for more critical views on European integration not fully considered in prior political debate.[30] Public opinion surveys at the time did indicate that German citizens had more preoccupations about the Treaty than the political debates reflected.[31] German politics was characterised by a large pro-European consensus and it could be difficult to raise critical arguments about European integration. In fact, within the German political climate of the time, influential political actors framed the choice between accepting and rejecting the Maastricht Treaty as a choice between peace and stability on the European continent on the one hand, and disorder

[27] See De Boer (n 1), 131.

[28] On the deliberations see inter alia: Beschlußempfehlung und Bericht des Sonderausschusses 'Europäische Union (Vertrag von Maastricht)', BT- Dr 12/ 3895 of 01.12.1992; Bericht der Gemeinsamen Verfassungskommission gemäß Beschluß des Deutschen Bundestages— Drucksachen 12/ 1590, 12/ 1670— und Beschluß des Bundesrates – Drucksache 741/ 91 (Beschluß), BT- Dr 12/ 6000 of 05.11.1993; Plenarprotokoll 12/ 110, Stenografischer Bericht der 110. Sitzung des Deutschen Bundestages am 8. Oktober 1992; Plenarprotokoll 12/ 126, Stenografischer Bericht der 126. Sitzung des Deutschen Bundestages am 2. Dezember 1992.

[29] De Boer (n 1), 130–140.

[30] De Boer (n 1) ch 4.

[31] R Knoben, 'Public Opinion in the European Union' in F Laursen and S Vanhoonacker (eds), *The Ratification of the Maastricht Treaty* (Brill Nijhoff, 1994).

and disunity on the other.[32] One parliamentarian went so far as to suggest that the choice against Maastricht was tantamount to opting for a return in the direction 'of the thirty years' war'.[33]

The Karlsruhe proceedings that led to the *Maastricht-Urteil* can be seen as having provided room for more critical viewpoints on European integration. First, the GFCC provided a forum to those who had concerns about the Treaty, and the proceedings generated significant public attention. Second, the Court itself provided such a more critical perspective by adopting a national understanding of democracy and articulating constitutional constraints on the course of European integration. There is also little evidence that the Court's Maastricht ruling constrained subsequent political debate in the direct aftermath of the case. The possible limits to European integration still seemed far away at the time and the Maastricht judgment could be interpreted by German politicians as offering support for their previously held viewpoints.[34]

Yet, while the limits to European integration set by the GFCC could still be considered fairly theoretical at the time of Maastricht, this appeared to be no longer the case when the German Court handed down its 2009 *Lissabon-Urteil* and several subsequent judgments on the Euro crisis. While the *Lissabon-Urteil* upheld the Treaty of Lisbon, the Court returned to the main principles of its *Maastricht-Urteil*, placing more stringent restrictions on European integration than before.[35] Particularly contested was the part of the ruling in which the Court judged that extensive competence transfers would not be permissible in certain areas, for example, decisions affecting the budget right of the *Bundestag*. Yet, when the Euro crisis began shortly afterwards, in the spring of 2010, it was the budget rights of national parliaments that were affected by the manifold European measures taken to tackle the crisis.

Within this context of the Euro crisis, the German Court continued to function as a forum for Euro-critical voices within Germany. All the major parties in the *Bundestag* remained strongly pro-European during this time, which meant that there were large majorities in support of most of the Euro- risis measures. Only in 2017 did a Eurosceptic party – the Alternative for Germany (AfD) – obtain seats in the German Parliament. Before that, politicians with more Eurosceptic viewpoints were instead minorities within the bigger mainstream parties, especially within the parliamentary groups of the Christian Democrats and the liberal Free Democratic Party (FDP). Given that the views of these minorities departed from the party line, parliamentary debates did not always reflect the full range of political positions on the Euro crisis measures.[36] The GFCC provided an avenue for these critical *Bundestag* members, as well as for a broader extra-parliamentary opposition to contest the Euro crisis measures. These measures touched

[32] C Schrag Sternberg, *The Struggle for EU Legitimacy Public Contestation, 1950–2005* (Palgrave Macmillan, 2013) 155.

[33] P Kittelmann, Plenarprotokoll 12/ 110, Stenografischer Bericht der 110. Sitzung des Deutschen Bundestages am 8. Oktober 1992, 9387.

[34] See Plenarprotokoll 12/ 181, Stenografischer Bericht der 181. Sitzung des Deutschen Bundestages am 20. Oktober 1993; Presseerklärung des Bundeskanzlers, Nr 386/ 93 von 12. Oktober 1993, reprinted in I Winkelmann (ed), *Das Maastricht- Urteil des Bundesverfassungsgerichts vom 12. Oktober 1993, Dokumentation des Verfahrens mit Einführung* (Dunckler & Humblot, 1994).

[35] BVerfg, Judgment of 30 June 2009, 2 BvE 2/ 08 ('*Lisbon* judgment').

[36] eg 'Streit um Rederecht für Euro-Rettungskritiker' *Handelsblatt* (Düsseldorf, 30 September 2011).

on the budgetary powers of the *Bundestag* and the Court's case law appeared to rule out more extensive European economic and fiscal integration. In fact, in an interview for the *Frankfurter Allgemeine Zeitung* of September 2011, the then President of the German Constitutional Court, Andreas Vosskuhle, stated as much. He declared that the room for further European integration under the German Constitution was 'probably largely exhausted'.[37]

The German example indicates that the role of facilitating opposition to European integration sits uneasily with the position of constitutional courts. Ultimately, constitutional courts interpret the legal framework that is supposed to provide the framework in which ordinary politics takes place. Their interpretations must therefore stand above the legitimate political contests taking place in the ordinary political process. One may of course conclude that the rulings of the GFCC on the EU were the only proper interpretations of Germany's constitutional framework and for that reason properly beyond political contestation. However, the German Constitutional Court's case law on the EU is highly contested by German legal scholars, even in the academic writings of Doris König, a current judge of the constitutional court.[38] A more deferential approach by constitutional courts towards the political process therefore seems appropriate. The Czech Constitutional Court and Danish Supreme Court have chosen this path, leaving their respective national legislatures with wide discretion in deciding on the desirable power transfers to the EU.[39]

III. Constitutional Courts as Counterweight to the ECJ?

The previous section discussed the pitfalls with a general role for constitutional courts in providing room for opposition to European integration, even if one accepts that decision-making on EU matters lacks sufficient political conflict. Yet, national courts could possibly avoid these downsides where they aim to correct the excessive power of the ECJ. While the constitutional courts' review raises problems when directed at the acts of political branches, this seems less of a worry when the national courts check the power of the EU's top judicial institution.

Such a case for national courts as a counterweight to the ECJ has been articulated by former German constitutional justice Dieter Grimm. In fact, he has argued that 'In the current constellation, national constitutional courts are the only available counterweight to the democracy-diminishing mechanisms at work in the EU'.[40] Grimm bases

[37] M Mann and I Kloepfer, 'Mehr Europa Lässt Das Grundgesetz Kaum Zu' *Frankfurter Algemeine Zeitung* (Frankfurt, 25 November 2011), at www.faz.net/aktuell/wirtschaft/eurokrise/im-gespraech-andreas-vosskuhle-mehr-europa-laesst-das-grundgesetz-kaum-zu-11369184.html.

[38] D König, *Die Übertragung von Hoheitsrechten Im Rahmen Des Europäischen Integrationsprozesses – Anwendungsbereich Und Schranken Des Art. 23 Des Grundgesetzes* (Duncker & Humblot, 2000). See for example p 503, where she states that 'the thesis that only strong national parliaments can provide sufficient democratic legitimacy cannot be convincingly justified with constitutional arguments' (my translation).

[39] The Supreme Court of Denmark (Højesteret), Case 361/ 1997, decision of 6 April 1998 (Maastricht) (summary translated in [1999] 3 CMLR 854); The Constitutional Court of the Czech Republic (Ústavní soud), judgment of 3 November2009, Pl ÚS 29/ 09 (Treaty of Lisbon II) [110]–[111].

[40] Grimm (n 5) 25.

this argument on the problems of over-constitutionalisation and the high-consensus requirements in the EU's decision-making processes discussed in the introduction. To recall, these features have turned the ECJ into a powerful institution that is difficult to correct politically. Political institutions have therefore only limited opportunities to address what Grimm sees as the undemocratic consequences of this non-political mechanism of decision-making.

Within this setting, Grimm argues that national constitutional courts offer a crucial contribution to European democracy by constraining 'the undermining of national democracy through European law, and to urge European institutions towards greater respect for the results of national democratic processes.'[41] Through identity and ultra vires review, national constitutional courts help safeguard that the EU – and the ECJ in particular – respects the Member States' constitutional identities, does not overstep its competences and would thus hollow out national democracy.

Grimm's reliance on national constitutional courts to correct the ECJ's power is nonetheless paradoxical. The excessive judicial power of the European court resulting from over-constitutionalisation is to be countered by the judicial power of national constitutional courts. The idea can be likened to combating fire with fire, which can be effective, but it carries the risk that the controlled fire burns out of control. While trying to counter the supposedly 'political' judgments of the ECJ, constitutional courts may fall into the trap of handing down 'political' judgments themselves, overstepping the bounds of legitimate judicial authority and worsening the problem of judicial power, instead of addressing it.

In this context, it is important to address in three ways the idea that constitutional courts should provide a counterweight to over-constitutionalisation and the powers of the ECJ. First, most of the case law by national constitutional courts does not concern merely the ECJ's role, but deals with constitutional questions of European integration more broadly. These rulings also have repercussions for legislative institutions at the Member State and EU level. The GFCC's case law presents the most obvious example, where key cases – *Maastricht*, *Lissabon* and several cases on the Euro crisis – concerned the ratification of Treaties. While the German Court does articulate limits to the ECJ's powers, these limits are rooted in a more general reading of the constitutional framework. That reading also limits the powers of the *Bundestag* and European legislative institutions, as these must respect German constitutional identity and competence limits as interpreted by the German Court. As Christoph Möllers commented in 2011, the GFCC seemed 'more ready to rhetorically fight the European political process than to effectively review the European courts.'[42]

A second and related problem is that the constitutional courts' review may in fact exacerbate the problem of over-constitutionalisation. While the power of the ECJ is one consequence of over-constitutionalisation, the more general problem is the skewed balance between law and politics at the EU level, resulting from the many policy decisions laid down in the EU Treaties. The Economic and Monetary Union (EMU) provides

[41] ibid 206. Komárek may be seen to offer some considerations that point in a similar direction: J Komárek, 'National Constitutional Courts in the European Constitutional Democracy' (2014) 12 *International Journal of Constitutional Law* 525.

[42] C Möllers, 'Constitutional Ultra Vires Review of European Acts Only Under Exceptional Circumstances; Decision of 6 July 2010, 2 BvR 2661/06, Honeywell' (2011) 7 *European Constitutional Law Review* 161, 167.

an example, where overriding importance is given to price stability at the expense of certain other possibly relevant considerations, such as high employment, or environmental sustainability.[43] Yet in this respect ultra vires review by national courts is liable to worsen over-constitutionalisation. The GFCC's *Maastricht-Urteil* is again instructive, as it is the case from which ultra vires review is commonly seen to originate.[44] The Court's reasoning there was that the EU's democratic legitimacy derives primarily from the national parliaments, given democratic deficits at the EU level and the missing sociological preconditions for well-functioning democracy beyond the nation-state. The statute by which powers are conferred to the EU is consequently of great democratic significance. It is through this Act that the German Parliament – the *Bundestag* – democratically authorises the Union's powers.[45] Yet, to ensure that it is truly the *Bundestag* that decides on the scope of the Union's competences, it is pivotal that these competences are sufficiently certain and predictable. Open-ended transfers of powers would give the democratically deficient EU potentially unlimited competences without democratic authorisation from the German parliament. This reasoning provided the basis for ultra vires review: the German Court would review whether the EU institutions remain within the bounds of their conferred competences.[46]

Yet, the result of this reading is that it makes the problem of over-constitutionalisation worse rather than better for the EMU. The German Court did not see as democratically problematic the elevation of contested goals and policy prescriptions to the level of constitutional law. Instead, the Court reasoned that abidance by them was a democratic requirement. Germany was allowed to participate in the monetary union precisely because it was conceived as a *Stabilitätsgemeinschaft*: a community based on stability. It was this orientation that made the development of the monetary union sufficiently certain and predictable. The Court thus considered that the Member States' duty to avoid excessive deficits or the prohibition for Member States to assume debts of other Member States were vital ingredients of this *Stabilitätsgemeinschaft*, not democratically problematic restrictions on government action.[47] Through the *Maastricht-Urteil*, the German Constitutional Court was able to offer its own interpretation of the EMU provisions and use them as the basis for future review of EU acts, including those of the political branches. The consequences of this vision became clear during the Euro crisis. When the economic and political assumptions underlying the EMU framework failed to match reality, European government leaders sought to solve Europe's developing debt crisis. Yet in this context, a number of German citizens immediately and predictably threatened to challenge mechanisms of financial assistance before the Karlsruhe court as an illegal departure from the *Stabilitätsgemeinschaft*.[48]

[43] M Herdegen, 'Price Stability and Budgetary Restraints in the Economic and Monetary Union: The Law as Guardian of Economic Wisdom' (1998) 35 *Common Market Law Review* 9; M Dani, 'Openness, Purposiveness, and the Realignment of the EU and the Democratic and Social Constitutional State' (2023) 24 *German Law Journal* 1099, 1118–20.

[44] Although the French Conseil d'Etat's judgment of 22 December 1978 (*Ministre de l'intérieur c Cohn-Bendit*) was probably the first ultra vires ruling by a national court.

[45] BVerfG, *Maastricht* (n 26) [37] and [46]–[47].

[46] ibid [48]–[49].

[47] ibid [80].

[48] M Brackmann and J Münchrath, 'Finanzhilfe für Griechenland: "Wir ziehen wieder nach Karlsruhe"' *Handelsblatt* (Düsseldorf, 22 February 2010).

A third problem is that even in cases where national constitutional courts point their review directly at the powers of the ECJ, courts still need to justify such decisions on the basis of underlying constitutional principles. The interpretation of these principles, in turn, is removed from democratic political contestation. In addition, where national constitutional courts judge an ECJ judgment unconstitutional, such a ruling has potential negative repercussions for the stability of the EU legal order.[49] Assuming these courts care about the stability of the EU legal order, they should take into account such possible negative consequences. As a result, the task of controlling the ECJ is complicated.

The response of the GFCC and the Danish Supreme Court to the ECJ's 2005 *Mangold* ruling presents one of the best examples of a situation where national constitutional courts have grappled directly with the ECJ's powers. The *Mangold* case concerned Directive 2000/78 on equal treatment in employment and occupation, the prohibition of age discrimination more specifically.[50] Mr Mangold argued that his employment contract was incompatible with the prohibition of discrimination on grounds of age. However, Germany had not yet transposed the Directive, as its implementation deadline had not yet passed. Moreover, the dispute was one between two private parties – Mr Mangold and his employer, Mr Helm – while the ECJ had only accepted the direct effect of Directives when invoked against state authorities.[51] These circumstances appeared a significant obstacle for Mangold to win his case. Nonetheless, the European judges considered that the principle of non-discrimination on grounds of age was 'a general principle of Community law', which the national courts had to apply and give priority over conflicting provisions of national law.[52] Many legal scholars saw the *Mangold* ruling as problematic. It sparked a particularly fierce reaction from Lüder Gerken and Roman Herzog, a former President of the German Constitutional Court. They criticised the European Court for no longer acting as 'part of the judiciary', but as the 'legislative authority'.[53]

Questions about the permissibility of the *Mangold* ruling ended up with the GFCC in the *Honeywell* case. Yet, when this case was decided in 2010, a majority of the justices declined to hold Mangold ultra vires. This majority also laid down stringent conditions for ultra vires control given its downsides:

> If each Member State claimed to be able to decide through their own courts on the validity of legal acts of the Union, the primacy of application could be circumvented in practice, and the uniform application of Union law would be placed at risk.[54]

For that reason, ultra vires review would have to be exercised in a manner 'open towards European law'.[55] Ultra vires rulings could only be given when competence transgressions

[49] Weiler and Haltern likened this option to the 'use of tactical nuclear weapons' carrying 'the risk of a nuclear domino effect'. Weiler (n 2) 320.

[50] Case C-144/04 *Werner Mangold v Rüdiger Helm* EU:C:2005:709, [2005] ECR I-09981.

[51] Case 41/74 *Van Duyn v Home Office* ECLI:EU:C:1974:133, [1974] ECR 1337; Case 152/84 *Marshall v Southampton and South-West Hampshire Area Health Authority (Teaching)* ECLI:EU:C:1986:84, [1986] ECR 723.

[52] *Mangold v Helm* (n 50) [75].

[53] R Herzog and L Gerken, 'Stoppt Den Europäischen Gerichtshof' *Frankfurter Allgemeine Zeitung* (Frankfurt, 8 September 2008) (author's translation).

[54] *Mangold v Helm* (n 50) [57].

[55] BVerfG, Judgment of 6 July 2010, 2 BvR 2661/ 06 (*Honeywell*) [58].

would be 'manifest' and 'highly significant in the structure of competences between the Member States and the Union'.[56] Before declaring an EU act ultra vires, moreover, the GFCC would have to give the ECJ the opportunity to state its view through the preliminary ruling procedure. The ECJ also had 'a right to tolerance of error'.[57] Based on these criteria, the Karlsruhe judges ruled that the *Mangold* judgment was not ultra vires.

Justice Landau dissented. In his view the *Mangold* judgment was ultra vires and considered the requirements of the majority 'excessive'.[58] These would render ultra vires review practically meaningless as a means for controlling the European Court. Relying expressly on the views of Grimm and Scharpf, he saw this outcome as problematic. Because political institutions lack effective means to correct the ECJ, national constitutional courts were critical to safeguard democratic legitimacy.[59] Nor could he accept that competence transgressions would have to be 'structurally significant'. The loss of competences usually resulted from a gradual process. The majority had ignored that minor competence transgressions 'accumulate to have significant consequences'.[60]

The controversy did not end with the German judges, however. The acceptability of the *Mangold* ruling also became an issue for the Danish Supreme Court in the *Ajos* case. The reason was that Danish employment legislation conflicted with the general principle on the prohibition of age discrimination as first developed in *Mangold*. The Danish Supreme Court, however, had reservations about applying this general principle in a dispute between private parties, because that would clash with the principle of legitimate expectations.[61] In a preliminary ruling, the ECJ had held, however, that the principle of legitimate expectations could not justify the continued application of the Danish rules.[62] Disagreeing with this outcome, a majority of the Danish judges then refused to follow the ECJ, effectively declaring ultra vires the European Court's judgment as well as the prior *Mangold*-ruling.[63]

Still, the conclusion of the Danish Supreme Court was not merely based on a democratic critique of the ECJ. The Danish judges instead justified their verdict with a more general reading of the constitutional relation between Danish law and EU law, similar to that of the GFCC. In the eyes of the Danish Supreme Court, the Danish Act of Accession served as the crucial basis for the effect of EU law in the Danish legal order. The Court therefore devoted significant attention to what had been discussed in the Danish parliamentary debates on the law on accession. The challenge with constructing the authority of the EU in this way, is that it is not directed at the ECJ as such. Instead, it seems to locate the authority of the EU as a whole decisively in the assent of the national parliament. Such a vision appears to favour a narrow interpretation of the EU's competences, including those of its legislative branch, reducing the authority of the EU to what has been accepted in the national ratification debates.

[56] ibid [61].
[57] ibid [66].
[58] Dissent Landau in BVerG, Judgment of 6 July 2010, 2 BvR 2661/ 06 (*Honeywell*) [95].
[59] ibid esp [99].
[60] ibid [103].
[61] See the preliminary reference as quoted in The Supreme Court of Denmark (Højesteret), Case 15/ 2014, decision of 6 December 2016 (*Ajos*) (translation at doms tol.dk/media/2udgv vvb/judgm ent-15-2014.pdf, 5 [6.12].
[62] Case C-441/14 *Dansk Industri v Estate of Karsten Eigil Rasmussen* ECLI:EU:C:2016:278.
[63] Højesteret (n 61).

The controversy over the ECJ's *Mangold* ruling illustrates the difficulties for national constitutional courts in checking the ECJ. First, they have to assess the possible repercussions for the EU legal order that come with an ultra vires ruling. As ultra vires rulings threaten the unity of EU law, national courts are faced with a dilemma between 'destruction and inaction'.[64] Here it seems hard to get the balance right. The German judges were criticised for falling on the side of 'inaction' with their *Honeywell* judgment.[65] Yet, when the GFCC did hand down its first ultra vires judgment in the *PSPP* case, this ruling was widely criticised, even as a 'bomb under the EU legal order'[66] and 'the decisive turning point in Europe's history towards disintegration'.[67] Secondly, if the goal is to check judicial power, national courts should refrain from relying on contested readings of the underlying constitutional framework that would restrict legislative choices.[68] In this respect, national constitutional courts appear to have distinguished insufficiently between the role of the ECJ and the EU political process.

So even if national constitutional courts could theoretically provide a counterweight to the ECJ, the example of the GFCC indicates how complicated it is to adequately fulfil such a task in practice. This finding provides reasons to doubt that national constitutional courts are the appropriate institutions to counter the power of the ECJ. Political alternatives seem better. Grimm himself has advocated a downscaling of the EU Treaties that would limit them 'to their truly constitutional elements and downgrade all other treaty provisions of a non-constitutional nature to the status of secondary law'.[69] Such a deconstitutionalisation would in turn make political correction of the ECJ easier. Scharpf has proposed the institutionalisation of a political override for judgments of the ECJ.[70] The advantage of such mechanisms would be their political nature: how to protect the space for democratic politics would itself be a political rather than a judicial question.

IV. Constitutional Courts as Bulwarks against Executive Dominance?

The previous sections showed that where constitutional courts review European law, they risk deciding contested issues on which there exists reasonable disagreement,

[64] Möllers (n 42) 166.

[65] ibid; Dissent Landau *Honeywell* (n 58).

[66] M Sandbu, 'German Court Has Set a Bomb under the EU Legal Order' *Financial Times* (5 May 2020), at www.ft.com/content/79484c01-b66b-4f81-bdc6-fd4def940821.

[67] M Wolf, 'German Court Decides to Take Back Control with ECB Ruling' *Financial Times* (16 May 2020), at www.ft.com/content/37825304-9428-11ea-af4b-499244625ac4. It also seemed that the Court had not abided by its own *Honeywell* standards: F Mayer, 'The Ultra Vires Ruling: Deconstructing the German Federal Constitutional Court's PSPP Decision of 5 May 2020' (2021) 16 *European Constitutional Law Review* 733.

[68] Both challenges were arguably nicely summed up by dissenting Justice Lübbe-Wolff in the case of the GFCC on the ECB's programme of Outright Monetary Transactions (OMT). There she criticised as an 'anomaly of questionable democratic character' the reliance of 'some few independent German judges' on 'the German interpretation of the principle of democracy' to 'make a decision with incalculable consequences for the operating currency of the euro zone'. Dissent Lübbe-Wolff in BVerfG, Order of 14 January 2014 2 BvR 2728/ 13 (*OMT referral*) [28].

[69] D Grimm, 'The Democratic Costs of Constitutionalisation: The European Case' (2015) 21 *European Law Journal* 460, 473.

[70] Scharpf (n 15).

limiting the room for legitimate political decision-making. This problem does not disappear when courts use democracy as a standard of review. Reasonable disagreement also exists about what democracy requires.[71] A particular difficulty in the EU is that there is disagreement about whether democracy is fully possible at the EU level. Such disagreement leads to diverging views on whether the EU's democratic problems should be addressed primarily through enhancing the powers of the European Parliament, or by giving intergovernmental institutions the main power, checked by national parliaments.[72] Courts that employ democracy as a review standard in relation to the EU consequently risk deciding deeply contested constitutional issues. This is precisely the problem with the EU-related case law of the GFCC, as it has cast doubts on the possibility of creating European-wide democratic institutions based on a contested understanding of democracy.[73]

Is there a way out of this dilemma? Is there still an appropriate role to play for constitutional courts in addressing separation of powers problems in the EU? It seems that the answer must lie in a type of review that facilitates democratic politics and political contestation, without constraining it. One way in which I believe constitutional courts can fulfil such a role is by countering executive dominance in the EU's decision-making processes. National constitutional courts could possibly do this by relying on democratic norms to demand better parliamentary oversight of the executive, without deciding the more contentious questions of EU democracy, such as the proper relationship between the EU and its Member States.

Member States' constitutional courts are not always capable or willing to engage in this type of review, as Cristina Fasone and Nicola Lupo show in a comparative overview from 2017. For Italy, they note, for example, that the limited rights of access to the Italian Constitutional Court make it 'extremely unlikely' that this Court would render 'a decision on the parliamentary powers in EU affairs.'[74] For Spain they consider that the Constitutional Tribunal was not confronted with this issue, primarily because of the lack of questions on this matter and the limited use of actions in which such questions could be raised.[75]

The GFCC, however, has strengthened the position of the national parliament vis-à-vis the executive in European matters. A number of judgments during the Euro crisis show how the German judges in this manner helped counter executive dominance by ensuring better parliamentary oversight. The German example suggests, moreover, that parliaments themselves may fail to protect their own position in relation to the executive. A reason is that a parliamentary majority commonly has an interest to support the Government.[76] In such a context, court interventions may be instrumental

[71] Möllers (n 19) 156–57; J Waldron, 'Democracy' in D Estlund (ed), *The Oxford Handbook of Political Philosophy* (Oxford University Press, 2012); Waldron (n 18) 282–312.

[72] For differing views see eg: Føllesdal and Hix (n 16); R Bellamy, *A Republican Europe of States: Cosmpolitanism, Intergovernmentalism and Democracy in the EU* (Cambridge University Press, 2019).

[73] Schönberger (n 19); Mayer (n 19); Wendel (n 20).

[74] C Fasone and N Lupo, 'Constitutional Review and the Powers of National Parliaments in EU Affairs: Erosion or Protection?' in D Jancic (ed), *National Parliaments after the Lisbon Treaty and the Euro Crisis: Resilience or Resignation?* (Oxford University Press, 2017) 69.

[75] ibid 70.

[76] P Lindseth, *Power and Legitimacy: Reconciling Europe and the Nation-State* (Oxford University Press, 2010) 178; E Benvenisti and G Downs, 'The Democratizing Effects of Transjudicial Coordination' (2012) 8 *Utrecht Law Review* 166–67.

in overcoming the unwillingness of a parliamentary majority to create strong parliamentary oversight.[77] German politics during the euro-crisis provides an example of precisely this phenomenon.

A first area in which the German Court strengthened the rights of the *Bundestag* concerned the *Bundestag*'s rights in decisions on financial assistance, first concerning the European Financial Stability Facility (EFSF) and later the European Stability Mechanism (ESM).[78] During the initial stages of the Euro crisis, the German Government had been unwilling to give the *Bundestag* an extensive say on decisions concerning financial assistance. Take the parliamentary debates of May 2010 on Germany's participation in the EFSF. At that time Finance Minister Schäuble still appeared mostly concerned about the EFSF's credibility in the eyes of capital markets, which a parliamentary veto on financial assistance decisions could endanger.[79] Instead, the Government preferred to restrict the *Bundestag*'s involvement in the EFSF mainly to a single approval of the mechanism. Although the *Bundestag*'s rights were strengthened to some degree during the parliamentary proceedings, they remained ambiguous. The legislation merely required the Government to 'endeavour to reach agreement' with the *Bundestag's* budget committee prior to giving financial guarantees and exceptions were possible.[80]

The *Bundestag*'s position in the financial assistance mechanisms became a topic for debate again in the spring and summer of 2011. The GFCC's judgment of 7 September 2011 on the EFSF and financial aid to Greece played a decisive role. There, the Court ruled that the legislation on the EFSF had to be interpreted in a specific manner in order to protect the *Bundestag*'s budgetary rights. It was not enough for the Government to merely endeavour to reach an agreement with the budget committee. The Government was instead 'obliged to obtain the prior consent of the budget committee', although the GFCC did retain the room for exceptions.[81] The judgment subsequently played a key role in the parliamentary debates on the modifications of the EFSF and the changes to the national legislation governing Germany's participation in the EFSF.[82] The ruling led to both enhanced rights for the *Bundestag* in decisions on financial assistance, as well as a change in rhetoric within the Government. Finance Minister Schäuble now declared that 'the budget right of the Bundestag is the basic principle of our parliamentary democracy'.[83]

Nonetheless, a major issue with the revised legislation remained. The legislation provided that the rights of the *Bundestag* plenary – which had been significantly

[77] Critical of this case law is F Meinel, 'The Merkel Court: Judicial Populism since the Lisbon Treaty' (2023) 19 *European Constitutional Law Review* 111, 124–26 and 128–29.

[78] For more examples and a more elaborate discussion see De Boer (n 1) ch 6.

[79] See Plenarprotokoll 17/44, Stenografischer Bericht der 44. Sitzung des Deutschen Bundestages am 21. Mai 2010 (EFSF second plenary) 4427; 'Bundestagspräsident blockiert Schäubles Blankoscheck- Pläne' *Handelsblatt* (Berlin/ Brussels, 24 August 2011).

[80] Gesetz zur Übernahme von Gewährleistungen im Rahmen eines europäischen Stabilisierungsmechanismus vom 22. Mai 2010, Bundesgesetzblatt I 2010, 627 (StabMechG) Art 1(4).

[81] BVerfG, Judgment of 7 September 2011, 2 BvR 987/ 10 (*Greek loan facility and EFSF*) [141].

[82] See BT- Dr 17/ 6945 of 07.09.2011: Antrag der Fraktionen der CDU/ CSU und FDP Parlamentsrechte im Rahmen zukünftiger europäischer Stabilisierungsmaßnahmen sichern und stärken; Gesetz zur Änderung des Gesetzes zur Übernahme von Gewährleistungen im Rahmen eines europaïschen Stabilisierungsmechanismus vom 9. Oktober 2011, Bundesgesetzblatt I 2011, 1992 (amended StabMechG).

[83] Plenarprotokoll 17/ 124, Stenografischer Bericht der 124. Sitzung des Deutschen Bundestages am 8. September 2011, 14551.

strengthened – could be taken over by a special committee of nine parliamentarians chosen from the ranks of the budget committee for situations of particular urgency and confidentiality.[84] Two *Bundestag* members of the Social Democratic Party – Peter Danckert and Swen Schulz – challenged the constitutionality of this special committee, also known as the *Neuner Gremium*, before the GFCC. The Court ultimately ruled in their favour. According to the Karlsruhe judges, the delegation of the rights of the *Bundestag* plenary to the *Neuner Gremium* violated the democratic rights of the *Bundestag* members. The Court conceded that the *Bundestag* plenary could in principle delegate rights to a special committee, and that the information provided to the plenary could similarly be limited. However, the need to maintain confidentiality could only be justified in very specific circumstances. Many EFSF decisions would require public preparation measures. This meant that there was no justification for keeping subsequent decisions secret. The Court also held that reasons of urgency could not justify delegation of responsibilities to the *Neuner Gremium*, as again, many EFSF decisions would require significant preparatory measures.[85]

The GFCC's ruling on the *Neuner Gremium* led to a further improvement in the *Bundestag*'s rights concerning decisions of the EFSF, as well as of the ESM.[86] In this way the Court can be seen to have countered executive dominance: decisions taken by executives would now be subject to more stringent parliamentary oversight. What makes the ruling on the *Neuner Gremium* a particularly convincing instance of judicial intervention is that the Karlsruhe court took into account countervailing considerations. The way in which national parliaments should be involved in EU decision-making is an issue on which different reasonable viewpoints may exist. Parliamentary involvement may curtail the effectiveness of a government operating in EU decision-making when its room for manoeuvre is significantly limited, which also may be detrimental to the national interest. Nonetheless, in the *Neuner Gremium* case the German court assessed the reasons for urgency and confidentiality and found that they lacked plausibility in most cases. The case thus presents an example of a court correcting curtailments of democratic oversight that lack plausible justification.[87]

A second area in which the GFCC helped strengthen the *Bundestag*'s position concerned the Government's information provision on legal instruments adopted outside the EU legal framework but closely related to EU law, such as the EFSF and ESM. A recurring problem during the Euro crisis was that the German Government provided little information on the negotiation of such instruments, limiting the ability of the *Bundestag* to debate and influence their design.

[84] Amended StabMechG (n 82) Art 3(1).

[85] BVerfG, Judgment of 28 February 2012, 2 BvE 8/ 11 (*Neuner Gremium*).

[86] See eg, BT- Dr 17/ 9145 of 27.03.2012: Gesetzentwurf der Fraktionen CDU/ CSU, SPD, FDP und Bündnis 90/ Die Grünen Entwurf eines Gesetzes zur Änderung des Stabilisierungsmechanismusge setzes (BT- Dr 17/ 9145); BT- Dr 17/ 9435 of 25.04.2012: Beschlussempfehlung und Bericht des Haushaltsausschusses (8. Ausschuss) zu dem Gesetzentwurf der Fraktionen CDU/ CSU, SPD, FDP und Bündnis 90/ Die Grünen— Drucksache 17/ 9145 – Entwurf eines Gesetzes zur Änderung des Stabilisierungsmechanismusgesetzes; Zweites Gesetz zur Änderung des Stabilisierungsmechanismusgesetzes vom 23. Mai 2012, Bundesgesetzblatt I 2012, 1166 (second amended StabMechG); and Gesetz zur finanziellen Beteiligung am Europäischen Stabilitätsmechanismus vom 13. September 2012, Bundesgesetzblatt I, 1918.

[87] Such an approach resembles the justification of judicial review offered by M Kumm, 'Institutionalising Socratic Contestation: The Rationalist Human Rights Paradigm, Legitimate Authority and the Point of Judicial Review' (2007) 1 *European Journal of Legal Studies* 28.

In the spring of 2010, the *Bundestag* received only limited information on the design of the Greek loan facility, the European Financial Stabilisation Mechanism (EFSM) and EFSF.[88] The problem re-emerged when the German Government fell short in informing the *Bundestag* on the negotiations about the ESM and Euro Plus Pact in the spring of 2011. The German Government repeatedly failed to provide key documents and often only provided information orally. Remarkably, the *Bundestag* obtained several drafts of the ESM Treaty from the Austrian Lower House of Parliament, rather than from its own Government. These shortcomings in the Government's information provision elicited significant criticism from various parties in the *Bundestag*, not just from the opposition parties, but also from those of the governing coalition. For example, the *Bundestag*'s EU affairs committee protested across party lines against the Government's failure to provide a draft of the ESM Treaty in the beginning of May 2011.[89]

Yet, ultimately, an intervention by the GFCC proved to be a decisive factor in strengthening the *Bundestag*'s information position. In a case brought by the parliamentary group of the Greens, the GFCC decided on 19 June 2012 that the German Government had indeed failed to adequately inform the *Bundestag* on the ESM and Euro Plus Pact negotiations.[90] That failure constituted a breach of the Government's constitutional obligations. With its judgment, the Karlsruhe judges laid down detailed requirements on the provision of information to the *Bundestag*, requiring that it be comprehensive, continuous, extend to informal meetings, and come early enough to still allow the *Bundestag* to influence European decision-making.[91]

This judgment ultimately led to an overhaul of the German legislation on the *Bundestag*'s participation and information rights in EU affairs supported by all parties. These changes clarified, among other things, that the Government's duty to provide information also applies to EU-related activities that strictly fall outside the EU legal framework, that information would have to be provided in writing, and that the Government would also have to provide information on 'unofficial' documents.[92]

The GFCC's judgment of 19 June 2012 can be seen as having provided an important check against executive dominance in EU affairs. The adequate provision of information is a precondition for democratic oversight and political debate on EU affairs. During the Euro crisis, Germany's parliamentarians had protested about the insufficient information provision by the Government, but ultimately failed to protect their own position. The coalition parties in the *Bundestag* would have had to engage in an open conflict with the Government, an option that one observer dubbed 'virtually impossible politically'.[93] Significant change only occurred after the Constitutional Court in Karlsruhe intervened.

[88] See also D Kietz, 'Politisierung Trotz Parteienkonsens: Bundestag, Bundesrat Und Die Euro-Krise' in Bertelsmann Stiftung (ed), *Politisierung trotz Parteienkonsens* (Bertelsmann Stiftung, 2013) 21–23.

[89] On these events, see BVerfG, Judgment of 19 June 2012, 2 BvE 4/ 11 (*Information on ESM and Euro Plus Pact Negotiations*) [2]–[42].

[90] ibid.

[91] ibid [117]–[132].

[92] Gesetz über die Zusammenarbeit von Bundesregierung und Deutschem Bundestag in Angelegenheiten der Europaïschen Union (4. Juli 2013) Bundesgesetzblatt I 2013, 2170 (EUZBBG 2013 version).

[93] Kietz (n 88) 27.

Comparative research indicates that partly as a result of the GFCC's interventions, the *Bundestag* emerged as one of the most powerful national parliaments in EU affairs.[94] The GFCC's strengthening of the *Bundestag's* information and participation rights helped to secure better parliamentary oversight of the executive operating at the EU level and thus safeguard the space for democratic politics on European matters. Moreover, such court-ordered strengthening of parliaments appears possible without constraining the room for parliaments to decide themselves on Europe's future development.

Yet, although the GFCC was instrumental in countering executive dominance in the German context, parliaments in other Member States were able to develop strong oversight positions without being so required by a court. Moreover, at least some of the political developments to which the GFCC responded appear to have been specific to Germany. Take the Netherlands, where there is no constitutional court and it falls to the Parliament itself to provide oversight of the Government's operations within EU affairs. Yet unlike the German Government, the Dutch Government did not seek to restrict the House of Representatives' involvement in decision-making of the EFSF and ESM. Nor did the Dutch Government consider that the intergovernmental nature of various crisis instruments constituted a justification for withholding information to Parliament.[95] The Dutch House of Representatives was better able to safeguard its own oversight position than the *Bundestag*, even though the *Bundestag* may have ultimately emerged as stronger after the GFCC's interventions.[96]

The Finnish Parliament, the *Eduskunta*, provides another example. The *Eduskunta* has been judged both institutionally the most powerful, as well as the most active in EU affairs compared to other Member States' parliaments.[97] In contrast to Germany, this strong position is not the result of intervention by a constitutional court. Key factors instead appear to be the constitutional provisions on the role of the *Eduskanta* in EU matters and the role of this Parliament's constitutional law committee.[98] This is a political committee with a quasi-judicial function, whose opinions have a high authority. Many of the crisis measures that formally fell outside the framework of the EU Treaties were treated as EU issues in Finland, because the constitutional law committee considered

[94] K Auel, O Rozenberg and A Tacea, 'Fighting Back? And, If So, How? Measuring Parliamentary Strength and Activity in EU Affairs' in C Hefftler et al (eds), *The Palgrave handbook of national parliaments and the European Union* (Palgrave Macmillan, 2015); O Höing, 'Differentation of Parliamentary Powers: The German Constitutional Court and the German Bundestag within the Financial Crisis' (2012) *OPAL Online Paper Series* 9/2012.

[95] On these issues see more elaborately: N de Boer, 'Judging European Democracy' (2018) (PhD Thesis, University of Amsterdam, 2018) ch 7, s 3. See also Tweede Kamer, 'Aandacht voor het parlementair budgetrecht in Europees perspectief. Rapport van een werkgroep uit de commissie voor de Rijksuitgaven van de Tweede Kamer der Staten-Generaal' (9 September 2014) Bijlage bij Kamerstuk 31 597, nr 7, 26–27.

[96] The German information arrangements are wider in scope and more precise, particularly on EU-related negotiations that strictly fall outside the EU Treaty framework. See also Commissie Meijers, 'De meerwaarde van een Nederlandse Europawet voor parlementaire informatievoorziening: een verkenning' (*Commissie Meijers*, 2016), at www.commissie-meijers.nl/nl/comment/de-meerwaarde-van-een-nederlandse-europawet-voor-parlementaire-informatievoorziening-een-verkenning.

[97] Auel, Rozenberg and Tacea (n 94) 79.

[98] P Leino and J Salminen, 'The Euro Crisis and its Constitutional Consequences for Finland: Is there Room for National Politics in EU Decision-Making?' (2013) 9 *European Constitutional Law Review* 451; T Raunio, 'The Finnish Eduskunta and the European Union: The Strengths and Weaknesses of a Mandating System' in C Hefftler et al (eds), *The Palgrave Handbook of National Parliaments and the European Union* (Palgrave Macmillan, 2015) 408–09 and 414.

them comparable to EU matters. Consequently, the Finnish Parliament kept both extensive information and participation rights in relation to negotiations on the Euro crisis instruments, as well as regarding decision-making within the ESM and EFSF.[99]

In sum, while the GFCC helped to counter executive dominance and strengthen parliamentary oversight during the Euro crisis, other Member States' parliaments were able to safeguard their own position in a better way than the *Bundestag*. The idea that parliaments cannot be relied on to provide adequate oversight of the executive is therefore too simple. Where parliaments decide on the proper arrangements for parliamentary oversight, formal rights are likely to be more meaningful in practice. Moreover, where a court mandates parliamentary oversight, it risks deciding against a parliament's preference for a reasonable alternative arrangement. For such reasons, constitutional courts should be careful to intervene in the political process. The case for judicial intervention is strongest when there are clear signs that the political branches have failed to safeguard democratic accountability.

V. Conclusion

Executive dominance and a lack of political conflict over policy decisions are two key problems in the EU's institutional set-up and functioning from a separation of powers perspective. Studying the case of the GFCC in this chapter, I have argued, however, that the review of European law by national constitutional courts does not provide a straightforward solution to these problems.

I first assessed whether national constitutional courts should serve as a forum for political conflict on EU-related politics – conflict that is not sufficiently present in the political process in the EU context. Yet, I argued, the risk is that constitutional courts will then end up making contested decisions on constitutional questions and actually restrict the possibility of political conflict over European issues. The GFCC's EU-related case law presents a troublesome example in which, because of the Court's contested and national understanding of democracy, precisely this risk materialised.

Review of European law by national constitutional courts is more easily justifiable when directed at the power of the ECJ. A challenge is nonetheless that it is complicated for courts to conduct such review properly. It requires constitutional courts to balance the harms for the EU legal order against countering the democratically problematic judgments of the ECJ. At the same time, courts will have to justify their review on the basis of a constitutional framework that is removed from democratic politics. The peril is that national constitutional courts adopt politically contested interpretations of this constitutional framework and thus limit the scope for legitimate political choices. So, although the position of the ECJ in the EU legal order raises serious questions from a separation of powers perspective, these concerns may be better addressed by political means than through review by national constitutional courts.

Nonetheless, section IV discussed how a number of judgments by the GFCC helped safeguard a space for democratic politics on EU affairs during the Euro crisis. The GFCC

[99] Leino and Salminen (n 98); Raunio (n 98).

did so by countering executive dominance. The GFCC's example suggests that national constitutional courts can invoke democratic norms to demand better parliamentary oversight of the executive, without deciding on the more controversial issues of EU democracy. The extent to which courts in other jurisdictions can and should perform such a role, however, still requires further research.

Possibly there are other ways in which constitutional courts could raise constitutional questions while not limiting the room for legitimate political decision-making. Recently, some scholars have embraced the idea of weak-form review for constitutional courts in relation to the EU.[100] Weak-form review is a type of review that allows courts to assess the constitutionality of legislation, but leaves it to legislatures to address judicial findings of constitutionality or allows legislatures to override the courts.[101] Judicial review critics favour weak review, because it obviates the main democratic objection to stronger forms of review, while allowing an enduring deliberation between institutions on constitutional norms.[102] Where national courts would weaken their review, arguably they could continue to facilitate opposition and contestation of European law, without overriding legislative decisions and undermining the stability of the EU legal order. Such arguments for weak review deserve further consideration elsewhere.

The focus on the German example in this chapter comes with certain limitations, which would also have to be addressed in further research. Firstly, the instances of review by the GFCC discussed in this chapter do not exhaust all possible scenarios in which such review may be exercised. Possibly there are other settings in which a national constitutional court's review can be justified more easily. Secondly, judgments of Member States' constitutional courts other than the GFCC may command less authority, both in the domestic and European political process. If so, a constitutional court judgment may be less of a constraint on political decision-making and more a catalyst of political and public debate. Thirdly and related to the previous point, in some Member States the quality of political deliberations on constitutional matters may be considered significantly lower compared to Germany. If so, deliberations in the judicial process could be more positively evaluated as compensation for a failing political process.

Still, as I have argued in this chapter, the German case appears to confirm the warnings of those who say that constitutional courts risk curtailing legitimate political decision-making. Constitutional courts may help safeguard space for democratic politics in EU matters in some cases, but it appears that the appropriate role of constitutional courts in addressing separation of powers in the EU should be a limited one. To address the issues of executive dominance and a lack of political conflict the solution lies not primarily with the courts, but in the political process.

[100] O Garner, 'Squaring the PSPP Circle' (*Verfassungsblog*, 22 May 2020), at verfassungsblog.de/squaring-the-pspp-circle; T Violante, 'Bring Back the Politics: The PSPP Ruling in Its Institutional Context' (2020) *21 German Law Journal* 1045.

[101] M Tushnet, *Weak Courts, Strong Rights* (Princeton University Press, 2008).

[102] R Bellamy, 'Democracy as Public Law: The Case of Constitutional Rights' (2013) 14 *German Law Journal* 1017.

16

Conclusions

CHRISTINA ECKES, PÄIVI LEINO-SANDBERG AND
ANNA W GHAVANINI

The analyses carried out in this edited collection and the research project it builds on give rise to concern about the dynamics of power within the EU in the twenty-first century. The chapters examine the three policy fields of of Economic and Monetary Union (EMU), migration and trade. Their results can be grouped into three categories of observations.

First, while the EU has always been executive-driven, its executive branch has been further strengthened. It appears sometimes fair to ask whether the legislature and the judiciary are able to and do exercise the autonomous influence and control functions that fall to them under a system of separated powers. Second, what adds to this pattern is, in practice, a lack of judicial control by the European Court of Justice (ECJ) in all three policy areas. While in classic accounts of the evolution of EU law the ECJ has been widely seen as disproportionately powerful, today it seems to fail to properly control the other EU branches in particular as regards matters that can be characterised as constitutional or going beyond mere technicalities. This results in an overly consensual mode of decision-making between the EU institutions, which is applied in particular in crisis contexts, and which also affects the European Parliament's preparedness to defend its own prerogatives. Third, the multilevel interaction within the EU legal order adds not only complexity but also may also affect separation of powers. The EU institutions and actors expand their powers at the expense of, above all, the national legislatures. This additionally dilutes competence divisions between the EU and Member States which further hinders clarity and visibility of who exercises power and how that exercise can be scrutinised and balanced by other actors.

While many of these difficulties can be traced back to the EU's constitutional design, they are further strengthened by the institutional practice ensuing in the interaction between the EU institutions and other European and national actors. This indicates that there is no easy solution. Treaty change – which carries its own well-known difficulties – might be necessary in order to create a stronger basis for interaction between the branches; however, without an institutional willingness to make use of and defend the powers allocated to each institution, any Treaty amendment would remain a paper tiger. Ultimately, separation of powers is not something that *is*, but something one *does*.

I. How Many Branches?

The EU does not offer a strong conception of separation of powers. In their chapter, Leino-Sandberg and Minkkinen argue that national contexts have often witnessed a move from a tripartite to bipartite governance models because of a merger of the political branches, deeply entangling the legislature and the executive. Our research in this volume demonstrates a more nuanced picture for the EU. What makes the EU different from national contexts is that the Council is partly a co-legislature and partly an executive. Within the Council, the two branches are therefore by definition deeply entangled. One of the most relevant questions addressed in many chapters is therefore whether the European Parliament is strong enough to balance the ever-strengthening executive powers in the EU.

Here our results are coloured by at least two factors. First, due to our choice of policy fields, we have focussed less on the traditional contexts of ordinary law-making because, particularly in the areas of trade and EMU, legislation is somewhat scarce. In trade, it primarily focuses on the implementation of trade agreements; in the economic field, the role of the EU is focused on establishing coordination mechanisms rather than substantive legislation, and in the monetary field, the show is run by the European Central Bank (ECB). In migration, our focus has been more on informalisation in the external dimension. While major legislative reform has been ongoing in this field,[1] the EU's new Migration Pact was completed in December 2023, too late to be studied in depth in this project. Therefore, we are unable to draw any broad conclusions about the extent to which the European Parliament is able to pursue its own agenda in legislative negotiations of migration files. Second, the three policy fields were chosen because of their topical relevance and relationship to recent or ongoing *crises*. Because of this crisis context, they have all three witnessed a strengthening of the European Council, which has impacted on the spectrum of choices available for the co-legislature.[2] Since the Member State governments are represented in both the European Council and the Council, this primarily impacts the European Parliament's position as a lawmaker.

In the contexts that we have studied, we do see growing executive powers that the European Parliament is struggling to balance and control and, in practice, often fails to control. What is more, while the European Parliament is known to have created and defended many of its institutional (procedural) prerogatives through interinstitutional litigation in the Court, we have in this project studied a consensual mode of decision-making that has often led it to support executive choices in substance. The EU finds solutions to crises at the cost of the rights of the European Parliament. The Parliament agrees to being sidelined and disempowered by accepting informal arrangements of information and consultancy without challenging the loss of its formal rights in court. These patterns are clearly visible in both the informal arrangements in migration and in Next Generation EU (NGEU).

[1] On this, see M Sormunen, 'Järjestelmä, oikeudelliset reunaehdot vai järjestelmään kohdistuvat odotukset? EU:n turvapaikkajärjestelmän vanhentumisen kolme tasoa' (2022) 120 *Lakimies* 513.

[2] For trade this was most apparent in the Brexit context. See C Eckes and P Leino-Sandberg, 'The EU-UK Trade and Cooperation Agreement – Exceptional Circumstances or a new Paradigm for EU External Relations?' (2021) 85 *Modern Law Review* 164.

For example, in the context of trade, the crisis results from the controversy emerging from the growing insight that ever-more trade and investment protection stands in the way of the green transition and hence contributes to the multiple planetary crises of the twenty-first century.[3] The autonomy of the Commission during the negotiations of trade agreements and in particular the lack of a structure allowing the European Parliament to instruct the Commission constitute a hindrance for collective will-formation. The same is true for the limited legal requirements for public debate and deliberation.[4] A concrete example that illustrates the Commission's position as the prime actor in treaty-negotiations is how it carries out sustainability impact assessments. When doing so, it has great leeway to frame and direct the political debate about the desirability and added value of trade and investment treaties.[5] In the field of EMU, the sovereign debt crisis (and the more or less permanent state of crisis following it) have led the ECB to expand its powers significantly,[6] while the COVID-19 crisis led to the adoption of the recovery plan NGEU, which, on the one hand, weakens parliaments as legislatives and budgetary authorities and, on the other, strengthens executives.[7]

Furthermore, instances of the use of Article 122 of the Treaty on the Functioning of the EU (TFEU) as a legal basis to tackle various kinds of crises have exploded in the EU during recent years.[8] It is a legal basis that allows the Council to approve EMU measures in a non-legislative procedure, raising concerns about the side-stepping of the European Parliament especially when the measures reach beyond the immediate context of a crisis. In the field of migration, already the Treaties degrade the Parliament position and involvement in emergency situations under Article 78(3) TFEU. Far from guarding what remains of parliamentary control, the Court has instead allowed the executive to cut additional corners vis-à-vis the European Parliament.[9] One area where this becomes particularly apparent is the external dimension of migration. Here, informalisation tends to empower the executive further and circumvent legislative and judicial control mechanisms as foreseen by the Treaties.[10] Crises have an impact on the functioning of separation of powers and more specifically the intensity of judicial review (see below in the next section).[11]

These developments highlight the dangers of interinstitutional consensus. While both the Treaty of Lisbon and recent Commission presidents have emphasised the close linkages between the Commission and the European Parliament, these linkages, especially in the absence of a government-opposition setting in and between the institutions,

[3] Ankersmit, ch 5 in this volume; Eckes, ch 12 in this volume.

[4] Ankersmit (ibid).

[5] Krajewski, ch 6 in this volume.

[6] Ronkainen, ch 9 in this volume.

[7] Fasone, ch 10 in this volume; P Leino-Sandberg and M Ruffert, 'Next Generation EU and its constitutional ramifications: a critical assessment' (2022) 59 *Common Market Law Review* 433; P Leino-Sandberg and T Raunio, 'From bad to worse: The continuous dilemma facing parliaments in European economic and fiscal governance' (2023) *Government and Opposition*.

[8] M Chamon, 'The use of Article 122 TFEU. Institutional implications and impact on democratic accountability' (Study requested by the AFCO committee, European Parliament, September 2023), at www.europarl.europa.eu/RegData/etudes/STUD/2023/753307/IPOL_STU(2023)753307_EN.pdf.

[9] See AW Ghavanini, 'The CJEU's give-and-give relationship with executive actors in times of crisis' (2023) *European Law Open* 284.

[10] Gnes and Sormunen, ch 4 in this volume.

[11] Ghavanini, Östlund and Waldenström, ch 11 in this volume.

also do away with one of the most important functions of separation of powers: the potentiality of conflict between the branches.[12] If political agendas and key solutions are agreed on informally prior to the negotiations, there is no divergence of positions. However, such divergence is central to a functioning democracy.

The discussion about the entanglement of the political branches also raises the question whether the Commission, staged as the super-executive of the EU, in fact, qualifies as a *political* actor at all. Several of the chapters have pointed to how the use of and reliance on expertise as a source of legitimation affects separation of powers and the interactions between the three branches. As is well-known, the executive traditionally relies on the justification of its powers on a claim to be best placed to develop and deploy sophisticated (technocratic) expertise. The institutional design of the Treaties places the Commission in an inherent trade-off between independent expertise and political legitimation, which is manifested in its oscillation between justifying its powers based on technocratic (sometimes legal) expertise and making attempts to strengthen its political representativeness and accountability. These two sources of legitimation may at times create tension, which we can see, for example, in the context of the rule of law crisis in the EU.[13] Institutional practices and series of events as outlined in the chapters of this volume exacerbate this tension in the three policy fields. The Council has access to expertise through national administrations and is therefore able to challenge the Commission's monopoly in providing it. We now also see the European Parliament increasingly developing its own in-house expertise,[14] highlighting how deeply political debates are often reframed as technical matters that can be outsourced and delegated to experts. It currently seems to be the Court that is alone lacking in this game. For example, in the field of EMU, the ECJ appears reluctant to engage substantively with expertise and instead relies heavily on expertise provided by the EU executive (see below). The expertise used to evaluate institutional action then naturally supports a specific institutional agenda that may define European interest narrowly or be unconvincing in the eyes of other experts or the broader European public.[15]

II. Judicial (Dys)function

Since the entanglement of functions within the Council and the comparative weakness of the European Parliament prevent the legislature and the executive from controlling and balancing each other, the role of the judiciary in the power dynamics of the EU becomes even more important. The ECJ could arguably seek to provide a reliable and strong counterbalance to the other two increasingly united branches. Our results, however, demonstrate that the ECJ has not taken up this task in any of three policy areas.[16]

[12] Leino-Sandberg and Minkkinen, ch 2 in this volume.
[13] Möllers, ch 3 in this volume.
[14] Morvillo, ch 13 in this volume.
[15] Ronkainen (n 6).
[16] eg Ghavanini, Östlund and Waldenström (n 11); Ronkainen (n 6); Eckes (n 3).

On the basis of the contributions to this volume, we can identify mechanisms through which the Court fails to fulfil its control function. First, as observed in the introduction, the ECJ's powers are in some respects exceptional as compared to the other branches as well as to other judiciaries. However, they do not include the ability to set its own agenda. In practice, judicial control within the fields of migration and EMU is almost exclusively the result of individuals bringing challenges before the courts. The Judiciary Dataset of the project on which this edited collection is based[17] comprises all cases decided between 2010 and 2020 that are categorised by the Court as belonging to one of the policy fields.[18] It includes only one interinstitutional dispute in the field of migration and none within the EMU.[19] In these two policy fields, it furthermore contains only a handful of cases in which state public actors bring challenges against the Union executive or legislative or vice versa: six cases within the EMU (of which two were found inadmissible) and three in migration.[20] This illustrates that actors from the legislative and executive branches appear in general agreement or at least are not willing to defend either their substantive preferences or procedural prerogatives beyond the political process.

As a result, the judical branch is sidelined and one important procedural guarantee for effective separation of powers is weakened. Whereas individual applicants bring cases to the ECJ, sometimes (particularly in cases concerning the EMU) directly before the General Court and sometimes (particularly in the field of migration) mediated through national courts under the preliminary reference procedure, these cases are substantively different from those that would have been brought by public actors, in terms of both purpose and argumentation. While these cases ensure that the Court has the opportunity to engage in judicial review, they typically do not allow it to engage directly with the process of collective will-formation in the way an institutional complaint would.

Only in trade do we see another trend. In this field, interinstitutional challenges, with many Member States intervening, surged after the entry into force of the Lisbon Treaty;[21] this is demonstrated in the SepaRope Judiciary Dataset where one out of three trade cases were interinstitutional disputes. Disputes related both to procedural prerogatives of the institutions under Article 218 TFEU and substantive issues.[22] This has given the Court ample opportunity to engage with the other branches. Rather than

[17] Separation of Powers in 21st Century Europe (SepaRope).

[18] For details on the SepaRope Judiciary Dataset and the case selection, see AW Ghavanini et al, 'An Empirical Approach to Separation of Powers Research in the EU' (2022) *CERGU Working Paper Series* 1.

[19] Case C-355/10 *Parliament v Council* ECLI:EU:C:2012:516, in which the Court annulled a Council Decision within the Schengen Border Regime on the basis that it should have been adopted by the legislature rather than the executive.

[20] Case T-496/11 *UK v ECB* ECLI:EU:T:2015:133; Case C-270/12 *UK v Parliament and Council* ECLI:EU:C:2014:18; Case C-223/13 *Netherlands v Commission* ECLI:EU:C:2014:83; Case T-261/13 *Netherlands v Commission* ECLI:EU:T:2015:671; Case T-676/14 *Spain v Commission* ECLI:EU:T:2015:602 [2015]; Case C-521/15 *Spain v Council* ECLI:EU:C:2017:982; Case C-482/08 *UK v Council* ECLI:EU:C:2010:631; Case C-508/10 *Commission v Netherlands* ECLI:EU:C:2012:243; Case C-431/10 *Commission v Ireland* ECLI:EU:C:2011:227. Additionally, two cases within EMU were removed from the register: Case T-45/12 *UK v ECB* ECLI:EU:T:2015:289; and Case T-93/13 *UK v ECB* ECLI:EU:T:2015:290.

[21] See C Eckes, *EU Powers under External Pressure* (Oxford University Press, 2019) introduction.

[22] Notably Case C-399/12 *Germany v Council* ECLI:EU:C:2014:2258 (*OIV* case) and, more recently, *Opinion 1/20* ECLI:EU:C:2022:485 on the Energy Charter Treaty.

independently scrutinising the exercise of EU institutional powers, the Court has tried to square the circle by reconciling the EU institutions' and the Member States' autonomy at the same time.[23] This pragmatic approach of the Court has fortified complex legal constructions that obscure who is finally responsible for substantive policy decisions.

Second, some of the executive practices explored in this volume undermine the Court's powers. Informalisation effectively removes executive action from judicial control, as the decisions made are not conceived by the Court as reviewable legal acts; it follows from established case law that the Court can only review acts that have legal effect. 'Fuzzy law' – ie, formally legal acts whose content or application offer broad options for action (and possible abuse), de facto functioning as a mere façade concealing a reality of alegality[24] – has formally binding status and is as such in principle reviewable by the Court. However, as the branch confined to framing its interventions in terms of legality and illegality, the Court is able to intervene only where executive action can be branded as 'illegal'. The indeterminacy that is characteristic of this kind of 'law' deprives the Court of workable benchmarks, rendering its intervention ineffective. Hybrid decision-making in all three policy areas entails that the Member States and Union institutions and agencies exercise of power in complex and often untransparent intertwinement.[25] This challenges the relatively strict division of competences between national courts and the ECJ. While the Court has at times been rightly criticised for stepping into the jurisdiction of national courts, the comparatively regulated processes of judicial decision-making entail that the judiciary cannot easily cooperate in the way needed to ensure that acts of hybrid governance does not fall between the chairs. Paradoxically, while more minor deviations from the prescribed modes of decision-making could have been challenged and struck down by the Court, the described practices digress so far from the constitutional framework that they risk falling outside the scope of judicial control.

Third and most importantly, however, the ECJ has been the architect of its own misfortune. The practices discussed above are outside the Court's own powers and undoubtedly make its role more difficult to fulfil. Yet, the resort to informal or unforeseen avenues of political decision-making must not necessarily be accepted as extra-legal by the Court. In other contexts, the ECJ has proven itself willing to pierce the veil as to the political branches' classification of legal (or not, as the case may be) acts. In the fields we have studied, it has however most often stayed faithful to the other institutions' preferences. The so-called EU–Turkey statement in the field of migration provides an apt example.[26] While this 'statement' could be construed as an international treaty with binding legal effects, the Court instead chose to rely closely on the argumentation provided by the Council and upheld the 'statement's' informal character, which led it to decline jurisdiction.

The Court's approach to expertise is similarly guided by the institutional actors appearing before it. As observed already in the introduction, the Commission and its legal service self-identifies as an *amicus curia* rather than as a party or an intervenient

[23] Eckes (n 3).
[24] Chamon, 'Regulatory Cooperation Chapters as Fuzzy Law' ch 7 in this volume.
[25] Coman-Kund, ch 14 in this volume.
[26] Westlund, ch 8 in this volume.

supporting one of the parties. Across all three policy fields, the Court appears to share this perception. It tends to defer to technical expertise as being either outside the jurisdiction of the Court or within the discretion of the executive.[27] While the Court could, at least in some procedures, nominate independent experts to bring in its own expertise to counterbalance that provided by the parties, it generally refrains from doing so, leaving itself at a disadvantage compared to the more knowledgeable actors appearing before it.

The Court also takes a backseat vis-à-vis the institutions in the matters that fall squarely within its expertise: legal matters. More often than not, the Court appears content to adopt the position taken by EU institutions. When the ECJ examines acts of the institutions and in particular of the executive, it tends to set a low bar for judicial review, limiting itself to verifying that acts are not 'manifestly' unlawful or applying similarly low standards.[28] In conflicts concerning the boundaries of EU competences, we observe a lack of commitment to protect the Member States' competences, with the Court often giving the powers conferred to the EU a broad interpretation. While the ECJ makes a distinct contribution and functions reasonably well on more technical issues, it tends to side itself or be placed on the side of the EU institutions, rather than the Member States.[29] The ECJ's willingness to facilitate the other Union institutions' preferred mode of decision-making entails that it fails to provide the counterbalance required to ensure either properly inclusive will-formation procedures or control of executive exercise of powers. Ultimately, the Court's deferential rulings contribute to a situation where the control of executive powers is left to other executive actors and their internal negotiations. The rarity of inter-institutional disputes – in which institutional loyalty would clearly have a less determinant effect for the ruling – exacerbates this behaviour. Control is delegated to the multilayered and polycentric landscape in the EU rather than the traditional separation between the different branches. What further adds to the problem is the lacking visibility of how powers are exercised in the EU,[30] which makes channels of political accountability difficult to exercise for the broader public.

III. Multilayered Separation of Powers?

The EU is a complex multilayered legal construction in which both the EU institutions and Member States' authorities enjoy autonomous democratic legitimacy and an institutional position to participate in top-level decision-making. This creates multiple forms of interactions not only between the three branches but also within and across branches between the two layers. Prima facie, one could assume that this contributes to procedures that ensure that different voices are heard in will-formation, as well as mutual control between the different actors. This assumption was to some extent borne

[27] Morvillo (n 14); Ronkainen (n 6).

[28] Ghavanini (n 9).

[29] On this, see A Ronkainen, P Leino-Sandberg and Anna W Ghavanini, 'The House Always Wins – an empirical analysis of CJEU case law relating to the Economic and Monetary Union (2010–2020)' (forthcoming).

[30] Gnes and Sormunen (n 10); Eckes (n 3).

out in relation to the migration crisis, where the opposing interests of the Union and of several Member States were visible in the political decision-making process, as well as in ensuing judicial challenges.[31] However, in trade, we can see that the EU and national executives do not necessarily control each other or bring in different points of view, but rather cooperate to expand their powers vis-à-vis the other branches.[32] The same pattern exists in EU economic governance and the structures created by NGEU: the EU and national executive act jointly at the expense of the powers of, in particular, national parliaments.[33] Those national constitutional courts that have been called to scrutinise measures formally adopted by the parliaments, but substantially predetermined by the government (in cooperation with the Commission) in the national plans, with little or no parliamentary control, have shown deference to the substantive loss of control by parliaments.[34] In practice, this broadens and strengthens EU action in areas where the EU does not actually have substantive competence (esp. structural policies) through financial incentives.[35]

In other words, the 'top-level split-executive' in the EU, ie, that the federate bodies are directly represented in the federal executive, may in principle offer another structure of control by autonomous actors. At the same time, the pure assumption that executive actors that stand in a non-hierarchical relationship to each other offer additional channel for disagreement and potential of mutual control can work to the detriment of separation of powers. It may and actually does lead the other branches, notably the judiciary, to refrain from exercising their own powers in an assertive manner. Furthermore, in practice, the split executive regularly allows the different, partially overlapping, executive actors to collaborate and accumulate even more powers, unchecked by the other branches. This has the effect of bolstering executive powers in Union layer, both vis-à-vis the national layer and vis-à-vis the other branches. The effect is rendered stronger by the ECJ's hesitation in practice to guard stringently the boundaries of EU and national competences and ensure compliance of EU actors with the procedural requirements of EU law.

Judicial review of EU law at the national layer cannot compensate for the shortcomings of the Union judiciary. The German Federal Constitutional Court has – as an exceptionally powerful national constitutional court – been understood as not only offering counter-limits to EU integration,[36] but also as strengthening national channels of control and influence. Yet, such judicial intervention also challenges the division of tasks under a traditional separation of powers conception. It draws highly political (and arguably distributive) decisions, which affect the whole of Europe, into the sphere of judicial reasoning of one specific national constitutional court, who reasons from the perspective of that particular national constitution.[37] In this respect, there are clear limits to how much the conclusions from the German context can be generalised:

[31] Ghavanini (n 9).
[32] Eckes (n 3).
[33] Leino-Sandberg and Raunio (n 7).
[34] Fasone (n 7).
[35] ibid.
[36] M Maduro, *We the court: The European Court of Justice and the European economic constitution* (Hart, 1998).
[37] de Boer, ch 15 in this volume.

not all Member States have a constitutional court, and those constitutional courts that exist are confined to their own constituting document. Some constitutions of EU states provide explicit and strong rights for national parliaments to engage in EU matters, while others are entirely silent on this question. This logically also affects the possibilities for a constitutional court to enforce those rights and protect the right of the parliament to deliberate on EU matters, if the constitution frames them as a competence of the national executive.

The research conducted within this project and presented in the contributions to this volume further demonstrate how judicial interventions lead the federal EU layer to expand at the cost of the federate national layer. In the context of EMU, for example, judicial reasoning offered in the context of reviewing the ECB's government bond purchasing programmes has provided the ECB with additional arguments and a convenient framing that push the boundaries of its mandate.[38] The classification as falling within the realm of 'EMU Constitution' provides a mandate for activities that arguably circumvent the prohibition on monetary financing and form part of an overall structure that compresses national fiscal policy competence.

In all three fields (most primarily in migration, least commonly in trade), the ECJ and national courts cooperate in the preliminary ruling procedure. This allows the national judiciary to rely on and refer to the ECJ's position vis-à-vis the legislature and the executive. The national judge can reasonably claim to have no choice when implementing preliminary rulings. This bolsters national judicial power in the confrontations with the political branches that enjoy stronger democratic legitimacy. Ultimately, this creates strong judicial control of national acts, both by national courts and by the ECJ, with the latter arguably overstepping its competences in order to contribute to that control. This double eagerness to control the political powers at the national layer is coupled, as discussed above, with limited judicial control of the Union policy.

Another result of the multilayered European and national legal spheres is that they interlock in complex legal constructions in order to ensure ownership and participation of actors from both layers and draw from the autonomous democratic roots of both layers to legitimise decision-making. These constructions are often pragmatic solutions to achieve the two objectives of ensuring ownership and participation, on the one hand, and democratic legitimacy, on the other. These pragmatic solutions are also often a result of political compromise, sometimes consciously construed in a way that obscures who is responsible and in charge of what. This regularly permits national and European actors to either claim ownership or blame responsibility on the other, usually towards their own (and hence different) audiences or constituencies.

One way in which we see this interlocking in all three examined policy areas is in hybrid forms of decision-making, where national and European actors engage in joint decision-making.[39] Hybridity and other ways of obscuring responsibility go against the traditional idea of separation of powers which demands that responsibilities are reasonably clearly allocated. Even if hybridity prima facie blurs the responsibility for the final decisions and outcome only within one branch, usually amongst executive actors,

[38] Ronkainen (n 6).
[39] Coman-Kund (n 25).

this may have the knock-on effect of creating serious gaps of control and untransparent channels of influence that escape judicial review and parliamentary scrutiny. Another manifestation of the interlocking of decision-making layers is found in the EU's participation in international treaty-making. Complex constructions are necessary to ensure the involvement of the EU and national executives in the highest level of political decision-making, while at the same time speaking with one voice towards the other partners to the international agreement. Ultimately, these complex constructions remove the EU further from the ideal of separation of powers that not only prevents concentration of powers in one single actor but also aims to ensure that responsibility is reasonably clearly allocated. In fact, the EU's multilayered legal order must guarantee an adequate separation of powers along three axes: first, the horizontal EU axis on which the Union institutions and agencies exercise the legislative, executive and judicial power; second, the horizontal Member State axis concerned with the exercise of Union functions by national bodies; and third, the vertical or perhaps diagonal axis on which these actors cooperate across the two horizontal layers as well as the three branches.[40]

Finally, and importantly, the research in this project has engaged with the limits of the capacity of legal and procedural rules to contain political disagreement and even obstruction. Certain tensions within a federation cannot be addressed by and through law.[41] Resolving them would require a unitary political decision-making body that is in the formal position to rein in the other centres of power when they challenge the core of cooperation. Without such a unitary top-level political decision-making body, certain tensions leave the EU in a stalemate.[42]

IV. Conclusions and Outlook

The EU does not offer a strong conception of separation of powers. This is partially by design. The Treaties have blurred the separation between the branches by creating the Council which has both legislature and the executive functions. The structural weakness of the Parliament, which prevents it from effectively balancing and controlling the executive, also stems from the Treaties themselves. However, the relational perspective adopted in this volume allows us to demonstrate how institutional practices further contribute to weakening the separation of powers in the EU. The judiciary tends to support the other EU institutions rather than offer an appropriate level of control. EU institutions are at times set against national actors, but often EU and national executive actors work together in a collaborative fashion rather than providing a counterweight. As this collaboration deepens into hybrid models of decision-making within the executive branch, the disadvantage of legislative and judicial bodies is deepened and their control functions risk becoming ineffective.[43]

[40] Coman-Kund (n 25), *cf* also Ghavanini, Östlund and Waldenström (n 11).

[41] Möllers (n 13).

[42] See Möllers (n 13) on the rule of law crisis and Eckes (n 3) on the withdrawal from the Energy Charter Treaty.

[43] Coman-Kund (n 25).

Unlike most nation-states, which consider themselves completed in an 'end of history' sort of way, the EU is open about being in a process of becoming. The EU is a political project that seeks a moving target, an 'ever closer union'. It is also existentially threatened by the risk of exit, which is an option under more or less constant debate in several Member States. This again is different from nation-states. Perhaps these differences can go some way of explaining why the EU does not feel comfortable to provide a stronger – potentially more conflictual – conception of separation of powers, which could unveil deeper controversies amongst institutional actors from different branches and layers. One could be tempted to argue that the EU has not yet reached a sufficiently mature, established state and therefore its institutions need to collaborate rather than dispute in order to build legitimacy and provide policy outcomes. Yet, as quoted in chapter one of this volume, 'Democracy is not about the States. Democracy is about the exercise of public power – and the Union exercises a huge amount of public power'.[44] This discrepancy between the factual exercise of power by the Union institutions and the lack of transparency and democratic structures that exist to control it has remained at the heart of each of the chapters in this volume.

We trace this reluctance to provide more stringent controls and space for democratic deliberation to a general 'fear of (national) politics' in the EU, which is seen as a threat to the efficient operation of EU institutions in solving problems on their agenda. The lack of political debates and controversy is one of the causes for the over-empowerment of the executive. As Christoph Möllers demonstrates in chapter three, the EU has a long tradition of reinterpreting political problems into administrative ones. He convincingly argues that in the current state of integration, translating political problems into administrative ones may be 'less satisfying and less acceptable from a separation of powers perspective than ever before'. He argues that while the idea of separated powers may not easily provide handy institutional solutions, it offers critical arguments for assessing institutional decision-making practices.

The chapters of Nik de Boer and Cristina Fasone point in different directions. While de Boer criticises constitutional courts for taking over the settling of deeply political questions from the political actors by reference to the case law of the German Federal Constitutional Court on EU law, Fasone concludes that national constitutional courts in France, Italy, Portugal and Spain, dealing with the Euro crisis reform of the economic governance and the initial implementation of the NGEU, do not in practice act as guardians of the democratic process or the budgetary prerogatives of parliaments. De Boer argues that the best contribution of constitutional courts to a functioning conception of separation of powers in the EU would be to strengthen national parliaments' position in a way that enables them to counterbalance the exceedingly strong EU executive, which has also been identified by the other chapters as the main challenge to the EU's separation of powers. In Fasone's chapter, we see that in some national contexts, judicial deference has strengthened the long-standing path to executive dominance.

This volume has examined many instances where the settling of highly political issues is gradually taken over by the EU's executive layers of decision-making at the

[44] JHH Weiler, 'Europe in Crisis – On "Political Messianism", "Legitimacy" and the "Rule of Law"' (2012) *Singapore Journal of Legal Studies* 248, 251.

expense of parliaments, be it the European Parliament or national parliaments. One telling example comes from the external dimension of migration, where Davide Gnes and Milka Sormunen (chapter four) alert us to the dangers and consequences of excess interinstitutional consensus. However, as demonstrated by several other chapters, the interinstitutional consensus is not only a question of Treaty design, but reaches much deeper, into institutional self-perception and behaviour of the EU institutions.

As regards the Court, for example, there is nothing in the Treaties that prevents the Court from engaging in a deeper review. The recent proposal to reduce the ECJ's workload in relation to preliminary references has been treated by some as allowing the ECJ to assume the role of a true constitutional court.[45] However, while a reduction of its workload in terms of 'less important cases' might allow the Court to engage more deeply in the remaining cases, it is far from certain or even unlikely that the current outlook of the Court is an effect of an excessive workload. The intensity of review provided by the Court is, rather, a result of its perception of itself and of the function that it serves in the integration process, which may ultimately not be all that different from the self-identity of the Commission. While both would certainly see themselves as playing key roles in ensuring that in EU integration 'the law is observed' (Article 19 TEU), they are also both ultimately committed to the goal of further integration. The Court rather explicitly concentrates its role on reining in Member States and seems largely oblivious vis-à-vis the judicial role of counterbalancing and controlling the political branches in the Union layer.[46]

Fundamental questions remain as to who sets that integration agenda and whether this agenda is the result of democratic, deliberative processes that have enabled the meeting of different positions in a manner that leave the ultimate power in the hands of EU citizens or, as critics would have it, the edict of a closed executive bubble in Brussels that refuses to make its choices visible to their constituencies and outside audiences. These considerations are of relevance in several of our studies that have focussed on measures taken in a crisis context. In these circumstances the EU institutions tend to act under what Somek has called a 'normativity of distress', which is

> manifest in the unheeded exhortation that 'something needs to be done', regardless by whom and how. The poignant exhortative tone reveals a built-in preference for quick action over deliberation. A society seized by anxiety experiences itself to be under Handlungszwang. Since the justification for action lies in its responsiveness to exigency it would not even make sense for it to stay within pre-established constraints. Wherever jurisdictional boundaries exist – be they officially classified as emergency powers or not – they are likely to be extended and transgressed.[47]

Crisis contexts are instances of a deep institutional consensus: a pressing problem must be addressed; a set goal needs to be achieved. It is revealing that the one inter-institutional

[45] D Petric, 'The Preliminary Ruling Procedure 2.0' (2023) *European Papers – A Journal of Law and Integration* 25.

[46] Noteworthy is the contrast between the general title and the content's focus on Member States in K Lenaerts, 'On Checks and Balances: The Rule of Law Within the EU' (2023) 29 *Columbia Journal of European Law* 25.

[47] A Somek, *Individualism: An Essay on the Authority of the European Union* (Oxford University Press, 2008) 233–34.

dispute we encountered in the field of migration occurred well before the migration crisis. During crises, exceptional and alegal solutions can be adopted because of the exceptionality of the specific file and the specific context.[48] Ordinary powers can be reinterpreted and procedures applied flexibly. This is also necessary since the EU has – unlike most constitutional democracies – few formal emergency powers. At the same time, the proliferation of crisis rhetoric is turning exception into normality. Many of these originally exceptional measures have changed the EU permanently and affected institutional roles as defined in the Treaties, moving its structures even further away from classic conceptions of separation of powers.

Against this background, it is interesting to examine two recent proposals for Treaty change. In September 2023, a Franco-German working group of experts published a report on EU institutional reform – a report that is careful to underline that it 'should not be considered as representative of the French and/or German official position'.[49] In December 2023, the European Parliament approved a resolution on proposals for the amendment of the Treaties.[50] What is common to both proposals is that they would not change the dominant emphasis on efficiency and functionalism. For the Franco-German working group, the top priority is EU enlargement, which needs to go 'hand in hand with reforms that increase its efficiency, its capacity to act and its democratic legitimacy, as well as empowering the rule of law'.[51] Aiming for quick interinstitutional consensus is of utmost importance. The Report specifies:

> The first goal is to strengthen the EU's capacity to take and implement decisions across all policy areas based on EU primary law, including those areas of cooperation which – because of the various crises – have de facto become EU powers. Given external and internal challenges, speedy decisions are of the essence.[52]

The Parliament appears to agree with this order of priorities: it suggested 'amendments [that] aim to reshape the Union in a way that will enhance its capacity to act, as well as its democratic legitimacy and accountability'.[53] Both reports include minor institutional changes aimed at reducing political gridlock. One communality is the suggestion to further expand the qualified majority voting in the Council, politicising the 'European Executive' (new name proposed by the Parliament for the Commission) in particular through a clearer appointment procedure of its President and strengthening the role of the European Parliament as co-legislator. The Parliament – logically – also asks for 'the right of initiative for legislation, in particular the right to introduce, amend, or repeal Union law, and to become a co-legislator for the adoption of the multiannual financial

[48] P Leino-Sandberg, 'Constitutional Imaginaries of Solidarity: Framing Fiscal Integration Post-NGEU' in R Weber (ed), *EU Integration through Financial Constitution: Follow the Money?* (Hart, 2023).

[49] O Costa et al, 'Sailing on High Seas: Reforming and Enlarging the EU for the 21st Century' (Report of the Franco-German Working Group on the EU Institutional Reform, Paris-Berlin, 18 September 2023), at www.auswaertiges-amt.de/blob/2617322/4d0e0010ffcd8c0079e21329bbbb3332/230919-rfaa-deu-fra-bericht-data.pdf.

[50] European Parliament resolution of 22 November 2023 on proposals of the European Parliament for the amendment of the Treaties (2022/2051(INL)), at www.europarl.europa.eu/doceo/document/TA-9-2023-0427_EN.html.

[51] Costa et al (n 48).

[52] ibid.

[53] European Parliament Resolution (n 49).

framework'. These reforms would strengthen the role of the Parliament in ways that are certainly justified from a separation of powers perspective.

Both reports also recognise the lack of clarity surrounding the EU's emergency powers. For the Parliament, this should be done by revoking Article 122 TFEU and substituting a reworded emergency clause that provides for full parliamentary scrutiny in Article 222 TFEU. The Franco-German working group refers to 'lessons taken from the various crises should be expressed in the wording of competence provisions' as regards banking, health and the EMU, but also suggests strengthening the EU's competence to deal with unforeseen developments. This way, the exceptional crisis measures approved in the context of earlier crises with reference to being exceptional and temporary would be formally codified in the Treaties and become the EU's 'new normal'.

Both reports also engage in the debate about the role and functions of the Court of Justice. The Parliament proposes that the Court should have jurisdiction for inter-institutional disputes and for abstract 'pre-emptive review of norms' at the request of a parliamentary minority, while the Parliament should also have standing to bring infringement cases before the Court. As regards the protection of national competence, the Parliament would allow the Court to 'monitor compliance with the principle of subsidiarity and [to] give preliminary rulings on whether the Union has acted ultra vires' as well as to hear actions brought on grounds of infringement of the principle of subsidiarity. The Franco-German working group is far less responsive to such concerns. It underlines how the 'CJEU is the court of competence, but its ultimate legal authority has been challenged on multiple causes, the most trivial being discontent with an actual or anticipated ruling'. The working group recommends an additional forum for judicial dialogue between the ECJ and national top courts – importantly, without the authority to take binding decisions, but instead for the purpose of bringing current informal contacts between the courts into a more formal setting. This would of course do little to address the questions of judicial review we have observed in our research.

This observation also applies to the reports more generally. They are conservative in the sense of preserving existing power structures and sensitivities and accept the EU's lack of maturity as a political system. The Franco-German working group is very explicit about its vision. It treats the EU's current status as a 'hybrid system in which the European general interest is put forward in three ways: by the European Commission, by citizens' representatives in the European Parliament, and by government representatives in the European Council and Council'. For the working group,

> given the political realities in Europe today, this threefold and hybrid logic should continue to provide the EU with a stable and effective political system. While our report seeks to help overcome shortcomings in decision-making and to further clarify the rules of the game, it does not include proposals that would shift the EU away from this balance.

Therefore, in both proposals, the problems of political and judicial accountability remain under the surface, unidentified and unaddressed. The EU was never designed for political accountability, and there seems to be little interest in changing this design. The same applies to better transparency over who exercises power. Our research has demonstrated a number of grey zones in which it remains unclear who is responsible for what, and who does or should be exercising which powers, including the blurring of powers and responsibilities in all three policy areas. In order to truly address these problems, any proposal for Treaty change would have to abandon the current focus on functionalist efficiency, which creates a mindset in which questions of democratic governance and control are second order issues and where strengthening separation of powers only comes at the cost of the Union's problem-solving capacity.

Most fundamentally, the specific considerations of functionalist efficiency are in practice very relevant in all areas we have studied, arguably even more in the EU context than in the national context. This, too, can be traced to the Treaties; while ost nation-states do not justify their existence with a particular purpose, the EU is explicitly goal-driven. Thus, the fundamental constitutional document provides political direction, and at the same time depoliticises that direction. Seen this way, it is less surprising that virtually all institutions collude and support each other towards attaining that goal, including in pushing the limits of EU competences. At the same time, the ever-present threat of withdrawal creates a need for a steady stream of positive results, constantly proving that the EU is capable of meeting its promise of problem-solving. Particularly in the (semi-permanent) state of multi-crises, the EU also needs to deliver desired outcomes *fast*. However, reproducing the functionalist logic, as the two recent reform proposals do, creates something of a hen-and-egg problem. Any legitimacy based on a functionalist logic can only be upheld by continuously delivering desired outcomes. This can at times only be done fast enough if it does not mind too much about democratic scrutiny and control. By contrast, more democratic scrutiny and control may paradoxically lessen the need for positive results by enhancing the EU's democratic, rather than functional, legitimacy.

Opting structurally in favour of a broad interpretation of EU powers is arguably more problematic in a polity that is not deeply democratically rooted. As observed in the chapter one, it is sometimes argued that the EU's *sui generis* nature and unique features mean that it does not need to observe the same democratic standards as states. We disagree. As the EU exercises public power that reaches deep into Member States and directly changes the legal positions of individuals, it is every bit as important to ensure that this power is not unduly concentrated in one actor, that popular dissensus is channelled into the process of collective will-formation, and that the perspectives of each and every actor is balanced and controlled by the others. While the EU institutions may be aligned around the common goal of an ever-closer Union, not all citizens or even Member States are necessarily on board with this goal. Alternative voices are currently being sidelined by the consensual mode of decision-making. Addressing these issues by Treaty reform would require a significantly broader outlook than is currently being discussed. However, even more substantial Treaty reform is not only unlikely, but also insufficient.

What is needed is a change of mindset, in which the current consensual decision-making is replaced with political debate and institutional rivalry – or even institutional conflict – reflecting the full spectrum of voters' opinions. More emphasis should be placed not only on problem-solving and providing results, but also on whose voice reaches into the institutional decision-making and in what way. Democracy is hard work. Seriously exposing and defending one's views in a deliberative process that includes contestation and takes opposition, including fundamental opposition, may take time. Ultimately, however, separation of powers requires precisely this: that power is shared between different branches that represent an exchange, at eye level, of different autonomously legitimised points of view. It excludes domination of one branch over the others and it requires stopping to regard democratic exchanges involving all branches, including the parliament, particularly at the national level, as just a complication to the efficiency of an otherwise goal-driven and expert-controlled process. Indeed, the ever-closer union of the *peoples* of Europe – the *demos* upon which democracy depends – might be better obtained by a little more institutional discord.

INDEX

www.ingramcontent.com/pod-product-compliance
Ingram Content Group UK Ltd.
Pitfield, Milton Keynes, MK11 3LW, UK
UKHW020845290926
15470UKWH00004B/1566

9 781509 971596